Judith

Judith
Sexual Warrior
Women and Power in Western Culture

Margarita Stocker

Yale University Press
New Haven and London

For Colin Sampson

Set in Monotype Ehrhardt by Servis Filmsetting Ltd, Manchester
Printed in Great Britain by the Bath Press, Bath

Library of Congress Cataloging-in-Publication Data

Stocker, Margarita.
    Judith: Sexual warrior, women and power in western culture/
    Margarita Stocker.
    Includes index.
    ISBN 0–300–07365–8 (alk. paper)
    1. Bible. O.T. Apocrypha. Judith—Criticism, interpretation,
    etc.—History. 2. Judith (Jewish heroine) 3. Women in the Bible.
    I. Title.
    BS1735.2.S76   1998
    229′.2406—dc21   97–45503
                                                           CIP

A catalogue record for this book is available from the British Library

2 4 6 8 10 9 7 5 3 1

Contents

Illustrations

14. *Judith and her Maidservant with the Head of Holofernes* by Orazio Gentileschi. (Wadsworth Atheneum, Hartford, CT. The Ella Gallup Sumner and Mary Catlin Sumner Collection Fund)
15. *Judith* by Jan Metsys. (Koninklijk Museum voor Schone Kunsten, Antwerp. Photo: © A.C.L. Brussels)
16. *Woman at her Toilet* (Judith Beautifying Herself) by unidentified Netherlandish painter after van Eyck. (The Harvard University Art Museums, Cambridge, MA)
17. *Judith and the Boy Hercules* by the Master of the Mansi Magdalen. (National Gallery, London)
18. *Judith and Holofernes* by Giorgio Vasari. (St Louis Art Museum, MO)
19. *Venetian Woman at her Toilette* by Paris Bordone. (National Gallery of Scotland, Edinburgh)
20. *Judith with the Head of Holofernes* by Johann Liss. (National Gallery, London)
21. *Judith Holding the Head of Holofernes*, attributed to Giovanni Antonio Pordenone. (Rijksmuseum-Stichting, Amsterdam)
22. *Mary Aubrey*, engraving from the series *The Crimes of Mary Aubrey* by J. Caulfield. (Guildhall Library, Corporation of London)
23. *Saskia as Flora* by Rembrandt. (National Gallery, London)
24. *Heiligenmartyrium* by Jaspar Woensam von Worms. (Wallraf-Richartz-Museum, Köln. Photo: Rheinisches Bildarchiv, Köln)
25. 'Westerwald' jug. (Musée Cluny, Ecouen. Photo: RMN)
26. Cabinet, French, *c.* 1675. (Rijksmuseum-Stichting, Amsterdam)
27. Whitework sampler (detail). (Fitzwilliam Museum, Cambridge)
28. *The Story of Judith of Bethulia*, a detail of a marble pavement in Siena Cathedral by Matteo di Giovanni. (Photo: Alinari)
29. *Judith with the Head of Holofernes*, a wax tablet by unknown artist. (Wallace Collection, London)
30. *Speculum virginum, 'Humilitas and virtuous women (Jael and Judith)'*, manuscript illumination. (Arundel MS44, f. 34^V. British Library, London)
31. *Justitie over enige Arminiaensche verraders* by C.J. Visscher. (Museum Catharijneconvent, Utrecht. Photo: Ruben de Heer)
32. *Charlotte Corday* by Paul Baudry. (Musée des Beaux-Arts, Nantes. Photo: Giraudon)
33. Cartoon by Nick Newman, from *Private Eye*, issue 838.
34. *Judith* by August Riedel. (Bayerische Museum, Munich)
35. *Judith of Bethulia*, a still from the film by D.W. Griffiths. (British Film Institute)
36. *Judith with the Head of Holofernes* by Mattia Preti. (Wallraf-Richartz-Museum, Köln. Photo: Rheinisches Bildarchiv, Köln)

Acknowledgements

Since I began this book in 1988, many audiences for papers delivered on my research have been responsive, interesting and helpful. I am also grateful to the library staff of Oxford University English, History and Social Studies, and Law faculties, Cambridge, Utrecht and Princeton universities and the Paris Arsenal; and staff of the Siena Pinacoteca, Amsterdam Rijksmuseum, Rubenhuis, Nelson-Atkins Museum, National Gallery London, Northampton City Museum, De Witt Library and Wallace Collection, amongst others too numerous to mention yet gratefully remembered.

The very extensive funding required for this project, and particularly for research abroad, was generously subsidized by the Leverhulme Trust and the Oxford University English Faculty, and I am also grateful to Oxford University for granting me some sabbatical time to write what turned out to be a much more comprehensive and demanding book than I had at first envisaged.

Margarita Stocker
Oxford

1

Beginning

One of the obscurer parts of the Bible, the Old Testament Apocrypha, contains one of its most striking stories. The Book of Judith opens with the Assyrian emperor Nebuchadnezzar's conquest of the Near East. As his forces mount the invasion of Israel, the town of Bethulia is besieged by his foremost general, the cruel and domineering Holofernes. The pass defended by the town is strategically vital: if Bethulia yields, the whole country will fall into his hands. Ground down by famine, the populace begs the city's elders to surrender, and they agree to do so within days should the Lord fail to rescue his people. When Judith, a respected widow, hears of this, she summons the elders to a meeting and upbraids them for their lack of faith. Who are they to set time-limits on God? She herself undertakes to save the city within five days, although she will not reveal her plan to them. However desperate the situation may seem, she avers, God shall overcome. Divinely inspired and fortified by prayer, she departs for the Assyrian camp. There, claiming to have foreseen Bethulia's doom and offering to reveal a stratagem for taking the city, she is welcomed. Holofernes himself, much smitten with her remarkable beauty, invites her to a banquet after which he intends to seduce her or, failing that, rape her. When he retires to his bed in an alcoholic stupor, they are left alone in his tent. Judith takes up his sword and decapitates him. With his severed head she steals back to Bethulia. When its general's corpse is discovered, the Assyrian camp is thrown into confusion. Meanwhile, displaying the head to the Israelites, Judith encourages them to seize their advantage by a rapid surprise attack. They are victorious, and she is fêted as God's agent and Israel's saviour. She is honoured in Jerusalem by a triumphal celebration; but when she returns to Bethulia, she also returns to her retired life, adamantly refusing all offers of marriage and living singly until her death. From start to finish, Judith is a self-reliant heroine. When everyone else was helpless and demoralized, she undertook to save them single-handedly. She did, as the Apocrypha makes quite clear, what no one else could have done. Further, Judith is astounding not only because of what she is, but because of where she is: we meet this peerless, man-slaying heroine within the Book most central to Judaeo-Christian patriarchy.

What the feminist novelist Rebecca West described as 'the obviously gorgeous theme of Judith'[1] has fascinated the western world. Over the centuries, it has remained more consistently popular and influential than anyone now imagines. Representations of Judith have been ubiquitous in all the arts: there are literally thousands of them. In literature there are epics, plays, novels and poems. The story's sensational aspects have been almost obsessively reproduced by numerous artists in the visual and plastic media. It has also been filmed, set to music, illustrated and lampooned. Unnervingly, it has even been consciously re-enacted in real life. The Book of Judith has had a profound and lasting impact upon Western culture..

Sexual Warrior follows Judith's curious, intriguing and unpredictable path through our history. Further, though, I have wanted to explore the multiplicitous meanings that we have attached to this story. *A propos* the nature of human perception, Georges Bataille once remarked that 'Only a spectacular killing . . . has the power to reveal what normally escapes notice.'[2] It is unarguable, at the least, that Judith's was a spectacular murder. Consequently, what I have set out to discover is 'what normally escapes notice': the submerged ideas, issues, anxieties and dreams that Western culture has invested in this image of the gorgeous gorgon.

Judith is, therefore, the story of an icon that has been at once central to and yet in some ways denied by Western culture, because it contradicts those conventional values that societies are accustomed to encode into their most cherished myths. Since we tend to perceive the world through mythic lenses, we subconsciously interpret its phenomena in accordance with myths which stereotype our responses to them. That reflex is, as we shall see, obstructed by a myth as counter-cultural as Judith's, challenging our assumptions about such elemental things as sex and death.

Ultimately, by describing concentric circles around the various aspects of this icon, I intend to present an alternative history of our most basic attitudes. Power, rebellion, passion, gender, belief, deviance, murder and terror are the subjects of this investigation. Viewing these through Judith's myth can, perhaps, open our eyes to the ways we imprison ourselves in our own mythologies.

2

The Gorgeous Gorgon
Women and Power in the Myths of Judith

Scratching the Surface

By beginning to explore some of the themes of the apocryphal story, we can anticipate some of the richly multifarious twists and turns in Judith's later history – although their full meaning will only emerge in other chapters. This is because Judith's story has multiple meanings and many faces, each reflecting something central to our culture.

Thunderstruck by our heroine, Israel's Assyrian enemies conclude that 'There is not such a woman from one end of the earth to the other, both for beauty of face, and wisdom of words' (11:21). Their reaction is not surprising, since, as the Book tells us, it was God himself who made her sexually irresistible on the Monroe scale. 'The Lord gave her also a special beauty . . . in all men's eyes.'[1] (Some translations of the Book of Judith omit this verse, doubtless because the translating cleric found the idea that God deliberately conferred sexual allure less than proper.) He made her a *femme fatale* – the Bible's premiere seductress, unequalled 'from one end of the earth to the other' – in order that she could not fail to entrap Holofernes, thus to kill him, and thereby save her city of Bethulia from his army; thereby saving, also, the whole nation of Israel from the Assyrian horde which had hitherto conquered everything in its path and which, had it taken Bethulia, would have taken the holy city Jerusalem itself; and the Temple would then have fallen to the heathen. Allegorically, the City of God – power and dominion of the Book's true God – is preserved by a good woman who murders the man besotted with her.

No wonder that the early Christian Fathers found this story a thorny subject for pious treatment. Their traditional view of Genesis was that man was seduced into the Fall by the dangerous sexual lure of womankind, yet in the Book of Judith God himself was not above using sexuality to vanquish the pagan and save the chosen people. And if Eve took the blame for bringing death into the world, the punishment for the Fall, the Book of Judith's female death-dealer was inspired to commit murder by the God who, in the Ten Commandments, forbade it. Judith's gender, vampishness and homicide defy all the normal canons of received Christian morality.

The misogyny of the Church Fathers, which is characteristic of the Christian tradition, found comfort in Eve, who misled her husband Adam and hence manifested the duplicitous character of womankind; and in such biblical sirens as Delilah, who betrayed Samson to slavery and blinding at the hands of his enemies. But faced with such a morally contradictory heroine as Judith, both godly and fatal, they perforce had to resort, with even more determination than usual, to the doctrinal allegories that jettisoned literal events of biblical narratives in favour of high-minded metaphors. Most commentaries, for instance, pointed out that, as deliverer of the chosen, Judith was a type foreshadowing the Virgin Mary, who was delivered of the Saviour. Judith's excessively mournful widowhood (locking herself away from the world, abandoning her fine house in favour of a miserable tent upon its roof, defacing her beauty with sackcloth and ashes, wearing a hairshirt, fasting habitually and praying frequently) was, according to St Anselm, a metaphor for the spiritual state of all true souls, widowed brides of the crucified Christ who will be reunited with their spouse only in heaven, and must mourn for him in the meanwhile. A model for Christ's lovers, Judith was consequently also a type of the Christian virtue of chastity. Warning widows against the heinous sin of remarrying, St Jerome cited her example of inconsolable fidelity to her dead husband. Like virginity, celibate widowhood kept in check both the supposedly congenital lubricity of women, daughters of the easy Eve, and the desires of men. Chastity and celibacy being the next best thing to outright virginity, Judith the widow (who could not, therefore, actually be a virgin) came to represent virginity's virtues too. Thus, even murder could be absorbed into a traditional morality, for, as St Jerome opined, in beheading Holofernes, Judith as Chastity had decapitated the sin of lust.[2]

This is, of course, much the allegorical equivalent of saying that she had castrated him. Jerome's patristic interpretation of Judith's story tentatively and inexplicitly foreshadows, as did many early views of Holofernes' fate, Freud's psychoanalytic interpretation, that, motivated by penis-envy, she figuratively castrated Holofernes.[3] Entranced by his own vision of the dominatrix, Jerome says, 'I see her hand armed with the sword and stained with blood. I recognize the head of Holofernes which she has carried away . . . Here a woman vanquishes men, and chastity beheads lust.'[4] Despite this emblematic finale, there is something suspiciously masochistic here, and Jerome's prurient antipathy to sex, symptomatic of his extreme asceticism, here foreshadows later, more explicit fetishizations of Judith. Naturally, theologians treat such matters delicately in all times, but we should not mistake their discreet phrasing for a failure to recognize the same things that strike us so forcibly now.

Similarly, Freud's interpretation of the beheading as metaphor for castration is simply using a different system of knowledge, a rival episteme to Christianity, to allegorize the event. He regarded Old Testament stories as similar to classical mythology, as cryptically encoded repositories of the fears, wishes and taboos of the human tribe.

This view of the Book of Judith as a fiction – albeit one of high cultural status and value – is something on which Freud and modern theologians could agree in part. The consensus view amongst academic theologians is that the Book of Judith was deliberately written as an exemplary moral tale, for its historical and geographical anachronisms and inconsistencies offer glaring evidence that it is unhistorical.[5] Most would agree that it was a deliberately constructed, consoling story written to address the concerns of the Jewish people in the second century BC, after the Babylonian captivity.

To this motive we can attribute the triumphal nationalism of the story, and its reassurance that God will always protect his chosen people. Judith is both a national heroine and a personification of the nation, her name meaning 'the Jewess'. This also emblematizes her Judaic piety: throughout the Book she is rigorously observant of the Law, and especially of dietary regulations. And they prove their magic, since it is her devotional regime that provides her alibi for escaping from the camp after the deed is done. At one level, the Book is a parable of what it means to be Jewish.

Thus it is a fiction of a particularly elevated kind, at once a national and religious myth and a novel, a literary artefact. In fact, its literary features are skilful and elaborate, designed to emphasize both the drama and the didacticism of the tale. Even comedy is not eschewed for this purpose, as for example when first the Bethulians and then the Assyrians are dumbstruck by Judith's beauty: all these hapless admirers 'marvel' at her because what they are seeing is, in effect, God's own idea of what is irresistible. No one can argue with that. Even her beauty, then, is a manifestation of God's omnipotence.

Off this parallel between desire and power spins the moral point. The Assyrians deduce from their helpless desire that they must massacre the Israelites forthwith, for if even their women can exert this kind of magic they are an infinitely dangerous people (10:19). This is ironic, since it demonstrates that even the pagan Assyrians recognize the true power of God when they see it. At the same time, though, the point is made with psychological accuracy, for the Book is portraying that antagonistic impulse that comes over coarser males when they think that the object of desire would not deign to give them a second glance. Like the Church Fathers, the authors of the Book know perfectly well which dark crannies of human psychology they are mining for their parable.

A particularly striking instance of this is the castration motif, recognized even by Jerome and other ancient theologians because the authors of the Book of Judith are very keen that we should see it. Castration is part of an image-pattern which is fundamental to the story's themes.

Highlighting these themes is a recurrent pattern of doubling of the characters. The story's great binary opposition is between Israelite and Assyrian, monotheist and pagan idolater, the divine God and the earthly emperor, Judith and Holofernes – in short, between the heavenly and earthly, the City of God (Bethulia/Jerusalem) and the City of Man (Ecbatane and Nineveh, the imperial capitals). This is the great contest between true and false religions: between the Lord who will allow 'no other gods' and Nebuchadnezzar, who demands of the conquered that they acknowledge him as a god. Both the emperor and Holofernes are guilty of hubris (9:9).[6] All the characters function symbolically within this scheme, belonging either to the Assyrian or the Israelite camp. On one side is God, whose champion in this mortal combat is Judith, seconded by her maidservant; on the other, the emperor Nebuchadnezzar, whose captain is Holofernes, seconded by his major-domo, the eunuch Bagoas. Each servant is introduced in the same way, as having the 'government' of all that belongs to mistress or master, for in effect they are avatars or aspects of their owners as well as literally slaves (8:10, 12:11).

However, the most striking of these binary oppositions is a battle of the sexes which is also the contest of godly with ungodly. To this degree the Book of Judith has a feminist premise, and female victory is God's triumph too. The Book is disarmingly frank about the nature of this battle. Holofernes is no pining swain, but will certainly resort to rape if his seduction techniques fail, techniques that the Book bluntly labels as intended to 'deceive' her into bed (12:16). He is also a macho misogynist, who reckons that if he does not sleep with Judith his troops will laugh him to 'shame', and that Judith herself will 'scorn' him as unmanly (12:12). These firmly drawn battle-lines between the sexes highlight the way in which Judith's actions invert and reverse those of the preening despot. Holofernes punishes Achior, his Ammonite captain, for telling the truth (the usual fate of truth-tellers) which he does not want to hear ('And who art thou, Achior . . . that thou hast prophesied among us . . .?', 6:2). In ironic counterpoint, Judith rebukes the elders for failing in faith ('And now who are ye that have tempted God this day . . .?', 8:12). She accuses them of hubris, which is precisely the sin committed by Holofernes when he scoffs at Achior's prophecy. Just as Judith rewrites Holofernes's speech into godliness, so her robust rebuke to the Israelite elders ('ye shall never know any thing') inverts the normal hierarchy, for as elders they should govern her, both spiritually and politically. As God's spokeswoman, she overrules the patriarchs of her own community, just as she vanquishes the imperial commander.

The structure of the plot reflects the same opposition between the sexes. Despite the Book's title, the eponymous heroine does not appear until the beginning of the eighth chapter. The reader's expectation of her is first deferred through seven chapters during which Holofernes's army cuts its ravaging, conquering swathe through the Near East, subjugating the nations. (Taking their cue from this, retellings of Judith's story often assumed epic form: the Anglo-Saxon poem, Du Bartas's Renaissance epic, J.M. Neale's micro-epic.) The introduction of Judith brings about a sudden change. It is as if an epic of international war abruptly turns, at the half-way point, into a melodrama of the sex war set in a bedroom. Like the protagonists, the plot itself is constructed on a dichotomy, between a narrative of public, political, masculine history and an intimate domestic drama of a more feminine cast. In literary terms it is half epic, half romance. The two flow together in the close, where the traditional ritual with which Israelite women land the hero's triumph in dance and song (as they do also for David in the Book of Samuel) is, because this hero is female, transformed into a feminine event.

This thematic gendering of the story is the overall structure in which the castration motif accrues its meanings. If Holofernes is metaphorically emasculated, this has been foreshadowed in the story by the fact that his avatar Bagoas is a eunuch. Similarly, it is also succeeded in the story by an event that moralizes the motif. Achior had been punished by exposure in the mountains for his impudence in warning Holofernes that the Israelites' God was powerfully protective. Having been rescued by the Bethulians, Achior is one of those who greet Judith on her return to the city, and when he sees his erstwhile master's severed head – a material symbol of God's power in action – he converts to Judaism. Or, as the book puts it he opts for circumcision (14:10). The symbolic castration in this rite is a formal submission to God: as it were, an acknowledgement of the greater virility or power exercised by the ultimate patriarch. Conversely, then, what the emasculation of the Assyrians means is that before the true power of the universal God these hubristic earthly potentates are quite simply impotent. Every time Judith fulsomely submits to Holofernes' commands, she avers that she will always obey her 'Lord' (12:14), knowing that Holofernes will identify himself with this supremacy, whereas of course for her there is only one Lord. The most striking element in the Book of Judith is that it is so conscious and deliberate in its acknowledgement of the phallic concept of power. If power is patriarchal, then the only possessor of supreme masculinity is God.

This is why, although she is the cynosure of universal desire, no one ever manages to sleep with Judith. Holofernes' fate is a classic instance, if we look at it from one perspective, of the association of the Freudian male castration-complex with the death-wish. Freud's rather literary notion of human psychology linked the fear and helplessness dissociable from desire with the death-wish itself.[7] Meanwhile, in this literary fable, Holofernes desires his own death, embodied in the castrating woman. Spiritually, this means that hubris is its own punishment, that evil brings about its own ruin. That Holofernes' servant, acting as pimp, is already emasculated is an indication that those who desire Judith will inevitably fail.

This is even true of her dear departed husband. Immediately after Judith enters the narrative we are told that he died of sunstroke, and told in a way that emphasizes an ironic parallel with Holofernes' fate; Manasses is struck in the head, collapses on his bed and dies, in partial inversion of the series that befalls her would-be lover. It is necessary to the story that Manasses be removed from the scene, so that Judith will have both the status in her community and the independence of a widow to facilitate her heroic action, for no self-respecting ancient Jewish husband would have permitted his famously faithful wife to sortie out in order to play games with enemy generals. More bluntly, though, God's plan requires that Manasses be deceased, so the Lord killed him off as surely as he killed Holofernes through Judith. Symbolically, Judith, as Jewry, is married to God alone. And as we know, he is 'a jealous god'.

Indeed, the narrative harps obsessively upon Judith's chastity, because it is the symbolic guarantee of all the values she represents, metaphysical, moral and national. In her prayer for inspiration, Judith recalls the rape of the virgin nation by a previous conqueror, and in her final song of triumph she identifies Israel with her own person, Assyria with the male who 'bragged that he would burn up my borders' and make 'my virgins as a spoil' (9:2, 16:4–5). Allegorizing the customary barbarity of rape inflicted upon women of conquered nations, the Book constructs Judith's own chastity as the nation's inviolacy (because it is under God's protection). Like the city of Bethulia, she is a besieged fortress (and would later be allegorized as Fortitude). That she returns to her eremitic life, adamantly refusing to remarry, symbolically conveys that in her celibacy Judith is living out the price of the nation's security. Thus 'many desired her, but none knew her' (6:22). As long as she lived (and lived thus) Israel was threatened by no more invasions (16:25).

The effect of this is as it were to demonize masculine sexuality: as the national penetration of invasion, as Holofernes and his false god's lust for power, as the rapine which is an intimidatory strategy of power politics. In these symbolic patterns the Book of Judith deliberately portrays sexual politics as a vehicle for its religious themes. When Judith decapitates Holofernes – man, lover, ruler, commander – she beheads patriarchy.

Spiritually, this is the defeat of an epitome of human power by the divine ruler. But of course there is a logical difficulty here, since God himself is a patriarch, in fact (as generations of conservative political theorists argued) the ultimate term guaranteeing all notions of hierarchy.[8] Judith's feminist defeat of the patriarch ruler Nebuchadnezzar/Holofernes could seem to challenge God's rule also, since their hubris was, by definition, an aspiration to the same power that he exerts. When Judith destroys a patriarchal power she inevitably challenges that of God as well.

This is why, despite its own thematics, the Book of Judith cannot afford to be feminist. It stresses that it is not Judith, but God, who has killed Holofernes – 'by the hand of a woman' (16:6). She was merely an instrument of the true patriarchal power, which punished those who aspired to his omnipotence. That she belongs to God in this instrumental sense is underscored by her chaste fidelity to him, her possession only by him. Chastity secures the fact that Judith is not a free agent. Thus, when as a reward she frees the slave maid who was her accomplice (16:23), Judith gives her something she herself does not have: freedom of action. For, by contrast, Judith locks herself up in seclusion. As the maid is an avatar of her mistress, so her manumission gives us the illusion that Judith too is free; but it is Judith who is, as she says, the 'handmaid' of the Lord, the hand that enacts his will. The maidservant's emancipation is a cunning literary effect, designed to reassure us that Judith's own bondage is freedom. In fact, though, her chastity functions to immure her within the power of God.

Further to elide any anti-patriarchal challenge to that, the castration motif was, as we saw, controlled by flanking negative and positive symbols, the pagan impotence of Bagoas and the Judaic consecration of Achior's foreskin. This sublimation of the motif is enhanced by the business of Judith's bag. In this she transports her kosher food, in order to avoid eating unclean items in the Assyrian camp. In it she also brings out of the camp the unclean item of Holofernes' severed head. The cannibalistic implication of placing this in her foodbag is one of the story's classic mythic-primitive ingredients, ingestion of the enemy being a traditional method of acquiring the power of his spirit. That subserves the religious point that godly power has ingested pagan. Hence the narrative's heavy preceding emphasis upon Judith's conscience about kosher food: we are meant to conclude that if she is chary about what she eats she will be able to resist this morsel too.

At the same time, though, the cannibalistic idea suggests the usual subtextual accompaniment to castration imagery, the voracious woman, all *vagina dentata*. Precisely because all these primitve images of potency and impotence are inexorably sexual as well, the idea that this victory is indeed anti-masculine cannot be evaded.

A similar effect ensues from the use of Holofernes' severed head as a primitive head-hunter trophy: on Judith's advice it is displayed by the Israelites, terrifying the Assyrian army into demoralized defeat. Like the head of Goliath in David's hand, Holofernes' is a warning to God's enemies. It performs the totemistic function of a deterrent. In classical myth, Medusa's head, petrifying onlookers, is displayed by the hero Perseus in the same way for similar reasons. In all three cases the 'Medusa effect' operates.[9] The totem stands for a supernatural power in a way that human beings can see and tolerate: it is, as it were, a sideways glance at godhead because looking at it directly would destroy us. However, in Judith's case the fact that the head's possessor is feminine underwrites the story's implications of castration, placing a gendered spin on the primitive symbol.

Of course, the femininity that overcomes masculinity is not intended to be feminist in principle. When Judith's triumphal song exults that 'the mighty one' was not defeated by 'young men' or 'sons of the Titans' or 'giants', but by a woman (16:7), the point is that he was defeated by a mere woman. His mightiness is made ridiculous by the weakness of its nemesis. 'For thy power standeth not in multitude' (9:11), which is why Judith iconized Humility in Christian tradition.[10] Like the boy David who slew the giant Goliath, Judith is the meek, weak and humble agent pitted against the mighty, for the feebleness of God's instruments insults his enemies' pretensions. Equally as their hubris is so utterly humbled, so God himself, we are intended to deduce, possesses the kind of power that requires no great armies and no muscles to exert itself. It just is. Ultimately, the weaker its instrument, whether an adolescent boy or a woman (much of a muchness, as it were), the more manifest is the hidden hand that activates them beyond their own abilities. Judith's femininity is a sign that God's virility is not to be doubted or contested.

However, it is not, in the end, possible for the Book of Judith to contain the significance of its heroine, despite its literary sophistication. Whilst it attempts to subordinate Judith to God's patriarchy by means of her chastity, this attribute is compromised by the fact that Judith has to exploit her sexuality in order to captivate Holofernes. A personification of Chastity who is also a deliberate seductress is a paradox. Despite the allegorized repetitions that moralize the castration motif, it nevertheless sexualizes the bedroom homicide. And these resistances to the story's overdetermination of Judith's chastity help to emphasize the battle of the sexes, which is itself the spine of the Book's spiritual message. A feminist implication to Judith's action is not repressible.

The Supernatural

Most important, and the key to the Book's inability to repress the feminist implications of Judith's role, is that the divine and supernatural are themselves feminized to a degree by the story. The habitual imaginative universe of the West tends, as Simone de Beauvoir suggested in *The Second Sex*, to posit a series of binary oppositions which are gendered, so that rationality, intellect and activism are regarded as masculine qualities, irrationality, emotion and passivity as feminine. These oppositions boil down to a programmatic distinction between that which is Self (the masculine subject) and that which is Other (the femine object). Consequently, the supernatural, which is assumed to be supra-rational, is often identified with femininity, just as muses, sirens and sibyls are traditionally female.[11] Judith was allegorized as Wisdom in the iconographic scheme of Christian Virtues, and as possessing the gift of prophecy.[12] Thus the feminine comes to represent the unearthly, the most pronounced form of Otherness to humankind. In the same way, we may recognize that the

Otherness of Judith's femininity to her patriarchal society, governed by male elders, emblematizes the sacredness conferred upon her by her God-given destiny.

In paintings of the murder – what I shall call Judith's acteme – this liminally metaphysical Otherness is often underlined by racial difference. As in Antiveduto Grammatica's Derby painting, the maidservant, Judith's double, is often portrayed as ethnically distinct, as dusky, oriental or black. Sometimes portrayed as the shocked witness of murder, the maid's natural reaction and her colour can be mutually reinforcing elements, as a contrast to her mistress, implying Judith's own Otherness, femininity as deviance. Another effect of the maid's doubling for her mistress is achieved when she is portrayed as a withered crone, counterpointing the heroine's beauty. This achieves the further effect of rendering her ageing, her evident mortality, a comment on the death of Holofernes: the crone is Death's presence, a *memento mori*.

Thus Judith as Death and as Resurrection – type of the Virgin who brought eternal life to humankind – presides over a tomb in the mausoleum at Pisa's cathedral. Like the Virgin Mary, typology contended, in decapitating Holofernes Judith trod on the head of the serpent Satan, which was Genesis's prophecy of Christian salvation. Her Christian significance as type of the Virgin thus makes her homicide – ironically – a sign of death-into-life, resurrection. This is why Nicholas Wespin's altarpiece at Crea in Italy portrays Judith's acteme as a foreshadowing of the Annunciation of the saviour to the Virgin, and why Judith appeared on medieval fonts (for instance, at Hutton Cranswick in Yorkshire) as a sign of the meaning of baptism. This was the Christianization of her Book's mythic motifs of taboo, cleanliness and purgation. In the Sainte-Chapelle in Paris, the stained-glass window that illustrates Judith's story centres on her daily bathing as an image of baptism, the 'death' of the carnal body and rebirth into the spirit.[13]

By these means the female pair become Death and its dealer, the agent of the supernatural and the personification of the mortal step over the threshold out of life into the dark mystery beyond. Both mortality and mystery, the ineffability of the supernatural *tout court*, are signified by feminine Otherness. Both the terror and the magnificence of Judith as Other signify the terrifying mystery of the invisible deity. The good murderess and sexy celibate embodies its strangeness, that 'God sees not as man sees'.

In this sense, by the symbolic logic of the Book of Judith, even the divinity is feminine when in epiphany on earth. Ironically, the Book's feminist implications are actually stronger because of its traditionally male-centred symbolic system. Abstractions are often allegorized in culture as female (Mercy, Charity, and so on), but Judith's role as the supernatural personified is not only of this kind. Once the earthly enemy is represented as masculinity, as is the case in her Book, the femininity of Otherness becomes a meaningful gendering. It supports that feminist substructure that keeps piercing through the tidiness of the story's symbolic construction.

Thus even the original story could not control the multiple significances of Judith. And, as we shall see, she has continued to be an exceptionally obstinate, problematic subject for subsequent attempts to reimagine her story in terms that would fit it neatly to the prevailing cultural climate. Implicitly feminist, iconoclastic, satirical and (in its homicide) amoral, the Book of Judith is a counter-cultural myth. Translating it into culturally orthodox terms is therefore inherently impracticable. Precisely the features that make the story fascinating are what make it impossible.

Biblical Femmes Fatales

It is by comparison with other icons, female and male, from the Bible and classical mythology that Judith's unique cultural positioning becomes clear. Significant differences from even her closest analogues – such as Jael, Lucretia and David – reveal why her myth is counter-cultural.

If she will not (so to speak) play ball with patriarchy, that is because she is distinctive amongst the women of the Old Testament. Like all ancient texts of wide cultural currency, only more so because of its religious status, the Old Testament generates mythic imitations of its plots and characters. Not one of its more famed heroines and villainesses is as complex and contradictory in mythic value as Judith.

Unlike her, even her closest analogues can be accommodated to cultural stereotypes without difficulty. Paintings of Judith and Salome are in some ways very similar, for instance; so much so that many of Judith have been mistaken for Salomes. Yet Salome is a villainess and, as I have explained elsewhere, her significance whilst complex is very different from Judith's.[14] Delilah's shearing of Samson's hair, and his subsequent blinding, have been habitually interpreted in the same way as Judith's head-taking, as metaphors for castration. Yet, since Delilah is a nefarious siren and a Philistine to boot, she is a stereotypical *femme fatale*, the Mata Hari of the ancient Near East.

Equally, the heroines analogous to Judith comfortably inhabit conventional females roles. Both Judith and Esther were regarded as types foreshadowing the Virgin Mary, for Esther too delivered her people from an Assyrian pogrom. Whilst they are often paired in iconography for this reason, the 'meek' Esther's implications are antipathetical to Judith's.[15] A dutiful second spouse recruited, by means of a beauty contest, to replace the divorced termagant Vashti, Esther is a domesticated consort and trophy wife. She saves her people by appealing to her husband, the emperor Ahasuerus, and is thus evidence in support of the time-honoured conviction that women possess power over public events by influencing their husbands. The more old-fashioned misogynist will still opine that women, if only the poor dear creatures would realize it, are actually much more powerful behind the scenes than they could ever be if holding public office *in propria persona*. Esther may be a queen, Judith a mere widow, but precisely for that reason Judith's self-election to political action marks her out as a much more challenging figure for traditional views of the public sphere as a masculine arena.

Similarly, Susannah, Judith's complement in the personifications of Chastity, is no sword-wielding defender of her own honour. Victim of voyeurism and false allegations, she is rescued from condemnation by a man who attests to her wifely fidelity. The Book of Susannah in the Old Testament Apocrypha is in fact an appendage to the canonical Book of Daniel. The Book of Ruth is no richer in assertive females. It is a textbook demonstration, so intended, of the way in which a woman may assert her right to be married and protected by a male relative, under the laws of the kinship system. This is not the same kind of assertiveness as is found in the Judiths of this world. So much, then, for the models of womanhood provided by the eponymously female books of the Bible. There is not much here for feminists to greet with joy, and on the whole they have not.

Once the apocryphal books were demoted from the canonical Bible – Jerome included them in the Vulgate only with reservations, Protestant churches eventually excluded them altogether – the Book of Judith, with its peculiar and minatory heroine, was rather conveniently marginalized. So were the apocryphal fragments that had fallen away from the Book of Esther, where that queen emerges as rather less compliant than she is in her canonical Book. In the excluded text she goes so far as to complain that God had decreed that she must sleep with the uncircumcised heathen. Although the apocryphal texts of Esther and Judith were excluded from the canon on linguistic grounds, one finds oneself wondering whether the Jewish authors who wrote in Greek were rather more sympathetic towards women than those who were writing in Hebrew. Linguistic censorship can itself be a form of heresy: if, that is, 'God thinks not as man thinks'. Whatever the case, the Bible's most feminist – and its most dubious – heroine occupies a marginal position within it, which seems entirely apt to her exceptional character.

Being located, as it were, on the threshold of the canon is also appropriate to Judith's liminal Otherness as a divinely inspired being. To let her in would be to permit entrance to a rather complex, counter-cultural view of how God acts in the world, as well as the counter-culture of feminism itself.

Jael

As it happens, Judith does have a foot within the canonical camp, in the form of Jael, who has often confused with her by those who do not know the Bible intimately.[16] Essentially Jael's role in the Book of Judges is merely a walk-on part (Judges 4:17–22). When the prophetess Deborah inspires General Barak to defeat Israel's enemy, the defeated general Sisera pauses in his flight to rest in the tent of Jael, a goatherd. (Doubtless he raped her first, in the normal way, but this is not mentioned.) As he sleeps, she kills him by driving a tentpeg through his forehead. Given the similar scenario, it is not suprising that representations of Jael often portray her as if she were Judith, and in literature and art the two have often been confused or compounded into a single figure, as we shall see.

But Jael is very much a truncated version of Judith. Her role is brief – two verses – because the national heroine here is Deborah, and the military hero Barak. Between them they divide the functions that Judith performs entirely by herself, from doctrinal instruction and strategic planning through to murder. Deborah is not morally ambivalent like Judith, because Jael does the dirty work for her, and Jael is not the prophetess-heroine precisely because she does do the dirty work. She is a goatherd, Judith is a lady. Put Jael and Deborah together, and Judith's ambiguity results. In sum, then, the canonical equivalent of Judith is not unduly disturbing because she is not an equivalent at all.

Jael's murderousness is, however, an aspect of Judith, one a canonical narrative can accommodate without much difficulty. Esther is a domesticated type of the queen of heaven, yet politically – both in the public sphere and in sexual politics – anodyne by comparison to the private citizen Judith. Judith's particularity is the more striking and definitive because only this biblical heroine is so ambiguous, and therefore resistant to stereotype. Since the Bible has been for many centuries the most powerful generator of Western cultural myths, this anomalous heroine was unleashed by an exceptionally authoritative and influential source. Feminists have often complained, and rightly, of the supports to patriarchy and misogyny that have been provided by the Bible.[17] But if Judith is a feminist heroine, it is to the Bible that we owe her counter-cultural myth. With one hand it gave us the Eves and Delilahs who demonize women, but with the other it gave us woman of independent mind, clever, rational, ingenious, resourceful, persuasive, courageous, self-reliant and indomitable.

We have no idea who wrote the Book of Judith, but its author (orthodox in religion, heterodox in imagination) devised a myth that would contest the Bible's own massively influential promulgation of deleterious female stereotypes. Judith's was a characterization that generations of writers, artists and historians would struggle in vain to acclimatize to cultural norms. Precisely because they encountered her in the seminal Good Book of the West, hers was an image of femininity that, however incommensurate with conventional ideas, they could not ignore.

It is our habit to view the world, and indeed ourselves, through mythic lenses. We refer what we see to pre-existent mythic stereotypes that have a firm grasp upon our habits of cognition. Unlike the myths of Eve and the Virgin Mary, Judith's affronts Western cultural stereotypes. As we shall see, the ways in which this counter-cultural myth has been re-used over time thus reflects our most fundamental beliefs and anxieties.

You Can't Keep A Good Woman Down

Of course, as one would expect, one of the story's more complex elements for interpreters has been its dependence upon sexuality. A *femme fatale*, as clever as she was lovely, and a powerful general, as cruel as he was extravagant – clearly these were the stuff of which myths were made, a biblical alternative to Antony and Cleopatra. But Judith's is a much more complex and interesting version of the clichéd cultural plot about mighty men felled by sirens. She was permitted to possess the sexual charisma of a Cleopatra without dying for it, as in such tales fatal women customarily do. Moreover, Judith was not a fatal woman in the usual, merely metaphorical sense, but despatched her quondam lover in a particularly bloody fashion herself. What better than a siren whose story was morally uplifting and theologically instructive? More than any other classic heroine, Judith offered remarkable scope to the exploitation of sexual tropes, with full authorization from the Good Book and Christian tradition. In this case, sensationalism was wonderfully licensed for anyone who chose to exploit it.

But if, despite its literary excellence, the apocryphal Book could not constrain Judith's significance, the only way for later interpreters to avoid the pitfalls of this complex narrative has been to select from it, to leave out much of what makes it unique. To use her simply as an icon of virtue – as Chaucer did in the *Tale of Melibee*, where she is Good Counsel, a variation on her icon as Wisdom – requires abbreviated allusion. At the other extreme, to recast Judith's story as a simple parallel to Delilah's requires radical surgery upon the plot. For instance, Chaucer's *Monk's Tale* constrains her example within the context of sexuality. In this, the fullest of the medieval poet's three allusions to the story, Holofernes is portrayed as an instance of the many great men ruined by women's wiles. The religious and patriotic contexts of the sexual occasion are omitted, because only in this way may Judith's exemplum be accommodated within the Monk's misogynist account of history. Once acknowledge that God and her country were on Judith's side, and the game is up. One is then left with the awkward fact that the fatal woman was a good woman too, and hence resistant to the stereotypes of 'cursed daughters of Eve'. Western culture has happily produced legions of sly seductive mankillers, but Judith, as good-bad woman beloved of God, occupies no such familiar cultural space.

Precisely Judith's authorization by God for deceitful seduction and murder was what made her more terrifying than any mere villainess. From this flows that transfixing combination of moralism and menace that underlies more complex treatments of the sexual theme than Chaucer's. In Jan de Bray's painting of Judith, caught at the moment when she raises the sword above Holofernes' bed, the snuffed candle on the table signifies both retribution – the extinction of the candle of his life – and the phallus. Accordingly the picture's composition placed the candlestick at an appropriate point against the background of Holofernes' serenely recumbent body. Symbolizing female sexuality, the basin next to it encodes both vagina and womb, fertility and life, whereas the snuffed candlestick symbolizes male sexuality and death. The painting is a representation of sex as a mediating term between life and death, as an expiration into orgasmic oblivion.

This theme is reinforced by the mature appearance of Bray's Judith and the childlike maid, respectively Maturity and Youth attending the deathbed that awaits all human beings. Bray's is one of many paintings of Judith that explore the existential elements encoded into her myth, its sublimated significance as 'divine retribution' *and* its primitive representation of the link between sex and death, eros and thanatos. Viewed in one way, the painting moralizes Judith as an appointed executioner of divine retribution; in another way, it implies a paranoiac vision of woman as man's enemy, as castrator and as the womb that is his tomb. The ambiguity of the painting is a consequence of Judith's own ambiguity.

The Two-Faced Woman

One way for interpreters to elide Judith's sacred-sinister ambiguity, and thus protect her heroic iconicity, was to edit the story in a different way. By concentrating on her public, political aspect, and abandoning the Christian context that made her so morally dubious, it was possible to disambiguate her to a degree. In one of Anteviduto Grammatica's versions of the subject, heroine and maid are portrayed as whispering together, dramatically highlighted by candlelight and the circumambient gloom of everpresent danger, in a way that implies women conspiring against the male. Yet Grammatica precludes our interpreting this purely in misogynist terms. Judith's antique armour and especially her helmet allude to her correspondence with Athene, the classical warrior-goddess who also personified wisdom. Like Judith, Athene was the guardian of her city, Athens. An equally popular comparison of Judith with the ancient warrior-queen Tomyris, another head-taker, had the same effect of focusing carefully upon Judith's public status as national heroine and guardian of her people. Thus a Renaissance wax tableau represents Judith as classicized warrior-maid, an image associating her with Athene and the Amazon, whilst other paintings signify both classical and biblical examples of female heroism as emblematized on her jewels or her armour. In such representations she is reinforced as a summation of female heroism, accruing the less ambivalent attributes of more standard heroines.

One of the major problems reflected in subsequent representations is that Judith's release from patriarchal controls itself renders her vulnerable to misogynist interpretations. The patriotic context is not intrinsically sufficient to protect Judith from stereotyping. After all, patriotism's virtue depends very much on which side you are on: the enemy may believe in his or her own patriotism too. It is only God's authorization that stands between Judith the sacred heroine and our viewing her actions in the light of normal human morality. Seducer, deceiver and murderer, she only transcends moral values if she is indeed God's instrument, in which case her crimes become heroic. Paradoxically, Judith can only be securely heroic if her metaphysical context remains in place, if she remains within the patriarchal order: yet the character of her heroism as feminist is what slips out of that order. The tension of feminist heroism within sacred context is actually vital to preserving Judith's icon from its defamation by stereotype. Reducing her from sacred agent and Israelite secret agent to private sexual predator does much more misogynist damage to her image than it does to biblical patriarchal values.

Conversely, however, this privatization and sexualization of Judith's acteme can exploit the same misogynist neuroses to feminist effect. It can be made an epitome of women's vengeance upon the males who abuse them, and the original Book's symbolic plot is such that Judith can even be interpreted as raping the would-be rapist. The Renaissance artist Artemisia Gentileschi (1593–1651) repeatedly returned to Judith's story for her most remarkable paintings, and her most violent representation of the acteme has been understood as reflecting her own experience of rape.[18] Her Holofernes is positioned to this effect, a foreshortening presenting his raised arms as thighs, feminized. This representation is exceptional, not only in its extreme brutality but in making the maid an active participant in the murder. The women's co-operation again implies a female conspiracy against the male. Another of Gentilechi's several versions of Judith shows only the maid and Judith, surreptitious and alert to the danger of discovery, liaising in the prosecution of their plan. The recurrent subtext of Gentilechi's representations of Judith is that women are capable of retribution upon masculine brutality, and if at one level this is evidently a wish-fulfilment fantasy, at another it is a reminder that God himself once empowered female vengeance. The advantage for a Renaissance artist of basing a feminist message upon the Bible was, in that much more religious age, that this particular virago carried divine authority. Gentilechi was not the only female artist to exploit that to a feminist end (Sirani was another), but she was the most comprehensively violent and antagonistic in her emphasis upon the bloodthirstiness of the event, precisely because she wished to evoke the spectator's fear of the homicidal woman.

Similarly, it is Gentilechi's portrayal of Judith after the murder, holding up her hand against the glare of candlelight as the kneeling maid stows the head, that most explicitly evokes Judith's sacred/sinister ambiguity. In the glare, her hand shades only one side of her face, dividing her between the light and the dark. The furtiveness implied by the composition enhances this effect. Gentileschi's Judiths have a tendency to underscore Judith's ambiguity precisely in order to suggest female subversion. Far from positing a difficulty, for Gentileschi Judith's moral ambiguity became the feminist premise.

This feminist construction of Judith is of course almost indistinguishable from the misogynist version that demonizes her. Its motivation is different, but its reception by the masculine spectator might not be. He may deduce that it is unwise to traduce women, or he may instead simply relapse into the received wisdom that 'women are like that': instinctively Furies, and therefore rightly severely controlled by the more rational male who is their master. Evocation of the Furies is something of a double-edged sword.

On the other hand, the sword is a vital ingredient in Judith's positive representations. Iconographically, it is usually a sign of retributive justice, of God's fiat. Hemessen's Judith, for instance, is a strapping heroic blonde beauty who fills the frame, her resplendent nakedness signifying *nuda veritas*, spiritual Truth. The most prominent element in the painting is her arm, foreshortened as it raises the sword, for this stance signifies the intransigence of justice, that it is no respecter of persons. Gazing out at the viewer with absolute candour, the heroine poses a challenge to him/her: do you understand what my icon means *for you?*

More pragmatically, in many representations the sword is the only indicator that the woman bearing the severed head is probably Judith the heroine, not Salome the villainess. The iconography of the standard representation of Judith is ambiguously suggestive of Judith/Salome (heroine/villainess) before it is ambiguously suggestive of Judith's sacred/sinister character.[19]

In versions of the acteme, the face of Judith's maid sometimes registers amazement, thereby highlighting Judith's lack of it, her unabashed concentration on the task in hand. This can function as a sensationalizing tactic, emphasizing that Judith is a deviant woman. Within the frame, the maid may represent the horrified viewer of the painting itself. Similarly, the ugliness of the crone can signify the twisted psyche of the beautiful protagonist. But in more sympathetic portrayals the maid's fear or horror emphasizes that Judith is exceptional, and hence underscores her heroism too. And many of these compositions enhance the effect of Judith's beauty by portraying her maid as wizened, as in Caravaggio's brilliant, disturbing and highly influential version. Given Caravaggio's true subject (of which more later), this is to contrast the white-clad Judith as Innocence with a scarified Experience and corruption. Such motifs, which vary in intensity from version to version, can be interpreted either positively or negatively, depending not only upon the artist's agenda but also upon the spectator's. One way or another, in Judith's representations the iconography of villainess and heroine tends towards merger.

On the whole it was usually the patron who commissioned the painting who dictated its subject: the vast number of extant paintings of Judith suggests that customers had a positive enthusiasm for her. Both Artemisia Gentileschi and her father Orazio had a profitable line in Judiths. Amongst the latter's versions is one that uses a deliberately mannered double-headed composition. Judith and her maid stare out of the frame in opposite directions: an exaggeration of their watchful alertness to possible discovery, which suggests fear. Like a Janus-face, the double-headed effect also implies Judith's two-faced nature, an exploitation of her duplication in the maid. But is this in fact a derogatory version of Judith, or is it a Salome, in which case these effects are justified? The clue is in the sword. Judith's grasp on it is implausible because she is also holding a salver in the same hand, and it may be a late addition. Probably this picture began as a Salome with Herodias, their anxious expressions registering belated shame. It may be that Orazio altered it at the request of a customer other than the one for whom it was originally intended; but the problem of divining the difference between a Judith and a Salome is not confined to such cases of revision. As in literature, if a painting's iconography is selective this obscures the crucial distinction between a heroine and a villainess and thus absorbs Judith into the swollen stream of misogynist images in Western art.

The iconic image of the woman holding the severed head is itself a moderation of the horror of the homicide. Judith's acteme enacts a murder before our eyes, whereas Judith holding the head is a kind of metaphor of the homicidal event. It partakes of the Medusa Effect, whereby the head becomes more totemic than human, showing death only obliquely and granting a psychic distance for the spectator. Because painting is not normally a narrative art, but a 'snapshot' medium, it often and easily effects an abridgement of Judith's myth that contains her ambiguity within sexuality and reduces her to simple criminality.

Rape and Lucretia

If the run-of-the-mill *femme fatale* defuses Judith's sexual challenge, her classical analogue, Lucretia, likewise sanitizes her political meaning. In art Lucretia has often been paired with Judith, as in Cranach's complementary paintings. But Lucretia is Judith's obverse as much as her analogue. Like Judith, Lucretia was an exemplar of chastity, and her story is also as much a political myth as a moral and sexual one. The crucial difference is that Lucretia's colludes with traditional cultural assumptions about femininity, even though its political theme is revolutionary.

The central event in Lucretia's story is her rape by Tarquin, son of the Roman tyrant.[20] Because she is a chaste woman, she confesses what has happened to her husband and her family, and punishes her polluted body by taking her own life. Punishing herself for her sexual victimization, Lucretia confirms stereotypes of women as passive and reinforces the sexual double standard. Her stabbing herself becomes a replicative penetration of her violated body: an eroticized event frequently exploited in prurient paintings of her suicide. Representations of the rape itself are also common in art. Titian's celebrated and much-copied version is typical of the sexual codes at work both in the myth and in these representations. Tarquin's knee thrusts aggressively towards the contrastingly naked, defenceless woman, mimicking the phallic sword. Supposedly pathetic, such paintings are equally voyeuristic fantasies of sexual violence.

What is interesting about these works for our purposes is the way in which this kind of Lucretian composition effects the reverse of the Judith acteme. Reproducing 'normal' sexual codes, a man with phallic sword assaults a naked woman on a curtained bed. The same thing happens in Judith's acteme, except that the gender-roles are reversed. (Hence the direct parallel between Titian's *Lucretia* and Francesco Rosi's *Judith* in the Louvre.) Lucretia's scene is the coded erotic norm that Judith's contradicts.

At the sublimated political level, both myths have the same moral. Yet the sexual code that produces that moral makes them crucially different as myths of gender. Although Lucretia is a victim, proof of the tyrant's villainy, unlike Judith she does not take her own revenge. That is undertaken by her bereaved relatives, who rise up against the Tarquins, abolish the monarchy and establish the Republic. Lucretia becomes the catalyst of Roman liberty. Thus, like Judith's, this is a myth of tyrannicide. The difference is that Lucretia is a passive conventional woman, her relatives the assassins, whereas Judith seizes her own role in public events to perform this function. Despite the fact that these are the complementary feminine biblical and classical myths of tyrannicide, it is the secular myth, not the Judaeo-Christian one, that literally de-activates the woman at its centre. This is another symptom of the fact that, as I suggested earlier, it is precisely the patriarchal Judaeo-Christian metaphysic that valorizes the woman in Judith's myth, overriding cultural assumptions. By contrast, Lucretia's characterization fully confirms stereotypical femininity.

Lucretia is Judith's analogue in chastity and resolution, but her opposite in terms of sexual narrative. Whereas Lucretia is a hostess betrayed by a guest, Judith is a guest who betrays her host; whereas Lucretia was a victim (finally of herself), Judith was victorious; whereas Lucretia was raped, Judith eluded her would-be ravisher; whereas Lucretia died, Judith killed. Lucretia's suicide echoes her violation, whereas Judith appropriates the phallic sword of Holofernes in order to kill him. The insistent refeminizing and repeated violation of Lucretia's body is reversed by Judith's mutilation of the man's. And whilst Lucretia offended Christian ideals of spiritual autonomy, so that Augustine condemned her suicide,[21] Judith exemplified them. Her story is not simply the mirror-image of Lucretia's: it implies the inversion of the whole range of masculinist assumptions there encoded. Judith's icon empowers the feminine whilst Lucretia enfeebles it.

At the political level, both myths established templates for the philosophy of tyrannicide. Both would be invoked when such revolutionary action was undertaken in subsequent times of crisis, as we shall see. But it is only in the myth of Judith that the violent political moral is given to the woman herself to enact, thus challenging both the political and the sexual orders. In her myth, but not Lucretia's, the parallel between the personal and the political aspects of autonomy is manifested. And whether in comparison to classical or biblical counterparts, the uniqueness of Judith's icon is her paradigm of a woman's ability to affect history. The single most important feature of her cultural image is its assertion of women's rightful place in politics, for it is in this arena, where the fact of power is entirely overt, that sexism is most severely tested.

Boys Will Be Kings: David and Oedipus

The parallel between political and personal in Judith's myth is also manifest in the essential myth of the patriarchal order, that of Oedipus, who killed his father and ascended his throne, marrying his own mother. From various perspectives, psychoanalytic, anthropological and literary, the myth of Oedipus has long been explicated as the founding myth both of masculinity and of political systems based upon promigeniture. For Freud it was the universal underplot of human sexual development. From the start, however, Oedipus's myth was simultaneously sexual and political, and for the ancient Greeks it was religious too. Like Judith's story, it functions on all three levels as a powerful cultural myth. The difference is that the Oedipal story mythologizes Western culture's central convictions about family, sex and power; whereas Judith's deploys them in order ultimately to contest them.

Retellings of familiar myths function within a culture ritually to reaffirm the beliefs and collective aspirations fundamental to that culture. For that reason there is a contiguity between the fundamental stories of patriarchy in Greek myth and in the Bible. The version of the Oedipal myth which appears in the Bible is the story of David, Judith's male counterpart as head-taker of Israel's enemy.

By virtue of his gender, however, David offers a mythic pattern much less challenging than Judith's. Like Oedipus, he usurps the place of the Father in order to assume his patriarchal role. In the Freudian analysis, the rebellious Oedipus represents the attainment of sexual identity, as the son contests

masculinity with his model, his father. He rebels against the patriarch only to
become him. Much the same mythic plot underlies David's story, symbolizing
its religious meaning. For David becomes the proxy son of Saul, by God's direction and increasingly against the king's will, until they confront each other as
king and rebel. Unlike Oedipus, when given the opportunity to kill Saul and
take his throne, David resists it: but that is because God has legitimated Saul as
king, and God alone will confer the throne on his heir. That is, whilst father and
son are bitter enemies and rivals for power in Oedipal manner, in the Judaic
tradition only God will kill the father so that the son can take his place, absolv-
ing David of personal guilt. Instead, the symbolic act of parricide is displaced
into the episode where the boy David slays the giant Goliath, representative of
a patriarchy that is God's enemy. In the same way, Judith as a rebellious daughter, or Electra figure, temporarily ousts the patriarchal elders of Israel, taking
the fate of the city upon herself, but the patriarch whom she actually kills is their
tyrannical enemy.

If David is the biblical Oedipus, Judith is his sister, the rebellious daughter
within the mythic system. It is for this reason that Judith and David share the
same iconography as audacious head-takers, grasping human authority by the
hair. In art they often form a male/female pairing, as in Michelangelo's ceiling
for the Sistine Chapel. And, as in Caravaggio's versions of David, both protagonists shared not only the iconography of the head's display to the viewer,
but also the stylistic conventions that would, for instance, habitually enlarge the
severed head of Holofernes in order to match the gigantic head of Goliath in
paintings of David. In both cases, the head's enlargement symbolized the
aggrandizement, the sin of hubris, that God's agent had punished. In the
reverse direction, Judith's iconography also influenced David's, so that the boy
hero was often portrayed in the act of severing the giant's head from his body
with Goliath's own massive sword, appropriating the phallic symbol of power.
In both iconographies, these motifs identified God's agents as tyrannicides, performing revenge upon an image of the cruelly autocratic Father.

The key difference between Judith and David is that, as a male, David is destined finally to be crowned with the power of the Father, completing the circle.
Judith's story does not culminate in her taking the patriarch's place as ruler, but
it would be mistaken to see this merely as the disadvantage of the female gender.
Of course it is that, but it is also why Judith's myth is peculiarly powerful. For
in her story the rebel is not finally absorbed into the political and familial system
he had once challenged, as David and Oedipus are. On the contrary, Judith
cannot be adopted into the system she opposed, because she cannot simply step
into the place of the man she killed. She cannot thus be compromised, and
power cannot corrupt her. Her revolt does not bring her either power or
material reward, and its altruism means that the rebel is never bought off, the
image of revolution never mitigated. Ironically, it is precisely because Judith

cannot achieve David's political eminence that her rebellious image is incapable of assimilation to the plot of patriarchy.

On both political and personal levels, the myth of Judith is counter-cultural because it is unreceptive to the pattern whereby society absorbs and placates its rebels. For this reason it is a radical and feminist alternative to the Oedipal myth, and to all that it signifies about the ordering of Western culture. Consequently, the often strange story of how Judith's myth has been used, in the past and in the present, forms an alternative history of our attitudes to sex, politics and power.

3

Her Virtue Was Vice
Christian Allegory and the Selling of Sex

Central to Judith's story are two difficult questions: Can a homicide be a good woman? Can a chaste woman be a seducer? The ambiguity of Judith's icon as the Good Bad Woman became clear early in European history, but its most striking manifestation emerged in the fifteenth century and flourished for the two hundred years of the Renaissance. In early medieval times Judith had begun a long reign as an image of central human virtues, of ideals which have in various forms endured throughout Western history.[1] Professing to teach human beings how best to live – according to Christian principles – the Virtues were codified in the emblems of iconography. This official, decorative, idealized Judith was nevertheless shadowed by a more secretive yet very popular existence in the subcultures of Western life even in the Middle Ages. Her double life was paradoxical in the extreme, since she was both a primary image of Virtue and a magnetic sign of Vice.

Can a cultural icon be both at the same time? What happens to a cultural myth when it becomes something we use to image others, or ourselves to ourselves; to label our actions and impulses, to explain ourselves to others, or most of all to sell something on the stock exchange of human relationships? What Judith's example shows is that, in exploiting cultural myths to our own ends, we are past masters at having our cake and eating it.

How to Be Good

In the early Middle Ages a massively influential Christian epic, Prudentius's *Psychomachia* (AD 405), established Judith's crucial role in the Christian imagery of human virtues.[2] It was crucial not only because she here became an image of fundamental Christian principles, but because – uniquely – she represented so many of them. In Prudentius's allegory her icon functions on several levels, as an image of the Virtues Chastity, Temperance, Justice, Fortitude, Wisdom and Humility. There were reasons why this spectrum of Christian ideals was compounded into Judith's form, but I have explained them elsewhere and they need not detain us here. What is important about Prudentius's multi-faceted Judith is that she summed up in a single figure the moral point that, whilst each of the Christian Virtues was intrinsically ideal and believers had to aspire to them all individually, ultimately the Christian Virtues were interdependent. The whole Christian person, that is, would be just if temperate and strong, and strong if just, and so on. A psychomachia is an allegorical representation of conflicting impulses in a single human personality. *Psychomachia* was an allegory of how they might be harmonized: of how to live well.

Prudentius's allegory begat the mass of paintings, statues, manuscript illustrations, tapestries and literary works that in the Middle Ages and the Renaissance memorialized Judith as these Virtues. Thus in the Italian *quattro-cento* Botticelli's *Fortitude* is essentially the same figure (and takes the same artist's model) as his *Judith*. Similarly, a fifteenth-century English work of polit-ical theory, *De Regimine*, instructed kings in how to rule virtuously, by evoking Judith as its role-model for Justice and Achior for Truth.[3] Like Prudentius's allegory, it acknowledged that in a Christian world-view there can be no bound-ary between the personal and political worlds that human beings inhabit.

De Regimine stressed that in order to be a good (that is, both beneficent and effectual) ruler, a king must first be a good man. An unjust man could not rule justly; a lecherous man could not administer laws that punished others for their sins; an intemperate man could not sit in judgement. The public virtue Justice and the private virtue 'righteousness' were one and the same, and neither could subsist without the other. Whether for a peasant or for a king, then, a Christian personality was ideally a seamless garment of virtues.

Judith's embodiment of the link between public and personal integrity was invoked by a play sometimes attributed to Shakespeare, *The Reign of King Edward the Third* (1596). Besotted with the Countess of Salisbury, a married woman, Edward III instructs his lackey Lodwick to write seductive verses on his behalf, but is horrified by the result. Lodwick's verses salute her as 'fair and chaste . . . / More bold in constancy . . . than Judith', complimenting both her beauty and her virtue as exceeding the biblical siren's. However, the Virtue of Chastity represented by Judith's sword is precisely what stands between the king and what he wants. Infuriated by this self-defeating compliment, he rants: 'O monstrous line! Put in the next a sword, / And I shall woo her to cut off my head' (II.i.167–71). The problem with Judith in seductive games like these is that she was indeed a splendid way of complimenting beauty, but also a reminder of Christian morality. She personified both the pulchritude that pro-voked Vice and the Virtue that defeated it.

In this case, Edward's offence is not merely the double adultery which he craves, but his traducement of the very laws that as a king he is obligated to enforce: 'violating marriage('s) sacred law' makes him a 'corrupted judge'

(II.i.260; II.ii.164). Similarly, the Countess's threat to kill herself reproduces the politics of Lucretia's suicide. As for *De Regimine* too, Justice is the Virtue represented by Judith (and the Countess, as her replicant) and is the central attribute of a good king. Thus the Countess accuses Edward of treason against kingship itself. On trial in this strand of the play is the personal integrity that guarantees a king's fitness for his public authority.

In refusing to recognize a distinction between personal and public virtues, *De Regimine* was highly traditional in its medieval Christian approach to the problems of political states. The most striking thing about it, I suggest, is that its refusal to recognise a boundary between personal lives and politics foreshadows the modern feminist tenet that 'the personal is the political'. For both philosophies, to erect a mental wall between the personal and public worlds is to evade one's responsibilities: to oneself, to other individuals, and hence to the mass of others whose lives are our public milieu. We will see much more of Judith's political faces in later chapters, but it is in Renaissance subcultures that her role in personal lives was at its most fascinating. As we shall see, the most personal things in life were here political too, and social and economic. Judith's role was not merely as the seamless garment of our ideal image, but a travelling icon of how we move through the various milieux that make up our lives, taking our myths with us.

Seductive Virtue

Like the celebrated courtesans of Renaissance Venice, Judith contradicts one of the cherished stereotypes of our culture, that beauty and brains do not go together. The most celebrated Venetian courtesans were renowned for their intelligence, cultivation and good taste, qualities that made them exceptional companions outside the bedchamber as well as within it. And whilst it might seem that they had little in common with the chaste heroine, they and their customers thought otherwise. Judith's erotic history shines a searching light on Renaissance sexual habits and fantasies, from royal bedroom to whorehouse.

In order that the apocryphal heroine could credibly dazzle and deceive the Assyrian general, she was granted both irresistible physical and exceptional intellectual attributes (11:21). Her medieval descendants had largely personified the intellectual and moral virtues. But one of her most ubiquitous Renaissance incarnations emphasized, by contrast, her allure and sensuality. Erotica featuring Judith played a complex and provocative role in sexual relations, both of the romantic and of the mercenary variety: overt and covert sexual messages were relayed through her representations.

There is something challenging to the normal perception of Christianity in the notion that the Creator actually set out to make a woman who was every man's wet dream. If the pagan goddess Venus and her human lovers offered a classical mythic fantasy of what intercourse with a goddess might be like, Judith's allure tantalized (in so far as monotheism allowed) with something similar, a divinely perfected sensuality. Renaissance paintings of Judith face us, in fact, with an immediate interpretative problem: are they pious representations of a cardinal virtue and/or sacred heroism, or are they, on the contrary, portraits of vice?

The ambiguity of the sacred heroine-cum-*femme fatale* is never more pronounced than in Renaissance portraiture. The rise of the individualized portrait likeness, increasingly suggestive of the sitter's personality, nevertheless did not spell the end of allegory and moralization. It was common to depict the subject in masquerade, as either a biblical or a classical personage, and also to place portraits of contemporary individuals within illustrations of biblical scenes.[4] Generally, of course, the individuals concerned wished to be portrayed as either exceptionally virtuous or legendarily beautiful characters. Judith was, gratifyingly, both. For instance, Da Sole's painting of Judith is a portrait of a contemporary woman, who in the guise of the biblical heroine is idealistically represented to the spectator. To wish to be represented as virtuous – especially, in a woman's case, as chaste – was a reflex of the prevailing, highly constrictive notion of women's virtue, that harped obsessively upon their sexual continence.

Of course, Judith was not the only biblical heroine whose personation would imply the sitter's virtue. On the other hand, she was unique in that she could encode a paradoxical characterization of the sitter, simultaneously complimentary and insulting to her. For example, Cristoforo Allori's Judith is a portrait of his mistress, the maid is modelled on her mother and Holofernes' head a self-portrait of the artist.[5] These personations wittily, if bitterly, record what Allori regarded as his mistress's heartless abandonment of him, suggesting that she is as pitiless as the homicidal heroine. At the same time, though, her appearance as Judith testifies to the mistress's fatal attraction, that she remains irresistibly desirable to the artist despite her cruelty.

Moreover, the Judith-mistress becomes paradigmatic, representing a universal and disturbing truth about sexual allure of this magnitude. It exerts absolute power over the desirer, independent of the woman's character and the man's own volition. In this context Judith personifies the fundamental nature of overpowering sexual desire, its tyranny over those human faculties, rational and ethical, that might oppose it, yet remain helpless before its tide. She personifies passion writ large as *amour fou*. In suggesting the mortal combat between will and desire, her ambiguity signifies the entrapment of human beings in their sexuality: their enthralment to the body.

Thus, in the apocryphal story, as we saw, Holofernes might be seen as embodying the erotic death-wish, the body willing its own destruction in the desperate search for gratification of its need. In painting, Holofernes's severed head, in the heavily sexualized context of the mistress's portrait, symbolizes that need

and the ultimate price exacted for it. In fact, of course, the heaviness of the price
– that this is a love the force of which is confirmed by its paying that price – is
itself an erotic idea. Legends of the great lovers usually end, fulfillingly, in that
dying for love, *Liebestod*, that implicitly asserts that love is everything.

Judith, then, is paramount amongst fatal women because, whilst she personifies the tyranny of desire, Holofernes' head images the way in which that desire
exerts itself, against reason and authority. Holofernes' political despotism and
hubris become, in his abasement, testaments to the brutal levelling exercised
upon us by a passion that is ours, yet that we do not in any sense own or control.
Judith herself images the force of conscious will (that which can plan, entrap,
deceive and kill) simultaneously as she evokes overpowering desire. The fact
that the Book of Judith portrays its heroine as an unattainable object of desire
underscores this frustration; which is why the modern American poet John
Crowe Ransom's 'Judith' makes her the embodiment of the impossibility of satisfying desires. Sexuality and its negation, desire and will are in permanent conflict within the ambivalent depiction of an erotic Judith, a conflict itself sexually
intense and provocative.

These multiple erotic motifs underlie a gnomic couplet 'Upon Judith' by the
English Cavalier poet Robert Herrick. Like other Renaissance lover-lyricists in
the bawdy Cavalier mode, he tended to personate his (probably fictitious) mistresses under classical names. But the unique exception to this in his poetry is
his Judith, so named to indicate her wiles and guile. Whilst implying her infidelity to him, the forename equally reflects his reluctant, yet inescapable, bitter
fascination with her. Both Herrick's and Allori's Judiths flatly contradict the
biblical figure's iconography as a Virtue. As Temperance, Donatello's Judith
had asserted precisely those rational, spiritual and moralized qualities which
were supposed to enable the righteous to resist their own basic urges.[6] In that
iconographic tradition Judith personified the impressive triumphalism of rigid
resolve against Vice; in the erotic tradition she symbolized the irresistible
temptation exerted by Vice. (Of course, Christian tradition has always regarded
sexuality as the paramount vice.) Whilst symbolizing what transcended the
flesh, she also embodied it in its most imperiously demanding form.

Having It Both Ways

For some Renaissance patrons of art, biblical scenes of the more torrid variety
– in which the Old Testament is rich – afforded pious pretexts for the possession and display of what was, essentially, expensive erotica. Some were displayed in bedrooms, like the titillating scene hung on the back wall of a
roistering youth's bedroom in one of Jan Steen's depictions of contemporary
life. So pronounced was this line in biblical decor that, during the Counter-
Reformation, the Council of Trent officially denounced lewd images of sacred

subjects.[7] Neither the Church nor the market was under any illusion about the real function of such artworks. Like many depictions of Bathsheba and Susannah (in which voyeurism was itself the subject), some representations of Judith were Renaissance variations of the pin-up.

With their slashed and pinked garments, bondage-style accessories and knuckle-duster gloves, the slyly impudent Judiths of Cranach are at the relatively decorous end of this spectrum. But Quentin Metsys's Judith, her transparent shift teasingly emphasizing her semi-nudity, is emblazoned as a *femme fatale* by the flaming red of her cloak, the colour of passion and blood. Her eagerness to display her trophy seems to surprise even her maid, who is waiting to package it for transport. As so often, the servant's expression is a comment on her mistress's character: here, in surprised awe of the sexual power wielded by one of her own sex, a power she herself does not possess. That juxtaposition is a method of emphasizing the exceptional sensuality of Judith herself. Divesting the painting of piety, it establishes the tone of the pin-up.

Another method, achieving the same end, was actually to convert Judith into a Bathsheba, the Bible's striptease artist and concubine, or Susannah, its other bathing beauty. Jan van Eyck's *Judith at her Toilette* is almost unique in conflating two events in the story, her toilette before leaving Bethulia and her bathing in the camp, in this determined effort to convert the modest widow to fullfrontal nudity. Like other images of bathing beauties, this painting was probably destined for a luxury bathroom.[8] In general, bathrooms were associated with illicit and unbridled sexual activity, especially because of the European habit of mixed-sex bathing, and the installation of bathrooms in brothels.[9] Since Van Eyck's was a royal commission, the painting was intended either for the apartment of a male member of the ducal family or for a mistress's suite at the Burgundian court. Like dimmed lighting, it was a mood-enhancer.

The artists most lucratively engaged in the production of Judithic erotica were the Metsyses, Netherlanders for whom biblical pornography was a family business. Like his images of Bathsheba, Jan Metsys's *Judith* approximates a centrefold nude, evidently *deshabillée* from a pre-homicide heavy petting session with Holofernes. (The specious religious gloss is provided by the crescent moon, signifying the Islamic enemy.) Her snidely satisfied expression is deliberately suggestive of the post-coital – but it is also intended, not so much to represent the horrible perfidy of womankind towards the defenceless male, but actually to appeal to that aspect of male sexuality that is aroused by fantasies of cruelty. In pornography of all times, that fantasy clearly draws the line between eroticism and mundane life, since the pleasure of imaginary domination often appeals even to those men who would most fear it when encountered in actual women. Hence the allure of the snide *femme fatale*, an image compounded of misogyny and adoration, which allows those who most dislike women nevertheless to project their own sexuality onto them, without compromising that fundamental loathing. In that light, the attitude that 'she's a bitch and I love her' is supremely logical. The erotic Renaissance Judith is one of those bitches, with the added ingredient of supernatural allure, which makes her a witch as well. Her image merges attraction and aggression, love and hate, atavistic antagonism and irrational desire, what is subliminal and what is fundamental: a classic recipe for sexual extremism demanded by the most potent erotica.

Not least, this strand of Judithic erotica was so widespread and popular – there are countless examples still extant – because it pictorialized the compelling fantasy that, if one's going to die for it, the sexual encounter must have been truly outstanding. The scale of the punishment implicitly suggests the magnitude of the pleasure involved. Male spectators of erotic Judiths were expected to empathize with the idea that Holofernes had had a very good time before he paid his dues.

Familiarity with the biblical story enhanced the lubricious potential of the image. The strongly sado-masochistic ingredients in Judithic erotica were the sexual analogue of the story's theme of divine punishment. A religious ambience actually underwrote the erotics of the image, for the more pious a culture, the more antinomian excitement may be generated within it by the lurid subtexts of religious imagery. (As T.S. Eliot said, blasphemy is a religious impulse.) For the Renaissance, irreverence and transgression against the most absolute of official authorities intensified the erotics of biblical pornography. The pious pretext for possessing it, and its often open display in the stateliest of function-rooms, were themselves piquant enhancements of bawdy irreverence: in effect, the sanctimonious display of one's enjoyable vices. If the Metsyses' Judiths were impudent, their owners were enjoying their own impudence too.

There were, however, more oblique, witty and sophisticated ways of eroticizing Judith than the Metsyses' centrefolds. Her iconography could be bent to subtle ends, visual equivalents of the polite yet bawdy *préciosité* of Renaissance erotic poems, such as Shakespeare's *Venus and Adonis*. This was a culture that delighted in the clever manipulation of iconography to diverse ends, not least sexual. In the iconography of the Nine Worthies – the pre-eminent warrior leaders in classical and Christian lore – David and Judas Maccabeus were often selected as Old Testament counterparts to such classical heroes as Hercules, possessor of superhuman strength. Similarly, Judith, Deborah and Esther were represented as the Three Worthy Jewesses in the alternative scheme of female Worthies, which became established in the Renaissance.[10] Judith herself was an apt female complement to Hercules, a warrior who, like her, was strongly associated with the cardinal virtue of Temperance. This explains why, in a panel painting that has puzzled interpreters, the Master of the Mansi-Magdalen paired Judith with the infant Hercules. Although a 'weak woman', Judith had displayed exemplary fortitude; although a mere boy, Hercules had strangled a poisonous snake. (Notice the implicit relation, in both cases – woman and child

– of fortitude (defensive) with violence (offensive). That is, *before* eros and thanatos there may be also eros and punishment.) The nudity of both figures falls within that iconographic tradition that suggests both classical heroism and the Christian *nuda veritas*, the fearless self-display of Truth to our scrutiny. The panel is in many ways a paradigmatic example of the Renaissance's fusion of the classical with the Christian. It directs towards the moral that the virtue Fortitude is the force that makes the virtue Temperance capable of controlling and defeating vice. One could sum up the message here as 'the force of temperance', personified in Worthies of both genders.

However, underlying this unexceptionate moral is another, quite contrary subtext for sophisticated spectators of the panel. Judith and the boy Hercules are represented in a way more conventionally applied to Venus and her son Cupid. In Cranach's multiple versions of this topos, the interplay between the naked goddess and the infant god of love provides a feast of *outré* sexual implications (including, of course, a teasing suggestion of incestuous attraction between them). The panel's reminiscence of this convention appropriates Judith to the sexual fantasia associated with her mythic antitype, Oedipus. On the erotic plane, the attributes of iconic virtue – her detumescent sword and Hercules' crested serpent – are variations on the phallic: jokingly inverted allusions to precocious virility, priapism, impotence and sexual exhaustion.

This was precisely the kind of irreverent, cod-moralistic bawdiness that appealed to the sophisticated palate of Renaissance courtiers. Subtextually, the panel suggests that, despite what po-faced moralizers say, the virtues of temperance and continence are distinctly overrated, and that the most gratifying form of 'fortitude' for any red-blooded male would be exceptional virility. This is the piquant subtext of the infant Hercules' strength, a randiness and performance capability beyond his tender years. Similarly, Judith's detumescent phallic object implies that this is a sexual superwoman who would exhaust the most virile of men – a twist on the usual castratory, voracious implications of her image. In these ways Judith's traditional emblematization of chastity and self-restraint is gleefully attached to an inverted moral, contradicting the panel's overt message by recommending satyriasis and nyphomania. Here as elsewhere, Judith's special place in Renaissance erotica was owing to her unique potential for permitting artist and spectator to have it both ways, or all ways.

Vanity Thy Name Is Man

Her appeal to the sexual fantasies of the Renaissance did not reside solely in the fact that her moral iconography could be turned to amusingly immoral purposes. For depictions of Judith could also turn the tables on the theme of the dominant woman, defusing her feminist potential. Such paintings could exploit standard generic tropes which allowed artists to transform Judith's image of woman triumphant into one that surrendered the moral and sexual high ground to the male.[11] This was doubly ironic, in that the sexual re-empowering of the male in such depictions ran counter to the original Holofernes' metaphoric impotence and castration.

One most unusual generic troping of her acteme confines itself to masculine reappropriation of only the moral high ground. Giogio Vasari's Judith is a fashionable classicized heroine. But the artistic genre evoked by Vasari's painting subverts this apparent heroization of Judith. The popular 'May/September' genre provided satirical portraits of lovers grotesquely mismatched in age. In most of these there is a clear implication that the younger partner is motivated by love of money, not wrinkles, and that the older partner is a fond fool. Received wisdom about these Renaissance toyboys and trophy bimbos suggested that their avarice and infidelity were only to be expected. Exceptionally, Vasari's Holofernes is white-haired; his mercenary young partner is a Judith tutored in duplicity by a calculating matron, the servant's incarnation here. (In fact she so much resembles Judith that she is clearly intended to be her mother. It was often supposed that grasping mothers pandered their beautiful daughters.) This May/Judith goes one better than adultery behind her ageing partner's back, murdering the old man for his fortune. This is a cynically contemporary story. The subject remains 'women on top', but the positive antique spin on this is counterweighed by the negative implication of the painting's modernizing generic conventions. Holofernes becomes an instance of the folly to which ageing men are prone when they dote on young women who are devoted to the main chance.

The moralistic genre in which Judith appears much more commonly is the *Vanitas*, the admonition to women against the sin of self-love. Like Bathsheba and Susannah, whose toilette at the bath lent itself to this theme, in such works Judith is portrayed as appreciating or enhancing her own beauty at the dressing-table. (Their pretexts are Judith's deliberate self-adornment to attract Holofernes and her daily ritual bath in his camp, in 10:3ff. and 12:7.) This perverse adaptation of Judith's toilette transforms the modest, self-abnegating, hairshirt-wearing widow into an instance of what was supposedly women's invariable weakness, vanity being an instance of their reputed triviality of mind. This sub-genre of Judithic Vanities has caused a good deal of confusion amongst art historians. Thus Paris Bordon's Judith has been pedantically renamed 'Venetian Woman at her Toilette'.[12] Certainly the painting is of a Venetian woman, but it is also, and no less, a Judith. Like Vasari's, such versions of the theme crucially re-orient its meaning, layering a contemporary over a biblical subject. In fact, there are few more striking instances of misogyny in action than this cheeky inversion of the modest heroine into a personification of women's 'frailty'.

Nevertheless, despite the moralism implied by a Vanity these version of

Judith could be as ambivalently bawdy as the Mansi-Magdalen panel and might perform a function quite contrary to their avowed purpose. A warning against narcissism is not by any means the unambiguous message of such versions. For instance, an expensive, intricately carved wooden handmirror, backed by a depiction of Judith, announces itself as a pious reminder to the woman who uses it that she is mortal and will age, and thus must avoid the sin of vanity, which otherwise the mirror might encourage. However, selecting Judith – the siren of irresistible charms – as the Vanity emblem is a sly ruse. It encourages the woman to identify herself with that overpowering allure, gives her an ideal of beauty to which to aspire, whilst simultaneously seeming to discourage precisely that aspiration. This was the product of a craftsman who understood perfectly that one does not get far with wealthy customers by instructing them to repudiate vanity, luxury and expense. The mirror is a luxury commodity which, carrying its pious but ambivalent message, belies its own luxury and indeed its own function. The purchaser acquired something that confirmed that she used a mirror whilst being virtuous enough to despise it.

Vanity paintings often juxtaposed the beautiful young protagonist with an aged crone, her servant or perhaps her mother, whose wrinkled visage implicitely suggested what the youthful beauty would come to in the end.[13] The crone embodied a *memento mori*, the immanence of death. Although Bordon's painting does not use this motif, it is very common in representations of Judith and her maid, even in those that are not Vanities. The grotesque crone/maid behind Judith in Bernardo Strozzi's painting could well be the heroine's face in advanced age, and the ugly mortality written on her face links the heroine's own ultimate dissolution to the murder she has just performed. One function performed by many representations of Judith is to pictorialize the horror of mortality. Jan de Bray's composition thus juxtaposes the virile young cavalier, Holofernes, with the mature charms of his murderess and the tender age of her attendant: a parody of a nuclear family, the agent of human generation, as well as a kind of 'Three Ages' of humankind. Such subliminal motifs universalize Holofernes' death, subtly suggesting that we sympathize with his mortal vulnerability.

This is one of the emotive reinforcements that can make a male spectator's view of a Vanity Judith a consoling and indeed self-affirming experience. Vanities at once extol and reproach the beauties they portray. In a patriarchal society, sexual attraction was usually women's sole means of power and advancement, and the one that they are generally acknowledged to possess naturally and, as it were, of right. What the Vanity genre was invented for was to suggest that this power over men was, if undeniable, at least transitory. More, the genre condemned this power as morally culpable. And most satisfying of all, it displayed the woman's charms to the appreciative viewer (like the voyeuristic elders in the Susannah versions), whilst offloading the moral dubiety of this voyeurism onto the object of desire itself. It was all her fault, and she would be punished for it.

Modern love poetry can imitate this phenomenon. J.M. Synge's poem 'Queens' compares his beloved to legendary 'Queens acquainted in learned sin' and 'Judith of Scripture', but since all are dead she for the nonce reigns as supreme ruler of love's kingdom.[14] The sting in the tail is that, of course, one day she too will lose her looks and pass away, and the poet's tribute is conditionalized by that: he resents a sexual power from which one day he will be freed. Resentment is just as strong an emotion here as desire, indeed characterizes it. There is a nasty little misogynist thought curled at the heart of the Vanity moral: that if beautiful women can torment men, Father Time will wreak vengeance on them in the end. The more beautiful they are (and that is why they are Vanity protagonists), the more they will suffer when age blasts them. Equally, though, a female spectator of a Vanity might absorb the lesson that, if tormenting men is her bent, she should get it done before old age sets in: make hay while the sun shines. That potential, subversive message for women means that even the Vanity Judith could not be so easily turned to anti-female purposes as the genre would seem to suggest.

Another subgenre of the Christian Vanity actually condemned the male rather than the female. According to the Apocrypha, Judith tore down Holofernes' canopy, symbol of his worldly pride, and his armour was presented to her, the customary donation of trophies to the victor, as if this had been a military overthrow (16:19). In many representations of her acteme Holofernes' armour is shown hung up within his tent. In the presence of Judith's triumph this feature becomes moralized as the display of the defeated general's armour: it is an ironic foreshadowing of Judith's formal triumphal festivity if Jerusalem. In the Vanity tradition, a still life of discarded armour was an emblem of the fall of Pride, and this motif was imported into Grammatica's version of Judith in Holofernes' tent, where she treads upon his fallen armour (fig. ?). This was one way of reminding the spectator that Judith's story was an instance of the humbling of the mighty by the meek, showing the futility of earthly glory. For men, of course, military acclaim was the traditional route to that glory, so that Holofernes' fall became an instance of a nemesis peculiar to the male sex.

In counterpoint to Holofernes's warlike accoutrements, Judith's charms are the traditional weapons of the female sex. Thus Du Bartas' epic *La Judit* (1574) depicts her toilette as a feminine equivalent to the Homeric epic's ritual arming of the warrior before battle. In such compositions as Grammatica's, the antagonists and their attributes suggest the symmetry in the battle of the sexes, and moralize it. There is, certainly, something realistic and reductive in the way this moralization depends upon a very pragmatic view of the relations between men and women. Such versions of Judith and Holofernes suggest that, if all the sublimated human aspirations to glory, power and idealized beauty are stripped away, this is what life comes down to: whose weapons are most effective, who wins these secret pitched battles in bedrooms. Judith paintings of this kind are about as cynical as pious moralism can ever be, and all the better for it. They are very much more convincing renditions of the biblical heroine than those that attempt to portray her as saintly and ethereal, for this tough heroine belongs in a world more complex and brutal than hagiography would suggest. Grammatica's coarse peasant maid in her sturdy boots is, again, a commentary on her mistress, suggesting that this is a heroine of the real world, not story-books.

Browsing in a Bordello

And indeed in the real world, someone will always want to make money out of unique commodities such as Judith. Artists who exploited her polyvalent significance were maximizing that commodity-potential; similarly, the fact that Judith's was a brand-image for exceptional sexual allure did not escape the professionals. Courtesans and prostitutes, at both ends of the sexual market, appropriated her image as a woman (almost) beyond price. For these commercial enterprises – both the brothel and the grander, self-employed courtesan – Judith was no more and no less than an advertising gimmick.

Even the famed mistress of the Italian magnate d'Este, the celebrated Laura da Dianti, chose to have herself painted as Judith. (The subject is too mature to be Salome, even though, as so often happens, the iconography employed in the painting is a conflation.) This self-presentation encodes not only the sexual charisma of the original, which Dianti is seen to reincarnate. It also deliberately emphasizes Dianti's wealth and social distinction by means of the rich clothes and furnishings in the portrait, and these motifs are reinforced by the prosperity and prominence that the Apocrypha had attributed to the original. Dianti does not wish to be mistaken for any run-of-the-mill courtesan, even if she wishes her sexual achievements to be implied: and this careful balancing act is what inspires her haughty, restrained pose. This is not a sales pitch but a public image, and therefore the more painstaking about the way in which it evokes the biblical prototype.

Courtesans of lower status were less reluctant to suggest that their Judithic allure was more hoydenish than the original. Even the rich, famed and cultivated courtesans of Venice – the Bangkok of the Renaissance[15] – needed to advertise themselves with a more crudely commercial intent. Thus Francesco Guardi's 'A Woman of Venice' (which was as much as to say, a courtesan) is significantly based upon Johann Liss's influential version of Judith. Liss and other Northern artists such as the Metsys brothers had a lucrative trade supplying decor for the courtesan's business, and many Judiths of this stamp were produced specifically for the Venetian market.

Yet even the courtesans' Judithic personations sometimes posited moralistic pretexts, which may at first seem puzzling in the circumstances. The Vanity toilette scene was particularly apt to courtesanal portraiture, since it extolled the subject's exceptional charms, and Bordon's 'Judith/Venetian Woman' is such a portrait. Her appearance reproduces the ideal codes of beauty promulgated by Italian artistic treatises, which especially emphasized crinkly blonde tresses.[16] The hair-teasing gesture that frequently appears in such toilette scenes (such as those by Titian) is very much a courtesan's trademark, suggesting a provocative autoeroticism.

As courtesanal portrait, the Vanity becomes not simply a compliment to her, but a generic technique for presenting her wares to the potential client. The intended spectator is no longer the run-of-the-mill voyeur at whom decorative soft pornography was aimed, but the customer in a sexual transaction. Pornography need not sell anything but the image, to be enjoyed either solo or à deux, which was the function of most biblical erotica; whereas these Judiths (as we shall see) were intended literally to sell the woman.

This is achieved by dovetailing several visual messages. The *memento mori* central to the official Vanity's message is, in fact, equally central to the *carpe diem* tradition. The first urges us to remember our mortality in order to despise the things of the flesh, whereas the second urges us to enjoy the things of the flesh before our mortality overtakes us. Both the Christian ascetic and the pagan sensual propositions spin off the same theme, the transience of youth and beauty. The courtesanal Vanity-Judith diverts the moral to an irreverently immoral purpose, parodic and witty, as classic advertising so often is.

In this transaction Holofernes' role as 'the client' exploited his Christian vice-role as Lust. (Thus in Marston's play *The Dutch Courtesan* (1605), a character named Holifernes Reinscure combines the eponymous first name with a surname that is slang for 'randiness requiring urgent treatment'.) Centred on the amusingly irreverent identification of prostitution with sacred heroine, this portrait genre exploits commercially the aphrodisiac potential of being tempted into exuberant transgression. At the same time, though, its parody of the Christian genre is also subtly functional. Like the male voyeur, who enjoys a double pleasure in the beauty and the feminine 'inferiority' of the Vanity woman, the spectator of the courtesanal toilette scene could feel both morally and sexually superior to that which seduced him. Insofar as this beauty was being offered to him for consumption it was deferent to him, inferior; insofar as it was the transient Vanity it was not threatening to him; insofar as this genre typed women as inferior and material it typed them as consumables *intended* for his pleasure; insofar as it implicitly condemned women, it subliminally transferred the potential squalor of the sexual transaction to the woman's account, not his. All in all, this was a commercial genre brilliantly aligned to the psychosexual needs of the client.

It was also cannily directed towards making him willing to pay dearly for the product. One of the functions of a toilette scene was to persuade him that he was dealing with the luxury end of the market. For this the expensive cosmetics and accessories of the toilette table, and the labour-intensive activity implied by them, provide a visual code. It announces that (a) all this is being done for his sake, and (b) it will cost him. For this purpose even the negro maid who appears so often in Venetian Vanities was a personification of expense, since negro servants were pricey, fashionable and desirable accessories for anyone with aspirations to stylishness in Venice. In Veronese's portrait of a courtesan-Judith, her black servant is performing much the same function as her jewels and her expensive clothes, styling her mistress as a luxury commodity. (This is a particularly entertaining variation on the traditional use of the maid as a commentary on Judith herself.)

Like Judith, the subtext of these portraits suggests, this courtesan is a heroine of the bedchamber. To this end traditional Judithic attributes are diverted to tease the viewer. The pearls worn by Veronese's Judith, for instance, would in a pious context signify chaste purity; they could also signify the tears of remorse and compassion, no doubt a great comfort to male spectators identifying with Holofernes. In the house of a courtesan – and bearing in mind here the peculiar positioning of Holofernes's head – the pearls suggest rather that she can be relied upon to 'take pity' on a lover, that is, give him what he wants.

More generally, a diverse range of decorative items made use of Judith to promote the appropriate ambience of seduction. Majolica, for instance, expensive ceramics often used for decorative purposes, was decorated with biblical scenes, and representations of Judith are common. Many very expensive examples depict Judith's acteme, superbly rendered by craftsmen of repute, sometimes as a Christian Virtue and sometimes as a female conspiracy against the male.[17] Majolica was to be found in any Italian establishment, respectable or otherwise, that aspired to civilized taste. That aspiration was just as potent amongst courtesans of various classes. (One scurrilous Italian biography of a courtesan specifies that when she lost her looks and hence her trade, she had to sell off her majolica collection too. This was the Vanity model couched in economic terms.) Although majolica items might be displayed anywhere within the household, one of their functions was as bric-à-brac for the deep shelves formed by the headboards of fine beds. This was a particularly suitable place, of course, for erotica, and some of the more explicit majolica versions of Judith must have been intended for bedrooms and, indeed, beds. These were mood-enhancers, which could also perform on occasion as eroticized vessels for food and wine. To some degree, however, the courtesan's majolica collection was also an investment, a hedge against impoverishment: such decorative items were diversely functional and economical. The commodification of Judith for the business of sex was impressively extensive and creative.

Shopping for Sex

Courtesanal portraits personating the sensual Judith were very much the preserve of the self-employed, who could afford to hire better artists. Much more
widespread were cheaper versions of the same portraiture, characterizing an
individual prostitute in a brothel and intended to hang within a series of portraits designed to suggest the specific appeal of each of its employees. The ante-
rooms of better brothels were, in effect, miniature galleries, displaying the
beauties available on the premises. The frontispiece to Crispijn de Passe's directory of European prostitutes, one of the vade-mecums used by sex tourists on
the Continent, illustrates the customer's privilege of browsing through precisely such a directory, seated comfortably in the gallery of beauties; the directory and the gallery are complementary versions of the same erotic catalogue.
They are also multi-purpose, being catalogues ('all of our wares are at your
command, dishes to suit every palate'), advertisements, teasers and aperitifs to
the main course.[18]

In Passe's directory, each portrait is accompanied by verses describing the
lady's peculiarities and individual talents. Portraits in bordello galleries
achieved the same end by presenting their subjects in a masquerade which
carried the appropriate implications. (Hence the bawdy subtext of the Judith in
Giovanni Battista Guarini's poem 'La Galleria'.) Judith's implications in this
role are clear, since they were not dissimilar from those suggested by Cranach's
Judiths. The customary accessories, heavy gold neck-chains and the like, when
associated with Judith's sword, sufficiently implied the character of a dominatrix. Courtesanal portraits of Judith suggest that this particular lady of the night
is especially skilled in sado-masochistic techniques. Baglione's turbulent, bare-
breasted Judith, flanked at the left by the hugely phallicized limbs of
Holofernes, looks like a specialist in rough sex.

In these bordello versions of Judith, her maid is again transmogrified,
becoming the bawd, procuress or brothel madam who attends a prostitute. In
Pordenone's version, a youthful incarnation of the bawd invitingly raises the
curtain on the bed behind Judith, a courtesan who (as was customary) displays
herself to potential clients at a window or on a balcony. Filling the frame and
curtained/tented, the bed's representation here exploits the similarity between
Italian beds of baldaquin design and the tent that is the scene for Judith's story.[19]
This similarity between Renaissance beds and war-tents is often exploited in
erotic versions of Judith to suggest the primacy of the sexual theme.

Like most such Judiths Pordenone's is suggestively *déshabillée*, and appears
to be listening to the maid's bawdy badinage. Tugging Holofernes' beard (in
Renaissance Italy, a lascivious gesture) is a sign of this Judith's lubricious intentions.[20] Similarly, the hirsute interpretation of Holofernes' head implies
bristling virility, an attribute often associated with hair. 'Be a real man with me'

is the message of this painting, despite its evocation of a heroine who trumped male valour. It is as if the heroine's 'masculine' vigour is being transferred to the male: thus she does not touch the sword, which lies horizontally on the balustrade, inviting the spectator to take it up himself: the latter is to be a Holofernes, becoming more priapic in response to female impudence.

Fede Galizia's Judith is another *déshabillée* harlot, whose salacious maid (the crone as bawd) has her finger to her lips. This should not be interpreted as in Artemisia Geutileschi's and Grammatica's versions, which suggested women conspiring against men in feminist revenge. Despite the fact that Galizia was a woman painter, this is a commercial, bawdy Judith, and a warning against our assuming that all women's Judiths are necessarily therefore feminist.[21] Galizia, like her subject, was a professional making her living, and the Judithic subject a commodity aimed at a particular section of the brothel's clientele.

Simultaneously with these developments in bordello decor and sex tourism, which in the case of directories was facilitated by the invention of printing, the Renaissance saw the birth of connoisseurship, the collecting of art and of 'curiosities' by wealthy consumers who then formalized their taste within private galleries and museums.[22] Representations of Judith are such standard fixtures in paintings depicting these galleries that the fashionableness of the subject is evident. For such premier royal collectors as the Hapsburg duke Leopold Wilhelm, governor of the Spanish Netherlands, there was a specific motive for acquiring paintings on such apocryphal subjects. During the Reformation, the rigorous hermeneutics favoured by Protestant universities had led to attacks on the apocryphal books as fictions, which should be purged from the Bible. Polemically, the assault on the Apocrypha, which was formally repudiated by the Synod of Dordt in 1621, was targeted at the 'Popish' accretions of ecclesiastical tradition.[23] In reaction, the Counter-Reformation was all the more enthusiastic about apocryphal themes in art. Good Catholics were urged to patronize artworks that supported Catholic emphases, and Leopold's liking for versions of Judith is an effect of this injunction.

His gallery also demonstrates the way in which courtesanal paintings could mutate into collector's pieces in respectable venues, reinventing a Virtue topic out of the Vice it was painted for. Several painted versions of Leopold's gallery show what was clearly a favourite painting, Carlo Saraceni's *Judith*. Holofernes' toothlessness and the maid's gripping the open bag in her teeth are inventive variations on the erotic Judith paintings' sexual motifs of orality. From pornography to state art, in one bound.

Paintings depicting royal and aristocratic galleries – Leopold commissioned no fewer than nine of his own – were exported to other venues, as advertisements for the connoisseur's taste, wealth and magnificence, all signs of power. The Hapsburg collections, in particular, were one of the more decorative constituents in an imperial display at Vienna of the might and reach of this royal house. The very display of artistic riches could itself be made another form of conspicuous consumption. For example, some of the 'cabinets of curiosities' housed in private galleries and museums were themselves richly decorated, in some cases with representations of Judith. One that paired Judith and Susannah was alluding to the biblical affirmation that 'the price of a virtuous woman (wisdom) is above rubies' (Proverbs 8:11), implicitly comparing women as a commodity to the cabinet's priceless contents. The acquisitive instinct embodied by such a cabinet was thus doubly commodified, inside and out.

And just as less wealthy courtesans aped the taste of the richest in their decor, so non-royal collectors aspired to collections modelled on the famed imperial prototypes. Representations of Judith were considered *de rigueur*, and suppliers were appropriately stocked to cater for the fashion: both a Mauritshuis painting of an artist's shop and Francken's *La Boutique de Jan Snellinck* display paintings and statuettes of her. The collection of the prosperous Antwerp merchant, Cornelis van der Geest, sported at least two Judiths, including Van Eyck's toilette scene, within the same painting of his collection.[24] Courtesanal Judiths finding their way into connoisseurs' galleries were metamorphosing from one commodity function into another. Whether in illicit or pompously displayed regal collections, Judith's image became a marker of taste, an ideological statement and a consumable: an instance of the social and sexual economies operating in the Renaissance. In that sense, she was evidence of the simple realities that underlay the highly civilized and artificial features that we associate with the Renaissance, its taste, aesthetics and canons of beauty. In the end, art and material realities are not as disjunct as we often like to think. The Renaissance Judith was an instance of art getting its hands dirty on life.

The Marriage Bed and Rembrandt

If Judith's image was used extensively in the sex business, this illicit trade did not deter couples from regarding her as an appropriate decor for the deep peace of the marriage bed (as the actress Mrs Patrick Campbell once described it). Like some other legendary heroines, Judith was an emblem for marital values that were given visual expression on the walls, furniture and bric-à-brac of Renaissance households. These items of decor were both aesthetic and ideological: didactic reminders of the meaning of marriage in this society. The subordination of wife to husband was axiomatic.[25] Any bride or wife who was in danger of forgetting her allotted role as the 'weaker vessel' in a couple would be preserved from constant reminders of it only if she were literally blind to her everyday environment. Wherever she went in her own house – supposedly the one place where she might exercise authority without overstepping the misogynist mark – there were reminders that her tenancy within it depended on knowing her place.

Stylish interiors from the *quattrocento* onwards often highlighted the aptness of a room's decoration for its function. Whilst erotic biblical scenes graced men's bedrooms and courtesans' suites, respectably didactic portrayals of Judith were used to reinforce official ideals of marriage as a social institution. In a Sienese palazzo, for instance, the decoration of a chamber for a wedding festivity involved a scheme of the Nine Worthies which instructed the new couple to emulate their private and public virtues.[26] Centring on Judith, an 'insertion' of the prime female worthy, the scheme combined private and public virtues in her person, as the type of a citizen with no formal public role, who nevertheless devoted herself to the communal good: a moral crucial to the political aspirations of a republican state such as Siena, where Judith's reign as an icon depended very much upon this ability to migrate between private and public worlds. The couple's entry into the marital state is thus characterized as their entry also into a world of public responsibilities, their absorption into the social fabric. Whereas the biblical Judith had challenged normal earthly hierarchies, this emblematic descendant reinforced them, especially in the depressing self-effacement entailed upon the 'good wife' in the Renaissance.

In this role Judith became a remarkably conservative icon, underwriting both the social status quo and the fairly rigid distinction between the public roles of men and the household-bound, privatized roles of women.[27] In the palazzo fresco she was an emblem of *his* rights and duties as public citizen (only allegorically feminine) and *her* obligations as the citizen's wife (chastity, largely). Judith's allegorization glosses over the way in which the man's sphere of action is expanded, whilst the woman's is shrunk, by the ideals of republican virtue. She does her bit simply by being a faithful and pious wife, whilst in a republican state any male citizen may regard himself as politically significant. Since republicanism was in fact one of the most avant-garde political systems of this time, its relegation of the female citizen sufficiently measures the distance between its public stance of political progressivism and its reactionary attitudes to gender. Redefined by Renaissance notions of femininity and marriage, Judith's political vigour became masculinized. A man's 'honour' inhered in numerous public and personal roles, including military, civic and political obligations, whereas to refer to a woman's honour was to allude solely to her reputation for chastity. It is difficult to imagine a more reductive and stifling conception of what a human being's aspirations might amount to.

However, in such a 'shame culture', a woman's reputation was an attribute of her husband or her father, and therefore her instruction in chastity could not be too rigorous. There were various ways of using Judith to instruct wives in fidelity through the decor that surrounded them. In wealthier Italian circles, for instance, it was customary to provide a newly married couple with a set of matching luggage, richly decorated chests or *cassoni*, which would thereafter furnish the marital bedroom. These were often decorated with instructive narratives. On *cassoni* illustrating the procession of exceptional women from Petrarch's celebrated fourteenth-century poem *The Triumph of Love*, Judith was an exemplar of sublime, divine beauty and of idealized romantic passion.[28] The ensuing Renaissance theme of Love's Triumph somewhat ironically converted a literal man-slayer into an object of desire whom brides might emulate. Husbands with an aptitude for iconography, however, were probably given pause by this idea.

During the sixteenth century the use of Judith as emblem for wives' proper virtues became particularly common in Northern Europe. This was largely because the rise of Protestantism, and its devotion to the Word, led to a greater emphasis upon biblical than upon classical prototypes for contemporary virtue. The 'conduct-books' that instructed women in virtuous behaviour, family values and the management of the household repeatedly emphasized that a woman's whole and appropriate destiny could be summed up in the 'three ages of woman', 'maid, wife, widow'. Moreover, in all three roles her behaviour was to be invariably 'chaste, silent and obedient'. Judith, of course, had been neither silent nor obedient, but she could be extolled as a model of chastity. Thus a 1594 elegy on the 'Virtuous Life and Godly Death' of an Englishwoman, Helen Branch, by the English translator of Du Bartas's *Judit* paralleled her 'threefold godly life' to 'virgin Ruth, wife Sarah, widow Judith'.[29] More encompassingly, in his epic, Du Bartas portrayed his heroine as emblem of all three ages of woman, and was at pains to transform her into the dutiful, middle-class Protestant wife.

This absolutely privatized view of women's functions in life effected a remarkable continuity between the old Catholic and the avant-garde Protestant social ideologies. Thus the Protestant commendations of Judith as model wife maintained the Catholic tradition exemplified by William of Shoreham's fourteenth-century 'Song to Mary', which termed Judith 'that fair wife'. Old Testament women, most of all Judith and Susannah, became popular icons of wifely virtue in Protestant homes particularly. Judith's representations are outnumbered only by Susannah's – Susannah's greater popularity was no doubt owed to the fact that her private virtue, unlike Judith's, was not accompanied by a public role, and that the victimized Susannah owed her rescue to a man. On Netherlandish decorated hearthbricks the whole narrative of Susannah was represented, even more commonly than Judith's acteme, and both appeared on firebacks used in France and the Low Countries.[30] Screens, ceramic tiles and painted or carved armoires were decorated with their stories and with Esther's: all impressing upon the devout household the values of chastity, fidelity and benevolent wifely influence on the patriarchal husband. Hedged about with such emblems, representations of the cultural categories that constrained and distorted their lives, early modern women lived out from day to day the social coercions of their time, with more or less kind or brutal husbands. This was a

satisfactorily patriarchal arrangement which Protestantism, despite its iconoclastic attitudes in other areas, was by no means anxious to disturb.

However, even in Protestant representations and domestic contexts, it was
difficult for anyone entirely to lose sight of the erotic Judith who was being so
splendiferously portrayed by contemporary artists. There was an affinity
between the Judith who decorated connubial interiors and the one who cavorted
in brothels. Her sensual aspects were, of course, just as stimulating to respectable couples as to others, and this was undoubtedly a contributory factor in her
appeal as an item of interior decoration.

A particularly intriguing case of Judith's role behind closed doors involved
that remarkably successful exponent of commercialized painting, Rembrandt.
His marriage to Saskia Uylenbergh was itself commercially canny, since he
hoped that her Calvinist family network would increase his market amongst the
Reformers. His own family was predominantly Catholic, and on occasion
Rembrandt had offended Calvinist opinion, as for instance when in the 1630s
he had illustrated the Book of Tobit from the Apocrypha. After Dordt, the
official Dutch biblical translation of 1636 demoted the apocryphal books, and
any interest in them was increasingly seen as an indicator of Popish convictions.

One of Rembrandt's portraits of his wife has been the subject of much scholarly dispute, which has recently led to the rejection of its old title, *Saskia as
Flora*.[31] However, x-rays of the painting reveal that Rembrandt had initially
portrayed his wife as Judith, which in fact provides decisive evidence that
the final version is a Flora after all. For both the classical goddess and Judith
were personations that conveyed the same message about Rembrandt's view
of his wife.

As Boccaccio's *De Claris Mulieribus* (Book LXII) had reminded artists, Flora
was the Roman goddess not only of flowers but also of prostitutes, and numerous 'fancy portraits' of courtesans evoked her in that role. As we have seen,
Judith was one of her biblical counterparts in the Renaissance sex business.
First as Judith and then as Flora, Saskia is being complimented by her husband
on her sexual allure.

It is clear why Rembrandt had to expunge his Judith. This was an apocryphal
subject, and hence offensive to Reformers and particularly to Saskia's own
family. Moreover, the compliment was too overt in a respectable bourgeois
Dutch context, whereas Saskia as Flora could be confused with those popular
exercises in 'Arcadian costume' which did not offend anyone. Generic ambiguity, religious dogma and the biblical heroine's erotic reputation colluded to erase
Rembrandt's Judith. But beneath the overpainting, she secretly attests to his
unexpected delight in the wife he had married for economic motives, and (one
must hope that Saskia felt the same) to the joys of the marriage bed. One thing
that Judith's image did not suggest was that it was characterized by 'deep,
deep peace'.

Erotic Horror

Both the bordello function and the anecdotal evidence of modern male spectators suggest that representations of Judith and Holofernes often carried an erotic charge. The fetishistic aspects of the woman holding a severed head are not wholly adequate to explain this. In fact, a remarkable diversity of erotic codes can be represented within a painting of this subject; it is their cumulative effect that makes a representation of this theme more than the sum of its (body) parts.

One of the more provocative subtexts of Judithic representations is of course based upon the male fantasy of being 'raped' by a woman, articulated in 'unreconstructed' Shakespeare's *Venus and Adonis*. To this end, Holofernes' posture and the feminized placement of his limbs can reinforce the phallic symbolism of the sword.

More interesting than the uses made of this subtext, however, is the intriguing question of why sex, death and shock, the three major constituents of paintings of the acteme, should have such pronounced erotic effect despite the story's menacing aspects for the male. It is the quality of erotic horror that embeds, as it were, these paintings in a deep undertow of perennial sexual fantasies.

A particularly interesting example of these is the sub-genre of paintings of Judith and David, such as Johann Liss's, which deploy a triple-headed composition for its *grand guignol* effect. The same grotesque effect is repeated in 'triple-headed' compositions of the triumphs of David and of Jael (for example by Salomon de Bray). Judith's, Holofernes' and the maid's heads are cramped together within the canvas in order to set up a play of vivid contrasts between male, female, young, mature, elegant, coarse, impudent, awed, complacent and insensible faces; and to suggest, in this unnerving collision of heads and expressions, a kind of dreadful psychic intimacy in homicide, which exaggerates the physical intimacy of sex.

The perverse erotics of this composition take their charge precisely from the displacement of intercourse by the more intense experience of death, and of ecstasy by shock and *rigor mortis*. Liss's is a particularly vivid execution of the common contrast between the maid's recoil and Judith's phlegm, which is intended to denote Judith's deviance. Her back to us, a rather vulgar Judith turns with a repressively unabashed gaze upon the spectator, as if to say, 'What of it?' (This is effective: try eavesdropping on the gasps emitted by unwary tourists in the National Gallery.) Whereas Vasari and Michelangelo (whom Liss was imitating) used Judith's rear view as code for her sinister aspect, Liss's Judith is, in addition, an unrepentant slut. The setting and iconography are so underplayed, the clothing so plebeian and the colouring so muddy that this could easily be not a biblical scene, but a genre picture of a murder in a cheap whorehouse.

Liss's treatment of the severed neck also distinguishes this painting from the more tactful eroticism of courtesanal Judiths. In these, as also in Cranach's half-figure Judiths, the alignment of the severed neck with the surface on which it rests tends to replicate the mouth, emphasizing orality. But a more frontal representation of the neck much more emphatically suggests an almost vaginal orifice, and most of all in Liss's brutally foregrounded version. Such treatment create a play of orifices and eyes across the compositions, from the rounded pumping pulp of the neck to the maid's eye and mouth, dilated in shock. If all of the potential erotic codes and subjexts are integrated into a version of the acteme, the composition becomes a positive riot of sexual stimuli.

These include both autoeroticism, suggested by a spasmodic Holofernes, and homoeroticism. Autoeroticism is the clear implication of many artists' tendency to make the head of Holofernes a self-portrait. Like Caravaggio's androgynous portraits of the boy David with the head of Goliath, the complementary composition of Judith plays to homoeroticism, both of the kind required by Caravaggio's homosexual patrons and of the kind that can be subsumed within masculine heterosexual attraction. Representations of Judith can concentrate three erotic urges into a multiply-suggestive composition.

Within these available codes, the apotropaic effect of a severed head assumes a complex function. According to Freud, the Medusa's head provided a fetish which substituted a woman's 'lack' of a penis, assuaging male fear of the 'castrated' being.[32] But we should not follow Freud's secularizing impulse too slavishly, by forgetting the supernatural fear and horror with which Medusa's and Holofernes' heads were associated. This, mimed within the paintings by the maids' expressions, is transmogrified by erotic codes into the sensory senselessness precipitated by the most intense sexual experience. Similarly, its facially distorting effects are approximated by a Holofernes in agony (such as Caravaggio's), just as its stupefied, desolating, debilitating aftermath can be echoed in his features as frozen by death. Visually, representations of Judith's acteme tend to suggest such a multiplicity of elements of erotic experience, and to do so in such a teasingly metaphorical manner – a kind of visual foreplay – that it should not surprise us one whit that she was so favoured by courtesans.

Further, the mythical Medusa's transfixing effect at one level characterizes sexual charisma itself, as both erotic and menacing. That is because sexual attraction disables the one who experiences it, is both unwilled and stunning. This abjection of the self is contradicted by a reverse impulse, just as forceful, which is responsive sexual aggression. That uniquely intense experience of psychic and physical energy and vulnerability is what Judith's irresistible sexual charisma was intended to evoke, and it is also the key to that compound of horror, awe, intensity and attraction which is extreme eroticism. In the most potent erotic representations of Judith what we see is – quite simply – a portrait of that.

4

Worshipping Women
The Battle of the Sexes in Reformation Europe

It was during the Reformation that Judith's significance reached its apogee. Never, before or since, has there been such an overwhelming profusion of her representations, in all the available artistic media, as there was in the sixteenth and seventeenth centuries. In the secular world outside church buildings, numerous paintings, frescoes, engravings, woodcuts, sculptures, ceramics, drinking vessels, seals, pieces of metalware, screens, tapestries, fireplaces, bits of furniture, pencases, mirrors, jewellery boxes and jewellery, as well as poems, ballads, plays and pamphlets, multiplied her images. In the Renaissance Judiths did furnish a room.

There were several stimuli for this obsession. An increasing fascination with images of strong women, *femmes fortes*, fostered the representation of the Bible's most ruthless heroine. This interacted with an intensifying debate about the character of the female sex, whose main function in life, Christian tradition suggested, was to lead poor witless men astray. The Protestant determination to make the Bible accessible to the laity led to its translation into the vernacular European languages, and hence made the whole rather shocking story of Judith very much more widely known. It was of a kind to attract strong interest and inspire imitations.

Above all, the religious schism between Catholic and Protestant exponentially increased the polemical importance of biblical narratives and images. Judith would become one of the key images of these virulent controversies, especially in those countries – France, England, Scotland and the Low Countries – where the religious divide caused massive political upheaval and bitter bloodshed. The Reformation was a time of profound and protracted crisis, political and cultural, such as Europe had not experienced for centuries, and which would not be matched until the Berlin Wall divided it in the twentieth century. It is at this time that Judith's image was most ubiquitous. The strong woman is strong meat, befitting a time of extremes.

This was especially the case because of the ferment of new ideas produced by Renaissance learning and Reformation radicalism. Accordingly, Judith's radical potential now began to have widespread and marked effects across the Continent. As Europe struggled through the rapid changes that would produce our modern ideas and our modern sense of individualism, contradictory images of Judith became reflections of its trauma. But they were also striking indices of the new era's febrile enthusiasms and its excitement at fresh possibilities. One of the morals to be drawn from Judith's head-taking was that you do not make an omelette without breaking eggs. And that, it seemed, was what the great chef in the sky had in mind for Reformation Europe.

Women Rampant

One instance of the enquiring spirit of Renaissance humanism was its interest in the question of what women were like, and what they were for. (The fact that these questions were asked is itself a measure of misogyny: they were not asked about the male sex, which was not required to find a justification for its existence.) Traditional attitudes to gender have always regarded man as a universal, woman as a category; hence the humanists' presuming to regard women as entirely homogeneous.[1] Prior to this, a long-lived genre of medieval writing had derived a good deal of amusement from purporting to attack women's congenital vices or defend their virtues, using legendary examples to typify the sex. Although in Book I of *The Fall of Princes* (1431–8) John Lydgate cited Judith as an example both in favour of and against women, his poem *Examples against Women* cited her as one of the striking instances of women's natural perfidy and their ability to bring men to ruinous ends. The villainess version won by a head. As a seductress, her figure also became contaminated with legendary illicit sexuality, so that a series of panels in Faversham Guildhall, carved in about 1530, collocated Judith and Holofernes, Helen and Paris, and Medea and Jason as archetypes of unfaithful couples – of disastrous intersexual relations. Judith even became a sign for marital strife and for the power-struggle with the shrew. Thus a misericord scene in Lincoln Cathedral has been variously identified as either 'Judith and Holofernes' or 'A woman beating her husband'.[2] The similarity between the two motifs is perhaps the most important aspect of this confusion. On the whole, the argument against women had more devotees than the argument for. (It comes as no surprise that there was no complementary genre of assaults on men simply on grounds of their gender.)

Highly conventional exercise though it was, this debate was nevertheless not merely theoretical, since it interacted with the gender divide in everyday life. The coercive pressures exerted upon women by a patriarchal society relied upon the common resort to mythic stereotypes. Religious doctrine affirmed that women were naturally subjugated to the rule of father or husband, just as the divine Father was the prototype for the subjugation of the people to their monarch. And early modern political theorists would develop ideas of autocratic rule which depended upon a parallel between government and family.[3] In a circular argument, the model of the father's authority within the family shored up the contention that monarchy was natural, whilst the familiarity of monarchism was held to prove that the patriarchal family was also divinely ordained. 'He for God only, she for God in him' went Milton's formulation of the original marital relationship in Eden. As a conventional proof of the naturalness of hierarchies, marriage was a political state.

However, whilst scripture was used to support the idea that women were destined to obey men's orders, at the same time scriptural authority could be used by women themselves, in order to resist the customary constraints on their lives. Even in the Middle Ages, Judith's example had already proved useful for this purpose. Thus the saint Christina of Markyate cited a vision of Judith, model of celibacy, in order to resist the marriage her parents had arranged for her.[4] This feminine exploitation of Judith directly contradicted the masculinist use of Judith as a model of woman's domesticated destiny. Similarly, Countess 'Judith's' resistance to Edward III on the principle of marital chastity ended his pretensions. Even the patriarchally imposed virtue of chastity could become a strategy for women's resistance. Scriptural prototype could work both ways, either to reinforce or to subvert pressures upon women. For this purpose Judith's radical and feminist aspects made her uniquely useful.

In the early sixteenth century the overwhelming consensus that women were the inferior sex was challenged by such humanist writers as Vives and Cornelius Agrippa, who argued that women had souls as good as men's and (heavens!) possessed skills beyond the domestic ones which were felt to be their natural limit.[5] In 1521 Christine de Pisan's *City of Ladies*, which used Judith to challenge women's privatization, was translated into English: an effect of the burgeoning interest in this controversy. The sizeable polemical literature generated by the *querelle des femmes* – the debate about the place of women – persisted for over a century, and the colourful and uncompromising Judith inevitably became a key example in the catalogues of females who were either famously virtuous or notoriously maleficent.

When a masculinist polemic cited a Delilah as representative of her sex, the best riposte was a Judith. Joseph Swetnam's *Arraignment of Lewd, Idle, and Froward Women* (1615) reviled Judith as an epitome of the perfidious temptress. In the riposte, Esther Sowernam's *Esther Hath Hang'd Haman* (1617) evoked a biblical prototype for women's heroism even in its title, but would progress to the harder case. Such strategies were key moments in the formal debate, since biblical exempla were treated as more authoritative than others. Sowernam seized on Swetnam's citation of Judith as a usefully weak point in his catalogue of villainesses: didn't he know the difference, Sowernam asked rhetorically, between a villainess and a sacred heroine?[6] The *querelle des femmes* divided Judith's ambiguity neatly down the middle.

Neither of these pseudonymous pamphlets should be taken at face value, or too seriously, for they were part of a profitable publishing industry exploiting a rich and popular seam of tabloid extremism. Even those purporting to be by women were probably written by male hacks; Swetnam's objective was to exploit the familiar misogynistic diatribe for all that it was worth. On the other hand, Sowernam's response is equally determined to pursue the contradictory argument much more forcefully than was usual. The pamphlet not only complains that women are better than men have always made them out to be, but that they are in many ways the superior sex: Sowernam does not merely rely upon the usual apologia, but also takes the offensive. By the early seventeenth century the journalistic controversy had persisted for so long that the stakes had risen. Above all, the claim that women possessed both the right and the ability to enter the public sphere had become much more insistent than in Christine's *City of Ladies*. Since Judith was a salient prototype for public activism, the effect of the extended debate was to problematize her gender as never before. She was not only a paradigm of woman as 'man's conqueror', but now evidently one who damaged patriarchal stereotypes of authority in both private and public life.

Within this context, it was possible to exploit Judith's story as a consciously feminist argument for women's high spiritual potential and their special favour in the eyes of God. This was particularly useful as a counterargument to the traditional view that women were spiritually weak and therefore rightly subordinated to men's governance. In her poem *Salve Deus Rex Judaeorum* (1611), Aemilia Lanier asserted that the Bible proved women to be distinguished exponents of Christianity. She is contemptuous of 'evil disposed men, who forgetting they were born of women . . . and that if it were not by the means of women, they would be quite extinguished out of the world, and a final end of them all, do like vipers deface the wombs within which they were bred . . . they have tempted even the patience of God himself, who gave power to wise and virtuous women, to bring down . . . the pride and arrogance of evil men.' In effect, she argues that it is not women but men who are spiritually weak, for power has led the male into hubris. And God's punishments are arranged in such a way as to ironize men's folly: they fall to the very sex that they are foolish enough to despise. Such was the fate of 'blasphemous Holofernes, [brought down] by the invincible courage, rare wisdom, and confident carriage of Judith'.[7] Appropriated to a feminist thesis, Holofernes' emblematization of Pride becomes the male's delusion of superiority.

In order to carry through her feminist argument Lanier necessarily propounds the importance of women to the public sphere, both in religion and in politics. Her poem is dedicated to the queen and numerous distinguished noblewomen, who are characterized as the public face of femininity. (As we shall see in the next chapter, behind this gallery lies the most significant reason for the debate's longevity and Judith's place within it.) By creating such a gallery of prominent women as the preface to her poem's assertive theme, Lanier is able to achieve a wholesale retrieval of women's status as both public and private beings.

This crucial rejection of women's exclusion from the public world was what made Judith's authoritative example so important to the aspirations of Renaissance feminism. When women wanted to come out of the bedroom closet they cited the woman who left hers to go out into the city and the camp where history was made. Each woman in Lanier's gallery was now an argument for seeing the once formal debate in terms of real status and actual events. What had been a game had converted itself into something more significant.

Moreover, the *querelle* would not have lasted as long as it did, had it not been addressing some actual anxiety. After all, the Renaissance was everywhere producing images of 'women on top'.[8] Paintings of Judith and other Amazonian women, numerous as they were, were only the tip of an iceberg. More generally available, sold even by itinerant pedlars to relatively poor customers, were cheap engravings and woodcuts of the same gallery of menacing females, from the ultimate shrew, Phyllis, who beat her husband the philosopher Aristotle, to the various harlots, hair-cutters and head-takers of the Bible. The Renaissance produced so many images of women's capacity to dominate men that, we must conclude, there was widespread anxiety that masculinity was under threat.

Equally common, however, were illustrations offering dominating women as admirable examples of their sex's potential for heroism. From murals to pencases, this theme ran rampant through Renaissance decorative art. For instance, it was in the early sixteenth century that the iconographic theme of the Nine Female Worthies first became popular.[9] Hans Burgkmair's much-copied rendition of the Three Worthy Jewesses was only one example of the way in which Judith inevitably became a premier image of women's assertiveness.

Another artefact feeding the increasing appetite for such images was a series of tapestries illustrating the Triumph of Christian Virtues: its most striking panel was devoted to Fortitude, an uncompromising depiction of Judith and her analogues (Jael and Tomyris amongst them) doing horrible things to men's extremities. This series of tapestries was a particularly fashionable and popular item, exported from the Low Countries to both France and England.[10] Alternatively, those who liked to surround themselves with images of legendary murderesses could opt for another fashion in interior decoration, the *salle des femmes fortes*. This was a room wholly decorated by an integrated scheme of representations of heroic women. Both at the Paris Arsenal and at the castle of Rocca di Soragna in Italy, the series of heroic women is dominated by Judith as its central, climactic instance. At the Arsenal Judith's is the only image that occurs twice, in both cases at the centre of the longer walls, whilst at Soragna the main wall is devoted to the largest fresco, of Judith. Here the feminist implications of the subject are particularly overt. The sleeping sentries reinforce the impression given by the recumbent vulnerability of Holofernes's body, that two women are mounting a female conspiracy against a male sex pathetically unaware of the enemy creeping up on their tents. Soragna's *salle* is a late example of this, from 1701, but the dominance of Judith in such schemes had become conventional by then.

Between 1500 and 1700 Judith was the most commonly selected figure for such schemes, and often for their centre, because she was the most uncompromising example of female heroism available to a time that automatically ranked sacred above classical heroines. As we have seen, it was the peculiar characteristics of her ambivalence as a holy homicide that had always distinguished her image as more extreme than that of other heroines. The more overtly feminist a version of the *femmes fortes* motif was intended to be, the more likely it was that Judith would dominate the composition. In short, she was the Renaissance's primary image of the strong woman.

Was the duchess who commissioned a *salle* similar to the one at Rocca di Saragna at a villa outside Florence in the early seventeenth century motivated to do so by her own feminine assertiveness, projected upon the walls of her palazzo, or at least by an aspiration to be like Judith, if only she dared or circumstances allowed?[11] Of course she was. Many such *salles* were commissioned by women, and for reasons that it is not difficult to divine. In *quattrocento* Italy, Isabella d'Este, Duchess of Mantua, was one of the most formidable and famed of ducal consorts. Her client, the artist Andrea Mantegna, produced several influential versions of Judith.[12] Those executed in grisaille must have been intended for a *salle des femmes fortes*, to accompany his renditions of other legendary women, such as Dido. Isabella evidently commissioned such a room – perhaps more than one. The number of Judiths that Mantegna produced whilst under her patronage is an indication that Isabella aspired to some Judithic qualities. Since she was an ambitious woman, her enthusiasm for *femme fortes* implies a determination to be more politically influential than the average ducal consort (and contrasts with Eleanor of Toledo's *salle* in Florence's Palazzo Vecchio, which centred on Esther as the model of a more amenable ducal spouse). In such cases, Judith was a role-model and self-projection that implied a woman's ambition for power and influence. To commission a decorative scheme devoted to heroic women was fashionable, but it was also a statement by the patroness about herself.

A similar phenomenon emerged in the household arts which were customarily permitted to women to practise themselves. Embroidery, for instance, was felt to be a naturally feminine occupation, both decorative and useful, and was practised by royals, noblewomen and the middle classes alike.[13] By the late sixteenth century they were often plying their needles enthusiastically upon images of *femmes fortes*, especially the biblical heroines. Thus a demure tapestry-work cushion cover at Packwood House shows Judith triumphantly carrying off the head of Holofernes. It is here, in an art so programmatically attached to traditionalist views of women as domestic creatures, that their predilection for producing images of female assertiveness seems most evidently to indicate stifled but subversive impulses to break free of the narrow domestic sphere; or, in the case of women already relatively independent – because they were rich widows or backstairs politicians – to express their knowledge of their own power in a way that was inexplicit and socially acceptable. A fondness for embroidering portraits of biblical heroines could, after all, be ascribed to piety, which, like embroidery, was a respectable activity for females.

It may well be the case that the two genres of representations of *femmes fortes* – the shrews and the heroines – appealed to two different constituencies, dividing along predictable gender lines. Perhaps women mainly provided the market for heroines, men for shrews. There was one thing the artists and pamphleteers producing for these markets could be sure of, though: that Judith's image would sell equally well to both the neurotics and the feminists. Exceptionally amongst the biblical sirens, Judith was a polyvalent image that the observer could perceive either way. Giorgione's Judith is a good example of this, for one can read her treading upon Holofernes' head either as an example of women's unnatural aggressiveness or as an exemplary instance of woman triumphant over the venality of men. Alternatively, one could choose to see only the moral Christian message, that Holofernes is an instance of wordly pride put in its place – on the floor – by godly humility. Few of the equivalent legendary females could be such versatile commodities for artists. At another level, this is the commercial plane of those Renaissance fears and fascinations for which she provided the salient magnetic object.

Why Fear Women?

What, though, were those fears and fascinations? As yet, the cause of the Renaissance *querelle des femmes* has remained obscure. It is difficult to believe, as has been suggested, that it was academic humanism that produced this long-running controversy over women's nature. What, in that case, prompted humanism's interest in this question?

It is in Judith's representations that we can find clues to the origins of the *querelle des femmes*. As we have seen, her representations reached out to two extremes of the stereotyping of women: the whore or reductively physicalized woman, as in the genre of prostitute Judiths, and the sublimated, powerful woman, as represented in the *femmes fortes*. The degraded image addressed a new phobia that overcame Europe around 1500.

As we saw, in the darkly eroticized paintings of Judith produced by the sex business, horrific motifs characterized sexual charisma as intrinsically menacing in the same degree as it was intensely erotic: a representation of the physical and psychic risk inseparable from extreme sexual experience. In this sense, the agony on the face of Holofernes represented both an orgasmic spasm and the oblivion of identity in orgasm. Significantly, in the Renaissance orgasm was identified with a 'death' (an equivalent to the modern sexual sense of 'come'), in recognition of this presage of one's own mortality. An implicit identification of sex with death is common in depictions of Judith's acteme, and the more pronounced in the more eroticized genre.

Like the *querelle*'s representations of Judith, these erotic depictions could be read in two ways. Whilst functioning as a form of advertisement and foreplay for commercial sex, by recalling the element of psychic risk in sexual encounters they also permitted the possibility of recognizing the physical risks – most obviously, of venereal diseases. Most of the courtesanal Judiths are contemporary with the *querelle*. They offer the underworld, provocative version of the theme of woman as dominatrix. A customary fear of women's sexuality and a parodic version of the *querelle*'s complaints about women's domineering impulses interact in a way that is diverted towards sexual provocation and seduction.

However, they also interacted with a more disturbing development, the epidemic of syphilis in Europe. It had been brought back from the New World by Columbus's sailors, spreading so rapidly in Italy, for instance, that it was already recognized and feared as early as 1495.[14] During the 1500s syphilis became a source of widespread anxiety, shadowing sexual encounters much as AIDS would in the late twentieth century. As was usually the case, since they were so thoroughly identified with the sexual function itself, women were blamed for the transmission of the disease, as if this were another of the 'curses of Eve' inflicted upon innocent and vulnerable men. Readily absorbed into the systematic neuroses of Christian anti-sexual imagery, syphilis was regarded as one of the torments of hell found in the 'hell-pit' of women's vaginas. No wonder the Renaissance abounds in images of women tormenting their menfolk, of Judiths deconstructing male bodies. Especially when luridly sexualized in gothic terms – as in Liss's squalid prostitute – the image of Judith's acteme could be an evocative allegory of women 'murdering' men by infecting them with a fatal sexual disease. Not least, the grotesque dismemberment of Holofernes allegorized the way in which syphilis slowly and painfully deconstructed both body and mind.

Judith's acteme was unusually appropriate to this neurotic subtext. She was woman in vengeful mood, a dominatrix, a divine nemesis upon a male's desire and pride, the scene of her homicide the bedroom. Was her method not insidious, secretive and fatal, like syphilitic infection? Thus, for instance, Liss's grimly chiaroscuro painting could be read in several ways: as a biblical scene, as a pornographic version of the *querelle*'s dominatrix theme, as a warning against dishonest prostitutes, as a moralization on disease as the wages of sin, or as an image the very squalor of which was designed to appeal to a particular erotic taste. Liss was called upon to generate many imitations of his *Judith* – and it was so widely imitated – because it proved so inclusive of the Renaissance responses to her ambivalent image.

Similarly, the fear of syphilis and the anxiety about 'women on top' were symbiotic: like Judith, a woman's sexual power (the only power she was felt to possess naturally) could literally kill you. This subtext was at work in a popular early seventeenth-century tabloid-style account of a notorious murder case in Valencia.[15] A concubine had murdered her faithless lover in bed, with the collusion of her maidservant, and thereafter had dismembered him. The way in which popular pamphlets retold this scandal observed rather precisely the archetypal plot established by knowledge of the story of Judith. She was a template of 'women's vengeance' for the Renaissance.

Judith was one of the most compelling images of the battle of the sexes: of erotic antagonisms, feminist aspirations and masculinist nightmares. It was the convergence of these profound, atavistic notions that placed her image at the heart of contemporaries' perceptions of their own era of dizzying change, for she could represent, simultaneously, both its terrors and its hopes. At times of deep cultural crisis, convictions about gender become the more energetically held or contested, because when all else seems in doubt (as the poet John Donne would opine) human beings look to the atavistic for reassurance that some things, at least, never change. The biological division between men and women offers itself as one of those few immutabilities; hence its hysterical reassertion by reactionaries whenever they fear that radicalism is making headway. Ultimately, Judith was a Renaissance obsession because she was a mutable sign of what was regarded as an immutable human fact. Within her image antipathetic forces of anxiety and reassurance, masculinism and feminism, conservatism and radicalism could find their own images reflected back at them. Projected onto the cultural plane, Judith inspired in the Renaissance what some women inspire in men: her fearsomeness intensified her fascination, because she was regarded as the epitome of the sensual woman as well as the strong one. As Lanier put it, she 'had the power'.

Revolting Judiths

Despite this atavistic role in Renaissance culture, Judith did not lose her subliminal and political significance: on the contrary, it was at this time that both became so prominent that her image could be said to have invaded the European scene, much as her original had stormed her way into the Assyrian camp. During the sixteenth century, her role as a stimulant for resistance, revolt, war and massacre would be repeatedly and strenuously invoked in the protracted struggle between Protestants and Catholics.[16] In Western Europe particularly, where Protestantism made its most forceful inroads, she became an icon of the most aggressive radicalism.

In the Low Countries, where Lutheranism became rapidly established, it was the Protestant impulse that underlay a new interest in Judith's iconography as Christian Fortitude. Burgkmair's series of Nine Worthy Women was heraldized by the shields of German city-states, an iconography that supported the political intentions of his patron, the Holy Roman Emperor Maximilian I. Old Testament iconography was highly favoured by Protestants because of their emphasis upon the doctrinal primacy of scripture and the aptness of its iconography to the religious conflict. Preference for Old Testament types over the Virgin Mary (tainted for Protestants by Catholic Marian 'idolatry') also helped to maximize Judith's appeal. But this was only the least compelling reason for Protestant interest in Judith, who rapidly accrued a multiplicity of special associations for Protestants.

The Reformation consciously overthrew the Catholic Church's emphasis upon the authority of the priesthood. Judith's rebuke to the religious elders of her community thus readily represented the superiority of a godly lay believer to fallacious churchmen. This episode was particularly significant when Protestantism portrayed Catholic clergy as the tools of Antichrist. Since Holofernes had long been identified with Antichrist, for instance in the medieval *Bible moralisée*, Judith's antagonists, both clerical and temporal, corresponded to the enemies Protestantism posited for itself: the Catholic Church and those 'Popish' rulers who outlawed and persecuted adherents of the new religion. Hence Judith's role as Truth and Faith in the uncompromising sermons of the English maverick preacher Hugh Latimer, who roundly rebuked both clerical and political corruption.[17] In such sermons it was the very fact that Judith was a mere widow and private citizen that underwrote an attack on the ostensibly superior yet venal princes of church and state. His Judith was – characteristically for Protestantism – thus both a spiritual and a political iconoclast, demonstrating that to be godly was to be a free spirit.

Latimer was one of the most influential of radical Protestant preachers and, once martyred for his faith, a legend. The reprinting of his famous sermons gave their allusions to Judith wide currency, and they reinforced her intrinsic suitability as an image for the vigour of the Protestant spirit. Symbolizing the resolute determination of the new religion to destroy the old order, Judith became a central symbol in the religious wars.

Although Luther had protested, in support of their exclusion from the Vulgate Bible, that the apocryphal books were not factual or true, he had also argued that they were doctrinally instructive, wholesome fictions.[18] Seizing on this loophole, Protestant groups throughout Western Europe found Judith such a useful weapon in their armoury of propaganda that they preferred to turn a blind eye to the rigorous biblical scholarship practised by their own side. Whilst the new religion was still fighting to establish itself, such fine distinctions had to give way to the pressing needs of wartime. Without any undue sense of strain, it was for a Lutheran court that the studio of Cranach produced its paintings of Judith.

Judith's Protestant career had its origins in the theories of political resistance evolved by Protestant intellectuals, who sought to find ways of justifying rebellion against lawful, but Catholic, rulers. They were breaking rather new ground here, and it took time for Protestant resistance theory to develop into full-flowered belligerence. Whilst many radical Protestants were Calvinists, Calvin himself had not been much help at first. Under pressure from the increasing necessities of radical Protestantism, Calvin gave way and conceded that resistance to a ruling power might be justified if the ruler were ungodly. His followers rapidly went beyond this moderate position. In France, where after 1560 Huguenots and Catholics clashed in recurrent civil wars, rioting and massacres, Huguenot theorists such as Du Plessis-Mornay would evolve a highly sophisticated political theory to justify rebellion.[19] One consequence of this radical theorizing was Judith's sudden rise to prominence as a personification of Protestant rebellion. The Continent's most admired Protestant poet, Guillaume de Salluste du Bartas, wrote his epic poem *Judit* (1574) at the behest of the Huguenots' leader. It transposed the apocryphal story into a closely contemporary allegory of the French Protestants' heroic struggle against the monarchy. Translated and read all over Europe, Du Bartas's poem became the most important single catalyst of Judith's symbolic centrality for Protestantism.

As in France, in the Netherlands the Protestant struggle became a matter of outright armed rebellion against their Spanish Catholic rulers. Du Bartas's poem was soon translated into Dutch, and French resistance theory found parallels in the radical literature produced in the Netherlands. Once William the Silent emerged as the leader of the Protestant revolt against the occupying Catholic power, the Protestant cause had developed an extensive iconography for its propaganda. Calvinists were urged to identify themselves with the chosen people of the Old Testament, resisting their pagan oppressors. Because of the Protestants' commitment to armed rebellion, it was the military aspect of Old Testament stories that lent itself most readily to their propaganda. Judith became an emblem of the cause.[20] Her signification already included, as we have seen, a combination of the civic virtue of Justice with the idea of tyrannicide. As the citizen-widow, she was thus an emblem of lay godliness who also implied divinely sanctioned revolt.

Consequently, such Netherlandish artists as Maerten Jacobsz van Heemskerck represented Judith's story as an archetype of the current war of liberation. Abraham Bloemaert's painting of Judith displaying Holofernes's head to the populace is very precisely addressed to the character of the Netherlanders' action as a popular revolt, a mass insurgence as distinct from the 'vested interests' of aristocratic rebellions, which (as often as not) run counter to popular interests. The essentially democratic implications that had long lain dormant in Judith's story had emerged into the light at last.

In order to grasp just how pervasive was the role of such images in the daily life of Reformation peoples, we need to recognize that political images from the Bible appeared in the most unlikely contexts. For instance, whilst it has long been acknowledged that the pottery produced in Germany in the second half of the sixteenth century, primarily at Siegburg, was of remarkable quality and in much demand elsewhere in Western Europe, its political significance has gone unrecognized. In fact, the highly decorated Siegburg *Schnellen*, imported into the Netherlands as drinking vessels and decanters, reveal a very high incidence of Old Testament scenes. Given the ideological requirements of Protestantism in the Low Countries, it should not surprise us that one of the most frequently represented figures is Judith. She is also represented in very diverse ways: singly, in combination with Justice and Lucretia (an emblem of republican freedom) or Esther (an emblem of deliverance). Other jugs illustrate the whole narrative of the Book of Judith. These beautiful yet utilitarian objects – most were intended for everyday use at table – are perhaps the most intriguing testament to the avid Protestant appetite for Judith.[21]

The German potters were supplying a wartime market in the Netherlands where Judith's significance as Justice and tyrannicide was highly active. In good Calvinist households and taverns serving the rebel army, politics were imbibed along with the beer and wine. This, too, was an implicitly democratic phenomenon: German Protestant dukes owned splendiferously ornamented Judith jugs, centrepieces for formal banquets, whilst even a relatively modest household could afford the cheaper versions of Judith *Schnellen*. In effect, these jugs were examples of the way in which religious commitment cut across the classes, unifying a society from top to bottom. In more than one sense, even in early modern Europe, Judith belonged to the people.

Since the Netherlandish revolt proved to be the most determined and successful of Protestant wars, its ideology and iconography were influential throughout Protestant Europe. Heemskerck's illustrations of Judith's story were widely diffused through the medium of engravings. Flemish glass was Europe's market-leader, and numerous roundels, often containing a whole cycle on the story of Judith, and sometimes based on Heemskerck's illustrations, were imported into England in order to supply Protestant enthusiasm for her image.[22] They were mounted both in churches and in private houses. Like Du Bartas's poem and German pottery, Netherlandish art both fed and fostered Judith's association with 'true religion' and political radicalism. The Old Testament images on some Tudor jewellery have been regarded (like the jugs)

as ideology-free, yet Judith's role in English Protestant polemic was so significant that we have to recognize the Judith scenes on locket-covers and hat-
badges as personal heraldries of the wearer's zeal for the true religion.[23] In
Germany, use of her image in official public spaces, such as the Regensburg
Rathaus, emblazoned a 'free' government's Protestant loyalties.[24] Her long
reign in Protestant art and artefacts, well into the seventeenth century, demonstrated that hers was an unusually striking, effective and successful propaganda
image which spanned public, ecclesiastical and private contexts. Judith spoke
very directly to the most urgent issues of the time.

This was owed, above all, to the heroine's exceptional resolution and ruthlessness. As the effects of the Reformation bit harder upon the conditions of
daily life – in riots, wars, shortages, penal measures against either denomination
– so animosities hardened and ideologies became more militant. Judith's bloody
activism strongly appealed to Protestants in situations of extreme conflict as the
personification of their own resort to desperate actions. In the Netherlands, for
example, the head-taking rebel heroine was a precise match for the unusually
determined and extensive Protestant iconoclasm, the festive riot of image-
breaking that denuded so many churches of their traditional decorations. A religious opposition to idolatrous images and an assault upon imperial authority
were implications that happily cohabited in Judith's image.

Nevertheless, for many years the outcome of the wars in the Low Countries
would be in doubt, and some towns found themselves conquered first by one
side, then the other. In such circumstances, it was useful if the emblems of one's
allegiance could have a seemingly innocent function. One of the useful aspects
of Judith's role, in this respect, was that she could appear to be merely an
instance of the popular decorative theme of woman triumphant. Despite her
particular significance for Protestants, possession of jugs and hearthbricks decorated with Judithic scenes could hardly be used as proof of subversive intentions. Piety itself was not an indictable offence. Judith was one of the images
that could contain subversive political intent ambiguously, yet without in any
way moderating the intrinsic forcefulness of the image. In both Jewish and
Christian traditions, after all, she had always been held up as type of exemplary
devotional habits. Here was wolfish militancy that could masquerate as a lamb-
like, churchgoing conformity when circumstances required. When religion was
such a dangerous business, declarations of allegiance in symbolic forms were
best chosen with care. Just as Judith had dissembled before Holofernes, so her
image could disguise its own subversiveness as mere biblical decor.

Once radical Protestantism had proved that much political capital could be
made of Judith, Catholics took the point. Judith appeared in cheap Italian black-
letter propaganda pamphlets, such as *La Rappresentatione di Judith Hebrea* (c.
1560), which was sufficiently popular to be reprinted three times. On the
Catholic as on the Protestant side, Judith was a fixture in popular culture as well

as in high theological debate. When the Jesuits launched their aggressive campaign of counter-reformation, which helped to recatholicize the southern
Netherlands, they also mounted a hostile takeover of Judith's symbolic value.
There had been a long tradition of popular urban religious drama in the Middle
Ages, of which the play *Judith Tua Holofernes* (recorded in 1404) was a French
example. In Protestant countries this popular form of entertainment was
hijacked for propaganda, so that a number of reforming plays about Judith were
written and staged in the Netherlands from the mid-1530s onwards.[25] In
England, a town play entitled *Holofernes* was still being performed as late as
1572,[26] and there can be no doubt that its continuing appeal was owing to the
story's identification with Protestant values. This was the year of the St
Bartholomew's Day Massacre of Protestants in Paris, an event that shocked and
horrified their co-religionists in England. Throughout Europe, Protestant
aggression towards Catholics hardened, and it was this that prompted renewed
interest in a town play about the bible's most remorseless avenger.

At the same time, academic religious dramas in Latin served a similar proselytizing purpose. One such was presented by Ralph Radcliffe in England, and
an avowedly political Judith-drama appeared in the Low Countries as early as
1536. Plays such as Sixt Burck's *Judith*, written in Latin, were largely limited
to educated audiences, but both in England and in the Low Countries Judith
dramas written in vernacular languages carried reforming, rebellious messages
from the intellectual centres of Protestantism outward to the masses. Apart
from performances in cities, some Judith dramas were also disseminated in
print – and widely read, as evidence of reprinting shows.[27] Aristocratic
Protestants, when the reign of Mary Tudor re-imposed Catholicism on
England, could nevertheless continue to promote their own religion by spon-
soring plays on pertinent themes, performed either in the privacy of their own
great households or in local venues. This was why at least two interludes about
Judith were performed during the 1550s: our records of these – probably merely
the tip of an iceberg – are a trace of the determination of English Protestants to
hold to the religion, even to advertise it in these coded forms, during the darkest
days of their persecution. By the later sixteenth century, then, Judith had
become a symbolic standard-bearer of Protestantism. Cheap black-letter pamphlets and popular ballads on the theme manifest how much this particular
story appealed to mass-market taste: Protestantism was on to a winner in the
battle for minds and hearts.

Once the Counter-Reformation was under way, however, its most dangerous
agents were prepared to learn even from their enemies, and one thing they
rapidly understood was how useful Judith's image was for propaganda purposes. The Jesuits observed the Protestants' two-pronged deployment of drama
for propaganda – aimed at both the opinion-forming, educated classes and the
masses – and found it good. Their school plays, in Latin, consequently included

a remarkably large number of scripts derived from the Book of Judith. There were at least ten Jesuit versions in German-speaking areas between 1565 and 1654.[28] During the Thirty Years' War these plays provided parables of the Old Religion resisting the 'tyrannical' Holofernes, personifying Protestant princes. Now that Catholicism could portray itself as an underdog, Judith's iconoclasm could be reversed, a challenge to the recently established Protestant regimes in Europe. Her iconography always worked most effectively for propaganda when 'her' side could portray itself as oppressed. She was an inspiring example of the worm turning.

It was, of course, precisely her embodiment of the humble and the oppressed that made her so appealing to popular taste. Aware that they needed to match the wide and deep penetration of urban populations that had been achieved by Protestantism, some Jesuit organizations disobeyed the order's rule that plays be presented in Latin.[29] Performances in the vernacular were, of course, much more effective at communicating the dramas' message to lay audiences. Notoriously pragmatic and uncompromising, the Jesuits left no stone unturned in the battle to restore Catholicism in Europe. If the lurid tale of Judith reached the parts others did not, and if disobeying their own Church's rules was a matter of the end justifying the means, they were nothing loath to present the story full-frontally, so to speak, in the language of the people.

In respect of their pragmatism, of course, Judith's duplicity was a particularly apt image for Counter-Reformation ruthlessness: and that was precisely why she became so strongly associated with the reputed amoralism of Jesuit fifth-columnists.[30] For Jesuits she represented their own adamantine commitment, whilst for their enemies she symbolized their amorality. For both sides these implications were often subtextual (after all Judith was a biblical heroine), but they put a topical spin on her intrinsic ambiguity. As the exponent of desperate measures, she represented, in effect, the high stakes for which both sides were playing in Reformation Europe. The very luridness of her story captured something of the spirit of the age.

In fact, by 1600 the Jesuits had managed to place their own stamp on Judith. The notorious political theory of the Jesuit Juan de Mariana, which was seen as epitomizing their Machiavellian support of sedition and murder in the service of the Catholic cause, was habitually associated in the popular mind with the image of Judith and her remorseless killing.[31] Whilst we shall see the effects of this in a later chapter, the Jesuits were only one example of the Counter-Reformation's attempt to repossess this potent political symbol for Catholicism. This effort was largely successful, since, once established in hegemony over their own polities, Protestants understandably became less keen on the radical implications of Judith. Fortunately, there was a good doctrinal excuse for this gradual Protestant retreat from Judith after 1600: her apocryphal origin. It is significant that, once the Dutch republic was secure, Judith's role in their proselytizing dramas was gradually overtaken by Esther, the canonical Bible's docile yet reforming wife. Judiths were unruly creatures, to be exploited when one's own objectives were disruptive, but discomforting once one had achieved power oneself. Back to her hermitage – or Apocrypha – she went.

Nevertheless, it was Protestantism that had provided the most powerful impetus towards Judith's centrality in Renaissance culture. That was because, for the first time, a pan-European movement had fused her spiritual with her revolutionary political meaning. As Lord Morley wrote to Henry VIII of England in 1539, celebrating his break with the Church of Rome, 'England is new born, newly brought from thraldom to freedom. For whereas there is nothing more sweet than liberty, nothing more bitter than bondage, in so much that death hath often been chosen to avoid servitude, what owe we unto you . . . [who] are by you . . . the bonds broken, set out of danger from the captivity Babylonical, so that we may plainly say as the Jews did to Judith: You are our beauty, you are our honour, you are our glory.'[32] Protestantism seized upon a combination of spiritual and political in Judith's significance, that had always to some degree been evaded before: her full potential to disturb the received order of things. For as long as Protestantism saw itself as the avant-garde, it looked in the mirror and saw Judith's face.

Hysterical Heretics

The Reformation released Judith's full potential to challenge the received order because it combined with her radical political and religious aspects a realization of her feminist potential. The face of Protestantism was not simply allegorically feminine. Within the symbolic systems of Renaissance culture Protestantism was a woman.

One reason for this was, precisely, symbolic: that Protestantism was engaged in deconstructing an international patriarchal institution, the Papacy. Judith's anti-patriarchal and iconoclastic implications were complementary aspects of her symbolic utility when Protestantism attacked the authoritarianism, hierarchy, pride and worldliness of the Catholic Church: the attributes of Holofernes in the Apocrypha.

Another reason for Protestantism's female face was not merely symbolic but also strikingly descriptive of its own history. Protestantism's most effective political ally was the power exercised by women. In France, the initial leader of the Huguenots was the indomitable Jeanne, Queen of Navarre, patron and friend of Calvin, who bequeathed this leadership role to her son, Henry.[33] In the Huguenot epic that she commissioned, Du Bartas explicitly identified her as the Protestants' own 'Judith' in the Wars of Religion. After Jeanne's death, her successor's wife, Marguerite de Navarre would replace her in Du Bartas's poem as the female arbiter Judith.[34] So vital had been Jeanne's role as a standard-bearer of Protestantism in Europe – much more militant, belligerent and indeed Protestant than Elizabeth I of England would ever be – that the Huguenot cause was symbolically female; and for propaganda purposes, its leadership perceived as descending in the female line (despite Marguerite's own religion). It was as if the Judithic characterization of Jeanne, which she herself had chosen, rendered the biblical heroine as at once the allegorically female Muse and the literally female general of the new religion's troops. This was a role-model carefully selected to present Protestantism as obdurate, ruthless and inevitably victorious.

Similarly, in England, it was Anne Boleyn, initiated into Protestantism by the Navarre circle, who actively promoted the new religion. When the propagandist Thomas Heywood came to record the history of Protestantism in England, he would characterize it as established by women, in the teeth of Henry VIII's 'tyranny': subtextually Henry is the Holofernes here. From Anne the mantle had descended to her successors as queen, Jane Seymour and Catherine Parr, to the briefly enthroned Lady Jane Grey, and then (triumphantly, of course) to Anne's own daughter, Elizabeth I.[35] In later sixteenth-century Europe, Elizabeth herself was regarded as the champion of Protestantism, to whom Huguenots and Netherlanders appealed for moral and material support. The female visage of Protestantism derived, logically enough, from the demonstrable power of women to promulgate the new religion.

As Heywood's paean to royal women acknowledged, it was particularly in England that Protestantism had a striking feminine genealogy. This was, in fact, a very useful theme for Protestant proselytizing and propaganda. Piety had always been regarded as a virtue particularly suited to women – to the lives of those whose destiny was to support, serve and care for men, whose destiny required a more active life. (Although of course whenever piety was actually a professional matter, an employment in the Church, it became a masculine fief.) To associate the idealized purity, modesty and piety that this society postulated as women's peculiar genus of virtue with the virtues of the Protestant faith was a way of idealizing the faith itself. Thus, for instance, Thomas Bentley's *The Monument of Matrons* (1582) recreated in literary form the circle of Protestant noblewoman that Queen Catherine Parr had gathered around her, citing the Princess Elizabeth and Lady Jane Grey as luminaries of this feminine religion. Celebrated as godly, talented, aristocratic and influential, they conferred their graceful feminine nobility upon the faith. In effect, it was as attractive and distinguished as they were.

That Christianity was, according to the gospel, the religion of the meek and the weak meant that Protestantism, if womanly, was closer to its essence than the Catholic Church, dominated by a papal father. This imagery thus supported Protestantism's claim to revive the original, true version of Christian belief. At the same time, the fact that all of the *Monument*'s paragons are aristocratic prevented readers from confusing the idea of spiritual humility with plebeian coarseness. Bentley's *Monument* thus had it both ways: the true religion was humble, but not too humble.

Yet this feminization was not wholly an emollient image, for Protestantism was still young, embattled, militant and aggressive. Consequently, the *Monument* combined its eulogies of royal women with celebrations of biblical heroines. Its Esther is intended as a counterpart to the women's royalty, its Judith – the most salient biblical figure here – a model for religious militancy. Similarly, many decades later, the poet Michael Drayton urged Lady Jane Devereux, scion of a great family of Protestant politicians, to be a Judith for her time.[36] The message of such works was clear: the true faith might be feminine, but if so it was a *femme forte*, capable of wielding the sword of the spirit. What Judith's image conveyed – what no other such prototype did – was that Protestantism was the religion of the meek (viz women), as Christianity ideally was supposed to be – but the meek were not to be messed with.

This self-fashioning of Protestantism's cultural image was not confined to the realm of propaganda and proselytizing. On the contrary: it reflected qualities immanent in Protestantism itself. In its purist form, this was a democratic, informalized, de-institutionalized – in short, privatized – version of Christianity. Rejecting the institutionalized and hieratic mediations that Catholicism had so long interposed between the believer and God, Protestantism contended that every lay believer was capable of direct communion with the deity, and of interpreting the Word without ecclesiastical supervision. The moment that any lay believer was accorded this kind of spiritual autonomy, female believers were also necessarily permitted access to scripture and the godhead, as never before. Not least, Latin, a language almost never taught to women, had limited their access to the Bible until the vernacular transitions were issued by Protestant scholars.

This effect is very deliberately advertised in Du Bartas's *Judit*. Private study of the Bible, and its reading to the household, were habitual Protestant routines, reflecting this religion's character as very much a lay practice. Thus it is in the course of her daily Bible-reading that Du Bartas has Judith come upon the example of Ehud's tyrannicide, the moment when God instructs her in the job he intends her to do, and when she finds her destiny. Du Bartes was well aware of how far Judith's activism breached the norms of gender in Renaissance Europe, and he had no desire to encourage this, even though he was committed to commending her political example. This deep contradiction at the heart of his poem undergoes, here, one of his ingenious attempts to repair it: adding to the apocryphal story, he says that his (meek and timid) Judith hesitated to think of herself as capable of following a man's example. Tyrannicide, she thinks, is man's work. It is only when she lights upon the verse recounting Jael's murder of Sisera that she feels emboldened to see this as work that a woman might do.

On the one hand, Judith's inspiration is intended as exemplary of a lay believer's autonomy within Protestantism; whilst on the other, Du Bartas is anxious to reaffirm that, even amongst the equality of the laity, there is an inequality of gender.

But such fine adjustments to the feminist potential of a Protestant Judith were at best makeshift repairs to an old order that Protestantism itself was otherwise enthusiastically dismantling. The fact was that it had, like an Oedipus, slain the papal Father. And, as usual, behind an Oedipus was the spectre of his female doppelgänger, a Judith. By rejecting the conviction that clergy should be celibate, Protestantism had driven a wedge into the immemorial Christian misogyny that regarded women (and the carnal Flesh that they embodied) as 'the devil's gate', as inherently predisposed to wickedness. If even clergymen could safely cohabit with women, this view of women was clearly acknowledged as, at best, partial. Both the practical and the feminist implications of clerical marriage were quite clear to Jeanne, the self-proclaimed Judith of Navarre: she enabled the escape of her niece, a novice nun, from a convent where she had been immured to prevent her marrying, so that she could marry a Protestant. As it had been for Christina of Markyate when she cited her vision of Judith, marriage was a religious issue that intrinsically involved questions of women's autonomy as well.

This was particularly important when women's lives were being more, not less, restricted to the private sphere than before. Economic and other changes would, by the later seventeenth century, markedly reduce most women's ability to undertake occupations outside their own households: they were becoming even more domesticated.[37] However, Protestantism could ameliorate this increasing privatization of women's lives. In the Netherlands, for instance, the denuding of churches was compensated by an increase in biblical decor within the home. As we have seen, that decor was characterized by a high proportion of positive images of biblical women, and one of the reasons for this was that house-bound women could be presumed by manufacturers to be enthusiastic purchasers of these images of feminine virtue and achievement. As much as ideology, commercial good sense dictated the extensive production of furnishings and objects for the home that were decorated with images of biblical women. Because Protestantism was the privatized religion, it was in this literal sense necessarily the religion of women, the private gender.

In turn, the panoply of feminine biblical images in Protestant households reinforced the perception that Protestantism was symbolically feminine. Women themselves – even women of great position – colluded in its feminization, for the pious decoration of their own privatized sphere thus became a kind of lifeline to the public world. The most significant thing about Reformation religion (and the thing most often forgotten by historians) was that it was the unique link between the public political and private domestic worlds. For even the most domesticated wife, the ability to proselytize the decor of her own home lessened the divide between her world and that much broader horizon granted to men. Moreover, the high incidence of Judiths in this domestic context attests to their interest in a role-model who was herself a transgressor of the divide between private and public worlds.

Thus one consequence of Protestant reform was that women had greater autonomy in their religious lives. And since in most respects religion was acknowledged as the ultimate arbiter in early modern life, autonomy in their religious lives had massive implications for women's freedom of action in general. In effect, Protestantism bestowed upon women the possibility of a stronger sense of identity.

The most striking example of this is Catherine, Duchess of Suffolk, who became a legend in her own lifetime. Sponsor of Hugh Latimer, promoter of Protestantism, succourer of Protestant martyrs such as her friend Anne Askew; distinguished fugitive from the long arm of Mary Tudor's persecution, Catherine's fame as an indomitable Protestant and colourful heroine inspired ballads, stage-plays and fulsome dedications in religious works. Her son, a hero of the war in the Low Countries, accrued greater status as a Protestant hero from her repute. She herself exerted both direct and indirect influence in order to ensure that she was identified with Judith as the spirit of Protestantism. The many visible effects of this self-elected role extend even to the tapestries in her great hall, her reissuing of the Apocrypha under her own imprimatur and the penning of a sonnet on Judith by her son's client, Henry Lok. By iconizing herself as Judith she moulded her own public image, in which feminine assertiveness, aristocratic power and the new religion were mutually reinforcing. In turn, that image increased her capacity to exert influence upon her contemporaries.[38]

Women such as Catherine became models for their sex, feminist because religious heroines. What the Duchess's life became for posterity was a manifestation of personal autonomy, at a time when, on the whole, women were not supposed to aspire to that. Marvelling at the Duchess's ability to resist the Marin 'tyranny', Lanier saw in her a woman who was 'unsubjected'[39] – a free spirit.

Ironically, Catholic propaganda colluded with Protestantism's feminization of its own image. During the Wars of Religion in France, it became an axiom of Catholics that the majority of Huguenots were women.[40] Records do not bear out this stereotyping: it was in fact one of those myths generated by deep-seated attitudes to gender. The contention that most 'heretics' were women was intended to characterize Protestantism itself as weak-minded and hysterical, supposedly feminine attributes. It was also intended to imply that heresy was disorderly, in the same way that women with the temerity to hold opinions were unruly – disobedient and unnatural. Thus, the thinking went, Protestantism was the kind of febrile nonsense to which only women would be readily susceptible.

However, the conviction that heresy was feminine hysteria had the inescapable concomitant that women were an obvious target for Counter-Reformation efforts. The Catholic Church resolved to win back women's hearts, making a concerted attempt to reinvigorate the Virgin Mary's role as a model and spiritual companion for women. Some of the Church's most severe strictures upon, and penalties against, women – even 'fallen women' – were mitigated.[41] At the same time, as we have already seen, Counter-Reformation art followed Protestantism's successful example by extolling heroic biblical women: the numerous Judiths painted by Counter-Reformation artists, and her evocation in Spanish Golden Age dramas, were effects of this counter-offensive to Protestantism's appeal to women.

The net effect of internecine Reformation propaganda was to produce, very much as a side-effect, a feminist phenomenon. In dismantling old certainties and challenging the patriarchal church, Protestantism had inevitably fostered a social rebelliousness as well. Conversely, at the pinnacle of society it had offered royal women an opportunity to assert themselves by identifying with the new religion and promulgating it. Piety ceased to be a natural, privatized, safe occupation for the 'second sex'. Arguing that it was piety itself that inspired them to be assertive, opinionated and activist, highly placed women could express the individualism that is conferred by making a choice – of religions. Consequently, like Judith's chastity, female piety could be transformed from a mode of conformity into a mode of resistance to the constraints upon women's lives.

We can see this strategy at work in Lanier's poem, where the celebration of Protestant noblewomen, the catalogue of biblical heroines and the trenchant attack on conventional misogyny coalesce to place a feminist spin on the idea of a feminine religion. It has long been axiom of feminists that in the Renaissance the Christian religion was thoroughly disadvantageous to women, because of the unrivalled doctrinal supports it gave to patriarchy.[42] However, this is a simplistic view, which underestimates both early modern women and the meritocratic potential granted by Protestant doctrines. Both theoretically and practically, women had new opportunities. The Reformation enabled, for the first time, a feminist ideology that – however often simply rhetorical, theoretical, conventional or cynically propagandist – could bolt itself onto the most powerful issue of its time.

5

The Monstrous Regiment of Judiths
Power and Gender in the Renaissance

According to the Apocrypha, a nation surrounded by belligerent superpowers would be best advised to find itself a Judith forthwith. 'The Persians quaked at her boldness, and the Medes were daunted at her hardiness . . . And there was none that made the children of Israel any more afraid in the days of Judith, nor a long time after her death' (16:10–25) – which is not surprising. Observers of the European scene in the sixteenth century might have echoed the sentiments of the ancient Medes and Persians. At times it seemed that, wherever one looked, there were new Judiths taking the fates of nations into their formidable hands. Yet this was in a period when European monarchies had for many centuries been almost exclusively male dominions, when the new female rulers were shocking anomalies, and when received wisdom remained that women were by nature neither eligible for, nor in their wildest dreams capable of, rule. They were not considered able to govern themselves, let alone nations. In France, for instance, the Salic Law excluded women from the throne. By all the canons of Renaissance thought about the natural and divine order of things, a female monarch was a contradiction in terms. Thus it was that the biblical Judith, a woman who had traduced the patriarchal order, became a byword in contemporary responses – by turns amazed, impressed and horrified – for the phenomenon of multiple female rule. For the first time, the last frontier of inequality, supreme political power, was thoroughly colonized by what the enraged Scottish Presbyterian John Knox described as a 'monstrous regiment of women'.[1]

Medieval Queenship

Judith had long been identified with queens. Ever since the early Middle Ages, when the desiccated cleric Rabanus Maurus had saluted the splendid Carolingian empress Judith as her reincarnation, this identification had been available.[2] It was a particularly strong theme in medieval France and Burgundy, where royal women were habitually compared to Old Testament figures and especially to Judith. Thus, early in the fifteenth century, the poet François Villon compared Marie d'Orléans to both the Virgin Mary and Judith, her anti-type. At the other end of the century, after the death of Edward IV of England, William Caxton defended his widow, the embattled, disempowered queen by comparing her to Judith in her chastity, power and legitimacy. Caxton was drawing on what was already a centuries-old tradition linking Judith to female royalty and the virtues of kings' spouses.[3]

On the other hand, there was an equally long-established and rather stronger tradition of depreciating royal women. Writers and artists had long revelled in depicting the weaknesses, sins and crimes of ancient queens – the Cleopatras, Didos and Jezebels. Wicked queens of the past did service beyond the call of duty in ancient and medieval European literature, keeping many writers gain-fully employed. But their uses went well beyond the arts. When, during the French religious wars, *Francogallia* was published in defence of the Salic Law in 1573, it cited a remarkably extensive and apparently horrifying catalogue of maleficent queens and the political mayhem for which they had been respons-ible.[4] Its readers might well have concluded that every political disaster in human history could – somehow – be laid at women's door.

The proposition that women might be allowed not simply royal status but real power was wholly contentious. As we saw, the boundary between public and private spheres was heavily policed as a gender-divide. Consequently the most celebrated of Burgundian writers, Christine de Pisan, had retold Judith's story in the *City of Ladies* (1405) in order to provide a role-model for women's right to enter the public sphere and influence practical politics.[5] Since the most prominent readers of this popular writer were the royal women of the Burgundian and French courts, this message may have struck them as manna from heaven. Certainly we should understand that this was Christine's most assertive contribution to the *querelle des femmes*, although it would not achieve its full impact until over a hundred years later. It was then that the conjunction between myth and history occurred, which brought Judith's icon of female sov-ereignty into active use in day-to-day politics.

Gynecocracy

In fact the reason why the *querelle* was so prolonged was because it was given new impetus by women's rise to power. By the mid-sixteenth century Reformation politics was largely dominated by women.

Some achieved this eminence by the time-honoured unofficial routes to power that had been women's best hope in the past. Catherine of Aragon, for instance, was made regent of England during Henry VIII's absence on the Continent. While in office she repelled a Scottish invasion. In Scotland, the widowed Mary of Guise became regent for her daughter, the infant Mary, later Queen of Scots, whilst in the Netherlands two female regents governed on behalf of the Spanish Emperor. Meanwhile in France, no one was under any illusion that the three sons of Henry II, who successively occupied the throne, were more than the puppets of their terrifying mother, Catherine de' Medici. When Henry IV was assassinated, his widow, Marie de' Medici, ruled as regent for her son, as did the next queen, Anne of Austria. Those female politicians did not intrinsically challenge the cherished conviction that women could achieve power only by dominating male rulers or receiving authority from them. What was striking about these women was rather their sheer number and the long duration of their authority.

However, in the eyes of male commentators, these were merely the supporting cast to a much more disturbing innovation, a remarkable series of queens regnant – those who held power entirely in their own right. Mary Queen of Scots, sole heir to her father and with a strong claim to inherit the English throne as well, was only one of these. Margaret of Austria was effectively the heiress to an empire. In France, Jeanne de Bourbon was queen of Navarre in her own right. The throne of Sweden, then a prominent power, would be inherited by Queen Christina. But the most remarkable case of all was England. There, in the fifty years between the death of Edward VI and the execution of Mary Queen of Scots, women ruled in their own right: Lady Jane Grey lasted only six days, Mary I a few years, but the reign of Elizabeth I was famously prolonged.[6] As if queens regnant were not sufficiently outlandish, for the same period every other claimant to the English throne was also a woman. In short, the sudden and ubiquitous advent of gynecocracy – supposed aberration – was such as to stun contemporaries.

What had hitherto been something of a parlour-game, arguing about the virtues and vices of womankind, rapidly became an issue of obvious and urgent political moment. Long consigned to the shadows of private life, women had now taken over the public world. What was worse, in many cases they had done so by the absolute and unquestioned right granted by the normal rules of succession: the aberration had come about by due process. Thus, if an aberration, it could not simply be dismissed as illegitimate. That was precisely why the queens regnant posed such a problem for anyone wedded to what were, after all, the normal cultural assumptions about power and patriarchy. Unlike Catherine de' Medici, they could not simply be dismissed as ambitious women who had seized an authority to which they held no right. They should not have been there, as Knox howled, but there they were all the same, by law and due succession.

Thus, although by the mid-century the humanist *querelle* had abated, it was revived by the *fait accompli* of gynecocracy, which had overturned the relative status of the sexes. And the controversy about women's natures was the more contentious, and the more productive of *mauvaise foi* about queens regnant, because the politics of religion at this time made even the traditional Christian views of gender less reliable criteria than they had been previously. Being ruled by the subordinate sex did concentrate the masculine mind.

One of the touchstones the debate lighted on, repeatedly and almost obsessively, was the biblical example of Judith. From the early Middle Ages until the early sixteenth century the feminine element in Judith's monarchic symbolism had lain dormant: until gynecocracy reintroduced it as the most compelling image of the woman in power. Once again it became a focus for all the issues – political, religious, sexual – thrown up by a woman's supremacy in societies designed for men. In the Renaissance, however, the stakes were very much higher than they had been before, since the Reformation itself was indissolubly entwined with female sovereignty.

Apart from the usual burdens of power in the brutal ethos of Reformation politics, queens regnant had to negotiate a minefield of cultural assumptions that made their reigns very much more problematic than a king's. In that minefield, Judith's image could be for them by turns a comrade-in-arms, an enemy or a minesweeper. Both the opportunities and the problems of power as wielded by a woman were already written into her myth, and Renaissance queens lived them out: sometimes painfully, sometimes triumphantly.

A Judith or a Jezebel

Henry VIII's will, which established the succession to the English throne, frequently flew in the face of logic, but it did result in a multiplicity of female claimants (somewhat ironically, given his obsessive pursuit of a male heir through no fewer than six marriages). Queens' legitimate and autonomous hold on power left patriarchal political theory in disarray. But this was not merely a theoretical matter, since subsequent sixteenth-century English and Scottish history was dominated by the succession issue. Amongst other things, the identity of individual heirs and claimants determined the religious complexion of the nation, and hence also recalibrated its role in international politics. The accession of Mary I in 1553 re-Catholicized England, whereas her sister Elizabeth I represented Protestants' best hope of a return to the 'true religion'. Consequently, the whole question of whether women should rule at all was crucially complicated by the religious affiliation of the queen in question.

The character of good monarchical government had already been linked to Judith's image by the iconography of the marriage festivities for Henry VIII's sister, Margaret, when she married the king of Scotland.[7] One of the tableaux presented during the procession had portrayed a series of Virtues trampling upon vanquished Vices, but its import was not merely moralistic. The political freight of this tableau dictated that the Vices included the tyrants Nero,

Sardanapalus and Holofernes, whose personal wickedness was identified with their bad government. Judith's figure thus signified here both the chastity of the good wife (Margaret) and her role as one of the beneficent influences upon her husband's government. Judith's private Christian virtue, Chastity, was thus identified with her public virtue, Justice, as constituents of wise rule in a Christian polity. So far, so allegorical: but subsequent events in Scottish and English politics would make her template for monarchy both more literal and more controversial.

The initial response to Mary I's accession put a brave face on the business of female sovereignty. But in fact contemporaries found it difficult to take the idea seriously. Male politicians had intrigued to promote rival female claimants to the throne under the firm impression that, once in power, they would do as their sponsors told them. It was inconceivable to them that a female ruler could exercise real authority. And this view seemed to be resoundingly confirmed, in the event, by the disastrous reigns of Mary I and Mary Queen of Scots. So much so, indeed, that even after many years of successful rule, Elizabeth I had to contend with some of her closest advisers' rooted misogyny, which led them to underestimate this consummate politician.[8] Their presumptuous attitude was sufficient proof that men were reluctant to believe that a woman's power could be anything other than men's power exercised by proxy. At Elizabeth's accession, contemporary scepticism was necessarily more acute than at Mary I's accession: she had a mountain of entrenched prejudice to climb. Where Mary (dominated by men) had failed, Elizabeth would not be expected to succeed in proving women capable of government. This phenomenon is fascinating, because no one had ever thought to question a king's competence simply on the basis of his gender. As is clear from the attack on gynecocracy in *Francogallia* – which was designed to discredit Catherine de' Medici – bad kings were simply bad; bad queens were bad because they were female.

In this ambience, Elizabeth's success owed much to Mary's misfortunes. Personally, she seemed a bright prospect after Mary, but also she had learned by Mary's mistakes what were the special pitfalls awaiting a female monarch. And the controversy that surrounded Mary's accession showed Elizabeth the ground-rules that she had to observe if she were to turn her femininity into an asset for her propaganda, and if indeed she were to survive the machinations of her enemies.

The Protestant intellectuals driven into Continental exile at Mary's accession were determined to discredit her and incite resistance to her in England.[9] The easiest argument to deploy against the Queen was the time-honoured, absolute criterion, that she was a tyrant. However, it seemed to Protestant polemicists that in this respect Mary's gender was a gift. If they asserted the entirely traditional view that women should not rule, this in itself stamped her as illegitimate, and illegitimate rule was *ipso facto* tyrannical. Rounded off with cries of horror at her persecution of Protestants, this characterization was seen to be confirmed by the bloodthirsty cruelty that was also a habit of tyrants. In Scotland in 1552, Sir David Lindsay had already attacked Mary of Guise by asserting that women should not 'Realms take in governing'.[10] The Marian exiles elaborated that theme with great enthusiasm. Thomas Becon's *Humble Supplication Unto God* (1554) was far from humble in its contention that women's rule was contrary to the laws of God and Nature. Knox, Gilby and Goodman made particularly vituperative use of the usual biblical examples adduced by such writers to prove that women's rule was evil in the eyes of God. Mary was, they averred, a Jezebel, fit to rival the Old Testament's most wicked queen.[11] In due course, Mary Queen of Scots, Elizabeth I and Catherine de' Medici would all receive the same dubious tribute from their opponents. The biblical identification was sufficient to convey the full horror of gynecocracy: unnaturalness, cruelty and lasciviousness were Jezebel's talents, and therefore female rulers' immutable attributes. While the Old Testament provided the exiles' bogeywomen, the New supplied their scriptural proofs that God had forbidden women to bear spiritual authority, and hence disabled them from government of any kind.

But, as usual, the Bible was a double-edged sword. The Old Testament supplied alternative, much more positive examples of women's authority, which were equally familiar to the exiles' readers. Judith had already been recruited to Mary I's cause. A ballad saluted her as 'our Judith'. As Mary processed to Westminster after her coronation, the Florentine's pageant had brought the Florentine Judith to an English monarch.[12] Their representation of Judith as 'the liberator of her country' alluded to Mary's victory over Lady Jane Grey's supporters and the Protestant cause. Judith's method of assassination – decapitation – aptly paralleled the beheading of the Duke of Northumberland in the previous month. To Judith's trophy spectators of the pageant could readily compare the severed heads of the rebels, which by custom were displayed upon the gates of London. The biblical precedent had now been conjured into life as a symbol of woman's rule and Catholic resurgence.

Since the Bible was the acknowledged arbiter of the controversy about gynecocracy, the anti-Marians had to find a way of dealing with the inconvenient Deborah and Judith. In his *First Blast of the Trumpet against the Monstrous Regiment of Women* (1558), Knox's strategy was to argue that God could of course create exceptions to his own rule against female sovereignty – and anyway, those exceptions were confined to ancient times, when the world was purer. Deborah was such an exception, and in any case not a ruler in the strict sense of the word. As for Judith, she was easily dismissed, because, as Knox piously opined, her Book was apocryphal.[13] This was an awkward way of pitting one department of Protestantism against another – Latimer's Judith was an image for the contemporary radical Protestant, we remember – in a way that could dispose of Judith's feminist implications.

The main thrust of anti-gynecocratic argument was that woman, having been placed by God in subordination to man, could not bear rule over him. There were other, practical arguments. Women, like children, were weak and incapable of authority; therefore, like child-rulers, their accessions would inevitably provoke faction, war and anarchy. Both the Marian exiles and the French opponents of Catherine de' Medici, such as Henri Estienne, rehearsed these arguments as if by rote. Further, should female rulers marry, their subordinate role as wives contradicted their authoritative role as queens. Inevitably, their husbands would rule them, and hence their nations. A foreign husband would thus subject the nation to foreign rule, as the Marian exiles argued, Mary I's Spanish husband did. Should the queen marry a native, however, the situation would be even worse, since someone who ought to be her subject would rule her, and the nation. Also, his compatriot noblemen would be envious of his elevation, and factional wars would result. (These were factors that would later count against Elizabeth I's desire to marry the Earl of Leicester.) In fine, whilst monarchs were required to marry in order to perpetuate the dynasty, a woman ruler could not do so without fatally compromising her authority and courting disaster.

Through the queen's female body the national integrity was, as it were, permeable: could be penetrated by foreign invaders and domestic usurpers. Adopting the traditional view that the kingdom was a 'body politic', Knox compared it to the 'natural body' of man: since man was the head of womankind, woman merely the body, female sovereignty placed the body over the head. Consequently the national body itself became female: weak, passive and impotent. As we saw, a similar mythology inspired the Book of Judith's determination to keep Judith celibate till her death, her body being the impregnable citadel of Israel's freedom. In precisely the same way, it was borne in upon Elizabeth I that she could never marry. Hoping against hope, she may have flirted with the possibility of marrying Alençon (foreign) or Leicester (native), and she certainly used her eligibility as a valuable bargaining-counter in international diplomacy. But she knew that being trumpeted as the Virgin Queen was a matter not so much of magical-maiden mythology, but of practical politics. This was the real-life version of being the national fortress, like Judith. That was one of the reasons why the Virgin Queen was hailed as a Judith by her contemporaries: she was condemned to the same lonely fate.

Elizabeth's Judithic destiny was inaugurated by the Marian controversy. In 1558, her accession deeply embarrassed those exiles who had railed against women's regiment, for this queen was Protestant. Suddenly female government had recommendations. Even Calvin himself had to eat humble pie on the exiles' behalf, if Europe's most powerful Protestant monarch were not to be alienated from the struggle to reform the Continent.[14] But Knox chose to brazen it out, maintaining that, whilst women's sovereignty was unnatural, he would deign to except Elizabeth from this rule because God had clearly chosen her to preserve

Protestantism.[15] (Although he also stipulated that, in return, she must admit that all other women were ineligible for the post.)

But at least one exile interpreted God's will differently. In *An Harbour for Faithful and True Subjects* (1559), John Aylmer defended female sovereignty, and in particular Elizabeth's, because she was a modern Judith. If God has chosen to give England a queen regnant, then his will is manifest and to complain of it blasphemous, Aylmer argued. As when the formidable Judith flayed those 'milksops', the Israelite elders, for their fear and faithlessness, Elizabeth has been chosen to rouse Protestantism and England to their triumph over the Holofernes of Popery.[16]

Yet Aylmer could hardly be accused of ardent feminism. In fact his argument rather depends upon the opposite point of view. Submission to Elizabeth is really submission to God, whose power is manifested in direct ratio to her impotence. As we saw, this is the case in the original Book of Judith; and Aylmer perceived the utility of that theme to his persuading Elizabeth's subjects to accept her peaceably. Therefore, if God enthrones 'a woman weak in nature, feeble in body, soft in courage, unskilful in practice, not terrible to the enemy', like Judith, then he is telling us that 'My strength is most perfect when you be most weak', and as in the Book of Judith, the lack of 'man or any wordly means' will precipitate the 'greatest wonders'. Under Elizabeth as Judith, Protestantism will win its war. Aylmer's was an ingenious argument, which depended for its force upon selecting the one biblical prototype that would make contesting a woman's sovereignty a case of doubting God himself. Judith's unwomanly victory became a prophecy of Protestantism's certain triumph, a potent emotive appeal.

Elizabeth's role as the Protestant Judith predated Aylmer's work. Whilst she was, during her sister's reign, kept out of the public eye at Hatfield House, a play about Judith is said to have been presented before her:[17] implicitly suggesting, even in these inauspicious circumstances, her role as the hope of the Protestant cause. During her reign the burgeoning of Judith's Protestant significance on the Continent would be matched by English propaganda about their own royal Judith, but this was not a role that Elizabeth herself relished.

Richard Barnefield's poetic compliment, *Cynthia* (1595), saluted Elizabeth as 'A second Judith in Jerusalem', her chastity the complement to her ability to rescue England from Catholicism.[18] This is the orotund way of saying that celibacy is a prerequisite of the role designed for Elizabeth by her subjects. Other loyalists emphasized rather Judith's militancy, as a model for the ruthless foreign policy that a good Protestant queen should pursue (and in which Elizabeth was unenthusiastic). In 1578, the city of Norwich, for instance, mounted a pageant that compared Elizabeth's virtues to those of Deborah and Esther, but their climactic biblical instruction was embodied in Judith, who combined their virtues with a commitment to violence.[19] Flanked by her more amenable biblical analogues, Judith's lurid example is as it were contained and limited by theirs: she becomes both more dignified and more decorous. Uses of Judith for Elizabeth's iconography are often tactfully adjusted in this way, to recognize a distance between them and to drain Judith of her more dubious implications.

Specifically, though, Judith's role here is to persuade the Queen of the godliness of force. 'Oh mighty queen and finger of the Lord,' says Judith to Elizabeth, 'be sure thou art his mighty hand.' If Judith, only a 'poor widow' and 'poor wight', could be God's swordwoman, then a queen of 'surpassing might' will be able to overthrow any tyrant with ease. Although the Book of Judith's point was the reverse, that the meek vanquish the mighty, once one was addressing a queen one rewrote biblical mores to fit the prevailing hierarchies. Politics, and especially the coded advice urging Elizabeth to be more zealous, overrode Christian ethics here.

The 'tyrant' to whom the Norwich pageant particularly referred was the Catholic Philip II of Spain, who would send the Armada against England in 1588. Similar sentiments inspired the naming of a ship commanded by Francis Drake, scourge of Spanish fleets, as the *Judith*. When the Armada was defeated, it seemed as if at last Elizabeth's reincarnation of Judith were amply demonstrated, in a Protestant victory over the world's mightiest empire. Fire-breathingly nationalist and zealous, a popular street ballad by the highly successful journalist Thomas Deloney extolled Elizabeth as the Judith to Philip's Holofernes.[20] Since popular propaganda habitually identified jingoism and Protestantism, Judith's double role as national heroine and exemplary lay believer was supremely suited to it. And unlike the Norwich pageant, far from wishing to moderate Judith's significance, the ballad rises to the occasion of victory by stressing her militancy, violence and relentlessness. Judith typified fanatic godly patriotism, in a way that could accommodate the Queen's gender. In the four street ballads identifying the two women, there was no compulsion to be as mealy-mouthed as the Norwich citizens. Whether or not the Queen favoured the gory comparison was irrelevant to the mass audience which responded enthusiastically to this street literature.

It is clear, in fact, that Elizabeth did not like biblical personations. From the very start of her reign her attitude to religion was irenic, because she was more interested in retaining the support of all sectors of the population. Her official portraits were carefully policed,[21] and it is surely striking that not one of them employs biblical imagery. Classical and other allegorical motifs were uncontroversial, whereas biblical ones were not.

In particular, because of her reluctance to indulge the common view that she must bear the mantle of zealous Protestantism, the evocation of the Queen as a 'second Judith' was unwelcome. (Some propagandists recognized this: thus a stage-play about the Duchess of Suffolk which uses her own preferred Judithic self-image treats her as a displaced, more satisfactory popular image of Elizabeth's national role.)[22] Whilst the popularity of Judith's icon was intensified by English nationalism, especially in times of political crisis, Judith was a role imposed upon the Queen by her Protestant subjects. It is true that Renaissance monarchs were accustomed to issue propaganda in a much more programmatic and draconian manner than their medieval forebears, but it is questionable whether this was merely one-way traffic. Even in Renaissance England, there were means by which the people could influence the monarch, and Judith's image was one of them, a kind of ballot-box. Just as the original Judith had rebuked the governors of her city, so in sixteenth-century England her image acted as the voice of the people. Not only in mythic terms but in practical politics, Judith gave the 'poor wight' access to the corridors of power.

Paris Is Worth a Massacre

In the meantime, in France, the extreme brutality of the civil wars had made the question of effective propaganda much more acute. Here, if anywhere, the relative success of a propaganda machine could be measured by the practical outcome of streams of official and unofficial tendentiousness: royal spectacles, paintings, woodcuts, memorabilia, pamphlets and handbills posted in the streets. To a situation of such remorseless violence and vicious antagonism Judith's image was all too relevant, and it did sterling work on both sides of the religious conflict.

In the previous century, France had already learned to identify itself with Judith. Hammer of the English, Joan of Arc had been the saint sent by God to deliver France and restore its self-respect; contemporaries hailed Joan as the 'second Judith'. In the year of her greatest military triumphs, a biography compared her favourably with Judith and Deborah, champion and prophetess. This tradition persisted throughout the two succeeding centuries. A fanciful portrait of the warrior maid, painted in the seventeenth century probably by Jean de Caumont, calls her 'une autre Judith . . . [who] coupa la tête à Holopherne anglois', and Le Moyne's royally-commissioned handbook, *La Gallerie* saluted her as a Judith.[23] *Alors*, France had produced a heroine who combined and surpassed the Bible's best!

France was already personified in Joan's historical embodiment of Judith. Here was another Reformation struggle in which the major antagonists were two queens: the Huguenot Jeanne de Navarre confronted the dowager queen Catherine de' Medici.[24] More militant than Elizabeth, and aware that Huguenots had little choice but to commit themselves to armed revolt, Jeanne had in 1574 deliberately announced herself the Judith of this army through the medium of the poem she commissioned from Du Bartas. His epic made Judith's the most controversial iconography in France.

Jeanne's self-identification with Judith built upon her popularity as an icon for Huguenots. Calvin had instructed Protestants to choose biblical names for their children, as a sign that they would live in the Word. In his city of Geneva, the theocratic heart of Protestant Europe, the name Jeanne had already become popular, doubtless in tribute to Navarre's Queen. But in the mid-century the majority of children baptized there, including those of Huguenot exiles, were given biblical names, predominantly from the Old Testament. Protestants were explicitly identifying themselves with the Israelites, their predecessors as the 'chosen people' of God. Judith, a given name unkown before the Reformation in Geneva, now became one of the most popular names for girls. The same phenomenon occurred amongst Huguenots in Rouen, one of the flashpoints in the religious wars, when these were at their fiercest between the mid-1560s and mid-1580s: only the name Mary (after the Virgin herself) was more popular than Judith. A similar fashion would also flourish in Puritan New England, perpetuating Reformation values: one Samuel Sewall named a daughter Judith after the maternal line but also because 'the Signification of it [is] very good'. In England, the use of biblical names was already under way in the 1540s: between 1560 and 1580 the 'Hebrew Invasion' in nomenclature reached its apogee, because this was when the radical Geneva Bible became the standard household Bible. Such nomenclature was a way of signalling denominational commitment. What Judith's name implied, apart from its Protestant associations, was the fierceness of that commitment.

As I have suggested elsewhere, the complex polemical freight of Judith's icon in France and England underlay William Shakespeare's mysterious allegorical comedy *Love's Labours Lost* (c. 1593–5). It also inspired the naming of his daughters, Susannah and Judith. In both cases – his dramatic manipulation of recent French history and his careful selection of given names – Shakespeare was offering a cryptic clue to his own secret Catholic leanings, paying a recusant compliment to Queen Elizabeth as Judith, and setting up a misleading marker of Protestant loyalty in the baptism of his children. (In the latter case, the name would return to haunt Shakespeare's own image in the twentieth century, as we shall see.) He was also suggesting a possibility of alliance between Elizabeth and Henry of Navarre, personated as Judith and Hercules, traditional counterparts in Nine Worthies iconography and, as it happened, these monarchs' personations in contemporary propaganda. His was a particularly slippery, sophisticated manipulation of Judith's role in the French wars.[25]

Naturally, Catherine de' Medici too paid close attention to the possibilities of iconography in her own propaganda efforts. A Machiavellian politician, her guiding principle was to maximize loyalist support for the monarchy, despite the fact that she was perceived as the perpetrator of a Catholic despotism. Consequently, with the same irenic intention as Elizabeth, she favoured secular rather than contentiously religious iconography. Centring on her status as widow of Henry II, this was designed to mollify her reputation as a foreign devil, presenting her rather as devoted to her husband's memory and thus – it was implied – perpetuating his policies rather than pursuing her own. It was open to her to choose Judith for her self-presentation as the virtuous widow. Instead she chose classical equivalents: for instance, in the temporary sculptures commissioned to celebrate her daughter-in-law's entry into Paris, both the widowed queen Artemisia and Lucretia were placed beneath the central figure of Gallia, a classicized personification of the nation.[26] The design associates the bride with Lucretian marital fidelity, and Catherine with Artemisia's supreme devotion to her husband's memory: presided over by Gallia, they are faithful to the national interest as well.

There were, however, several problems with this kind of sophisticated, classicized iconography. It might speak clearly enough to courtiers, but no one else was likely to understand it. Indeed, it is clear from the occasional hiring of interpreters to explain sophisticated spectacles to visiting diplomats that even the most educated spectators could not be relied upon to comprehend the ins and outs of classical iconography.[27] Much more likely to communicate directly, with both courtiers and plebeian spectators, was biblical iconography, which was widely disseminated in churches, pulpits and the popular arts. That was especially true of an image as sensationalist as Judith's.

Therefore it is not surprising that Catherine's propagandist iconography failed to achieve common currency, whereas Jeanne's, exploiting a striking biblical image, had immediate and wide appeal. Catholic propagandists recognized this and were more enthusiastic than Catherine about applying it to women's rule. For instance, in Scotland the Regent, Mary of Guise, had ruled very much in the interest of her native France, and of Catholicism. At her funeral service in Paris in 1561, she was memorialized as the Judith who had held back the tide of Reformation there.[28] *Pace* Catherine, Catholic zealotry acknowledged that this image had a force that should not be relinquished to the other side.

It is curious that scholars have failed in the past to differentiate between the relative potencies of classical and biblical motifs in the explosion of propagandist spectacle that occurred in the Renaissance. But that is because they have concentrated on the art of propaganda at the expense of the propaganda of art. The salient criterion for the success of any propaganda exercise is not its aesthetic quality, but its political efficacy. In France as in England, the most effective way of influencing all classes of opinion, from the aristocratic to the mass, was to exploit biblical themes.

For some time Judith therefore proved a strong ally in the Huguenots' campaign for full rights and freedom from persecution. Her aggressive aspects were exploited when her use as a prototype for Jeanne also subsumed its commendation of armed rebellion and tyrannicide. Manifestoes and justifications were needed if these illegal activities were to be presented as political, not criminal.

The sanctification borne by Judith's example was immensely helpful in this respect.

However, once a series of assassinations, the St Bartholomew's Day Massacre in Paris, and the extremism of the Catholic League had made the other side seem the more criminal, Catholic propagandists expropriated the Huguenots' bloody Judith. Justifications by Catholics of acts of terrorism and assassination perpetrated by their own side cited Judith's precedent for extremism and holy homicide. Just as they had supplied the need for propagandist images of Judith in the Netherlands, German potteries now supplied jugs decorated with Judith's story, as well as similar jugs portraying League leaders, to Catholic France. These 'Westerwald' jugs represented Judith's whole narrative cycle, because it amounted to an instructive template for fifth columnist activity. These jugs recalled the assassination of Henry III of France by a Catholic, and commended the adoption of systematic extremism by the Leaguers.[29] Things had reached such a pass by the 1580s that both sides in the religious wars needed to invoke Judith's sacred Machiavellianism in order to cosmeticize internecine terrorism. To cite Judith was to incite the spilling of blood.

Queen of Bleeding Hearts

Just as Catholic propagandists exerted themselves to wrest Judith's image from the Protestant cause, so the government was able to repossess her image from the rebels. In the early Middle Ages Judith had been regarded as the soi-disant patron saint of French royal consorts. By 1600, that association had been revived as a cultural datum. The standard appearance of French playing-card packs had been conventionalized, and in these the Queen of Hearts was identified as the biblical Judith.[30] Queens consort in France were to be identified with Judith as Love – as the loving spouses of the king. (Shakespeare imitates this when he makes the Princess of France, the Judith of *Love's Labours Lost*, the play's queen of hearts.[31] This represented a very curious convergence of Judith's erotic reputation in the more louche areas of Renaissance life, and her long history as a political icon in France.

But her role as queen of love did not signal a less bloody conception of the apocryphal heroine: quite the contrary. Du Bartas's epic had experienced some difficulty in rendering Judith's characterization, as both ideal woman and murderess, coherent. In his preface, Du Bartas confessed that he thought a female hero an improper subject for epic, the genre devoted to war. The deep contradiction at the heart of his poem results from Du Bartas's inability to reconcile the model tyrannicide Judith and his anti-feminist assumptions about demure feminine psychology. Because he feels that Judith's acteme is not heroic in the true, bellicose manner, he compensates by turning Holofernes into a *miles gloriosus*, whose pagan pride is manifested by his habit of boasting of his military

prowess. This enables Du Bartas to import into the poem long passages of reminiscence about horribly brutal battles – directly inspired by what he had wit-
nessed during the French wars – balancing the heroine's furtive act of murder
in a bedroom with more traditional epic fare. Meanwhile, both Judith and
Holofernes are made to conform to Renaissance stereotypes of gender. In poetic
terms, that means that she must be transformed into the unattainable
Petrarchan mistress, all rose cheeks and snowy breasts, whilst he becomes the
unrequited Petrarchan lover, suffering exquisite torments of maddened desire.
In religious terms, Du Bartas's characterizations make good sense. Holofernes'
raging lust is intended to be metonymic of evil, whilst Judith's beauty, idealized
in the manner that meant most to Renaissance culture, carries the implication
that her wondrous face reflects a spiritually pure spirit.[32]

But precisely the emotiveness attached by Renaissance poetry to the
Petrarchan couple works against Du Bartas's religious theme. Good Protestant
housewives and Petrarchan mistresses were prevailing stereotypes of women,
but to make Judith both at once was a contradiction in terms. Equally, we are so
accustomed to identify with the agonized Petrarchan lover's point of view – so
brainwashed by the poetic convention – that the emotional sympathy generated
by the poem is appropriated by Holofernes. By attempting to accommodate the
story to Renaissance ideologies of gender, Du Bartas creates more problems
than he solves. By suppressing the story's feminist implications he renders it
emotionally and spiritually inconsistent. A writer committed to retailing the
whole story – as Du Bartas was, both by Protestant respect for the Word and by
commitment to its political theme – cannot avoid its intractability to emollient
stereotyping. Judith's story exposes ideology for what it is.

It was, of course, precisely Judith's resistance to tame domestication that was
her appeal for the more independent-minded aristocratic women of the
Renaissance. By the end of the sixteenth century, some queens were no longer
so reluctant as Elizabeth I of England to be identified with her. When Marie de'
Medici became the second wife of Henry IV of France, Jeanne de Navarre's son,
she found herself at a court that had long been dangerous, and after Henry's
death her assumption of the regency on behalf of her infant son was controversial. All the traditional arguments against women rulers were rehearsed
against her, and especially that a female ruler would be too weak to resist the
centrifugal force of France's long-standing divisions. Fated to be a foreign
consort where another Medici queen had long been hated and feared, what
Marie needed was a public image that asserted her strength of character and
natural authority. In this respect she learned by Catherine's failure that a classical personation could not equal the currency of a biblical one. And the
appropriate biblical prototype was one she had been familiar with in her native
Florence: the city's favourite female image of political fortitude, Judith.[33]

When Marie embarked on her campaign of self-aggrandizement she already

had in tow a crew of distinguished artists, amongst them the great Catholic propagandist Rubens and the Mannerist Vouet, to paint Judiths for her. Her most
ambitious project, her personal palace at the Luxembourg, was fronted by a
sculptural gallery of assertive *femmes fortes*, including of course Judith. One of
the biblical heroine's most evidently apt aspects for Marie was her character as
a widow-in-arms. Eclipsing Catherine de' Medici's classical Artemisia, Marie's
Judith asserted the naturalness, sanctity and, above all, the fortitude of a
widowed regent: that she was capable of managing a fractious France.

Courtiers and subjects took the point of this public image. When the Keeper
of the Paris Arsenal commissioned the decoration of his daughter's bedroom,
he paid close attention to the book in which Marie's gallery of *femmes fortes* had
been widely disseminated. Pierre Le Moyne's *La Gallerie* illustrated the sculptural design at the Luxembourg, and supplied each engraving of a *femme forte*
with an account of her story, an application of her example to historical heroines and a moralization of her significance.[34] As by custom, Judith was compared particularly with France's premier national heroine, Joan of Arc. Inspired
by Le Moyne's work, the chamber at the Arsenal was decorated with a frieze of
painted panels, which alternated biblical and classical heroines with historical
personages and focused on two crowned Judiths. In the ceiling Mary is portrayed as Queen of Heaven, Judith's antitype and Marie's patron saint. Judith
as image of heroism and of French royalty anchors the scheme as a compliment
to the Queen, and proffers a role-model for the Keeper's daughter. To Marie
and her strong predecessors we can, I think, attribute the increasing French
literary fashion for representing such 'masculine women' as Judith.[35] When
feminism was endorsed by the ruler, it became fashionable.

In the Arsenal's deliberately violent rendition of the theme, bristling with
weaponry and gore, Judith was the epitome of the armigerous woman, because
in France bellicosity was a required ingredient of female rule. In other venues
Marie de' Medici might portray herself as bringing about the much-desired
peace, but to have relied entirely upon irenic feminine images would have been
unwise. The Luxembourg was, essentially, her monument to might. After so
many decades of bloodshed on the European continent, this was a time for
queens to come out of the closet and reveal themselves as Judiths by nature.
Being Queen of Love was all very well, but being the Woman of Blood had more
mileage in the world of *realpolitik*.

Le Moyne's book was popular elsewhere, so much so that in England Thomas
Heywood plagiarized the idea. In his version, which also celebrates Judith of
course, the climax and close of the series is England's Elizabeth, warrior-queen
of the Armada victory.[36] Here as at the Arsenal, Judith's historical avatars
become her companions-in-arms, part of the universal army of Amazons which
marches through history. At the Arsenal, following Le Moyne, the inclusion of
Joan of Arc and Mary Queen of Scots amongst the *femmes fortes* is particularly

significant. Joan is present both as a saint and as the scourge of the English, whilst Mary, in classic Counter-Reformation terms, is seen as a Catholic martyr murdered by the Protestant Elizabeth. Religious zealotry and patriotism thus converge in the central figure of Judith as God-given national heroine. The overall effect of such galleries is not merely to provide a prototype for ambitious Renaissance queens, but to absorb the achievements and attributes of historical heroines to the repute of Judith herself.

In the sixteenth century Judith had become a summation of historical acts of female heroism, as well as her prototypical self. After 1600 it would become increasingly difficult to separate Judith's image from a penumbra of celebrated or reviled historical women. They became, as it were, a part of herself.

Murdering Mother

Bloodshed was common enough in Renaissance politics. It was generally believed, for instance, that Jeanne de Navarre had been poisoned by Catherine de' Medici. This was one of the many graphic events that enlivened Christopher Marlowe's populist play *The Massacre at Paris* (c. 1593), which dramatized recent French history for an English audience fascinated by the Reformation struggle being waged across the Channel. Naturally, England often had a diplomatic or military stake in French politics, the consequence of which was a continual flood of inflammatory pamphlets translated from the French.[37] The literature on resistance, just war and tyrannicide that bolstered their co-religionists' activities in France, and in which Judith figured prominently, aroused an intense interest in Elizabethan England. The radical ideas fermenting in France became as familiar to English readers as the lurid events of which they heard such regular reports.

Because Du Bartas was a particularly magnetic figure for Protestants, he appears in Marlowe's play despite taking no very perceptible role in its action. Regarded as the international laureate of Protestantism, he was the leader of its effort to equal in 'divine poetry' the achievements of such Catholic luminaries as Tasso. Consequently Du Bartas's essay in the paramount poetic genre, the epic *Judit*, was greeted with enthusiasm all over Protestant Europe and admired even by Catholics. In France alone, it inspired several similar epics on the same theme, some by women.[38] Like its heroine, it thus lived a double life, as both prime aesthetic artefact and incendiary political tract.

In 1584, ten years after its initial publication, *Judit* was translated into Scots English and published at Edinburgh; extracts would also find their way into major English poetic anthologies, such as those by Bodenham and Allott in 1600. Inevitably, the 1584 translation was the most important fillip to Judith's currency in England as the epitome of Protestant heroism, and powerfully combined with Elizabeth I's Judithic repute. But this is not its most interesting feature. In fact, the very publication of *The History of Judith* in English was a political act, with both overt and covert meaning.

The translation had been commissioned by James VI of Scotland – who would, as James I, eventually succeed Elizabeth on the English throne – from his court musician Thomas Hudson. Hudson was no poet, as his *Judith* attests (and Joshua Sylvester's sensitive 1621 translation, *Bethulia Delivered*, would supersede it). It is indeed rather strange that James VI did not translate it himself. Ambitious for poetic acclaim, James was a great admirer and patron of Du Bartas, had entertained him fulsomely at the Scottish court and had already translated the Frenchman's *Lepanto*. Whilst so industriously practising the poetic art himself, James fostered a florescence of Scottish Protestant poetry at his court. Written in Scots English, the works emitted from this circle amounted to a programmatic attempt by James to portray himself as arbiter of the Reformation's 'divine poetry' in its English form. It was the cultural tactic accompanying his boisterous diplomatic campaign to ensure that Elizabeth would name him as heir to her throne.[39] By the same token, since James was regarded as the most likely Protestant claimant to succeed her, the English kept a beady eye on his activities and pronouncements.

It was, therefore, the hapless Hudson who found himself ordered to undertake a task for which he possessed neither the equipment nor the experience. Du Bartas's original Preface, faithfully translated by the literal-minded Hudson, made clear that this was a work promoting tyrannicide. With due attention to saving his own skin, Du Bartas protested there that the poem had not been his own idea (perish the thought) but foisted upon him by royal command. Hudson prudently repeated much the same thing in his own prefatory statement to the translation, that the work (wholly beyond him, he modestly if accurately protests) was instigated by his king. In both cases, the poets are careful to distance themselves from the inflammatory political theme intrinsic to the work. Further, they took care to include fulsome loyal tributes to their own monarchs, in order to except Jeanne and James from the story's lese-majesty. Thus Hudson follows up Du Bartas's finale, which declaims death to ungodly tyrants, with a peroration extolling James's rule. The contrast is meant to deflect the anti-monarchical moral from the works' own patrons.

Perhaps, one might think, this would be a good reason for James's having translated the work himself, just as he had various other works by Du Bartas. Faced with the possibility of being identified with the tyrant Holofernes and tempting his gruesome fate, James's best form of defence against any such imputation on himself would have been to articulate the attack himself – to be the author. But this did not suit James's purpose, which was not primarily literary, despite the work's contribution to his cultural campaign for the English throne. Its overt message to an English readership, directed to their appetite for information about James, was that he was a committed Protestant, committed indeed to the Reformation values represented by Judith and Du Bartas. But this message had been conveyed before, in other signs of James's enthusiasm for the French poet: the difference lay in a specific commitment to Judithic values. And in 1584 the major propaganda value of these was to distance James from his mother's reputation.

Mary Queen of Scots, the strongest Catholic claimant to the English throne, had fled to England when she was deposed in James's favour. Her deposition had been justified on the basis that she was a Popish tyrant, a thesis pursued by James's tutor, the internationally celebrated scholar George Buchanan, in his *De Jure Regno* (1579). The theme of Hudson's *History of Judith* was similarly inflected: James's most daring tactic in the campaign for the English crown.

In England, the exiled Mary was a constant focus for Catholic recusant subversion and international conspiracies to overthrow Elizabeth in her favour. Fears of such subversion were particularly strong in 1584. In the previous year, Walsingham had uncovered the 'Spanish enterprise' to place Mary on the throne. In January 1584, the Spanish ambassador was confronted with the plot and sent home. By the summer, fears that Elizabeth would be assassinated by a Catholic reached their apogee. Pro-Mary conspiracies were 'an horrid piece of Popish malice,' said the contemporary historian William Camden, 'for they set forth books wherein they exhorted the Queen's gentlewomen to act the like against the Queen as Judith had done with applause and commendations against Holofernes.'[40] At such a juncture Judith's incendiary role was inevitably revived.

Further revelations of Jesuit conspiracy followed, and in October Elizabeth's Council drew up a Bond of Association, the purpose of which was to kill any potential successor who should attempt her life – meaning, of course, Mary. In November, Parliament embarked upon a furious burst of legislation to protect Elizabeth from Catholic treason, and pressed for Mary's trial and execution. Yet Elizabeth, not so much out of compassion for her cousin as because she knew all too well that to kill a monarch was a dangerous precedent for herself, was extremely reluctant to authorize either. What James hoped to achieve by issuing *The History of Judith* under his imprimatur was a coded message to Elizabeth and her ministers: that to execute Mary would be to commit a just tyrannicide upon the great white hope of Popery. By doing so, he hoped to remove the major obstacle between him and the English crown – not simply Mary's life, but also the Popery with which she was indissolubly associated. In short, James was instructing Elizabeth to kill his mother.

Inevitably Elizabeth's ministers had been somewhat concerned about what their putative future king might feel about their executing his mother. James did of course register the protest at her condemnation that was required of him, since he could hardly be seen to approve in public, but his protest was carefully worded. He himself admitted that in issuing his protest he had been merely satisfying expectations of his filial duty, for 'My religion ever moved me to hate her course, although my honour constrains me to insist for her life', and he stressed his 'hatred' of his mother's religion.[41] Similarly, he had not himself translated *Judit*, and thus could not be held to be the author of a work recommending sovereign-killing. That precedent would be just as dangerous for himself as regicide was for Elizabeth. Nor could he be definitely identified as the author of an anti-Marian message. All that was needed to counteract his official protest to the English was his imprimatur on a text already known to carry an explosive political message.

It may well be that James justified to himself his matricidal intent by recalling that, as her Protestant detractors always claimed, Mary had colluded in the murder of her husband by her lover. Vengeance for his father and the great prize of the English throne were the two birds that James was killing with one stone. If we consider that Judith and Oedipus were essentially mythic complements, we could speculate on the possible psychological gratifications of punishing the mother for the father's death and her adultery, which had brought the son one throne and gave promise of another.

Leaving that aside, though, it would seem that once James had gained the English throne, even loyalists allowed themselves to reflect a little upon his personality. In view of his homosexuality, misogyny and covert support for his mother's execution, one wonders how he reacted to the pamphleteers who urged him to become a Judith to the Pope.[42] In view of the biblical heroine's gender and James's epicene reputation, it is not surprising that these exhortations tie themselves into syntactic knots trying to evade a too obvious sex-change between the king and his female personation. As Jacobean propaganda often did, these androgynous allegories attempt to remake James in the image of Elizabeth, to make him seem equal to her Judithic leadership of the foremost Protestant nation.[43] (A similar phenomenon – following in the wake of an Iron Lady – would dog Mrs Thatcher's successor in the 1990s.) At one level, these are coded requests for James to prove himself a zealous international champion of Protestantism: requests that would become increasingly desperate as his reign continued.

That ironic reversal of traditional assumptions about vigorous leadership, feminizing the male monarch, was the more piquant because of James's liaisons with dominating male favourites. Perhaps these loyalist Judithic allusions had as subtext a reassurance to knowing readers that even a homosexual man could, like this 'weak woman', be rendered heroically virile by the Lord. Certainly Judith-James complemented the virulent, warlike Judith adopted by contemporary queens laying claim to masculine courage. By now decades of gynecocracy in European countries had made it imaginable that even a king and patriarch could be urged to emulate a woman, without bothering to translate her first into a sublimated Virtue. It was Judith's zeal, not her piety, that James lacked. What Judith now signified was the nature of public action itself, so that, albeit for only a brief span of time, it was as if the public sphere had become feminine.

It had taken a century of female rule to establish this cultural motif in Europe, and – of course – it would vanish soon enough. Female power would once again be regarded as naturally the exception to the rule, and Elizabeth I would be remembered as the paradigm of that exception, whilst her many compeers were largely forgotten. In order to collude with anti-feminism, a politic enough course on her part, Elizabeth herself always insisted that she was an exceptional, masculine woman, with the 'heart and stomach of a king'.

Feminist ideas have never managed to strike sufficiently deep roots in Western culture to enable them to outlive specific historical circumstances. Who now remembers that, whilst men wrote the books – the Luthers and Calvins – the great split effected by the Reformation was often in practice dominated by women? Governing, intriguing, speechifying, canvassing, horse-trading, financing, head-chopping and poisoning, they were indeed like Judith who, after Ozias the elder had made the pious pronouncements, actually did the dirty work.

1. *Judith with the Head of Holofernes* by Lucas Cranach.

2. *The Return of Judith* by Sandro Botticelli.

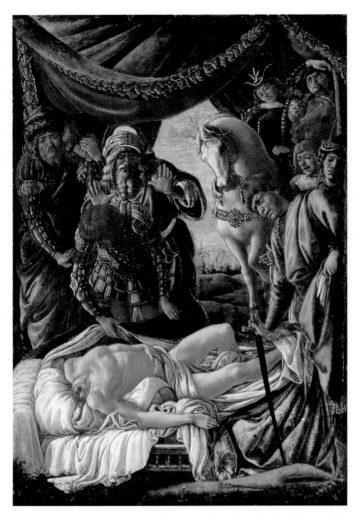

3. *The Discovery of the Body of Holofernes* by Sandro Botticelli.

4. *Judith and Holofernes* by Francisco Goya.

5. *The Marriage Contract* from *Marriage à la Mode* by William Hogarth.

6. *The Archduke Leopold Wilhelm in his Picture Gallery in Brussels*
by David Teniers the Younger.

7. *Judith and Holofernes* by Michelangelo Caravaggio.

8. *Jael, Deborah and Barak* by Salomon de Bray.

9. *Judith* by Gustav Klimt.

Hanging's Too Good for Her
Assassins, Tyrants and Executioners[1]

During the early modern age – between 1500 and 1800 – Judith's icon became a sign of death inextricably linked with rituals of power. Her myth was a template for the primitive rituals underlying public spectacles that were designed to manifest the power of the state. The reason why the Book of Judith became so central to political rituals was its heroine's status, as a model for political murder, and particularly for tyrannicides. Hence the broken sword in Mantegna's painting, icon of a just political murder. Inspired by Judith's sanction as God's assassin, a number of obscure, disturbed and fanatic individuals attempted to change the course of history by stepping into her shoes.

The Idea of Tyranny

On 10 September 1419, by prearrangement, the ruthless Duke of Burgundy, John the Fearless, met his rivals for power in France, the Armagnacs, for a parley on the bridge at Montereau. This location had been selected to preclude the possibility of an ambush by either side. However, the Armagnacs had nonetheless planned to separate John from his attendants, which they did and then murdered him.[2] They had their reasons, and seemingly John's own sanction. French politics had been dominated by the power-struggle between John and Louis, Duke of Orléans, until in 1407 John had hired thugs to murder Louis in Paris. When John was called to account, the famous jurist Jean Petit argued in his defence that this was a justifiable murder because a tyrannicide. That God sanctioned such an action was evident, he said, from Judith's precedent.[3]

Throughout Europe, the irony of this double assassination, in which John had been killed by his own argument, struck home. Petit's defence had been sufficiently shocking, but the second assassination underscored the dangerous potential of the Judithic idea. Her icon stood both for the original crime and for the vengeance exacted for it. John's murder may stand as a symbolic event subsuming Judith's multiple roles in issues of sovereignty, freedom and coercion.

During the Middle Ages Judith's potential as a radical icon had been understood but suppressed. It was not until Orléans's murder that John of Salisbury's radical political theory in *Polycraticus*, written over two hundred years earlier, became better known. By Judith's example John had justified the tyrannicide of ungodly kings – tyrants – because a Christian's duty was to a higher power than any on earth.[4] In medieval and Renaissance Italy Judith was a common and potent symbolic figure, and it was the doctrine of tyrannicide as embodied in Judith that inspired one of the Italian *quattrocento*'s most celebrated artefacts, Donatello's sculpture of Judith slaying Holofernes. In both Florence and Siena her icon had stood for the freedom of these city-states. Even the positioning of Donatello's sculpture in the Piazza Vecchio was directly related to the political complexion of Florence at the time, which was why the sculpture took to peregrinating about the city's civic centre.[5] Later in the century, in England her icon of tyrannicide inspired a slyly subversive work by the country's first printer, William Caxton, in resistance to the usurper King Richard III. The latter was an instance of the new prominence of Judith's role as tyrannicide from the fifteenth century onwards.[6]

John of Salisbury's theory of Christian resistance had been an unexploded bomb until Petit's defence of John the Fearless had been reprinted and read throughout Europe, ensuring that the Judithic authorization for tyrannicide became widely known. The proof of the pudding – that the argument was effective – came in two forms: the Duke of Burgundy had been acquitted of murder, and then he had been killed by the same token. A historical precedent had been set for justifying political assassination, and thus began Judith's long and bloody career as the inspiration of assassins who could make the mighty sleep uneasy in their beds. From potent ideas flow bloody consequences: that is how history is made.

Thus it was in the Reformation bloodletting that God's assassin truly came into her own. As we saw, in the French religious schism both sides grasped the value of Judith as a propaganda tool and incitement to violence. Even though Du Bartas's Protestant epic *Judith* was the seminal manifesto for this role, ironically most of those who were incited by her example were Catholics. In 1584, a cabinet-maker's apprentice, Balthasar Gerard, entered William the Silent's house in Delft and shot the Dutch Protestants' leader through the lungs and stomach. A Spanish agent, Gerard was inspired by Judith's godly tyrannicide, as transmitted through the Dutch translation of Du Bartas.[7] In 1584, the year when the poem was published in English, Elizabeth I was said to be menaced by Catholic assassins thirsting to imitate Judith's feat by murdering Europe's premier Protestant monarch. Five years later, while Paris was in the grip of religious frenzy, it was besieged by its own king, the excommunicate Catholic Henry III. A mad monk Jacques Clément inveigled his way into the king's tent and stabbed him mortally. Despatched on the spot by the king's attendants,

Clément was eulogized as a Catholic Judith in the camp of the heretic Holofernes. The victim's successor, Henry IV, sometime Huguenot leader and now a Catholic convert, was the object of a failed assassination attempt by Jean Chastel, celebrated as a Judith by the demagogic author of Pierre Boucher. In 1610, however, Henry IV finally met his fate as a Holofernes – his 'role' in Shakespeare's *Love's Labours Lost* – when a vagrant named Ravaillac leapt into his coach and stabbed him to death. In 1610 this event caused shock-waves comparable to the impact of Kennedy's assassination in 1963. Once again the minds of contemporary observers automatically turned to the fearsome impact of Judith's example. The theory and the practice of Judithic murder went hand in hand.

The Jesuit zealot Juan de Mariana's justification for godly tyrannicide, drawing on the Old Testament, became a byword in Europe for extreme Catholic Machiavellianism. From the first, Mariana's views were linked to Judith's myth in public perception. Thus an English pamphlet invoked Judith in the context of the English Catholics' Gunpowder Plot of 1605, and the Counter-Reformation Douai Bible stressed that Judith's Book was about defeating 'persecution of a cruel tyrant'. One of the many polemics provoked by his influence, *Antimariana*, characteristically saw hers as the most dangerous incitement to regicide.[8] By the early seventeenth century, assassination seemed to be positively fashionable, and Judith was its *éminence grise*.

Although most closely associated in the popular mind with the terrifying and insidious image of clandestine Jesuit tactics against Protestantism, Judith was a model for both Catholic and Protestant rebellion, resistance and assassination. By 1600, Judith thus occupied a remarkable position within the propaganda of international conflict. Both sides subscribed to precisely the same justification, as God's assassins of each other. Their competing claims to her icon might have been comic, had they not been indissociable from actual and terrible events.

This irony was probably Du Bartas's fault. When Henry III was assassinated, it was a highly influential popular pamphlet, *Martine Mar-Sixtus*, supposedly written by Pope Sixtus V, that eulogized the assassin as the Church's champion in its darkest hour, its Judith.[9] However, the pamphlet was probably a forgery by a Protestant, designed to defame the Pope. The author chose Judith for this purpose because she had already, through Du Bartas's agency, become the primary image for tyrannicide amongst Protestants themselves. *Martine Mar-Sixtus*'s excessively extrapolated comparison of the mad monk to Judith was mock-serious, intended to guy the assassin by comparing him to a mere woman, and to discredit a Pope who would be prepared to divert biblical authority to such manifestly bloodthirsty ends. The 'Pope's' cynical exploitation of Judith's Book was designed to manifest Catholic distortion of the Word of God. Its effect was quite otherwise, however, for the pamphlet buoyed up a genuine Catholic enthusiasm for Judith as an inspiration for extreme political acts. Good ideas were welcome, even if the Protestants' laureate had had them first.

The irony of Judith's twofold role in the Reformation schism was redoubled by the curious relationship between assassin and victim. Whilst a model for tyrannicides, simultaneously she was, as we have seen, a prototype for monarchs such as Elizabeth I, who were themselves named 'tyrants' by their enemies and hence became targets for tyrannicide. Killed by the Judithic Gerard, William the Silent was himself leader of a cause that had used Judith as an icon of just rebellion in the Netherlands.[10] Ideologically the victim was Judith too. Which was the true Judith entirely depended upon which side had one's allegiance. The significance of this is more than that her myth was protean: she signified the problematic nature of the Reformation schism itself. Since Protestant and Catholic were both Christians as well as deadly enemies, they had just as much in common as they had against each other. This conflict within a single religion, fought out as civil wars within France and the Low Countries, was a war of mirrors, in which the antagonists needed to define their own respective identities in order to hate each other sufficiently. A powerful political image from the book they competed over, the Bible, was bound to play a crucial if ambivalent role in the conflict. The troubling alter-ego relationship between the antagonists was manifested when a Spanish fleet defeated the Turks at Lepanto in 1570. Europe breathed a sign of relief at this decisive repulsion of Islam, Protestants for the nonce accepting that a Catholic victory was in fact a triumph for all Christendom. A Netherlandish Catholic gratefully donated to the church of St John in Gouda a magnificent stained-glass window, portraying Judith's story as the European defeat of Islam, signified by the crescent flag flying over Holofernes' camp. This motif was common, appearing in paintings such as Jan Metsys's *Judith*. Judith symbolized the unity of Christendom as well as its deep division. The ambivalence always immanent in her icon now reflected the schizophrenia of Reformation religion.

The fundamental reason for Judith's importance in political iconography was that her symbolism was vividly apt to a time when violence was endemic. Between Catholic and Protestant there were international wars, as between Spain and England; civil wars, as in France; rebellion, as in the Netherlands. But interdenominational violence also broke out in unofficial forms, so that in France, for instance, for forty years there were recurrent riots, murders and massacres in urban centres; and throughout Western Europe, outbreaks of iconoclasm, assassinations and terrorism (such as the Gunpowder Plot). Formal military campaigns and mass executions were performed against a backdrop of widespread unofficial bloodletting. In the political realm such a distinction between official and unofficial violence is crucial, for it establishes that one side in a conflict is defending legitimate power, the other perpetrating an outrage. What is in question is political authority itself.

Yet Judith's icon suggests that no such distinction could hold, for it was invoked equally by sovereigns, rebels and assassins. Authority and its subversion were both dependent upon the same validating concept – sanctification. But since there was only one source to which monarchs could appeal for this, the apparent will of God, subversive movements could readily challenge authority by kidnapping God for their own side. The struggle to own God was the struggle for power. If religion appeared to shore up the state, it also threatened it by the same token. Thus the very foundation to which states appealed for their authority was built on sand.

Further, the distinction between official and unofficial violence also gave way. For example, the apparently lawless massacre of Protestants in Paris on St Bartholomew's Day in 1572 was incited by the king's own agents.[11] This was government-inspired violence, in direct contradiction of the governmental duty to keep order in a state. Executions were formal, legal, ritual punishments: legitimate homicides by the legal authorities. But when Mary Queen of Scots was beheaded, Catholics questioned whether Elizabeth I possessed adequate authority to execute a foreign head of state. Herself menaced by Judithic tyrannicides, Elizabeth in executing Mary was regarded by militant Scottish Protestants as implementing a Judithic tyrannicide. In political theory and religious doctrine this dubiously legal execution was proximate to illegal assassination. From this point of view (the view from which its authority was derived) an execution by the state was indistinguishable from a murder of the state's representative. Elizabeth I and Gerard were both tyrannicides, mirror-images of each other.

The same ambiguity inheres in the concept of a tyrant. In Catholic propaganda Elizabeth I was a tyrant Jezebel, as was her antagonist Mary Queen of Scots in Protestant propaganda. Who was a tyrant and who a tyrannicide depended entirely upon one's point of view. A tyrannicide can be said to take place only when the victim has already been identified as a tyrant. Identified thus by whom? On what authority? By which criteria? The naming of a tyrannicide depends upon a definition of tyranny. This is the first problem we encounter in the concept, that it is blatantly ideological in definition.

Yet rebellious religionists found in the charge of tyranny their most feasible justification for armed rebellion against legitimate governments. To accuse the ruler of tyranny was the one *casus belli* that had a long and weighty tradition of Western political thought behind it. Casting about for religious concepts that would answer their pressing need to authorize rebellion, early modern theorists fell with relief upon the idea of tyranny, and set themselves to define it in terms that identified it with the regimes they opposed. The effort to pin down the term 'tyranny', to construct a photo-fit picture of the enemy, was vital because upon it rested a whole complex structure of ideas about authority and legitimacy. The difficulty of distinguishing between an Elizabeth and a Gerard, monarch and criminal, was where the whole system of power showed its Achilles heel. That was also, it transpires, where Judith's iconography was invoked. If we can understand what Judith denoted within that system of power, we will be able to understand the system itself.

The concept of tyranny is in fact fundamental to ideas of power and legitimate authority of any kind, for tyranny is the term for excessive power and coercion. The idea of tyranny presupposes a definition of legitimacy, which it exceeds. In the story of Lucretia, oppression consisted in the invasion of the people's rights by the tyrant, an idea given physical manifestation by Tarquin's rape of Lucretia. Her body symbolized the property rights, indeed the autonomy, of her family and hence of all subjects. It bore their honour and their autonomy in vulnerable form. Similarly, Judith, desired by the would-be rapist, embodied Israel itself. As a paradigmatic tyrant, Tarquin personified his irresistible appetites – his many 'lusts' – and their depredation of his people. Like Holofernes as Lust, the sign of Tarquin's tyranny is his willingness to satisfy his drives at his subjects' expense. Lucretia's mutilated corpse, signifying both those lusts and their violation of the people, thus signified the condition of the Romans themselves under tyranny – the body politic victimized. In turn, the people's recognition of what her body signified inspired revolt. In the female body oppression was materialized: it signifies that on which a tyrant exercises tyranny. In this way, that body actually *defines* a tyrant, within both the founding myths, biblical and classical, of tyrannicide.

Thus, in *King Edward the Third*, the chaste body of Countess 'Judith' was the object of Edward's desire, but when she fends him off by threatening to stab herself rather than submit, he comes to his senses and hails her as 'better' than Lucretia (II.ii.168ff.). In short, Edward manages to restrain his own tyrannical impulses.

Since they were legitimately the kings of Rome, the Tarquins were tyrants by oppression, as distinct in classical political theory from tyrants by usurpation. Both types of tyrant are invaders, conquerors and appropriators, thieves on a giant scale. That is particularly clear when the tyrant is a foreign invader: Nebuchadnezzar in Judith's story. The tyrant by usurpation appropriates power that rightly belongs to another, a legitimate monarch; the tyrant by oppression, whilst a legitimate ruler, de-legitimates himself by engrossing the rights of the subject (against molestation, injustice, theft and so on), as Tarquin did. Metaphorically engrossing and gross, tyrants were monstrous consumers because excessive in desire. Grossness of appetite, whether for food or sex, figured the despot's infinite and uncontrollable lust for power. The tyrant's voracity in all things was epitomized in its most literal form, gluttony. Thus the stereotypically tyrannical Duke in *The Revenger's Tragedy* (1606) voiced his 'long lust to eat' the Lucretia-like wife of one of his noble subjects (I.iv.32–3). When he has succeeded in raping her, Tarquin-like, she kills herself, Lucretia-like, and like Lucretia's relatives a group of nobles swear vengeance upon the tyrant. This was a classic plot for the representation of tyranny, because it identified the tyrant as what he was. Be re-echoing the Lucretian and Judithic myths of tyranny, writers could construct a convincing photofit of the oppressor.

This is why Du Bartas's *Judit* has as its centrepiece the banquet to which Holofernes invites Judith, prior, he thinks, to raping her. The episode in Book III is preceded by a lengthy (and otherwise puzzlingly venomous) diatribe against the deadly sin of Gluttony. Holofernes is presented as guilty of this sin *above all*, because it is a key ingredient in his delineation as a tyrant. To establish this metaphor of gluttony is vital to Du Bartas's thesis, endorsing Huguenot revolt in France. Similarly, Holofernes' banquet was represented – in the Judith series at Rouen Cathedral, for instance – as a sign not only of the personal vice of gluttony but also of the political crime of despotism. The tyrant's lechery and gluttony fused in the object of his desire, the woman. That which the tyrant eats/consumes is the female body that he rapes/consumes. Her body politic thus figures his parasitic relation to his subjects: he sucks the life out of them, which is why Lucretia dies.

Moral definitions of tyranny and tyrannicide depended upon these metaphors. Holofernes was recognizable as a tyrant because he first feasted and then intended to treat Judith's body as dessert. As a tyrannicide, she conducted an exact metaphoric reversal of his behaviour. As he would have raped her, she decapitated/castrated him; as he would have consumed her, his head became a comestible for her foodbag. The way to define a tyrant was to fit him to the archetype of greed, and the way to characterize his nemesis was to parody and invert his habitual behaviour.

This iconographic plot, the consumer consumed, was a staple of tyranny's representations. So when the aptly-named Vindice slays the Duke in *Revenger's Tragedy*, he relishes the fact that 'those that did eat are eaten' (III.v.159). Metaphorically, the tyrant must be eaten if tyrannicide is to be complete. Just as the head symbolizes the seat of power, so cannibalism figures its extirpation. In this play we can see how the cultural myths of tyranny and their primitive bases were perpetuated in Renaissance *mentalité*. The morality, and hence the politics, of the confrontation between monarch and assassin were defined by this mythic, Judithic ritual. To repeat the ritual was to define the event.

As we have seen, when a tyrant indulged in rape he was figuratively performing rapine upon the nation itself. In the fundamental plot of tyranny the female body thus symbolized the body politic. This symbolism reflected, of course, patriarchal convictions about the nature of power. The ruling head of the body politic was masculine, the corporate body of the nation feminine; an imagistic system that depended upon the classic opposition between the masculine (rational, commanding, the brains of the business) and feminine (physical, obedient, the brawn). For symbolism of gender is fundamental to political

concepts and in particular to that of tyranny. Power being perceived as masculine, the power-crazed tyrant was masculinity run amok. Conversely, his oppo-
nent was symbolically feminine.

This partly accounts for Judith's popularity as the personification of tyrannicide in the Renaissance: her feminine gender was a prerequisite of the metaphoric plot of tyranny. For the ritualized acts that identified a tyrant Judith's
myth was a template. And it was not merely reproduced in the literature on
tyranny. In Renaissance politics, the founding myths of tyranny were playing
themselves out in events.

Executions

If Renaissance ideas of authority depended upon the metaphor of the body, this
dependence was not merely a metaphor. In Renaissance politics, rituals of
power depended upon real human bodies for their effect.

According to Michel Foucault, power reveals itself by marking bodies,
making itself 'legible' upon them. In 'The Spectacle of the Scaffold', Foucault
argued that the horrific nature of the early modern executions was carefully
planned to demonstrate the 'technology of power'. The ability of the governing regime to enforce its authority was manifested by the *way* in which it implemented capital punishment. The ritual execution's formalized atrocities,
inflicted upon the victim's body, were designed to display *in extremis* 'the disym-
metry between the subject who had dared to violate the law and the all-power-
ful sovereign who displays his strength'.[12] In other words, the astonishing
cruelty of the event had a pragmatic intent. It confirmed the absolute authority
of the king.

Whilst Foucault is correct to see the scaffold as a spectacle of power, he is
unable convincingly to explain the role of religious ideas in Renaissance punishments. This is because he belongs to a French intellectual tradition that
accredits itself by its hostility to Catholicism. The fact is, however, that religious
ideas were fundamental to the way in which early modern executions displayed
the nature of power. Equally important was the iconography, biblical and classical, in which the Renaissance expressed ideas of power. The key to this spectacle's meaning lies within the iconography that was, as we have seen, essential
to the myth of tyranny.

First, the precise character of the atrocities inflicted upon the criminal's body
was itself meaningful. The very worst tortures were reserved for regicides. For
instance, when the English cleric Hugh Peter was executed for the regicide of
Charles I, he was hanged, drawn whilst still alive, and quartered, his genitals
severed and placed in his mouth. This execution ritual was the norm in England
for regicides. On the Continent, the ritual was similar but often with the addition of further grisly refinements. Thus, in France, Ravaillac underwent various

localized tortures before dismemberment was carried out by hitching his limbs to four horses, which were then driven off in opposite directions, tearing the body asunder. At this point the executioner handed over his function to the crowd, who were permitted to make off with the pieces, mangling them further, dragging them through the dust, burning them, or even cooking and eating them.[13] In this way the people themselves were recruited to the punitive process inflicted by the ruler, their integration with him represented by co-operation in the destruction of the victim's body. The whole intention of the ritual event was to maximize the pain and extend the process of execution: to figure in the manner of death the outrage that the regicide had committed against his anointed king, and hence against God himself.

This process had begun before the execution, during the customary application of torture to extract a confession. Subsequent to execution, the criminal's severed head was often either impaled on a stake and paraded about, or displayed upon a city gate, there to decompose. With a similar motive of deterrence, the spectacle was perpetuated by its illustration and description in broadsheets and pamphlets, so that those who had not been present would nevertheless absorb its meaning. For the spectacle was designed to be as minatory as possible, to convey most emphatically and broadcast most widely the power of the state which the criminal's act had challenged. Through the medium of the victim's body that message was conveyed.

Modern study of torture has suggested that its supposedly pragmatic purpose, the extraction of information, is merely a pretext for its true function, which is to confirm the power of the regime by unmaking the victim's body.[14] In this way the body in pain becomes the verifier of power, the power of the regime. Its pain attests to the regime's ability to enforce its will. Therefore the more the body is deconstructed, the more it attests to that enforcement. The more decisively the body is unmade, the more emphatically an image of power is manufactured. In this way power, which is an invisible quality, materializes in the visible suffering of the body. The maimed, distorted, scarred body is thus imprinted with the marks of power. The body makes power recognizable.

If we bring that insight to the Renaissance scaffold, we can see that this is how the power of the regime revealed itself, in the multiple atrocities of the execution ritual. Ravaillac's, Gerard's and Peter's bodies were the body politic made real. If the body politic was what the sovereign ruled, then his absolute power was imprinted upon its rebellious limbs by this ritual.

But there is more to this than the literalizing of a political metaphor. Since political ideas tended to rely upon religion to sanctify authority, there was a significant religious dimension to the execution spectacle. As we saw in the feats of Judith and David, the omnipotence of God is revealed by the *absence* of power in a woman or a child. This absence figures his presence. In a similar fashion, the absence of the sovereign from the Renaissance scaffold is actually the condition of his power's display. He does not himself deign to inflict punishment, for he has executioners and torturers to do it for him. His is the invisible hand behind the executioner's. As the instrumental executioner performs the ritual of power, its instigator the sovereign is so potent that his power is present even while he is absent. Executioner and people toil to render his power visible upon the victim's body, while his lack of participation paradoxically manifests his omnipotence. The deconstructed body attests to it, just as the severed head of Holofernes was an apotropaic sign of God's retributive power. The malefactors' heads displayed upon city gates performed the same function, which was at once primitive and political.

There are a number of Renaissance paintings that confirm these dynamics in the spectacle of punishment. Some depictions of Judith's acteme lay out Holofernes' body in the prostrate suffering posture of the execution's victim. Beheading him, Judith is being characterized as God's executioner: figuring his invisible power just as the state's executioner figured that of the regime. For the highly realistic paroxysms of Holofernes' body the painters could imitate those viewed at public executions. From there and from city-gates both the painter and the viewer were familiar with the appearance of severed heads. For this reason Holofernes' head and bloody neck had to be convincingly executed (!) to accord with the viewer's own experience; and it was possible to make it convincing because the painter shared that experience. Similarly, the radical foreshortenings of Holofernes' body in contemporary Mannerist art closely imitate those woodcuts used in the better-quality broadsheets representing public executions. From such stories as Judith's came the models for the Renaissance spectacle of retributive punishment, identifying the ruler with the punitive God of the Old Testament. The paintings and the executions are wholly symbiotic.

Although execution scenes were common in art, for the most part they were presented as highly realistic depictions of the martyrdom of saints. St James, for instance, offered a potential subject for decollation scenes (beheadings by professional executioners), imagined as contemporary executions. Jaspar Woensam von Worms's *Heiligenmartyrium*, depicting a mass execution of 'holy martyrs', in fact has specific contemporary reference to the persecution of Protestant 'heretics' in Germany in the mid-sixteenth century. Surrounded by soldiers, the executioner prepares to bring down his axe upon the man kneeling at the block, whose head will join the pile of heads and corpses below the scaffold. The power that instigates and presides over this scene is represented only by a pennant carried by a soldier in the background, bearing the insignia of the Hapsburg emperor. Where he is absent, the sign of his power is nonetheless present in the decapitated corpses, and heraldized by the pennant positioned behind and above them in the painting.

Of course, von Worms's painting, like those of St James, celebrates martyrdom, not the power that inflicts it. Its imitation of the power-dynamics of the scaffold is intended to reinforce the heroism of martyrdom, by connoting the terrifying power that it has defied. In this respect the painting highlights an inherent ambiguity in the spectacle of the scaffold. Its punitive character was in fact derived from the Old Testament ethic of equivalent revenge, 'an eye for an eye'. By multiplying tortures exponentially, however, the public spectacle signified that this was not merely a case of death for death, the regicide's for the king's. Since the king was more than a man, God's viceregent, so the punishment must be more than death. Its excess, drawing out the process in escalations of pain, figured the excess and transgression of this particular kind of homicide. On the regicide's body was delineated not only crime but sin, that which he had already publicly repented in the ritual *amende honorable*. But repentance was not sufficient to it. The torments of hell were imported into this life as the tortures of the scaffold. As a contemporary said, the regicide deserved *more* than the pains of hell.[15] In this way the sanctified power of the monarch was made visible on his body.

Yet this political logic was suborned by the way in which the spectacle might be interpreted. If the execution of St James were portrayed in contemporary guise, it made the contemporary execution spectacle *itself* look like a martyrdom. It also made the instigating power look like tyranny, like paganism. The painters' habit of representing martyrdoms by imitating the torments inflicted by contemporary regimes tended to identify actual executions, not as the punishment of a malefactor, but as the voluntary self-sacrifice of a persecuted martyr. Such scenes of holy martyrdom, which look exactly like contemporary public executions, were commonly available as cheap prints to the populace. A black-ink version of *The Martyrdom of St Simeon the Prophet*, for instance, shows him strapped prostrate on a trestle, straddled by the executioner who, with the aid of his assistant, is sawing him in half from crotch to head.[16] Broadsheets of executions were executed in the same style. A Dutch example used a series of pictures, cartoon-style, to represent each major stage in the ritual of punishment. The enlarged central panel shows the executioner quartering the body like an expert butcher. Imitated in artistic representations of martyrdoms, these archetypes of power as just retribution were thus identifiable with *wrongful* persecution and illegitimate power. In this way the spectacle of power subverted itself.

A similar problem arose from the official religion itself. The spectacle of the scaffold had to be fetched from the Old Testament ethic of just revenge, because the New Testament urged mercy instead. In the gospels, indeed, Christ had been crucified as a criminal, another judicial atrocity. The ignominious, atrocious death of a martyr replicated Christ's. Ignominy was glory. To interpret the spectacle of execution in christological terms would thus subvert its intention to display absolute and righteous power. The spectacle would be contradicted by the very sanctifying order it was invoking.

Whilst they said they were determined to be Judiths, Gerard and his fellows were required to pay a price that she herself had escaped. They were aware of how much they would suffer on the scaffold. Consequently they were also aware that to bear it with fortitude would confirm their sanctification. During his mutilation, Gerard chanted prayers. A French conservative angrily observed that these assassins were so convinced of their Judithic mission that they were emboldened against the intended 'ignominy of the punishment'.[17] In other words, its ignominy was contradicted, rendered morally positive. The cruelty of the spectacle also reinforced this. When their co-religionists were executed for treason, Catholic propagandists execrated the 'heathenish' cruelty of a Protestant regime.[18] A martyr's mutilated body bore material marks of exceptional spirituality, ratifications of sainthood. Whilst in the spectacle of execution the victim's body was the ground of power's display, equally it could be the ground of resistance, in the same religious terms. In these terms, on which it depended for its own righteous authority, the spectacle of punishment was intrinsically ambiguous.

If the spectacle's cruelty was a problem, laying the regime open to charges of heathenism, the regime could nevertheless not afford to dispense with it. For the point of the tortures, branding, pincers et al. was to imitate, rather precisely, what the infernal torments of hell were imagined to be like. Paintings of hell had long established in the popular mind that these were the torments inflicted upon the damned. By replicating these upon the scaffold, the regime signified to the spectator that the criminal was condemned by divine as well as human law. He was already, in effect, one of the damned in hell. Further, Renaissance minds were wedded to the idea that moral turpitude was faithfully reflected in physical ugliness. Transforming the victim's body into a grotesque distortion of itself had the symbolic objective of making him look like what he was, not human but demonic. Once rendered grotesque, revealed as a demon, this evil spirit was exorcized. The process of exorcism was what was being carried out when the victim's body was deconstructed: dismembered, reduced to friable substances, burned to ashes, consigned to rivers. This was a ritual of purification.

The spectacle of unmaking by *dismemberment* was usually reserved for two categories of criminal. Paradoxically, these were both the tyrannicide and the tyrant. The French populace understood the ritual of tyrannicide so well that it was able to implement it outside the judicial process and independently of public executions. In the early seventeenth century it was the popular view that the royal favourite, Concini, was responsible for government oppression. When he was ambushed and shot by the Captain of the King's Guard, the corpse was borne off by an exultant crowd of Parisians and subjected to the ritual of hanging, mutilation, castration, *amende honorable*, parading through the city, complete dismemberment and the feeding of its organs to both dogs and humans.[19] For the most part these were constitutive phases in the public execution of a tyrannicide. When tyrants fell they were subjected to precisely the same ritual punishment as tyrannicides.

Let us not imagine, however, that Concini's mutilators had to be taught this ritual by the previous execution of Ravaillac or any other French assassin.[20] The rituals of tyrannicide, like its doctrines, go back as far as ancient history, and were of course recorded in those classical texts that were enthusiastically studied and disseminated in the Renaissance. In ancient Rome, the fall of Sejanus had been marked by similar primitive rites. Ben Jonson's *Sejanus His Fall* (1603) described the popular festival of tyrannicide, 'the acts of furies'.[21] Sejanus's statues were symbolically beheaded, his corpse was 'rent . . . limb, from limb' and the flesh dealt out to the perpetrators in small pieces. His body was so comprehensively deconstructed, 'torn, and scattered . . . he needs no grave' (V.vi.761–833), as if he had never existed at all. Like the tyrannicide's, the tyrant's body was emphatically unmade.

A similar ritual was inflicted upon a supposed oppressor, Admiral Coligny, by Parisian Catholics in 1572, with such additional traditional refinements as throwing him, half-dead, out of the window, and castrating the corpse. The Christian element was superadded when a pious commentator observed that this form of punishment was merited by his 'ill life'.[22] The tyrant's fate, like the tyrannicide's, is an exorcism.

Similarly, both rituals are morally ambiguous. Jonson points out that the symbols of revenge turn back on themselves, as the oppressor himself becomes a body signifying inhumanity: 'since never slave / Could yet so highly offend, but tyranny, / In torturing him, would make him worth lamenting.' (839–41). In its potential appeal to compassion, the ritual deconstruction of a tyrant was as ambiguous an event as that of a tyrannicide.

Whether in political events or in histories or in fictions, tyrants and tyrannicides repeatedly became doubles of each other. This is a problem of some magnitude, since, as we have seen, the mythic rituals of power were designed to make it possible to distinguish who was who, oppressor and oppressed, in politics. Yet the ritual itself confused the issue by likening the tyrant to the tyrannicide.

We can begin to understand why this was so if we explore the Judithic underplot of such ritual events. Complementing a classical tradition of tyrannicide, the biblical model for the French ritual was in fact the Book of Judith. There the mythic plot of tyrannicide was played out as the private person targeted the powerful one; decapitated the tyrant's naked body, tore down his canopy of state, carried off his head to show it to the people (as Renaissance executioners did) and ordered it displayed upon the city walls. She transported it in her foodbag, as if it were a comestible; thus even the cannibalism of the more frenzied crowds had its subtextual prototype. As the tyrant ate, so is he eaten. By

the same token, visual representations of Judith's acteme had a symbiotic relationship with both the official and the 'spontaneous' popular performances of
ritual executions. The fact is that such spontaneous riots were not spontaneous
at all: either they performed the familiar mythologized ritual independent of
governmental blessing, or (as in the case of the St Bartholomew's Day
Massacre) they were actually incited by the regime. Hence in reports and 'eyewitness' accounts of such events we hear not unmediated reportage but versions
of the myth. For instance, two conflicting accounts of Coligny's murder nevertheless include all the usual tropes associated with the ritual.[23] In that sense they
are efficiently doing their job, which is to record not facts but the ritual.

   In the ritual, as we have seen, tyrannicide was characterized as 'the eater
eaten'. Both tyrant and tyrannicide were cannibals, because both were killers,
consumers of human lives. The tyrannicide as avenger made himself into the
image of that which he assassinated. Thus it was possible for a political ballad
to identify the two rather startlingly: when the Scottish regent Moray was assassinated, it was not Moray but his tyrannicide who was designated '*Tyrant* and
traitor'.[24] This moral ambiguity echoed that of Judith's myth. Holofernes the
tyrannical patriarch could be read as like God the righteous patriarch, which
was why Judith was 'God's assassin' in all senses. Similarly, in the Renaissance,
the 'Judith' William the Silent was assassinated by the 'Judith' Gerard. The
problematic identity between tyrant and tyrannicide was already present in
Judith's myth.

   Thus from the symbolism in the founding myth we can deduce why the
Renaissance identified them. This was because the iconographic identifying
marks of the tyrant were exactly replicated by those of the tyrannicide. The
political meaning of their iconographies was also the same. For instance, both
were represented as upstarts, transgressing their place in the hierarchical order
of things. Like Judith, Gerard, Clément, Chastel and Ravaillac were private
persons, without public status: that was one of the reasons why they were compared to her by their contemporaries. Yet although they were nobodies, they
could nevertheless kill a king. And since he was God's viceregent on earth, they
were like her an assassin of God himself. An absolutist pamphlet found it
inconceivable that Ravaillac, 'a man of nothing, a nothing and not a man', could
have unmade, 'undone', a 'sacred person'.[25] The great man was simply erased,
in a moment, by a nonentity. This was the most dramatic and effective challenge
to every principle of hierarchy, to the carefully structured system of power:
'Great men were Gods, if beggars could not kill 'em,' as *Revenger's Tragedy* put
it (II.ii.93). This rupture of all principles of hierarchy was why the assassins
were demonized. Only the fact that Clément was 'an infernal fury', in human
disguise merely, could account for this blasphemous act.[26] This was also why it
was so important for the regime to confirm that demonization of the assassin by
transforming him into a damned grotesque on the scaffold.

But the political objective went further even than this. If one saw Clément as demonically possessed – 'in whose heart Satan lodged' – then one denied that any ordinary *human* subject could challenge the power of the regime. Ravaillac too was merely Satan's 'instrument', and the 'author' of his act was hell's own king.[27] In other words, like Judith in her Book, the regicide was not intrinsically powerful over an earthly potentate, but merely instrumental to a supernatural one. Like the power behind the scaffold, this too was invisible. Thus assassins, like Judith, were returned to subjection under the rightful power-system. This obsession with dehumanizing, instrumentalizing, demonizing the regicide is precisely a strategy of power. It attempts to deny agency – power which is to say, *effective* power, or potency – to a prodigious agent.

But this attempt to draw an absolute moral distinction between the ruler and his assassin was abortive. For it was, in fact, quite usual to demonize the tyrant. In 1637 Henry Carey described the tyrant as a pervasive force of evil, whose crimes offended both God and man. Edward Sexby added in 1657 that the 'tyrant' Cromwell was primarily guilty of the sin of hubris, complaining that tyrants generally think themselves gods.[28] Of course, the same hubris characterized Nebuchadnezzar, demanding worship as a god, in the Book of Judith. His desire to be God is the most glaring symptom of tyranny.

The dismemberment of the fallen tyrant exorcized this evil spirit who had thought to rank with God himself. The clinching identification of a tyrant was that the ritual of tyrannicide was effected upon him. It is the proper end of his destiny as a tyrant, the verdict. If tyrants and tyrannicides shared the same definitive ending, dismemberment, so they were thought to share the same original motivation. Both were regarded as hubristic.

This view was born out of the moral casuistry applied to tyrannicide. Obviously, those who wished to support tyrannicidal rebellion were anxious to find ways of justifying murder for this purpose: *Killing Noe Murder* (1659), as one of them put it bluntly. Some argued that a wrong was permitted if performed to a good end. God had chosen and inspired tyrannicides, such as Ehud and Judith.[29] In order to justify the political principle, Du Bartas's poem is careful to argue out the ethics of Judith's action before she performs the murder (VI.111ff.). His heroine questions whether she is violating the sacred laws of hospitality; no, because God's law overrides humankind's. Is she a traitor? No, because loyal to Israel. Is she a murderer? No, because God himself commands her to kill. Having decided these questions to her satisfaction, she prepares to 'make this bloody tyrant die'; implying that his own homicidal character merits the death warrant. Biblical examples did indeed imply that God sanctioned tyrannicide if he endowed the instrument with a special mission.

But who was capable of being certain that God had chosen him or her in this way?[30] It was more likely to be human egotism that imagined such prodigious agency from God. Conservatives and revolutionaries could agree on this point.

The self-elected instrument of God must beware 'his own arrogance that swells within him, that he does not confuse himself with God'.[31] If he thought himself a Judith, he was probably guilty of hubris, the sin of the tyrant himself.

The language of this proposition in the Huguenot tract *Vindiciae Contra Tyrannos* is heavily dependent upon oral and sexual metaphors. The tyrannicide's fake inspiration relies upon his own 'creations', which 'conceive vanities and beget lies' – a monstrous illegitimate birth. These echo the femininity of Judith, the tyrannicide's model, and her transgression of women's normal role. Similarly transgressive, the deluded tyrannicide is like a woman rebirthing herself as a monster. Both Ravaillac and the English assassin John Felton were brought to admit that they had suffered from this delusion,[32] fashioning the punished body of the tyrant into a 'lie': a fake spectacle of God's power. As a person who confuses himself with God, the tyrannicide switches into the self-deifying tyrant. Thus in theology, demonization, punishment and desecration of the body, tyrants and tyrannicides are doubles in representation. Far from drawing boundaries or defining legitimacy, their representations converge, and subvert the signifying system of power-relations. The instability of the term 'tyrant' is also, inexorably, the radical instability of the term 'tyrannicide'.

What this unreliable distinction implies is the unreliability of any ideological term. For upon the distinction tyrant/tyrannicide, mutually defining terms, rested a series of moral problems clustering around ideas of justice, rights and authority. The tyrannicide appeals to a transcendence of normal morality (which condemns homicide) through public and divine values. In turn that appeal presupposes that both public and religious absolutes are accessible to definition, that the perpetrators knew which side of the conflict God had sanctified. Since both sides claimed such sanctification, this appeal problematized rather than clarified the system of public values. On the other hand, in the absence of an appeal to such an absolute authority as the divine – which the Bible suggested was always different from and often in conflict with normal morality – there are no definitive categories upon which to rest any claims to authority. Thus the political distinction between tyranny and tyrannicide is even more problematic in modern societies that no longer possess a consensus of religious beliefs, in which only secular morality can be adduced to justify acts of authority or subversion. When the United States invaded Panama (a violation of international law) it justified its actions by news bulletins. In doing so the USA begged as many questions as it professed to answer. Was it playing the role of a Judith or a Holofernes?

Power and Gender

Implicit in *Vindiciae*'s sketch of the tyrannicide was, as we saw, a feminine troping of the 'conception' of the crime. This was only one instance of the symbolic gendering of concepts of power. We saw that the iconography of tyranny figured it as masculine, the opposing tyrannicide as Judithically feminine. Any such assassin was thus symbolically feminine. The feminization of the tyrannicide was a significant part of the way in which the Renaissance mythologized power in gendered terms.

The feminine concept of tyrannicide was particularly useful to Protestant politics. This was because Protestantism itself had been represented as the feminine religion. During the English Revolution, for instance, French political theory, especially on tyrannicide, had a revived influence upon English politics. Despite her apocryphal status, there were still ways of inserting Judith's example into the current cultural ferment of Protestant England. In 1611, the publication of Nicolaus Seravius's Latin commentary on Judith had in fact been inspired by the European reaction to the recent assassination of Henry IV.[33] Similarly, two commentaries published at Lyons in 1648 and 1653 were clearly inspired by the shocking current events in England. The second infiltration of Judith's icon was by way of reprints of older works on Elizabeth as Judith, a Protestant heroine who was often contrasted to Charles I and his alleged crypto-Papist tyranny. The translation of Le Moyne's *Gallery* into English, *Elogium Heroinum* and Shirley's tome on heroic women – all including Judith as a major prototype – swelled the field of pamphlet literature on women, which received new stimulus from the social upheavals. Revolting women (both parliamentary petitioners and sectarian preachers), the Protestant repute of Elizabeth and the controversy over the Catholic queen Henrietta Maria's role in the conflict comprised the complex relation between revolution and femininity that made Judith's icon a political sign. Even texts of biblical commentary or conventional pro-feminine eulogy concealed political intentions by assuming her long prehistory in Reformation polemic. Either side could use her. For Protestants, though, her image perpetuated the feminine genealogy of the reformed religion. Whereas Elizabeth was eulogized as a pacific queen, Charles was execrated as a 'Man of Blood'. Her, and Judith's, feminine gender counterposed the masculine tyrant. Thus the feminine tradition that was part of Protestantism's self-constituting mythology was a useful way of asserting a moral distinction between the two sides in the conflict.

Whereas the Bible had permitted a firm distinction between Judith and Holofernes, during the Renaissance God's assassin and the demonic despot merged into one. The firmness of the Book of Judith's distinction, however, rested not only upon the asserted authorization of Judith by God but also upon the imagistic patterning that distinguished tyrant from tyrannicide by their respective genders. The original distinction subsisted because Judith assumed death's power by stealing the tyrant's in the form of his sword: it was not intrinsic to her sex, but a necessity of resistance. Judith's return to privacy signalled that she remained essentially feminine. When Renaissance political semiotics suggested that power was masculine and the subjects it ruled feminine, they replicated the contrast between Judith and Holofernes, Lucretia and Tarquin. Lucretia's body was the body politic raped by the tyrant, Judith's embodied Israel's femininity as against Holofernes' virulent masculinity. Tyranny was masculine, that which it depredated and that which opposed it were feminine. Similarly, Renaissance political thought attempted to fix the unstable terms of tyranny and tyrannicide by figuring them upon the female body. Tyrants both rape and dismember: in hagiographies of female saints torture substitutes for rape when the virgin martyr resists the tyrant's advances, and ultimately she is executed, usually by beheading. Such narratives imply that torture, dismemberment and rape are homologous activities of tyranny, all signifying engrossment and invasion. Thus, in political narratives, what befalls the female body symbolizes what is happening in the state.

However, distinction by means of gender encountered an awkward problem. Supporting an image of the tyrant's dissipation was a traditional charge of 'perversion', of effeminacy as well as concupiscence. In classical tradition the emperor Nero was portrayed in this way, whilst in Du Bartas's *Judit* (V.200ff.) we are treated to a condemnation of courtly dissipations and a juicy description of the effete Sardanapalus, portrayed on a tapestry in Holofernes' tent. If in fact both tyrant and tyrannicide were potentially feminine, distinction by gender dissolved in the necessity to defame an effete tyrant's power as subject to the supposedly female sin of passivity – a metaphor for irresponsible government.

In Shakespeare's *Titus Andronicus*, the tyrant's sons rape the rebellious Titus's daughter Lavinia in order to signify to him their coercive power. They cut out her tongue and lop off her hands supposedly to prevent her identifying her rapists by either spoken or written testimony. But the political meaning of this mutilation reinforces the political meaning of the rape: to dismember the female body politic is the action of a tyrant. But if Lavinia is a combination of the mythic rape-victims Lucretia and Philomel, her mutilated body is also, like theirs, itself physical testimony to the fact that the ruler is a tyrant. In that respect, the tyrant's enforcement of his own excessive power is self-defeating: it creates the symbolic witness to its own evil.

In a later Jacobean tragedy, John Fletcher's *The Maid's Tragedy* (1608–11), Evadne, the ruler's concubine, attempts to cancel her transgression against her husband's honour by killing her lover. Having been the permeable, contaminable container of his honour, she had like Lucretia been penetrated by the tyrant. In a reversing revenge, she stabs the Duke. In this she is, as it were, a sullied Judith. When her husband rejects her act of expiation, she stabs herself, thus destroying (purging) the contaminated vessel of her body. Now she is a sullied Lucretia. Evadne has carried in her person the corrupted body politic.

Thus in Renaissance drama mythic patterns of rape and dismemberment manifest to the audience the political meaning of the play. And the sex of the bodies that reveal power-relations is important, because women were made the measure of power by their subordination and, in the case of tyranny, by their victimization. Their permeability, their vulnerability, their instrumental embodiment of a husband's autonomy are the vehicles of political significance.

What can disturb this mythic political moralism is the apparent similarity between public and personal acts of revenge. When Titus kills the rapists and serves them up to their parents at dinner, the cannibalistic feast is what punishes by parody the tyrant's own gross appetite. Similarly, in the Book of Judith, the fact that Holofernes does not rape Judith, and that she therefore has no personal motive of revenge, is vital to her portrayal as a public heroine whose motive is the defence of her people. Personal revenge, the righting of a wrong by a wrong, is theoretically more problematic than public revenge, which is done not for selfish reasons but for the public good, to remove a public enemy. The perceived moral difference became very important, for instance, when John Felton assassinated the Duke of Buckingham in 1628. Whether Felton's motive was personal vengeance or political principle, a matter in doubt at the time, was crucial to the moral and public interpretation of the killing.[34] Only if an observer were able to portray Felton as fitting the iconographic pattern of tyrannicide could his motive become mythically defined as altruistic.

In drama, the mythic pattern could be confirmed by means of gender. For instance, Evadne's motive in killing the Duke is hopelessly compromised by personal motives, sexual and marital. But when she obligingly removes her contaminated body from the scene, the impure instrument of tyrannicide and the corrupt body politic are also eradicated. What remains – as in Lucretia's story – are the vindicated, restored masculine political rights of her husband and his compeers. Neither Evadne nor Lucretia could be permitted, in this mythic plot, to survive, because their bodies had been vitiated by the tyrant's evil spirit. Killing them off eradicates the vestiges of his evil. In Evadne's case, her double role – as possessed by the tyrannical spirit *and* as a tyrannicide – implies their identification. That problem of their similarity is also disposed of when she dies by her own hand. Only the permeable female body permits this symbolic moralism to work effectively.

The gender tropes of the drama were consistent with those deployed by contemporary observers to describe and analyse political events. Myth governed both texts and events, shaped events into the forms provided by its own pre-existent 'fictions' of meaning. Representing tyrannicides as feminine could provide a way of ratifying their sanctification. Thus the Catholic Jean Boucher eulogizes Clément, the lowly friar who killed a king, by troping him as Judith, who as a physically feeble woman was an equally unlikely candidate for such a glorious and bloody act.[35] In other words, since only God could have activated him, Clément's action was sanctified. This feminine troping confers sanctification upon the same assassin who was demonized by conservative writers.

By contrast, the latter found it useful to masculinize the assassin, like the tyrant, in order to codify what had befallen the body politic. After Henry IV's assassination the conservative writer Henri Estienne asserted in his *Marvaylous Discourse* (1575), that only bloody vengeance upon subversives could prove that France's aristocracy were not 'Frenchwomen, but Frenchmen'. A successful regicide has feminized the nation, by removing its patriarchal head. Ravaillac removed its masculine authority, just as Artemisia Gentileschi's painting revealed the feminizing of Holofernes's limbs by Judith's murderous vigour. Revenge for this would recuperate virility for the victimized and feminized nation. Thus the plot of tyranny and tyrannicide is a matter of assigning gender to the people, the assassin and the victim in order to validate their respective authorizations as political actors. The ideology of tyrannicide is defended or attacked or avenged by strategies that use the body as verifier – the *gendered* body.

One might have thought that, should a female tyrant arise, this gendering would become a conceptual problem. A striking example of the way to portray a woman as a tyrant was Henri Estienne's attack upon Catherine de' Medici. Naturally Catherine is seen as an instance of Wicked Queen syndrome. Whilst she is said to display the usual symptoms of tyranny – libidinousness, despotism, appetitiveness – Estienne's most powerful mythic image of Catherine is as Medea, rending the state limb from limb.[36] Dismemberment of the body politic is, in effect, the equivalent for a female tyrant of the male tyrant's rapine. His political mode is penetration, hers deconstruction. It is significant that she desexualizes this body before, Judith-like, she dismembers it. There is ready comparison with the feminization of Holofernes's body in Judith's portrayals. Assuming that a 'weak, passive' woman cannot rape a man, Estienne's strategy is to homologize national rape as dismemberment. Whereas Henry IV's body was portrayed as the manhood of the body politic, for Estienne the body politic is a male dismembered by the ruler's femaleness. The tyrant is assassin of the masculine body of France, a female Other who unmans and unmakes it. Estienne's re-gendering of the body politic as aristocratic virility makes Catherine, his throat-cutter, a Judithic severer of the patriarchal head. Envisaged as Judiths, both female tyrant and male tyrannicide represent the same Other to the political mythology of the Reformation. The Judithic tyrant is an alter-ego of the Judithic tyrannicide.

The Appetites of Women

Like Estienne's, François Hotman's attack on Catherine's tyranny in *Francogallia* portrayed female rule as characterized by bestial appetites for sex and blood. Important to the efficacy of such propaganda was the fact that the political idea of feminine bestiality was already firmly locked into all the cultural paradigms of the Renaissance, whether public or private. A perspective on Renaissance notions of the body offered by Mikhail Bakhtin suggested that they resided in an opposition between 'classical body' and 'grotesque body'.[37] The first is highly finished and impermeable, perfect; whereas the grotesque body is unfinished, uncontainable and overflowing. As we have seen, the fundamental problem for female rulers was that their bodies were regarded as permeable by a foreign masculinity: if they married, their foreign husbands would master the national body. Stereotypes of gender were built on a similar opposition to the classical/grotesque, in which women were characterized as sexually voracious, garrulous, excessive and unruly. Public punishment of shrewish wives just required them to be bridled; women's libido was similarly described as head-strong like a horse in need of bridling. To explain the female tyrant's excess Hotman quotes Cato: 'If you loose the reins with women, as with an unruly nature and an untamed beast, you must expect uncontrolled actions.'[38]

The radical instability of this sign follows upon women's portrayal as a prin-ciple of unnaturalness because they are excessively natural – appetitive. Yet naturalness was customarily construed as good. The same contradiction inheres in the strategy of identifying tyrants by their appetites. Those very naturalizing strategies, whereby absolutist theorists attempted to ratify patri-archal power, produce contradictions in the images of power. The strategy then is to make naturalness excessive, and therefore transgressive: women are too natural, therefore transgression tends to acquire gendered characteristics. So tyrannicides too could be re-gendered, as 'not a man', as female trans-gressors of the received divine, social, natural, sexual and physical orders: as Judiths.

Assassins disrupted the state's natural order by feminizing the ruler's body. This process had to be reversed if the state was to re-empower itself. In the public execution of the assassin, the state attempted to return power to its proper gender, masculinity. The scaffold was a scene of invisible masculine power asserting itself. What it exerted itself upon was the criminal's body. In order for the supposedly natural sexual dynamics of power to display them-selves in this event, the criminal's body had to be feminized. If the criminal had feminized the nation and the ruler, then the latter had to become men again by contrast to the offender becoming a woman.

This process began when the criminal was portrayed as a Judith, as a self-elected assassin and feminine transgressor. Then, on the scaffold, the execu-tioner's tortures proved that the criminal's body was vulnerable, permeable, violable like a woman's. Just as the assassin had penetrated the ruler's body, feminizing it, so the burning pincers that pierced and mutilated the assassin's body subjected it to the same metaphoric rape. Dismemberment completed the mythic ritual of rape, death and dismemberment. The execution process added up to parodying, and hence inverting, the process of tyrannicide itself. It thus necessarily involved restoring the correct genders to the powerful and the powerless. The assassin, punished, ceased to be male-penetrative and became female-penetrated. The fact that such rituals often included castration made the feminization of the punished body more emphatic. By making the tyrannicide's body grotesque, the ritual revealed it as the grotesque body of the female. The assassin's challenge to power had consisted of erasing the patriarch. He had acquired a potency that threatened the whole system. To prove that this could not be done, and thus must not be attempted again, the assassin had to be rendered impotent. Which was why the scaffold rendered him feminine. By contrast, the power that executed him was remasculinised. It retrieved its authority.

As we have seen, power's supposed masculinity habitually displayed itself upon the feminine body politic. On Lucretia's body it became visible. Precisely this imagery was enacted in the execution of tyrannicide. As we saw, the tyrannicide's body on the scaffold represented the vitiated body politic, punished and purged. On his body, as on Lucretia's, the regime displayed its power – and in the same way, by mutilating and metaphorically raping it. Thus his body, feminized, came to represent the feminine body politic. It became the obedient female of patriarchy. Its violation proved that the ruler still ruled, that it was passive to his will.

This brings us back to the question, asked by Foucault, of how bureaucrats and spectators could tolerate the spectacle of such cruelty, could, in fact, be comfortable with it. But the question assumes that these spectators should have felt that it was excessive. As I have said, this was only the case if the criminal could be construed as a martyr, in which case, the excessiveness of his suffering was appropriate because it simply confirmed the martyrdom. In no other sense did contemporaries find the Renaissance execution an *extreme* demonstration of power. Since power was customarily imagined in these violent masculine terms, what happened on the scaffold was the making vivid of the normal status quo; a natural metaphor made real. That is why we hear so little from Renaissance spectators in the way of criticism, disapproval or revulsion at these spectacles. They only complained of cruelty when they had a propagandist motive for doing so. That was because what they saw was, in their *mentalité*, natural to power.

Judith and Rape

As we have seen, paintings of Judith's murder of Holofernes tended to reproduce the semiotics of executions. Holofernes's prone or prostrate body was feminized by its posture; equally when his severed neck was presented frontally, the feminizing effect was enhanced by its quasi-vaginal appearance and by the portrayal of Judith's rampant swordsmanship. As in art so on the scaffold, the aims of the execution scene were to re-empower masculinity and to remasculinize power. In both contexts the same cultural mythology dictated the terms.

Whether in the divided Europe of the Renaissance or the disintegrating Yugoslavia of the late twentieth century, atrocities of dismemberment and rape have been strategic actions. These technologies of power have remained in essence the same in all times, features of the *mythos* of tyranny. We can compare them to the way in which feminists have perceived the modern character of patriarchy. They have repeatedly insisted that the tendency to regard rape as a sexual crime is disingenuous, an attempt to except it from other crimes committed upon the body, such as grievous bodily harm and murder. According to Susan Brownmiller, rape is simply – and thus horrifically – a crime of violence. As an instance of coercion and oppression, like other violent crimes, it is an infliction of power upon the victim: within a patriarchal society, it functions as the action of last resort to confirm the power of men over women.[39] In other words, any patriarchal society ultimately depends upon fear of rape to exert control over women: rape is the event that exposes the workings of patriarchal domination. (The point is not that 'all men are rapists', but that for women any man might be, which in practical terms achieves the same effect.) This argument has often been dismissed as extravagant and paranoiac. But by comparing it to the technologies of power in the Renaissance, we can see that it is not simply credible but compelling. The Renaissance scaffold exposed the workings of power in precisely this way. As torture, dismemberment and sexual mutilation were like the technologies of Renaissance power, so rape, clitoridectomy and sexual murder are modern crimes of torture, a contemporary technology of power.

This also throws light on the reason why some men fail to recognize that rape is a serious crime. (The inability of some male judges to acknowledge this has become notorious in Britain.) If one is accustomed to thinking of sex as penetrative-aggressive, then rape seems merely a more forceful version of the norm. It may even seem *more* natural than seeking a woman's consent first. Just as in the Renaissance the technologies of power were viewed as natural to it, in the same way under patriarchy rape is regarded as natural. The mythology of power underwrites it.

By reversing the spectacle of power enforced, representations of Judith's acteme could signify much more than a merely exceptional example of 'women's revenge', the revolt of the underdog. Rather the opposite: by inverting the sexual power-dynamics of the scaffold, the female executioner depicts power itself as feminine by nature. Judith's acteme is not merely a raid on patriarchy, but an appropriation of the very spectacle that is its guarantee. Since the fact of spectacle is vital to the power asserted on the scaffold, so the Judithic spectacle is more than a metaphorical image: it counteracts and denies the actual *practice* of power endemic in Western society.

Parricide and Marricide: Beatrice Cenci and the Woman of Valencia

As a paradigmatic instance of society's power-relations generally, the public execution and its Judithic implications were as dear to artists as they were to political theorists. During the Renaissance *querelle des femmes* both male and female feminists had complained of the 'tyranny' and 'despotism' exercised by the male upon the female.[40] As we saw, politics depended upon patriarchal images of the family to underwrite the monarch's power as 'natural' – it was paternal, and regicide was 'parricide'. Equally, political terminology was retrojected back into the household by the feminist debate. Husbands were, they complained, given such tyrannical power over wives and children that they could mistreat them – whether psychologically or physically – with impunity. In seventeenth-century England the law case that bore out this contention was that of the Earl of Castlehaven, who was executed for marital rape, incestuous rape of a minor and sodomy. But the most notorious example of patriarchal tyranny concerned the father of a young Italian noblewoman named Beatrice Cenci. In 1599 Beatrice Cenci was beheaded for the crime of parricide. Since it was well known that her deceased father had been a tyrannical paterfamilias, the legal system was in this instance at odds with popular opinion. So cruel and irrational had he been in his treatment both of his wife and of his children that they had been driven by desperation into a familial conspiracy to murder him, of which Beatrice herself was the instigator.[41] The populace sympathized with his murderer, and the spectacle of Beatrice, as beautiful as her name implied, on the scaffold became the stuff of tragedy. This was, indeed, an instance of the way in which the scaffold' significance could be inverted, a replication of the 'virgin martyr' effect. Her crime, her early death and the pathos of her execution, attended by thousands, became a byword for tragic eroticism.

In Caravaggio's *Judith and Holofernes* of 1600, the virginal young blonde murderess has been identified as Beatrice Cenci.[42] The aged maid can thus be seen as her mother and co-conspirator. Transmogrified as Judithic, Beatrice's act becomes a just revolt against patriarchal domination, a tyrannicide in the private domain. If we regard the painting as a legitimated execution scene, the sharp rapier-like character of the sword is explained. Whereas the Bible specified a heavy war-sword such as Holofernes would naturally have used, a 'falchion', the thin sharp blade suggests the Renaissance weapon used for execution of nobles granted a degree of mercy. It was such a sword that Henry VIII ordered in advance for the execution of Anne Boleyn, so that she would die more quickly. Beatrice-Judith's is the sword of a legitimated private justice, visited as if by the public authorities. In this way Caravaggio uses the technique of importing execution-scenes into Judith paintings as a way of subverting the state's own 'just verdict' upon Beatrice. Like her own action, the painting is a judgement against patriarchy.

Just as Judith's myth was read into Beatrice Cenci's history, so in a popular French Renaissance account of a 'true' murder we can see Judith's myth shaping the story. In Valencia, a nobleman had secretly married his 'concubine' but thereafter publicly married a noblewoman. In revenge, his first wife pretended to welcome him to her bed; then, 'assisted by a bondwoman of hers', she tied him to the bed and stabbed her sleeping husband in the throat. She then stabs him repeatedly in the body, 'in fury' pulls out his eyes 'cuts out his tongue, and then his heart, which she tears in pieces, and mangles him in diverse parts of his body.' Finally, with her maidservant's help, she defenestrates the remains. She is gratified by 'so extraordinary a revenge'; equally, the spectacle in the street below, it is implied, is a cynosure for all men fearful of women's maleficence: 'day being come, every man runs to behold the bloody spectacle.'[43] This imaging of 'women's revenge' in the bedroom is thus conflated with tyrannicide motifs of dismemberment. In these images, as in the plot of this reportage as a whole, we can see how the facts were filtered through the lens of Judith's acteme, mutilating the man on the bed. Moreover, the detail that the woman freed and paid her maidservant as a reward for complicity is a direct echo of Judith's manumission of her own 'bondservant' in the Apocrypha. It may be, indeed, that here we are looking at the popular news story that lies behind some painted representations of Judith.

The exceptional detail in Artemisia Gentileschi's painting of Judith's acteme is the active co-operation of the maid who holds the man down. Artemisia's subject is indeed 'women's vengeance' for male perfidy. In a similarly unrepentant spirit, the woman of Valencia, although 'condemned to lose her head, went . . . cheerfully to execution . . . to the great amazement of all the inhabitants of Valencia.' Like the mangled corpse, this spectacle too suggested that women might not after all suffer remorse after their revolt against their masters. Supposedly a warning against 'secret marriages', the story was in fact retold as a warning against women's capacity to be Judiths to Holofernean husbands. It reveals the continuum between public and private politics that transforms a bed into a scaffold, and *vice versa*.

Charlotte Corday and the French Revolution

As females, the woman of Valenicia and Beatrice Cenci were of course more literally Judiths than the male assassins so named, even though their crimes were perpetrated in the private domain. But in due time a female assassin of the public sphere joined their cohort. Just as Balthasar Gérard was inspired by Judith's example to kill William the Silent in 1584, so in 1793 Charlotte Corday was inspired by her to kill the demagogue Citoyen Marat. By this time the French Revolution had entered the phase of the Terror, a systematic legal application of massacre in which many revolutionary leaders themselves would perish. All the customary iconicities of violence and revolt repeated themselves during the events of the Revolution. Queen Marie Antoinette was demonized as the foreign corrupting principle, a luxuriant embodiment of vice and exploitation. In what one deduces was an attack on her by proxy, a mob attacked her lady-in-waiting, the Princesse de Lamballe.[44] This assault applied misogynistically the classic process of tyrannicide to tyranny's embodiment: stripping the body, dismemberment, the impaling of her severed head on a pike and mutilation of the genitals: her labia were severed and used as a mock-moustache by one of her murderers. When Louis XVI was guillotined, his head was displayed to the people by the executioner Sanson as an icon of tyrannicide.[45] His own name, a variant of Samson, supported the implications of biblical iconography.

For such events the Revolution had already subsumed the iconography of Judith as justified revolt. In 1789 her story had been dramatized for the Parisian stage, alluding to the current upheaval.[46] When the Revolution swept away the monarchy, even playing-cards underwent a signal change. As we saw, queens in the French suits had been portrayed as Judith. In revolutionary card-packs the queen's function was replaced by that of Judith herself, holding in her hand the severed head, icon of tyrannicide. It was an especially appropriate image at a time when France fell under the rule of the guillotine, feminized as 'Madame Guillotine' or 'The Widow'.[47] As the latter sobriquet suggests, the guillotine itself was an icon and instrument of Judithic import, a twin of the female allegorical figure of Liberty. Emblematized as the sturdy woman of the people, the Marianne with bared breasts famously portrayed in Delacroix's painting, Liberty like the revolutionary Judith – as in Hemessen's – bared her breasts as a symbol of freedom and truth, of *nuda veritas*. Like her, the guillotine was the great 'equalizer', the first engine of execution specifically intended to humanize death for all criminals by beheading them cleanly and quickly: all classes, from monarch to peasant, would expire by the same method. Metaphorically, too, the symbolism of head-severing was iconoclastic of all traditional authorities. Symbol of 'freedom' and vengeance against the *ancien régime*, the guillotine was the Revolution's Judith.

These feminine symbols of revolution inverted the imagery of the *ancien régime* scaffold. Whereas there the masculine power of absolutism had confirmed its power upon the body of the feminized patient, in the revolutionary scene that popular feminine body bestowed a fatal equality upon everyone. At the foot of the guillotine, watching the severed heads fall into the basket, *sans-culotte* women sat and knitted; afterwards they became a notorious image of the bloodthirstiness of the Revolution, its savagery epitomized by their Fury-like femininity. Similarly, early revolutionary societies included associations of women, but these were increasingly defamed and excluded by the men of the revolutionary Convention. Again, the female revolutionaries were identified with the ravening mob of women who marched on the palace at Versailles, 'Megaeras' of bloodlust. On the one hand, femininity signified the revolt of the body politic against its masters, an imagery promoted by revolutionary propaganda. On the other, hostile European powers of the *ancien régime* characterized the French Revolution as an anarchy fitly represented by the bloody heads and writhing corpses produced by the guillotine. Severed heads symbolically underwrote the ambience of 'cannibalism' that Carlyle and other commentators attributed to revolutionary bloodlust.[48] If the people's Revolution was politically feminine, that femininity was death, the *femme fatale* of the guillotine. The political ambiguity of that symbolic engine in effect replicated the ambivalence of Judith herself. In one way or another, the Revolution was a Judithic scene.

As always, however, Judith's icon was a double-edged sword. The demagogue who had profited most by the Terror, the radical journalist and Convention member Marat, used it against the Girondin party, of which Corday was an admirer. A genteel young woman in provincial Normandy, Corday chafed against her helpless witness of the Girondins' persecution, convinced that Marat was the instigator of a ruinous civil war. Educated religiously in a convent, Corday had thought of becoming a nun, but she was also a zealous Republican. In the Bible she discovered the role that would combine her religious and her political idealism: Judith's example revealed to her how she might take a hand in the destiny of France.[49] By assassinating the tyrant Marat she could remove the villain who had driven the Revolution onto the wrong course, could rescue 'Liberty' itself.

Travelling to Paris, she purchased a knife and tricked her way into Marat's home. Even in this her method was Judithic. Just as the biblical heroine had offered to reveal to Holofernes how he might gain entrance into the city, so Corday offered to inform against Marat's enemies, the Girondins in Caen. Like Holofernes, Marat was not suspicious of a woman, despite his fear of assassination. Her youthful femininity reassured him that he faced no danger from this intrusion, that he might indeed indulge his fancy for female pulchritude. Precisely the same thought had made his mistress the more obdurate in her attempt to prevent Corday's seeing him. As was his custom, Marat was seated in his slipper-bath, a treatment for the painful skin disease that plagued him and compelled him to conduct his paperwork in this strange venue. The high slipper-bath also constrained his movements, making it more difficult for him to resist Corday when she pulled out her knife and stabbed him, efficiently and mortally, in the lung. There was a certain poetic justice in her timing, for Marat had been noting down the names of Girondins and reportedly exulting at the prospect of their imminent decapitation. The Judithic character of the scene underwrote this irony of his 'headtaking'.

Corday had resigned herself to the inevitable price of her assassination, condemnation and death. Although she defended herself against the furious assault of Marat's mistress and neighbours, she surrendered calmly to arrest, and during the trial she remained composed and unrepentant. She even attempted to cut short the judicial masquerade by stating firmly that she had indeed killed Marat. As with the Judithic tyrannicides of the Renaissance, the authorities refused to credit that this female nobody could be an autonomous agent rather than an instrument of vested interests: but she insisted that she had acted at no one's instigation but her own. Refusing to allow her action to be appropriated to other than a political, altruistic motive, she declared: 'I killed one man to save a hundred thousand . . . I never wanted energy.' This resounding confirmation of a Judithic motive – the deliverance of her people – was not welcome to the revolutionary government. During her trial and incarceration Corday's conduct emphasized her lack of remorse, ensuring that her assertion of her own idealistic political motive would remain current afterwards. She was immediately dubbed a Judith, and in 1797 a play published at Caen celebrated the Girondist heroine as *Charlotte Corday ou La Judith moderne*. She took care to fix the meaning of her action in her own behaviour, much as Lucretia had 'guaranteed' her purity to afterfame by her suicide.

In England, anti-revolutionary propaganda seized upon Corday as a heroine, an avenging angel against 'that monster of atheism and murder, the regicide Marat'.[50] Amongst the flood of memorabilia that rapidly followed news of her murder was an elaborate etching of Corday's trial by the virulent cartoonist James Gillray. Fearlessly confronting a pack of ruffianly judges, she places her hand on her heart and condemns the Revolution that they represent: 'Wretches – I did not expect to appear before you – I always thought that I would be delivered up to the rage of the people, torn in pieces, and that my head, stuck on the top of a pike, would have preceded Marat on his state bed.' In other words, she had envisaged suffering the traditional ritual punishment of a tyrannicide. She goes on to suggest that, in an obverse of the Holofernean head as sign of deliverance, she had envisioned that her own severed head would 'serve as a rallying point to Frenchmen, if there still are any worthy of that name'. Implied is the feminization of the nation that Henry Benevent had also thought to be signified by a tyrannicide. But the point here is rather that Corday's female fortitude mocks by contrast the feminine cowardice of a nation that colludes with its own terrorization. A similar inversion of meaning is effected when Corday asserts that, condemned now, she will soon be regarded as a heroine of the Revolution: her remains will 'soon have conferred upon them the honour of the Pantheon; and my memory will be more honoured in France than that of Judith in Bethulia.' Heroization as a Judith was echoed in the English identification of

Corday as 'A Second Jeanne d'Arc',[51] her historical Judithic predecessor in the deliverance of France.

The hagiography of Corday portrayed her as a tragic beauty as well as a heroine, eroticizing her image just as Beatrice Cenci's had been. For Thomas Carlyle, the most influential English historian of the Revolution, the imagined murder scene was one of adversarial opposites: 'beautiful Charlotte . . . squalid Marat!'[52] Contemporary English propaganda often emphasized Marat's ugliness and his disfigurement by disease. In Gillray's cartoon the body is both cadaverous and leprous, whilst in Isaac Cruikshank's Marat is a repulsive and corpulent figure carrying the marks of dissipation. Cruikshank's work dates from soon after the first arrival of the news from France, when there was some confusion about the circumstances of the murder, so there is no bath in these scenes. Instead, both in Cruikshank's cartoon and in a group of pottery figures memorializing the event, the dominant Charlotte is shown standing over a dying Marat who has fallen at her feet, his degradation comically exaggerated by the cartoonist as Marat's bouncing to the floor, legs in air.[53] Here too, however, the English view of the heroine exploited her Judithic character. Cruikshank's Marat is characterized by homicidal wickedness, a list of planned murders pinned upon his wall; and Corday's is like the Apocrypha's 'hand of a woman', for as she says, 'Down, down to Hell and say a female arm has made one bold attempt to free her country.'

By contrast, in France the official response to the murder was to capitalize on Marat's potential as a martyr of the Revolution. In death he was fast accruing a cult as the 'people's martyr'. His body lay in state in a desecrated church for the veneration of the populace, his wound displayed as if the stigmata of the Revolution's martyr were to replace in the new age those of Christ himself. In September 1794 Marat was officially invested with a crown of immortality.[54] It is somewhat ironic for the fervently anti-religious revolutionary regime that both its own hero and his murderer, heroized by its opponents as virgin martyr and Judith, depended for their political functionalism on hallowed religious iconography.

There was something of a *pietà* also in Jacques-Louis David's officially commissioned portrait of the dead Marat, modelled on Christ's figure in the traditional compositions. David's painting shows Marat slumped over the side of the bath, on which still rests his worktable, symbol of his dedication to public business. Marat's unrealistically smooth skin and classicized limbs are in effect a representation of the authoritarian 'classic body', offered for reverence by the populace. As Kenneth Clark suggested, classical style in art usually appeals to totalitarian regimes.[55] The transmogrified Marat of David is an instance of this effect. With it can be juxtaposed those representations of his assassin that democratized Corday, actually the descendant of a noble family. Brard's portrait applied to Corday the selective heroizing strategy

David had applied to Marat. Omitting the man's corpse, Brard shows Corday as a young woman of the people, in mob cap and knotted shawl, the knife in her hand ready for the defence of their freedom. Whereas David's interpretation, intended for a prominent position in a public building, represented Marat as an embodiment of selfless revolutionary authority; by way of contrast, Brard's Corday was the champion of the people against the tyranny of their new masters. This is the furthest development of Judith's implicit underplot: democratic assertiveness.

The prevailing tone of Corday's representation was tragic and romantic. A contemporary sketch of her in the tumbril taking her to the guillotine shows her as the still centre in a turbulent crowd, her hand on her breast, her eyes raised heavenwards: the red bloom of her rough dress contrasts with the gloomy chiaroscuro of the crowd and an aureole of raidiance lightens the sky behind her.[56] This characterization of Corday as virgin martyr became something of a cult. Later, an artist from her home province, Court, portrayed her at the entrance to Marat's rooms, her eyes raised heavenwards, hand on heart, a cross on her breast: the virgin martyr preparing for her act of Judithic Fortitude. Such romanticized interpretations of the serene young woman who met her fate on the guillotine cheerfully were of the kind that we have already seen in the Renaissance, subverting the intention of the spectacle of execution.

In theory, the executioner's display of Corday's severed head to the spectators should have signified condign justice exacted by the Revolution for the murder of one of its heroes. It was intended to function similarly to the display of Louis XVI's head on the scaffold. However, in the latter's case the gesture immediately tapped into long-established images of the tyrant decapitated. In Corday's case the severed head should have been a symbolic response to her Judithic act and reputation. Whereas in imaginary terms her act implied that she was a Judith grasping the severed head of Marat, so the display of her own head on the scaffold should directly have inverted that icon: the executioner holding the head of a Judith. In a sense, the masculine/feminine dynamics of the traditional spectacle of execution had always been straining towards this image, the inversion of the tyrannicide's/Judith's icon. The spectacle in essence had always been driven by what we might characterize as a desire to invert Judith's revolutionary icon.

But the intended meaning of the spectacle failed to function. As he held up the head to the crowd, the executioner performed a symbolic rebuke for Marat's murder by slapping Corday's dead face. His rudeness offended the spectators, who felt the pathos of Corday's helpless humiliation.[57] A legend sprang up to the effect that the dead face had blushed in maidenly embarrassment at this outrage. The legend was perpetuated by the medical controversy that raged over the guillotine. Whereas the guillotine's champions contended that this was the most humane method of execution yet devised, other medical

experts argued that consciousness remained in the severed head and that therefore the sentient human being still suffered pain after decapitation.[58] Such a
view, that the head remained alive, issued from an atavistic belief in the symbolic value of the human head as seat of consciousness and intellection, indeed
of the mind/body relation and hence of the soul: upon its apparent concentration within itself of what might be imagined as 'humanness'. The apparent
proof of survival offered by the legend of Corday's blush made her, in effect, a
personification of the human being's unique animation by the soul. In the nineteenth century Corday would remain a crucial piece of medical evidence, as we
shall see. However, this process had already begun when, after her execution,
her corpse was subjected to an autopsy, which confirmed that she was a virgin.
The medical examination supported her posthumous reputation as a virgin
martyr and coalesced with her head's signification as the soul in pain. Instead
of confirming the condemning authority, the executioner's performance of a
spectacle of 'Judith's icon inverted' instead inverted the meaning of the
scaffold itself.

That Corday's Judithic significance would continue to exert its effect was
immediately confirmed. On the day following the execution, an admirer named
Adam Lux published a defence of Corday. Horrifying his friends, who feared
his self-destruction, Lux announced that he would be proud to die like Corday
and indeed for her.[59] He was duly condemned and executed, an event that as he
desired implied a ratification of her own idealism. It suggested, as intended, that
Corday did indeed represent a constituency, as she had claimed. In a sense Lux's
reaction to Corday's death – symbolically to the significance of her severed head
– replicated the way in which Achior had been converted by Judith's display of
her trophy. It was as if events fell into consonance with the mythology generated by the apocryphal Book.

Similarly, Corday's murder of Marat inspired numerous representations in
engravings, drawings and paintings. Just as her action had imitated Judith's
acteme, so these representations of Marat's murder are divided by the Judithic
ambivalence. Some celebrate Corday as an embodiment of 'Liberty', whereas
others underline the sinister implications of a Judithic acteme, the harpy or
fatal woman. The latter versions tend to emphasize violence, as in an engraving of 'La Mort du Patriote Marat', showing him pathetically constricted
within a slipper-bath, a vigorous Corday grasping his arm as he struggles, her
other hand driving the knife into his breast.[60] It was reputed that Corday wore
a bonnet with green ribbons on the day of the assassination. This hat often
appears in hostile portrayals, its black stovepipe eminence elongating and
maturing her figure to intimidatory effect, as in this engraving. Her high-
fashion presentation emphasizes a highly artificial femininity which effectively
denies her innocent maidenhood and youth. A more sympathetic portrait by
Paul Baudry shows Corday in the same dress but significantly bareheaded. The

appearance of Marat's body slumped in the bath, his head in the foreground, is diminished by its radical foreshortening, a technique copied from some artists' Holofernes. At the right, Corday shelters in the corner from the assaults of his friends (out of frame). The full-length Corday in her shimmering silk dress is a tragic romantic heroine, neither exultant not ashamed but transfixed by her incredible act and awaiting with trepidation her gaolers; on the wall behind her the map of France signifies her patriotic motivation. Another painting from the revolutionary period, now in the Musée Carnavalet, is particularly Judithic and also elevating. A three-quarter-length portrait of Corday, in a gleaming white dress, shows her with an expression of resolution as she stands at the head of the bathtub, Marat's head and shoulders in shadow at the lower right: she is purity and idealism. It is a composition derived from Judith paintings, contrasting the assassin's lambent whiteness with the dusky, truncated, prostrate body of her enemy, and the vague treatment of the bath deliberately confuses it with a bed. As in many paintings of Judith's acteme, the curtain behind the heroine suggests the tent of Holofernes. There are also similarities with Caravaggio's Judith/Beatrice and her significantly white attire. This is the virgin martyr of the Revolution: Judith's acteme translated into historical event.

During the revolutionary years popular plays re-enacted the event, which has been frequently dramatized ever since. Corday's most celebrated impersonation, in Ponsard's *Charlotte Corday* (1850), was by an actress of the Comédie Française whose professional name was Madame Judith. A contemporary drawing by Laurent Gsell of 'Judith, dans *Charlotte Corday*' is thus encoding more than a theatrical role for its French audience. As soon as the medium of cinema became available, four films about Corday were produced between 1897 and 1919 by French, German and American companies. In the later twentieth century her best-known representation has been in Peter Weiss's political play, *Marat/Sade* (1965), which has also been filmed. In a production redolent of 'sixties 'liberation', here the Marquis de Sade and Corday represented as it were the primitive underplot of sex and death playing beneath civilized modern life. Even Picasso produced a drawing, *Le Meurtre*, which portrayed Corday as a Fury, teeth and breasts bared in a primitive homicidal rage.[61] As in Munch's painting of her, a political threat has been defused because reinterpreted as individual sexual hysteria (as in many modern representations of Judith herself). At the opposite end of the imaginative spectrum, the representation of a political idea, an *al fresco* parody of David's painting, Alison Watt's *Marat and the Fishes*, was commissioned to celebrate Glasgow's year as 'European city of culture' within the European Community; whilst a 1989 pamphlet, at the bicentenary of the French Revolution, saw Corday as 'Judith' the spirit of Freedom.[62] Corday is at once an embodiment of the atavism repressed by sophisticated modern societies – a Fury or a madwoman – and a personification of the political abstractions by which such societies formalize themselves. In both roles she is depersonalized, either an animal or an allegory.

The extremes of Corday's representation are those of a Judith of the modern age: at once a personification of abstract idealism, and of that threat of reversion to the primitive which is perceived as lurking under 'civilized' life, and which at any moment may break out in violence. Our culture can only assimilate such a remorseless, impervious political figure as Corday by seeing her through the counter-cultural myth of Judith. Corday deliberately elected for that personation, understanding that she must control her mythic afterlife if her political intent were not to be obscured. In her, as in the ambivalent original Judith, a remarkable innocence, conjoined with defiance of normal morality, was able to demolish the mythic structures on which power depends.

7

The Dark Angel
Romantic Criminals and Oriental Others

The Romantic Criminal

The French Revolution's anti-authoritarian ideals of liberty and equality, which Charlotte Corday had seen herself as defending like a Judith, were a beacon for radicalism all over Europe. The Revolution had proved that it was possible to overthrow the oppressive governments that had constituted the *ancien régime* in Europe. Complementing this new optimism about political change was the Romantic cult of the individual. A Rousseauist worship of the natural, spontaneous and atavistic elements of the personality, and a fascination with the psychology of exceptional individuals, were essentially reactive responses against the increasing social organization and urbanization prompted by the Industrial Revolution. As industrialized society became more mass-oriented and regimented, there was an exponentially more anxious search for models of ways in which great individuals might make an impact that could change the course of history. This tendency would make Judith a surprisingly compulsive figure for the nineteenth century. We tend to think of this period as a time of complacency and repression but its air of confidence was accompanied by sub-terranean anxieties.

It was these anxieties that, as so often, emerged in the century's images of Judith. She marked the point of conflict between ideas of mass liberty and ideas of individual freedom. There is an inherent conflict between the two strata of freedom: since mass societies, and especially democracies, require the sub-ordination of the individual will to the majority. Political reforms, such as the 1832 Reform Bill in England, and collective insurrections, such as the European revolutions of 1848, repeatedly raised questions about the nature of authority, hierarchy and leadership.

Carlyle, who in his *French Revolution* (1837) had vividly recorded the terri-fying vision of an anarchic irrational tide of mass violence sweeping through history, also penned the great work of cultish individualism *Of Heroes and Hero-*

Worship (1841). There, by contrast, the great men who are seen to break out of the herd and rise to despotism – the Cromwells and Napoleons – are objects of idolatrous fascination. They might be monsters, but as movers of nations and riders of history they confirm the power of the individual personality to transcend impersonal forces. As technology advanced at dizzying speed, bringing with it ever more machines and communications and transportation systems, Carlyle's heroes were reassuring confirmation that nevertheless man was the most complex, interesting, powerful dynamo of all. And the masses, terrifyingly inhuman when they broke out into irresistible violence, were susceptible to control by a single, exceptional human being.

It is in Goya's turbulent, plebeian *Judith and Holofernes* (1820–2) that we see the vengeance of the Spanish peasantry upon their oppressors.[1] Finally penetrated by the revolutionary spirit, the people of Europe's most doddery despotism have finally turned on their masters. For Goya Judith retains her original role as the woman of the people and for the people, the nemesis of power. As the original biblical heroine personified her nation, so Goya's embodied the sudden irruption of a long-repressed popular rage. It is Carlyle's nightmare of atavistic mass violence, but from the opposite point of view: Judith's identity conveys it as divinely chthonic vengeance, justified by the supernatural laws of blood. It is atavistic because entirely natural, fierce because provoked beyond further endurance. This was Judith as a mass yearning for freedom that could not be denied.

But she could also embody equally aptly the character of an individual sharply differentiated from the mass: the Corday/Judith who, despairing of her pusillanimous countrymen, slew a demagogue. Both she and Goya's Judith represented faces of Liberty, but in ways that spelled out its contradiction between the convictions of the haughty individual and the energies of the insurgent crowd. Corday's was an individualistic political act, which presupposed that her convictions about freedom were superior to the prevailing popular mood. Her ideals were meritocratic and middle-class; she elected herself to a political achievement on behalf of 'thousands of Frenchmen', as she put it. Goya's Judith is the collective spirit of thousands of Spaniards doing it for themselves. As conceptions of what Liberty means, and how it is achieved, they contradict each other. For Carlyle the choice was clear: if history was characterized by great tides of change, then these were harnessed by the great individuals, whose rampant humanity overrode the inhumane anarchy of the Revolution's masses. It was the Romantic individualist in Carlyle, as much as the Englishman, who admired the isolationist heroism of Corday.

Whilst Romantic individualism tended to align itself with revolutionary ideals – so that the poet Byron died in Greece, having joined the native resistance to the Turks – this ideology concealed its own contradictions. If revolution was effected by mass movements, what was the relationship between the typical Romantic hero, an exceptional individual, and the other individuals in the mass? How were the equal rights of fraternity reconcilable with the Romantic's conviction of his own special subjectivity?

The Romantic poets' images of themselves were of the isolationist tendency: wandering lonely as a cloud, staring off into the distance from the lonely eminence of mountaintops, and so on. And along with that went an egotistic masculinity, most evident in Byron's *Don Juan* and his own Juanism. Libertinism was only one effect of the Romantic determination to throw off society's moral shackles. The Romantic hero was distinguished from the general run of humanity by his greater sensibility, imagination and audacity: antinomianism and charisma were his stock-in-trade. As a natural aristocrat, he was exempted from all normal social laws, and indeed, lawbreaking was his way of showing his independence of petty rules, his aspiration towards a higher, transcendent truth. If he was 'mad, bad, and dangerous to know', as Lady Caroline Lamb said of Byron, that was because heterodoxy, transgression and excess were symptoms of a unique personality in exuberant revolt against authority and his elders: against 'the Law of the Father'. In short, he was an Oedipus.

According to Harold Bloom, the Romantic poets regarded their literary precursors as fathers, against whom they needed to revolt to find their own voices.[2] If Oedipal and parricidal motifs were fundamental to Romantic ideology, they were also of course fundamental to the contemporary revolutions. The series in which Goya's Judith appeared, for instance, insistently repeated imagery derived from the myth of Saturn, the divine Father who ate his own children to prevent their decapitating him and usurping his place. Shadowing the revolutionary Oedipus, his female complement, the Judith, is the daughter as democratic parricide.

The competing, Romanticized, naturally aristocratic version of Judith is reflected in Shelley's drama about Beatrice Cenci, the parricide who inspired Caravaggio's Judith. In *The Cenci* (1819), she becomes an example of the Romantic Criminal. That figure was always both sublime and sinful, his transgressions effects of nobility, and his tragic doom was a measure of society's inability to comprehend or contain him. Shelley's heroine is a rare early example of this figure translated into his feminine counterpart. Cenci's parricide is presented as a nobly Oedipal act, defying the festering corruption of 'the paternal power' – an unholy alliance of parent, ruler, Pope – in what is presented as 'the great war between the old and young'.[3] The Fathers hate the innocence of the young, which implicitly reproaches their own corruption, and the condemned Beatrice becomes their scapegoat. Hence her characterization as a fallen angel, an angel precisely because criminal in a society where the moral norms have been perverted. Beatrice's is 'a high and holy deed', a transgression that transcends human laws. Shelley's play suggests that the distinctive individual, precisely because superior to her social conditions, is inevitably bound to a tragic doom that is society's revenge upon what overreaches it. If one were to reinterpret the Book of Judith as a Romantic text, it would share Shelley's theme. The Romantic Criminal is a tragedy in herself, born to a greatness for which she must pay dearly. In fact, that she is tragic is proof that she is great.

That paradox is like the paradox of her personality, the diverging 'sympathies and antipathies' that Shelley saw as provoked by Beatrice, a guilty innocent who paralyses our responses to her. We will see this repeated in the novelist Nathaniel Hawthorne's conflation of Cenci and Judith. Similarly, Carlyle portrayed Corday as 'cruel-lovely, with half-angelic, half-daemonic splendour',[4] ambivalence beatified. It is no coincidence that the ambivalent Corday and Cenci were seen as Judiths before they received the accolade of Romantic Criminals. As the sanctified murderess, her ambiguity was an *éminence grise* of this archetype, which would come to haunt the Victorian imagination.

As Shelley observed, the portrait of Cenci that was attributed to Guido Reni had become a cult, seeming as it did to delineate a moral mystery, hidden in 'the most dark and secret caverns of the human heart'. The cult of personality fixed upon such a figure because she threw into high relief the moral extremes of human capacity, within a single psyche. In the same vein, the Victorian novelist Anthony Trollope would write of the fascination exerted by the Romantic Criminal: 'artists in all ages have sought for higher types of models in painting women who have been violent or criminal . . . Look at all the Judiths . . . and the Charlotte Cordays.'[5] Corday's self-elected role as Judith thus replicated the original's ambivalence as part of her own double-edged repute, and like Judith's other historical avatars she merged with her myth. Centring on a compound figure of Judith-Jael, the extremism and radical moral ambivalence of Judith and her avatars became the type of the Romantic Criminal.

Whereas previous eras had often sought to simplify and partialize her, suppressing her ambivalence, Romanticism revelled in it. Once the quiddities of human personality had become the cynosure of culture, the Criminal its most resplendent image, Judith's problematic character became an attraction in itself. And what this transgressor provided for the Victorian imagination was a peculiarly intense exemplar of the essential self.

Such an intense image of the human self and its lurid magnitude counterbalanced the increasingly anxious Victorian reaction to a fossilizing, regimenting, modernizing age. As government and the exercise of law became more efficient, bureaucracy more extensive and society more bourgeois, so the Romantic Criminal asserted at the imaginative margins of life an obstinate solipsism. A throwback to darker, more primitive, more colourful times, the legendary Romantic Criminals returned the imagination to a dangerous freedom from modernity.

The creed of Shelley's Beatrice is 'Be faithful to thyself': not to state, or church, or family. Sited at this point of conflict between individualism and

social organization, Judith (and her analogue Jael) became a focus for strangu-
lated protests against the conformism of Victorian life.

Hebraism and Orientalism

As one might expect, this phenomenon is most pronounced in the realist novel,
a genre in which the Victorians excelled and which readily reflected upon the
society that it purported to portray in such detail. There are many Judith-Jaels
in Victorian fiction, but a particularly significant example occurs in Charlotte
Brontë's bleakest and perhaps best novel, *Villette* (1853). Her protagonists are
women whose bourgeois social position and economic powerlessness reveal
most acutely the difficulties of feminine individualism within Victorian society.
Villette's heroine, Lucy Snowe, like Brontë's more famous creation Jane Eyre,
undergoes her own version of the exceptional person's *Bildungsroman* without
the advantages of the Romantic male. Poor, unattractive, intelligent, committed
to the Protestant work ethic, Lucy as an English expatriate in the dull Belgian
town of Villette is implicitly compared to the Israelites sojourning in the desert,
exiled from hope. Whilst much of the novel turns upon a hostile portrait of
Catholicism,[6] Lucy's inner life, by contrast, is Protestant in the Hebraic
manner: as vivid and turbulent as the Old Testament itself.

If her external behaviour is stoical and self-effacing, Lucy's inner life is
extremely passionate, and the conflict between the two requires repeated and
vigorous exertions of self-repression on her part, especially when she falls in
love with the unobtainable Dr John Bretton. She longs to release the passionate energy upon which she habitually imposes a 'catalepsy' of social conformity.
'This longing', she says, 'it was necessary to knock on the head: which I did, figuratively, after the manner of Jael to Sisera, driving the nail through their
temples. Unlike Sisera, they did not die: they were but transiently stunned, and
at intervals would turn on the nail with a rebellious wrench: then did the
temples bleed, and the brain thrill to its core.' On an everyday basis Lucy does
herself this psychic violence, Jael's murder replaying endlessly within. When
she is calmer, 'My Sisera lay quiet in the tent, slumbering', only to awaken once
more when libido and aspiration – 'masculine' urges, in this world – revive.[7]
What the scene of Jael murdering Sisera encapsulates for the novel is the superego's repression of the id. The woman from Judges, an executioner, figures the
Law of the Father, of Jehovah, quelling the desires which are the self at its most
needy and greedy. The 'stern woman' Jael is, in effect, Lucy's conscience.

That her id is figured as male and martial implies that part of what Lucy
wants, and as a Victorian woman cannot have, is a masculine freedom of action.
Instead her aggressive instincts have to be introverted, redirected to the violence of self-control and self-repression. By contrast, the rebellious pagan
Vashti, from the Book of Esther, becomes the novel's image of a woman's

passion unleashed, rendered powerful by sexual charisma. Lucy can only cope with Vashti's image – of what she herself cannot be – by repudiating it as 'demonic'. It is the image of her own repressed rage: 'Hate and Murder and Madness incarnate.' Biblical images are the vehicles by which Lucy construes her own identity. Primitively original yet also authoritative, they manifest her personality in atavistic as well as moralistic terms. Vashti is the Romantic Criminal bursting to get out of the cold, modern, English Lucy Snowe in provincial Belgium. Lucy's biblical projections of her own riven identity are the key to her psychic life as a Romantic protagonist who has the misfortune to have been born female. As masculine women, Jael personifies both Lucy's strength and the patriarchal social organization that commands her to be strong only against herself. Jael is the Law, but also Lucy's internalization of the law, her socialized identity. The homicidal scene is an image for the way in which social norms redirect the strong woman's force from resistance to those norms, into the effort to conform to them. Jael is a woman's internalization of patriarchy.

Thus, whilst Trollope's Judith-Jael is a Romantic Criminal, Brontë's is the social and moral Law. For Victorians, Judith-Jael could function as a representation both of the antinomian self and, simultaneously, of that authoritative society against which the self chafed and rebelled. Brontë's deployment of Jael as a figure for the paradoxes of socialized identity is not eccentric. The notion that Victorian society was 'Hebraic' in character was to some extent implicit in its culture, and duly rendered explicit by the cultural critique of that Victorian sage, Matthew Arnold.

Arnold exhibits the Victorians' drive to analyse history and culture systematically, organizing historical and cultural phenomena into categories and movements. As archaeology and geology began to reveal that the world was much older than had been generally believed, and than the Bible suggested, the Victorians' sense of history was elongated. Increasingly the development of civilization came to be seen as a vast progressive movement over time, from primeval origins to the thrusting modernity that Victorians themselves inhabited. Evolution, which Darwin brought to controversial public attention in 1859, presented the development of the human race as progressively evolutionary and biologically determined. As religious orthodoxy receded before these challenges, so science increasingly usurped its place. The accompanying ideology was highly determinist, submerging individuals within newly authoritative categories of race and gender. History seemed to teach that the various races all underwent a pattern of rise and decline. If biological evolution was a process implying cultural evolution too, then eugenics offered the possibility of maintaining an upward arc for the white race.[8] Once biology was regarded as the key to genetic, social and cultural progress, the old biblical icons of womanhood were embedded in an increasingly antiquarian view of the Old Testament, which regarded it as an anthropological record of a primitive desert tribe. A nomadic goatherd, Jael suited this primitivist vision rather better than the urban Israelite Judith, which is perhaps why Judith's image was so often merged with Jael's in Victorian culture.

Their role as signs of identity and authority was conceptualized in terms of Hebraism and orientalism, two crucial constructs in the Victorian analysis of civilization. In the key chapter of his *Culture and Anarchy* (1868), 'Hebraism and Hellenism', Arnold diagnosed an imbalance in the national character as the crux of society's malaise.[9] Assuming that history is composed of a series of great ethnic trends, Arnold argued that since the Reformation the English had espoused a puritanical, Hebraic ideology. Impelled by conscience and the work-ethic, Hebraism's goals were behaviourist, ethical and productive. As a result the English had become a race of pragmatic doers, unaccustomed to thinking. By contrast, the Hellenic cast of mind was reflective, intellectual, meditative (and pleasure-seeking). If England is to come to terms with the way the world is changing, Arnold contends, it must become more Hellenistic. This is the age-old cry of despairing intellectuals against the philistinism so deeply engrained in the English. But Arnold's specific target was the prevalence of evangelical, middle-class values, which years of frustrating public employment had brought him to hate. Brontë's *Villette* conveys that *mentalité*, and Lucy Snowe's Jael is an image of the Hebraic conscience. It nails one down.

In Arnold and Brontë we can see how neatly the Old Testament Judge/Murderess fitted into Victorian ideology, even at its most self-critical. She is an image of the impact of Hebraic mores, of identity as constrained by social practices. As sign of identity, Jael-Judith inevitably occupied a complex position in Victorian culture, where its strains showed.

One such strain marked the Victorians' perception of Judaism. Arnold's formulation of Hebraism appeared at a time when the presence and status of Jews in England was a political issue. In the 1850s and 1860s, the public debate about whether Jews should be granted political rights clarified and articulated ideas about Judaism as both religion and ethnicity. If the end of time was near, as some thought, then the question of the Jews' collective conversion to Christianity intruded, since this was a prerequisite of the millennium. There was disagreement as to whether giving the vote to Jews in England would discourage them from returning to their homeland and thus frustrate the prophesied movement through repatriation to conversion. It was Jews' commitment to the homeland, Zionism, that inspired the most common argument against enfranchisement: that Jewish loyalties were racial and supranational, rather than patriotic, and that consequently English Jews could not be politically responsible voters. Such antagonists insisted that Jews were a dangerously unpatriotic group whose loyalty to Jews in other countries would be problematic in time of war. In this debate, though England was more tolerant than most European countries, racist attitudes did surface.[10]

The Victorians subscribed to orientalism, an attitude to the Near East that simultaneously exoticized and denigrated it. The Orient offered to European travellers visions of sensuality and excess which supplied their fantasies of a life untrammelled by Christian mores. As a racial and geographical Otherness, the Orient also supplied images of supposed backwardness which defined and high-lighted what Europeans saw as their own sophisticated attainments in civiliza-tion. Eastern despotism, specifically the Ottoman Empire, supplied an image of a polity regarded as outmoded in Europe; Islam was regarded as cruel; and Eastern social organization was metonymized as the harem, salacious, indul-gent, hierarchical, secretive, carnal and immoral.[11] The key point, I suggest, is that the Orient was viewed as a temperamentally anachronistic, as if it were the past geographically embodied in the present; as if it were the material, physical, pre-modern evolutionary stage of culture which a technological, industrial, enlightened Europe had outstripped.

As the imperial nations, the British and French ruled over the East and went slumming in it. Its harems and its slave-mentality were bywords, and both were mingled in that ubiquitous art-salon subject, 'the slave market', where female pulchritude was displayed and commodified. Amongst other things the Orient was a pretext for pornography masquerading as culture – as anthropology, geography and history.[12] In this respect it was a mental site of submissive femininity, embodied by compliant but mysterious courtesans and ravished slaves. In this light, the biblical Book of Esther became archetypally orientalist, portraying as it did Ahasuerus, a despotic Eastern potentate, his absolute power over life and death, his expectation of female submission, his corrupt courtiers and his ability to summon troops of nubile virgins at his pleasure. As he put them through their paces in his quest for a new wife, Ahasuerus epitomizes the exotic economy of the harem, itself the sign of orientalism. In *The Woman's Bible* (1899) he would be portrayed as the epitome of the orientalist tyrant. Chassériau's *Esther's Toilette* (1841) had already portrayed the mental paradox offered by Judaism in this context: as a Jewess in a harem, Esther inhabits a fertile ambiguous space in which Western canons of beauty and orientalist stereotypes of sensuality may meet.

For in this economy of imagination Jews were both Eastern and Western. Although comment on orientalism has tended to stress its cultural construction of Arabs (and males), in fact Jews too were still regarded as Eastern. This ethnicity was indeed emphasized by the alteration in attitudes to the Old Testament: German and English theologians were emphasizing its antique and anthropological character. Influenced by these, *The Woman's Bible* stressed that much of the Old Testament reflected primitive tribal superstition rather than true revelation: 'How little these people [the ancient Israelites] knew of the Great Intelligence behind the laws of the universe, with whom they pretended to talk in the Hebrew language.'[13] Such attacks on the authority of the Old

Testament identified Judaism itself as outmoded, anachronistic, the product of contingent historical conditions that had long since passed away. Jewishness itself thus became an orientalist anachronism.

But, like the Old Testament, Jews were problematically placed on the occidental/oriental divide. European Jews in particular were problematically placed as an ethnically oriental people domiciled in the West, whose religion was moreover closely linked to Christianity. In the context of the Victorian mania for origins, it was more, not less, evident that Judaism was the precedent for Christianity. To repudiate the Jews entirely would be to reject Christianity's own history. And the apocalypticism that captured the popular mood in the mid-century underlined this, for if one believed that the end of the world was nigh then, as a good Christian, one had to hope for the conversion of the Jews that had been prophesied in the Apocalypse. The Zionism of George Eliot's *Daniel Deronda* (1874–6) reflected this, and its heroine is modelled on Esther. Judith was a more important figure, however, because Victorians subscribed to the idea that they were the New Israel,[14] that God was an Englishman.

These ideas inspired the strange metamorphoses the apocryphal story underwent in J.M. Neale's poem *Judith* (1849). Neale was then a figure both celebrated and controversial, and his poem is, like him, utterly of its time. It is an apocalyptic vision of international conflict: in fact a tacit allegory of the Crimean War, which had become a nightmare for the English. Visionary historicism portrays the war as one of the latter-day conflicts, and thus implies the inexorable victory of the allies, which must have been a comforting thought, given the gloomy prognosis at the time. As the New Israel, Victorian England is pitted against the orientalist empire of Russia. (Neale has to juggle the metaphors very deftly in order to avoid turning the reader's mind to the fact that Turkey, England's ally, was usually regarded as the orientalist Other.) The New Israel's Judith vanquishes the Eastern despot in his depraved, dissipated court. Identified with the 'Lion of Judah', she is also subtextually the British Lion. As Neale's poem attests, there were times when invoking the shared spiritual identity of English and Israelites came in useful.

Nor could European Jews easily be regarded as culturally Other. During the enfranchisement controversy, the historian Thomas Babington Macaulay had insisted that assimilation had clearly fitted English Jews for the native status that would be acknowledged by electoral rights.[15] Although enfranchisement was eventually obtained, the cultural construction of Jews as contradiction, as oriental/occidental, persisted. In fact, it was exaggerated by the growing interest in ethnicity and anthropology, and by the kind of influential German scholarship that would later provide some of the intellectual bases of Nazism. As 'racial characteristics' became the object of pseudo-science, the full weight of the cultural idolatry of 'progress', 'modernity' and 'scientific objectivity' was thrown behind dubious eugenic contentions that were used to justify racism on rational grounds.[16] In 1840 August Riedel's painting of Judith had already manifested the orientalist influence: whereas earlier artists' Judiths had exhibited a wide variety of physiognomy and colouring, his is emphatically Semitic in appearance. It is an early example of a tendency that would culminate in the mad theories of Otto Weininger.

Weininger was familiar with the work of those other Germanic intellectuals, Nietzsche and Freud, and also with Darwin: Weininger subsumed the most prejudicial trends of nineteenth-century thought. His *Sex and Character* (1904), widely read and rapidly translated into English, made explicit a link between antisemitism and misogyny. Weininger saw individuals as constituted of varying combinations of both male and female characteristics: will, force and intellect were masculine characteristics, whilst passivity and feeling were feminine. In this determinist model of gender, he identified Man as 'form' to Woman's 'matter'; therefore all human beings of whichever sex contained both genders. On the other hand, it was clear that Woman included the lower, Man the higher, characteristics. Man was Will to Woman's Involition, and these Ideas were reflected in the behaviour of real men and women. Since Man represents the higher human characteristics, Woman is merely an animalistic simulacrum of his humanity. She wishes to be 'made' by him, to be possessed, to be treated as the passive instrument of his will. Of this masquerade as Man by Woman the hysteric is living proof: hysteria is Woman's ridiculous attempt to be like Man. In fact, Weininger explains, 'Woman is nothing', a chaos like the formless matter that existed before the Creation, whilst Man is the formative principle. Only he, then, can possess individuality and personality, forming himself by the operation of Will. Meantime, she is matter to his form, slave to his touch. It follows that women, incapable of individuality yet worshipping it (Man), must be masochists by nature, and sadism appropriate to men's power. Woman is object to Man's subject, and thus comes into being as an imitation of the personality she cannot herself possess.

One can see why Judith as Romantic Criminal individualism would disrupt Weininger's system. Weininger is particularly concerned to undo the Judithic icon. His characterization of Woman as a psychological blank firmly locates subjectivity, individuality and power in manhood alone: forceful women are a figment of men's imaginations, both literally (Man forms Woman) and metaphorically (male artists imagine Woman as simulacrum of Man). Any woman who appears to possess a personality is in fact an actress, making a desperate attempt to be what man intrinsically is. 'The most notable examples of the sex (I have in mind [the playwright] Hebbel's Judith . . .) . . . at the last moment . . . will kiss the man who ravishes them, and succumb with pleasure to those whom they have been resisting violently . . . Her shrieks and ravings are not really genuine.'[17]

Weininger selects Judith for debunking precisely because of her representation of woman dominant, intelligent, resolute and activist: she sums up everything that for Weininger is exclusively masculine. To unmask her is to dismiss women's claims to autonomous identity. That was what Judith as Romantic Criminal represented, obdurate and transgressive individuality.

As we saw, this was for Romanticism very much a male preserve, and that was why Weininger chose to refer not to the original Judith, but to the eponymous heroine of Friedrich Hebbel's play of 1840. The play's fame was such that when Germans thought of Judith they thought not of the Bible but of Hebbel. His view of Judith was that she epitomized Judaism.[18] That and his deceptive misogyny are the keys to his determination to transfer the heroic motif from Judith to Holofernes in his treatment of the story of the stage. Consequently, Judith's triumph over him has to be inverted into his triumph over her. He becomes a bombastic Romantic hero, an historical superman in the Carlylean mould. So exceptionally clever, forceful, brutal and charismatic is he, that the rest of humankind are pygmies in his sight; his hubris is a tragic condition of his uniqueness. Because his will is irresistible (foreshadowing Weininger's Man-Will), he has despaired of meeting an antagonist worthy of him, but Judith he recognizes as an exception to human mediocrity. She, however, is an hysteric, left virgin by her deceased husband because he did not possess sufficient masculine will to overcome her resistance. She wanted to overcome, since she possesses natural sexual desires, but her own will was too proud to submit to him. Unfortunately, in the circumstances, Holofernes as superman is virility personified. Whilst she has the determination to kill him, Judith is unable not to desire him. It is vital to Hebbel's demolition of Judith's rivalry to Man that this desire should not be resisted. Having slept with Holofernes before killing him, Judith discovers to her horror that she is pregnant. At the end of the play she is left with this permanent reminder of his domination of her desire, and also with palpable proof of what her society will regard as her shame and mendacity. Judith pregnant is Judith overcome, both by man and by social ostracism. In Hebbel's play it is all too clear that this is a 'phallic woman', motivated by penis-envy, whose rebellion against the proper norms of her gender is appropriately punished. Pregnancy refeminizes her and compels her literally to reproduce Holofernes, cancelling her destruction of the most heroic of men. It is man who is the great individual, and woman who learns that to worship him is a fate she cannot escape. In the form of Hebbel's Judith, Weininger expels the female Romantic Criminal so that his system reserves all self-individuation as strictly male territory.

The new psychology at the turn of the last century always referred to biology as the ultimate authority. Weininger's biologism was matched by Freud's view of woman's reproductive function as her whole destiny. Aptly, then, Hebbel's pregnant Judith manifested women's containment: try as she might to be the

Romantic hero, even she suffers the nemesis that teaches woman what her place must be – her womb. Hebbel's plot illustrates Weininger's view that women are under the curse of Genesis, in which Eve's punishment included both her desire for her husband and the sufferings of childbirth. Hebbel, Weininger and Freud exemplify the tendency of patriarchal ideologies to remake themselves in apparently new disguises.[19] The Bible had ceased to be absolutely authoritative, yet its determination of women's character and role was immediately substituted by pseudo-science.

It must be granted that such revisions of the ideological status quo had their casualties, since it was necessary for their own proponents to credit the new absolutes. Weininger had posited that Jews were biologically too feminine. As himself partly Jewish, Weininger realized that by his own lights he was a defective being, and shot himself. Defining Jews as the defective race and women as the defective gender, Weininger closed the circle of compounding them in one image of Otherness. When he instanced Judith as a type of women's defectiveness, even at her best, Weininger's subconscious recognized that she was not only a type of the phallic woman but also a type of the Jewess. If Jews were psychobiologically feminine, then Judith typed the race as the gender. In a way which Nazi propaganda would eventually render explicit, the Jews were regarded as a simulacrum of true humanity, which was the Aryan superman.

Anglo-Saxony

As if the contradictory ethnicity of the occidental/oriental Judith were not enough, Victorian culture further compounded this by identifying her as Anglo-Saxon as well. Arnold's Hebraism suggested a mental consanguinity between Englishness – as the national character that created the age of enterprise and empire – and Old Testament Jewry. On the basis of an identification between muscular Victorianism and ancient Israel it was possible to regard Judith as an ideal model of patriotism in the Hebraic prehistory of Victorianism. Most mid-century Victorians saw England as the New Israel, the identity on which Neale's Judith had turned, but they also saw it as Anglo-Saxon. In that light, too, Judith was English.

By the middle of the century, J.M. Kemble's bestselling work *The Saxons in England* (1849) had acquainted a wide public with the trend in German and English scholarship, which was to seek an antique model for a common racial heritage in the concept of Anglo-Saxony.[20] This assertion of an ancient Anglo-Germanic hegemony in Europe was in effect a way of suggesting that 'the northern races' were entitled to political dominance of contemporary Europe, as if by inheritance from their early progenitors. This is the explanation for the unprecedented strength of Victorian interest in an Anglo-Saxon poem about

Judith. A fascinated return to the surviving Old English texts renewed philolog-
ical and historical scholarship in those countries that perceived themselves as
members of the Anglo–Saxon community. L.G. Nilsson's edition of the Anglo–
Saxon *Judith* in 1848 was followed by two printings of A.S. Cook's 1888
American edition and by T.G. Foster's edition in 1892. They were contributing
scholarly ballast to the Victorians' construction of a myth of national identity,
confirmed by anthropology and dignified by antiquity. (Hence the establishment of Anglo–Saxon studies in the appropriate universities, such as Oxford).
A.S. Cook's edition was a particularly loaded example of the politics of scholarship. By identifying *Judith* as an allegorical representation of an historical
Anglo–Saxon queen, he was feeding the popular tendency to regard Queen
Victoria's reign over the British Empire as a modern counterpart to the beneficent power of her ancient predecessors. Anglo–Saxony and queenship were
seen as complementary, and the cult of Anglo–Saxony as confirming England's
right to lead (and own) most of the world. At one level, Judith was the Empress
of India. This was quite a contrast to the Semitic, orientalist Judith who was
also flourishing elsewhere within the same ideological envelope, embodying the
Otherness against which Teutonism defined itself.

The Anglo–Saxonist Judith also reflected the political complexion of
Englishness. As in Kemble's work, it became fashionable to regard England's
supposedly uniquely enlightened political constitution with a long tradition of
British liberty, derived from the freeman of Anglo–Saxon times. In Neale's
Crimean *Judith*, for instance, the national pride of England/Israel calls on the
eponymous heroine to a global 'mission', to defend the 'free-born rights' of
other nations as well as her own.[21] When specific national crises impelled
writers to summon up the image of Anglo–Saxony, the Old English Judith could
personify both the race and its commitment to liberty.

Although Neale's poem reflected this jingoistic concept in its most conservative form, the figure of Judith was as usual a double-edged sword. Much more
radical, subversive ideas about the nature of liberty could fasten onto her image.
As the revolutions of 1848 seemed to suggest that the whole Continent was
drowning in a tide of political radicalism, the Chartist movement inspired fears
of a similar upheaval in Britain. A curious product of this radical mood was a
novel that now looks like just another Victorian recitation of a scriptural theme,
this time as a popular exotic romance of the East. But *Judith, Prophetess of
Bethulia; A Romance from the Apocrypha* (1849) was anonymous for the very
good reason that it was an incendiary tract in pious disguise. Its Judith is a passionate patriot, passionate indeed in a way that substitutes for sexuality, making
her 'throb and burn' and 'shudder' at the 'invasions' of this 'love . . . that occupies my being'. This appropriation of Judith's chastity to sublimated love of
country is intended to suggest that the 'greater cause' must override and if necessary traduce mere human relationships.[22] The subtext of these exultant arias

on patriotism is highly topical, a manifesto for insurrection within the New Israel, England. The romance's political moral is that liberty must be achieved by revolution (a violence for which Judith's is a precedent), a course that would necessarily traduce social ties. This pulp 'romance' was devoted to informing its readers that Englishmen should follow the example of the continental revolutionaries of 1848, and do so the more resolutely because England was the natural home of freedom. Judith is made a 'Prophetess' in order to be harbinger of a revolution that has not yet occurred, the English version of 1848.

The clues to the romance's subtext lie in its contradictions. Its Judith, who of course as a childless widow has no 'domestic ties', gets very impassioned about the necessity for her to sacrifice these non-existent ties to her country's good. Similarly, because this is a romance, Judith finds love with Achior; but the novel's politics have demanded that she be portrayed as sexually inaccessible because her passion is patriotism. Most disingenuous of all is the work's preface, which professes great anxiety to justify the way in which its fictionalization might be felt to have transgressed against the dignity of the scriptures. This is a massive diversionary tactic, fussing about the Apocrypha's status in scripture in order to distract attention from the really subversive, political intent of the author. Even if this squib did not in fact instigate an English revolution, it did at least revive the radicalism implicit in Judith's image, in a way that inverted the more complacent visions of Anglo-Saxon Israel prevailing at the time.

It was, in fact, in the Germanic context that a subversive version of Judith's story scored such a popular success as to become afterwards a classic work. The political turbulence of 1848 in the Austro-Hungarian Empire inspired the actor Johann Nestroy's *Judith*, a parody of Hebbel's play, in which the literary burlesque is also an assault on the authoritarianism of Hebbel's Holofernes. He stands in for the dominant Austrian officer class, mocked and humiliated by a fifth-columnist Judith. Her transgressiveness is exuberantly projected on several levels, calculated to offend as many Austrian shibboleths as possible.[23] Her Jewishness challenged antisemitism; the fact that she was not a woman but a transvestite (Judith's bother, invented for the purpose) made the male officer's desire for 'her' itself a source of mockery; and the transvestite performance of Judith made her character into an actor, a proxy in the drama for Nestroy himself, identifying his iconoclastic drama with Judith's iconoclastic feat. For to parody the idolised Hebbel's play was itself, given its profound implication in ethnic ideology, to deride Teutonism.

By the mid-century Judith had acquired a role as a national identity, Englishness, and as an international ethnicity, Anglo-Saxony, which was in implicit opposition to her other incarnation as Romantic Criminal. Against those intrinsically conservative collectivities, the Romantic Criminal was a projection of the lone asocial individual who most resisted immersion in the mass. (We could in fact see Nestroy's transgressive Judith as a politicized Romantic

Criminal, assaulting the polity, the army and society, in short institutionalism.) And the opposition between Nestroy's and Hebbel's dramas was, in little, the contrast between one Romantic stereotype, the charismatic individual become fascist, and another, the antinomian criminal. Hebbel's Holofernes and Nestroy's Judith were contradictory effects of the same Romanticism, personifications of its ambiguous and dangerous politics.

In sharp contrast to the antisemitic Germanic psychological tradition, the ideology of Anglo-Saxony exalted Judith as one of its models of distinctive national character. Yet both movements were products of the same eugenicist impulse. As part of the Anglo-Saxon heritage, Judith expressed national identity just as much as she represented orientalized Otherness. She was culturally positioned at the point where powerful trends in modern thought stumbled on their own contradictions.

8

Judy and Punch
Marriage and 'Fallen Women'

Judith's revival as a symbol of political liberty was more than matched by her prominent and curious role in attitudes to private life. From the mid-eighteenth century onwards, surprising transformations in her cultural mythology reflected sea-changes in attitudes to marriage, sexuality, feminism and prostitution. Judith's images, multiple and diverse, became a catalogue of prejudices, anxieties, inhibitions and protests about the relations between women and men.

In the eighteenth century the modern view of marriage, as an intimate companionate relationship as much as a social and economic arrangement, was becoming more prevalent in England.[1] Probably it is precisely for this reason that marriage became, at the same time, the subject of a hugely popular and persistent form of caricature, the Punch and Judy show. The idealized view of marriage propounded in eighteenth-century advice-books and fiction bred its parodic alternative, which was imported into England from the Continent and met with immediate success. It has been such a staple ingredient of English life ever since (even if nowadays usually associated only with seaside venues) that its very familiarity has disguised its meanings.[2] In fairs and street theatres it functioned as a rudely comic, plebeian reassertion of marital stereotypes: the brutal, macho Punch versus his shrewish wife. The upper classes may have been getting more sentimental about marriage, but the lower classes were having none of it. Punch dealt with his shrewish wife, his inconvenient baby, a policeman and the hangman in a thoroughly manly fashion, by murdering them. He was very much the king of his domestic castle.

By the 1820s, the puppet wife's name had changed. Having been Joan, the traditional sobriquet for a lower-class woman, which implied coarseness and earthiness, she was renamed Judy.[3] On the face of it, she is a long way from being like the apocryphal heroine, chaste widow as she was. But Punch's dog, Toby, was named after the apocryphal Book of Tobit. No one has before noticed that the wife Judy was also named after an apocryphal character: Judith's Renaissance role in the battle of the sexes, and as an image for marital strife, had resurfaced in a different form of caricature. The reasons for the puppet's renaming in the 1820s lay in the history of Judith's image during the later 1700s.

The Domestic and the Shrew

When adultery and prostitution were regarded as commonplace, the marital ideal of intimacy required stronger emphasis from its defenders; equally, the calculating economic marriage, once so readily accepted as the upper-class norm, came under fire from bourgeois critics. Indeed, the companionate marriage was itself a product of a society in which the middle class was increasingly prosperous, and in which it was beginning to enforce its own values as the dominant values in English society. Those are evident in Hogarth's highly successful series of satirical prints, *Marriage à la Mode* (c. 1743), which portrayed the inevitably disastrous effects of an arranged marriage. In the initial scene, the parents – a *nouveau riche* and an impoverished aristocrat – negotiate the marriage contract, which will exchange money for title. Meanwhile the prospective bride and groom sit on the sidelines, the paintings hanging on the wall behind them offering ironic prophecies of the disasters that lie ahead. A painting of Judith with the head of Holofernes foreshadows the fact that the wife's future adultery will precipitate the killing of her husband in a duel. As it happens, the contemporary art critic Horace Walpole attributed a print of Judith and Holofernes to Hogarth, who had unsuccessfully attempted a career as painter of biblical scenes.[4] By incorporating such scenes as paintings-within-pictures, Hogarth redirected their purpose to social commentary. Once *Marriage à la Mode* became one of his most popular, most widely reproduced series, Judith was launched as an epitome of incompatibility and disastrous marriages. She was a complement, for Hogarth's customers, to Mrs Judy Punch's role amongst the lower classes.

The Punch and Judy theme has an intriguing role in Hogarth's next series, *An Election* (1754). In 'Canvassing for Votes' the inn sign portrays Mr Punch bribing voters, as 'Punch candidate for Guzzledown', and in one version part of the inn name is 'TOBELLO'. Turned to political satire, the names of Punch and his dog Toby invite us to conclude that the madam of the brothel, patronized by soldiers, is a satiric Judy. Thus political corruption is identified with prostitution, in a 'family' of national vices. Both as prostitute (another revival of her Renaissance guise) and as plebeian, Mrs Judy retained some of Judith's political as well as her sexual aspects.

By the Victorian period, the embourgeoisement of English marriage had been achieved. Idealization of the domestic hearth now centred on the image of 'the angel in the house', as celebrated in Coventry Patmore's eponymous series of poems (1854–63) on his own marriage. The domestic angel became the icon of true womanhood: chaste, demure, loving, supportive, self-abnegating, knowing her place.[5] Victorian marriage drew more definitely than ever before the boundary between men's public arena of business and politics and women's private domain of hearth and cradle. It is notorious that Victorian women were infantilized and invalidized by such constrictions, which left them without intellectual and active outlets. They were casualties of the new forms of collectivity demanded by modern social organization. A concomitant of increasingly rigid social formations was even heavier reliance upon the tradition binary oppositions that had underpinned orthodoxies about women's sub-ordination. When women were regarded as possessing purely 'private' func-tions, those were restricted to sexual and reproductive roles. Thus there were spinsters (unproductive and anomalous), wives (proper sexual objects) and whores (improper sexual objects). The latter were habitually known as Magdalens, as in for instance Wilkie Collins's *The New Magdalen*.[6] Whether Madonnas or Magdalens, women were categorized along a single faultline, the legality or otherwise of their relationship to men. (No one would have dreamt of classifying men exclusively according to their sexual histories, of course.) Naturally, biblical images were used as authoritative models for the positive and negative polarities of woman as sexual outlet.

Much has been made of the Madonna icon for the angel in the house. But in a Protestant country suspicious of Catholic imagery the Virgin Mother had her drawbacks. Another, more aptly Hebraic image was supplied by the Old Testament. Its most domestic story, the Book of Ruth, was a fertile source for those anxious to connect the Victorian angel to her authoritative origins in antiquity. In J.M. Neale's prizewinning poem *Ruth* (1860), that authorization is at work, shoring up the ideal of the angel in the 'domestic heaven' against the emerging challenge of the New Woman, the Victorian feminist. As so often in his poems, Neale was responding to the issue of the moment. In 1854 he had himself identified with Judith, whose resolution he saw as that characteristic of martyrs. This odd inflexion to the story was motivated by his sense of his own perpetual role as a focus for storms of controversy about Church politics. But whereas Judith was hospitable to his masculine self-image, the domesticated Ruth was quite good enough for women. More generally, though, Ruth and Judith would evolve into oppositional prototypes for women's sexuality.

As cultural icon, the domestic angel was intended to be attractive to women themselves, which was of course the best guarantee of their compliance with it. (Hence even the feminist Women's Bible regarded her as the type of the ideal wife.) The domestic angel knew that she was loved and respected as long as she fulfilled her function: to nurture her children and solace her husband: her func-tion was fulfilled by supporting and uplifting him in his. Bluntly, and this thought underlay many rebukes to the liberated New Woman, this was the work she was paid for. Neale stresses that marriage redeems the refugee Ruth from her rootless, poverty-stricken state as 'the alien one' in Israelite society.

Encoded in that emphasis is a subtle threat to the woman who demands independence: only marriage will give her a home to call her own, a shelter from economic and social ostracism. Such subtle threats implicitly acknowledge the point – made by J.S. Mill in *The Subjection of Women* (1869) – that Victorian marriage was a power-relation.[7] They were tantamount to an admission that women's subordination originated in, and could be enforced by, economic coercion. Understanding that they themselves might lose the only security provided for women in Victorian society, feminists were circumspect in their assaults upon the invidious conditions of marriage. But the bravest did indeed state that wives were simply legalized prostitutes, regarded largely as sexual outlets and 'paid' for their services by their husband's financial support. A similar accusation was made by Mill, and it was a particularly problematic line of argument for Victorian orthodoxy, for the feminists were articulating a similitude between those supposed and cherished opposites, Ruths/angels and 'fallen women'.

Upon that opposition Victorian marital ideals and social convictions depended, so much was at stake when some women refused marriage's romantic wrappings. Whilst maintaining a decorous personal life, Elizabeth Gaskell was adept at addressing such issues in her novels, which repeatedly focused upon social problems. Her very popular *Ruth* (1853), the story of a woman impregnated and deserted by her seducer, overtly challenges moral orthodoxy by conferring on the fallen woman the name more appropriate to the domestic angel. The pitiful case of the fallen Ruth is intended to evoke the traditional pun in her nomenclature ('ruth' as a synonym for compassion).[8] Further, Gaskell deliberately makes her vindication of the seduced woman a collision of iconic representations. To call her Ruth rather than Magdalen was an explicit refusal to maintain the artificial distinction between wife and prostitute. It collapsed the moral/immoral dichotomy in a way that exposed the contradiction in Victorian attitudes to sexuality. The fact was that whether married or not, women were paid sexual vessels and reproduction machines, and the iconic binary opposition between Ruths and fallen women was a cultural myth designed to obscure that fact.

Women were of course encouraged by such romantic visions as Neale's to internalize the values that determined their subordination: to regard their condition as both natural and privileged. To this end biblical models were very useful, since they inserted social shibboleths into the realm of piety. Faced with a Judith, Neale referred her heroism to himself; faced with a Ruth, however, he firmly placed her virtues on the shoulders of women. Unlike Judith, women were supposed to stay at home whilst public activities and business were the domain of men. In order for the Victorian cultural myth of womanhood to achieve its ends, it was necessary to re-position Judith. In public allegories she could still be used for masculine patriotic iconography in the mid-century, but significantly this motif becomes increasingly scarce after the advent of the New

Women's claims to political rights. In America and England, the women's movement was well under way in the 1850s. After 1860 Judith was reinterpreted in ways that emphasized her as exemplary of womanhood's privacy: of marriage and sexuality. At the same time, since she thoroughly contradicted the passive ideal of femininity, her figure was gradually demonized.

When Mill and female agitators were complaining that battered wives were commonplace, were indeed instances of the inequalities of marriage, Judith had already been established as a vulgar icon of wifehood. Mr Punch's battered but shrewish wife had been rechristened Judy. The masculinist and proletarian associations of the Punch and Judy ménage now contaminated her name with coarsely domestic significance. Literate culture acknowledged as much when in the 1860s the satirical magazine *Judy* was set up as a competitor to the long-established *Punch*. Thus in one of her personifications, Judith had dwindled into a wife. That is why, in Mill's attack on Victorian marriage, he can use Deborah, but *not* the similar Judith, as a radically alternative icon of women's fitness for public life. Judith has been compromised by the appropriation of her name to domestic subjugation.

This appropriation of the public heroine to the most simplistic private space – caricatured marital discord – was the more effective and important because of the actual alienation concealed within Victorian marriage. In Mill's view, Victorian men and women were effectively strangers: as one might expect, he explained, the slave-class had incentives to understand their masters, but the masters had no need to understand the slaves. As a result, he contended, Victorian men knew nothing about women other than those in their own households (and prostitutes, of course), and even these they did not understand well. The favourable conditions for mental intimacy were absent even where physical intimacy was normal. To this unwitting ignorance Mill attributed the categorization and derogation which homogenized men's perception of the female gender. Such categorization was simplistic and programmatic because nothing compelled men to know better.

But Mill's argument was only part of the story. Nineteenth-century social organization, which generally meant that men went out to work and women stayed at home, reinforced a divide between their worlds, one public and one private.[9] Consequently, in their perception of women English and American men were more reliant than ever before on the categorizing impulse. Just as everything else was being classified, scientized and commodified by novel technologies and philosophies, so the classification of women at once mimicked this mania for organization and reassured Victorians that the mysterious opposite sex was easily understood. Women were both a mystery and an intelligible quantity. Amongst other things, this conserved one compartment of experience as reassuringly familiar in what seemed to be a world of distressingly rapid change. Wherever there is ignorance, imagery tends to substitute for analysis. In

Victorian culture iconic dichotomies performed this function. One of these was the familiar paradigm Virgin versus Whore, but others occupied more complex sites. Complementary pairs of iconic women supplied a social iconography that functioned to fill the gap between the sexes. Over the brutal truth of an instrumental view of women, Old Testament nomenclature threw a pious cultural disguise.

As in the political uses of Judith, however, her Victorian image exposed the contradiction in the binary opposition between icons of womanhood, the Ruth/wife and Magdalen/prostitute. Judith was the figure who straddled their opposition, for she could figure both Mrs Judy and the fallen woman, revealing the uncomfortable fact that the moral distinction disguised what were simply different forms of degradation.

How Is Judith Fallen

During the eighteenth and nineteenth centuries, venereal diseases were treated in Lock Hospitals, most of their inmates being prostitutes. They were pious institutions – if also in a sense prisons – and in the 1760s the London Lock Hospital boasted a preacher so celebrated that his audience was swelled even by respectable and fashionable members of metropolitan society. Whilst Lock Hospitals generally bore an atmospheric burden of illicit squalor, the London hospital was redolent of piety in its most fashionable, enlightened form. For the preacher, Martin Madan, was a member of Lady Huntingdon's Connexion, an influential evangelical movement that was then at its height.[10] His sermons on the duty of repentance amplified their reflections upon the sins of prostitution by animadverting to the laxity of contemporary morals generally. The London Lock Hospital, an institution expressive of fear of venereal disease and of the 'wages of sin', gave public and institutional incorporation to the sexual underworld. It was also a site for confrontation between the libertine ethos and Christian revival. It was customary to mount entertainments to benefit hospitals, and the London Lock Hospital received the proceeds from such an entertainment in 1761: an oratorio of *Judith*.

Following the fashion for oratorios on sacred subjects, H.W.'s *Judith: An Oratorio, or Sacred Drama* was published in 1733, and the 1761 Lock Hospital benefit was a performance of Thomas Arne's oratorio *Judith*.[11] Afterwards, published copies of the Arne version were sold to benefit the Hospital; and the same work was re-used in another benefit context when the foremost actor of the day, David Garrick, mounted a Shakespeare centenary festival at Stratford-upon-Avon. Neither H.W.'s nor Arne's oratorios is intrinsically interesting as drama, being in the innocuous, official religious style favoured at the time.

In the visual arts, as a result of the aesthetic of 'decorum', representation of biblical heroines was not as common as it had been, and when painters did essay these subjects the results tended to vapidity: Giovanni Pellegrini's Judith, for instance, is remarkably limpid and demure. At a time when the real energies were secular, biblical heroines had only two kinds of appeal: official and sickly piety, or unofficial ribaldry. The success of Arne's oratorio was, in fact, owing to its ability to conflate the two.

The oratorio's reprinting in 1764 and 1773 and its selection for Garrick's ambitious festival bear witness to its appeal. Beyond that, the work's interest has more to do with the context of its benefit performance at the London Lock Hospital. The oratorio's audience included the inmates themselves. Staring at these unfortunates was one of the gratifications afforded to the rest of the audience at Lock Hospital events. Thus the oratorio celebrated Judith as an exemplar of resolute chastity in a place where the consequences of unchastity were physically manifested to the eye as the marks of venereal disease: where the 'weaker sex' displayed the heraldry of (so the thought went) moral irresolution. The absence at the centre of the libretto – the murder, which occurs offstage – implied the deadly act of illicit intercourse, which with equal stealth brought suffering and fatality on the hospital's inmates. As Holofernes' death is represented only by the production of his head in the final scene, so physical symptoms betrayed a carnality otherwise secret. Pregnant or diseased prostitutes and 'fallen women' manifested tangible proofs of what was perceived as their own immanent depravity and of having served the depraved purposes of others. In the interaction of theme and venue the pious point was made. As the traditional personification of Lust's nemesis, Judith confronted her frailer sisters, turning their membership of the audience into a spectacle in its own right.

In this also resided its squalid glamour, as a pretext for the respectable shudder at concupiscence. Coyly Ozias asks Judith, 'Daughter . . . how scap'dst thou undefiled?' (III.i) Legitimate contact with what was depraved was provided by a Lock Hospital benefit on a torrid religious theme. That the treatment was decorous and impeccably classicized in the polite manner was both appropriate to piety and sufficient to the purpose, for it was the location that achieved the effect. Not without shrewdness, then, the 1764 edition specified in its title that this was 'Judith, an Oratorio, as perform'd at the Lock Hospital Chapel', a collocation of words that signified to the purchaser very precisely its conjunction of piety and charity with sexuality and morbidity. This was commercial advertisement at its subtlest.

Gradually, by the mid-nineteenth century, attitudes to 'fallen women' had become more humane, the widespread concern for social conditions having embraced – as it were – them too. Now there was a tendency to regard them not so much as immoral by disposition, but as unfortunate victims of predatory men or of poverty: as Gaskell's novel exemplified. It followed that moral repentance and social reform might, indeed, be most effectively iconized in the form of contemporary Magdalens. If they were not, as earlier moralists had thought, irredeemably evil by nature, but victims of social injustice, then these women were capable of being rescued by the exertions of philanthropy. The biblical Magdalen had long been regarded sentimentally as a repentant fallen woman who seemed to have more intense access to Christian spirituality precisely because of her former sins. For Victorians, prostitutes embodied the affinity of sex and crime. By the mid-century Romanticism had been so assimilated to the middle-class *mentalité* that the Romantic Criminal, formerly aristocratic in conception, could be recuperated for respectable bourgeois sentimentalism as the fallen angel of spiritualized sexuality. Which is why Judith too could become an icon of fallenness.

Thus James Fenimore Cooper's dark, tempestuous, promiscuous temptress in his mythic American novel, *The Deerslayer* (1841), was named Judith, and she explicitly names the apocryphal progenitor as her inspiration.[12] Her iconic opposite here is Hester, a child-woman who is similarly explicitly linked with the biblical Esther. English Victorian novels would also make the affinity of sex and crime in the fallen Judith evident, as we shall see.

It might seem unlikely that the significance of Judith's name could be inverted from chastity to promiscuity, but in fact the Janus nature of Judith's signification invited precisely such an inversion. Her icon had always been at once erotic and punitive, provocative and retributive. Even Mrs Judy Punch tapped into this role, as domestic virago: the antagonistic female in the universal battle of the sexes, the shrew or dominatrix, the wife as a man's domestic nemesis. Similarly, Victorian sex was always conducted under the sign of death: the potential mortality of a wife in subsequent childbirth, or of the prostitute or her client from syphilis.[13] Victorian pathology readily connected sex with punishment, and that subtext underlies the use of the sobriquet 'Judy' to designate loose women, whether prostitutes or not, in popular slang from the 1820s onwards. (As a pejorative term for a proletarian woman, it still persisted in a film made in the 1950s.)[14] Thus a prurient schoolboy joke underlay the Victorian establishment of an Etonian tradition, which dubbed a lane in the school 'Judy's passage', and inspired a short-lived pupils' magazine of the same name.[15]

Loose women and plebeian mates (Mrs Judy Punch) were not in popular parlance always distinguished from one another, not least because of the prevailing assumption that most working-class women were sexually available. What the name Judy represented was woman as a being utterly dominated by the sexual function. An old proverb held that 'Joan is as good as my lady in the dark'. The sentiment was modernized for Victorians by Kipling's famous lines, invoking their new sobriquet for the plebeian woman: 'the Colonel's Lady an' Judy O'Grady / Are sisters under their skins!'[16] Naturally, these lines rapidly became proverbial, for they summed up womanhood as a genus crossing class-boundaries, because femininity was sexuality – and no more. How far was Judith fallen!

On the other hand, this thoroughgoing containment of women within their sexual relations with men made Judith's two iconic roles – the Missus and the prostitute – a logical pairing as the two faces of Victorian femininity. Because logical, that pairing also exposes the contradiction in their habitual opposition of wife and prostitute. In fact, they were both Judy. What her anomalous position in Victorian social iconography tells us is that caricatures, where common prejudices so often disport themselves without hypocrisy, demonstrated women's general subjugation, whatever their class or marital status. The cultural myth of Judy confirms that Victorian feminists were correct in their refusal to credit the married/fallen dichotomy.

Judith Fights Back

Judith's absorption into the constricting social iconography of womanhood was unfortunately aided and abetted by the women's movement: ironically enough, since Judith if anyone would have been a potent prototype for claims to women's social and political equality. Early in the century, for instance, the radical millenarian Joanna Southcott, subject of a Victorian cult, had cited Judith as a model for her own role as a female messiah.[17] But the Victorian feminists were educated middle-class agitators, conscious of cultural mores that made Judith problematic for successful propaganda. There were two reasons for their aversion to her: the demotion of the apocrypha from Anglo-American bibles, and the eugenicist ideal of womanhood to which feminists were committed.

By 1860 it was clear that the Apocrypha was heading for extinction, as far as its popular currency was concerned. It was already being omitted from English bibles, and would soon be banished from its traditional places in the liturgy by the reformation of the Book of Common Prayer.[18] As long as the Apocrypha had remained in reasonably wide circulation, literate culture remained in touch with the pattern and sometimes the detail of its narratives. In the early 1800s, however, the Protestant exclusion of the Apocrypha became more systematic in all the countries coloured pink on the map. Catalyst of this process was a controversy that blew up in the British and Foreign Bible Society in the 1820s. Whilst, on irenic principles, the Society had habitually published bibles that included the Apocrypha for use in some foreign countries, its Scottish wing, being more fervently Protestant in hue, decided that the time had come to exclude the non-canonical texts. Intellectually, the reformers were influenced by eighteenth-century scholarship and polemic, which had attacked the Apocrypha on rationalist principles. Voltaire had been the most forceful of the sceptics, and from his derisive assault upon the fabulism and superstition that he diagnosed in the apocryphal stories it was clear that these offered a weak flank to those who wished to discredit Christianity. (Voltaire had been particularly scornful of the Book of Judith, whose heroine's dubious sexual morality, he gleefully opined, was less than pious; the idea of female heroism was to him a manifest improbability.)[19] Confronted by the obdurate theological objections of the Scottish reformers, the Bible Society in London capitulated. In the era of empire, this decision to formalize the Apocrypha's exclusion determined that henceforth its cultural currency would decline. Victorian theological scholarship transmitted to the public the view that, in the words of Sir William Smith's influential *Bible Dictionary* (1907) the Book of Judith was amongst 'the earliest specimens of historical fiction'.[20] Smith's terse characterization of it as a romance was a sign that the Apocrypha was becoming demoted to the status of 'literature'.

According to the novelist Arnold Bennett's *Journal*, by 1918, the only copy of the Apocrypha that a country-house guest could locate in her neighbourhood was owned by the housekeeper. Although he had been struck by a fresco of Judith in Italy, Bennett did not know the story until the celebrated actress Lilah MacCarthy (who had already played her in Sturge Moore's inert verse-drama *Judith*) persuaded him that its sensationalism, in the form of his prurient play *Judith* (1919), would relaunch both their careers. The avantgarde Bloomsbury Group exploited Judith's image precisely because her non-canonical status liberated her for secularist aesthetic activity.[21] The Apocrypha was not only literature, but increasingly rare literature at that. In ecclesiastical contexts Judith's image was only kept alive by such means as Howells's setting of part of her Book as church music. There as in culture generally, her figuration was gradually becoming more detached from religious ideas and more attached to self-consciously creative reworkings.

Indeed, the 1820s controversy appears to have inspired a revival of interest in Edinburgh, since in 1830 the Royal Academy of Scotland commissioned William Etty, that enthusiastic depicter of massive female flesh, to execute three large paintings of the Book of Judith. Decorum prevailed, since the slaying itself was omitted; but Etty's choice of three unusual moments from the story suggests a renewed sensitivity to its narrative details. The occasion to look out and read the story, as distinct from absorbing it as diffused cultural information, could (ironically enough) prove more creative than the received clichés encouraged by familiarity. (The commission appears somewhat suspicious and may have signified some political in-fighting within the Scottish academic establishment at the time of the Apocrypha controversy.)

In this transitional period, from the 1860s to the 1920s, it was as her canonical alter-ego, Jael, that Judith retained a foothold in formal religious and doctrinal contexts. In predominantly Catholic countries, of course, Judith's figure still retains its place in bibles and its institutionalized religious context; but even Catholic theologians accept the consensus that the Book of Judith is a 'novel', not historically 'true' but nevertheless doctrinally significant. When reissued in study-guide versions, her Book is nowadays generally presented as a meaningful text the authority of which does not rest on fundamentalist premises. On the contrary, theological exegesis stresses its specifically Judaic character, as a template for the customs and value of perfect piety, idealized in Judith's character as a paradigmatic good Jewess.[22]

But we should not underestimate the cultural robustness of the Judithic figure even in Protestant contexts, and even when confused with Jael's brief Testamental appearance. In the early 1900s Sunday Schools sometimes awarded medals to conscientious pupils, and in Norfolk I have seen one such medal commemorating Jael. Since the late Victorian effacement of the Apocrypha, Jael has done Judith's work wherever Judith could not do it herself. As a result, from that period English iconography has habitually compounded the two figures. (Which is presumably why many of those who enquired what I was writing about for this book then responded, 'Oh yes, the one with the hammer.')

It was for feminists that Judith-Jael's figure became most unacceptable, in a way that directly reflected the increasing Victorian emphasis upon her Judaic character. Their rejection of Judith-Jael as a prototype for women was eloquently expressed when Elizabeth Cady Stanton, the most famous of American feminists, led the team of women who compiled the *Woman's Bible*. The compilers were careful to reflect the very latest biblical scholarship (thus deliberately evincing the intellectual authority of which women were capable) in order to demystify the texts that were traditionally adduced in order to prove that it was God, not man, who had put woman in her place. Consequently the *Woman's Bible* excludes the Apocrypha, and its interpretation of Judith-Jael is conveyed through the canonical half of the compound figure.

Stanton and her team consider Jael's homicide the most offensive example of unthinking 'Hebraism', quite 'revolting under our code of morality'; an instance of the way in which a tribe made their god like themselves, a 'god of battles' and hence ruthless, anti-Christian.[23] Jael herself they regard as manifesting a woman's internalization of Hebraic patriarchy, masculinist, militarist and inhumane. Like Brontë, they interpret her as both sign of the Law of the Father and internalized oppressor of the feminine mind.

Their own feminist philosophy was, however, deeply implicated in the masculinist 'progressive' ideals promulgated by eugenicists such as Weininger. To assume that women were defective human beings, as the psychologists did, produced a contradiction in their view that the human race might be perfected by genetic means, for after all women were (somewhat inconveniently) the means by which the race reproduced itself. A way had to be found, then, of incorporating women into eugenic improvement, which simultaneously would offer them an apparently dignified role in the process of accepting their own defectiveness. The solution was to inform them that they were elected to the sublime role of motherhood, charged with producing the healthiest and most carefully nurtured infants and thus occupying a decisive place in the onward march of the race. This was, of course, the eugenicist philosophy later propounded by the Nazis, who established baby-farms for Aryan mothers. But that extreme outgrowth of eugenicism both represents its fascistic potential and serves now to conceal its widespread acceptability in Western thought before the Second World War. In turn-of-the-century Britain and America eugenics and the new 'sanctification' of motherhood were both regarded as progressive ideals. In 1913, the first full-length Hollywood film, D.W. Griffith's *Judith of Bethulia*, identified Judith as sublime matriarch of her nation and deliverance as a birth. Similarly, the feminist *Woman's Bible* was fully committed to the view that sublime motherhood was women's vocation and a means of asserting women's dignity as fully human beings meriting every civil right accorded to men.[24] In one sense, they had fixed upon this ideal as the most culturally efficacious way of reconciling public opinion to feminist demands, because it was in tune with the times. On the other hand, it subserved an ultimately oppressive and masculinist tendency which revealed itself most completely in Nazism; it contained women within biologism, encoding their imprisonment within their gender more effectively than ever. Eugenics thus achieved the ambivalent work that characterizes all successfully naturalized ideologies: it persuaded the rebellious to regard themselves as fortunate in resubordinating themselves to it.

For this reason Jael-Judith was not a heroine of late Victorian feminism. Her homicidal act and her barrenness both tended to type her as the reverse of the creative mother-figure. Thus, for feminist resistance to Judaeo-Christian tradition, she was made to function in a manner quite opposite to the liberating rebel celebrated earlier in the century. Whereas Romanticism had conferred on Judithic figures the transcendent will of the Romantic Criminal, for the 1890s feminists they conveyed social control that was patriarchal and antediluvian, orientalist. Ironically, then, 1890s masculinists demonized Judith as an instance of women's destructiveness,[25] whilst feminists demonized her as an instance of their victimization.

Meredith's New Judiths

Someone placed between these positions – a male feminist – felt neither threatened by Judith's formidability, nor self-conscious about her awkwardness for the strategies preferred by the feminists. Both the fallen and the chaste versions of Judith's icon were represented by the wayward but much-read author, George Meredith. Partly because of the difficulties of his own first marriage, Meredith was preoccupied by marital problems and sexual mores. He wrote a series of difficult and heterodox novels that challenged complacent Victorian attitudes to personal and national politics. His view of the New Woman, in particular, was unusually sympathetic, and by the 1890s, when his reputation as a major writer had been fully established, he was well known as an ally of the feminists.[26] His movement from the iconic female pair in *Rhoda Fleming* (1865) to that in *One of our Conquerors* (1891) is also a movement from the chaste virago version of Judith to a more socially challenging, fallen Judy.

Rhoda Fleming relates the seduction of Rhoda's sister Dahlia by a socially superior seducer, Edward, and her subsequent abandonment and ruin. (Its original title was the more feminist *A Woman's Battle*.) In other circumstances a prime candidate for domestic angel, Dahlia is fair, feminine and meek, a Ruth *manqué*, whereas Rhoda is dark, proud, determined and tempestuous, a Judith. Edward's own stereotypical view of womanhood is iconized by the portraits in his rooms: one that suggests Dahlia's radiant innocence, which supremely fits her as a lamb to the slaughter, and another 'of a dark Judith, dark with a serenity of sternness'. Commenting on the temperament of Edward's mistress, Mrs Lovell, the dark Judith is used here to suggest both her sexual fascination and its habit of destroying promising young men: Edward himself had been a victim. But his libidinous misogyny misjudges Mrs Lovell and also fails to identify Rhoda as the Judith who will punish his transgression against her sister. This is foreshadowed when Edward's brother meets Rhoda and adjudges her 'a young Judith'.[27] As a reviewer noted at the time, Rhoda is 'stern, earnest, of the Hebrew or Puritanic complexion'.[28] In fact, Meredith is exploiting the Victorian Hebraic epitome implied in the biblical Judith's name to characterize his heroine Rhoda, as both intransigent rectitude and women's revenge. In a society designed to favour aristocratic males and permit them to escape the consequences of their peccadilloes, the Rhodas/Judiths are, Meredith suggests, agents of a rough justice.

A much more complex use of these themes is at work in *One of Our Conquerors* (1891), Meredith's most abstruse and ambitious novel – an instance of 'the penitential exercise of reading his works', grumbled a reviewer[29] – but also his best. Only part of the puzzled contemporary reaction was owing to its 'perverse' style: much more unpalatable was its systematic attack on Victorian values, political and sexual. The novel suggests that the nation worships false gods, venerating Mammon and mistreating women. Its anti-hero, Victor, is ironically named, one of our (apparent) 'conquerors'. Although a massively successful entrepreneur in a manner approved by his society, Victor has feet of clay, and his meretricious way of life finally brings ruin and death. Such admired materialistic heroes of Victorian Britain (Victor's Britain) are, in fact, conquerors of the nation itself, who will precipitate national ruin too. Victor's bullishness is portrayed as what Arnold would have designated Hebraic. His fatal secret is that he and his 'wife' Natalie are not in fact married, a fact that if known would consign her to the shunned status of fallen woman, jeopardize her daughter's chances of a good marriage and shatter Victor's social pretensions. The novel insists that society's view of sexual irregularity is foolish, malicious and destructive. Such shibboleths substitute human pettiness for authentic moral codes; Victor's success at 'respectability' is built on sham, the kind of sham that also condemns the 'fallen woman' for his own mistakes and immoralities.

In this context of radical critique, the fallen woman herself becomes a symbol of subversion. For her to overcome her ostracized status would be an optimistic sign of the possibility of change, and would itself represent an oblique revenge upon the oblique iniquities of respectable society and its 'great men'. Whilst Natalie is a collusive victim, and her daughter Nesta a New Woman, the true subversive here is another fallen woman, Mrs Marsett, the common-law wife of an army officer. Marsett is explicitly a Judith, whilst the self-destroying Natalie is implicitly her obverse, the Lucretia type. It is Marsett who rails against the bad faith of the social system: 'when men get women on the slope to their perdition . . . they do as much as murder. They're never hanged for it. They make the Laws! And then they become fathers of families, and point the finger at the "wretched creatures". They have a dozen names against women, for one at themselves . . . men have the power and the lead . . . and then they turn round and execrate us for not having what they robbed us of!' Herself named Judith, Marsett is complaining of being called a loose woman, Judy being one of those 'names against women' deployed by the Laws of the Father that dominate this society. 'Judith. Damnable name! . . . I did something in scripture. Judith could again . . . I loathe my name; I want to do things.'[30] What she wants to do is the social equivalent of Judith's murder, in retaliation for the 'as much as murder' that men perpetrate against women.

This she achieves, not by homicide, but by forcing her lover to marry her and thus admit her to the respectable circles that have ostracized her. Indirectly, this event triggers Victor's downfall and Nesta's liberation of herself from parental control. Mrs Marsett is the Judith to his Holofernes, just as he is the modern equivalent of ancient conquerors. And metaphorically she becomes the mother of Nesta's independence, replacing her failed counterpart Natalie. New Women are born of Victorian Judiths, and in a visionary finale Meredith sees the future of progress – achievable only by social reform – as dependent upon them. Meredith's clever, trenchant novel thus also contests the 1890s ideology of self-abnegating motherhood, in favour of the self-assertive Mrs Marsett. Merging the revolutionary Judith with the Fallen Judy was a remarkable stroke in the politics of progressive reform: it excavated a weak point in current ideology about both nation and womanhood.

Since *One of Our Conquerors* became standard reading for intellectuals of the next generation, it was also in time an effective agent of change. In the early 1900s H.G. Wells and Siegfried Sassoon would hail Meredith's work as prophetic of a new age, rejecting Victorian sham. 'It is one of the books that made me,' says Wells's self-projection in *The New Machiavelli* (1911).[31] A massively popular pundit, Wells helped to shape Anglo-American attitudes in the twenti-eth century; Judith had done her part in radicalizing the rising generation of leading intellectuals. But this male receptiveness perpetuated her ambiguity. A lecher *extraordinaire*, Wells may have regarded every woman he seduced as a potential Judith Marsett and hence credited his own conviction that he was liberating his victims.

9

Reader, I Murdered Him
Criminality and the Uncanny

Judith as Jael

In Victorian culture the mythology of marriage and the mythology of murder were often combined. In the puppet-show, Punch murdered Judy and their baby, but in the mythology of criminality it was the wife who was more likely to murder her spouse. From the late seventeenth century onwards, a rich folklore about murderous wives, derived from both fact and fiction, evolved a mythic archetype of the Murderess as Judith-Jael.

Essentially the Murderess Judith was an image of individualism, the husband was the authority against which she revolted. By the nineteenth century, this figure would come to reflect *in extremis* Victorian culture's struggle to constrain individualism, iconized by the Romantic Criminal, within a modern bourgeois society dependent upon widespread conformism to maintain itself. Consequently Judith's most significant guise became her romantic criminality as Murderess, an icon in which she and her alter-ego, Jael, were compounded. This was only partly because Jael was the canonical guise for Judith; more importantly, the imagistic compounding of the two permitted a stress on Judith's more sinister aspect. Unlike Judith, Jael's character had not been elaborated by the Bible in ways that made her so complex. She could more easily partialize Judith as vengeful murderess. In this role Judith-Jael became a focus for profound anxieties in Victorian culture.

For the prevailing bourgeois morality, which lacked the theological sophistication of the Renaissance, the fact that she had murdered Holofernes was more tendentious both morally and sexually. In 1828 this was already overt: 'she acted the part of a bawd, was guilty of notorious lying, and murder' declared one biblical commentator.[1] And Judith's imaging as the Romantic Criminal correspondingly underplayed the religious context sanctioning her action. Romantic Criminals were antinomian misfits, not providential instruments.

At the same time, interest in actual female homicides was increasing.[2] There had since the Renaissance been a roaring trade in cheap pamphlets about male-factors, which female homicides represented the most titillating end of the criminal spectrum. Not only did women who murdered men (especially if these were their husbands) appear shockingly insubordinate; not only did they seem unnatural exceptions to the supposedly more law-abiding character of their gender; but the particular form of punishment accorded homicidal wives added its own lurid ingredient. Because husband-murder was petty treason – the familial equivalent of treason against the king – the early modern wife's insub-ordination was punished not by hanging but by burning alive. One may judge how powerful a taboo was at stake in husband-murder by the horror of the stake. Like the Judithic regicides of the Renaissance, it carried metaphysical associa-tions mystified in its punishment. As well as being illegal and immoral, it was counter-cultural. Perhaps, then, it was only a matter of time before the myth of Judith became associated with husband-murder. The specific conjunction of circumstances favourable to the perceptible emergence of this association occurred in the mid-nineteenth century, on both sides of the Atlantic.

The Poisonous Wife

That the association was already latent in perceptions of female homicide is evinced by the case of Mary Hobry, an immigrant French midwife who mur-dered her husband in 1688. A particularly notorious case, this inspired no fewer than four competing penny-dreadful accounts of the murder, and subsequently went down in the annals of lurid crime.[3] Two concede some sympathy to Hobry, inasmuch as they mention the long history of brutal abuse which had motivated her crime. She was a slave in 'bondage': 'so that groaning under the burthen of my afflictions, I knew not what course in the world to take, to ease myself of that miserable bondage I was in'.[4] In her state of desperation she is tempted by the devil to her evil act. On the other hand, the pamphlets are insistent that she repented before her death, acknowledging that her sufferings cannot condone her 'unnatural' offence. Moralizing the occasion, as is their wont, the pamphlets suggest that it is a wife's duty to sustain whatever her husband might inflict upon her, patiently and without complaint. In one account, this bleak injunc-tion to battered wives is humanized somewhat by 'Hobry's' appeal to all couples to treat each other with patience and affection.[5] All four, however, pronounce (in one case, in verse) as a moral absolute that marricide is unnatural and blas-phemous whatever the circumstances.[6]

In effect, Mr Hobry is bifurcated: as a vicious man, he receives no sympa-thy; but as a husband, he is a cultural idol. Thus the pamphlets offer two inter-pretations of the event, in tandem. One is narrative specific to the case, in which the extenuating circumstances are explained, although they are not allowed to extenuate; the other is a universalizing interpretation, which sees all marital relationships as a hazard, and offers the unconditional pronouncement that husbands are sacrosanct. Such works are intentionally titillating, but it is not their intention to challenge the most cherished cultural assumptions. Titillation rather demands that they emphasize Mr Hobry's violence and his wife's victimization, so we need not assume that their sympathy is necessarily genuine.

Whereas these accounts bifurcate Mr Hobry into Vicious Man and The Husband, person and function, Mary went further, dismembering him completely. On the night of 26 January, he had returned home drunk and beaten her, a regular occurrence. But this time she was determined 'to be revenged of him', and after he had fallen asleep she strangled him. In order to facilitate disposal of the corpse, she then hacked up the body with a hatchet, helped by her accomplice Dennis. In the publicity created by the case it was rumoured that Dennis was her son. Presumably he is intended by the representation of a young boy in the most elaborate illustration which was published. Other images were generally rather crude woodcuts, including the scene of her burning. In the more sophisticated engraving, however, Mr Hobry's headless body is sprawled on a table, naked but for a corner of cloth which decorously covers his genitalia. Whilst Mary hacks off a leg, shadowy demons inspire her efforts, and on the right stands Dennis, holding in his right hand the severed head.

Several aspects of the murder-scene suggest that the engraver was imitating what he knew already, the printed illustrations of Judith's homicide. The foreshortening and classicized articulation of Hobry's headless body are reminiscent of Holofernes' in such representations, as Mary's posture and placing are reminiscent of Judith's, and the table takes the place of a bed. The inspirational demons are counterparts of the inspiring angel in Da Sole's contemporary painting, for instance. Most of all, Dennis's posture, the gesture of his left hand and his grasp on the hair of the severed head suggest a boyish rendition of Judith/David displaying the head. In this way, the engraving is like the 'narrative pictures' of the Middle Ages and the Renaissance, by seeming to combine two iconographic data. On the left, the engraving imitates representations of Judith in the act of murder, whilst on the right, it imitates those of the head's display. The engraving places a mythic cast on the event, a Judithic exaction of 'women's revenge' seconded by the suggestion of the boy's Oedipal, Davidic collusion with her. This is a way of conveying the Freudian family romance: the fear that such occasions represent the revolt of the family against the Father.

In the engraver's application of his trade's conventions, Hobry's murder becomes a contemporary version of a recurring scene, woman as murderer, just as Caravaggio had portrayed Cenci's parricide as Judith slaying Holofernes. By doubling his rendering of Judith-conventions, the engraver intensifies the metaphysical associations attached to this instance of petty treason. paradoxically, the sacred ambience thus imported into the scene produces not sanctity but evil. At least, that is the intention: the demon with scrawny dugs recasts Judith's crone-like maid for this purpose. On the other hand, a reminiscence of Judith, however demonized, always carries with it an uneasy recollection that she had been vindicated. Consciously or not, the engraving retains something of the double narrative of the pamphlets, where compassion for Mary runs parallel to her condemnation.

In the Victorian period, this uneasy vilification of Judith as female homicide became overt. Her image darkened, and became more and more closely involved in the theme of 'women's revenge' against the husbands who ruled them. Mary Hobry's vengeance for years of mistreatment was explicitly recognized as such even in 1688. The Victorians, however, were to become increasingly paranoid about women's revenge: its frequency, methods, atavism and malice. Consequently, there are two Victorian Judiths, distinguished by their sphere of action, much as Mr Hobry had been. On the one hand, there is Judith as Liberty, heroine of 1848, her public face. On the other hand, there is Female Vengeance, her private face as the domestic demon.

Disguised Judiths: Romantic Opera

This bifurcation is anxiously insistent in Henry Chorley's oratorio *Judith*, created for the Birmingham Music Festival in 1858. This was another hospital benefit, and the subject was calculated to appeal to the well-educated middle classes of the city. In European opera Judith was a popular subject, adaptations of the Old Testament being fashionable.[7] Chorley was influenced by Metastasio's *Bethulia Liberata*, and despite the music critic George Bernard Shaw's disgust, Hubert Parry's oratorio *Judith* continued to be revived as a work suited to prominent cultural festivals.[8] Musical adaptations of the subject carried cachet in this context, as Arne's had a century earlier. Judith's story conjoined high seriousness with a spicy subject, also partaking of the illicit ambience bestowed upon the Apocrypha by Victorian moralism. Thus in George Eliot's *Middlemarch* (1871–2), the laddish Fred Vincy's unfitness for an ecclesiastical career is demonstrated by his aversion to reading the Bible – except the juicy Apocrypha.[9]

Its steamy associations reinforced the trend to deny its authenticity as scripture. In 1858, faced with the censor, the producer of Giacometti's tragedy *Giuditta* argued that the play should be permitted because the story was fictional, not biblical. The Lord Chamberlain replied, judiciously, that he would forbid a play about Judith – but would permit one that used the same story.[10] There were two consequences of such hypocrisy.

First, Judith plots increasingly appeared in other guises. Many nineteenth- and twentieth-century versions of the story are 'displaced' in this way.

Paradigmatic of this process was Puccini's canny transformation of the story into his great popular success, the tragic-romantic opera *Tosca* (1900). Its translation of the story into a passionate episode of love, tyranny, rebellion, torture and rape in nineteenth-century Italy built upon those basic themes of the Book of Judith and its heroine's long-lived political significance in Italy: part of Puccini's motivation was nationalistic. Tosca's given name is Floria, a slight variation on the Italian Judith-Flora. When she stabs the evil oppressor Scarpia she is doing her job as Judith Murderess. The *fin-de-siècle* take on this, however, turns the rational biblical heroine into an emotional, somewhat shop-soiled, superstitious and turbulent diva – the earthy Judy seen more positively as generous passion. It takes an enthusiast for Judith to spot her in Tosca's form, as one odd Frenchman did.[11]

But Puccini did not leave his interest in Judith there. A mysterious, incomplete opera which has been thought to derive possibly from the *Arabian Nights* is, in fact, an orientalist combination of their ambience with the Book of Judith, which was often a subject for orientalization between the mid-nineteenth century and the 1930s.[12] Puccini's last opera, the brutal yet sublime *Turandot* (1926), achieves that paradoxical emotional effect by exploiting Judithic ambiguity. The heroine is a beautiful sexual hysteric (shades of Weininger here) who tests her lovers to destruction; when they inevitably fail, she has their heads chopped off. The only lover to escape this Judithic execution is the one whom, finally, she can identify as 'Love' itself. Exotic, allegorical romance has transported the story of a Judith redeemed from celibacy to the Orient. Here the Victorian orientalized Judith is both terrifyingly alien and the ultimate object of desire, its value ratified repeatedly by the mortality that is its price. Like Holofernes, its hero is impelled by the death-wish of unqualified desire, but (and this miracle is what renders the story uncanny) it is his willingness to pay the price that enables him to fulfil his desire. It is a weird allegory of what 'true love' might really mean. For Puccini – whose own amorous history was turbid – it seems to have meant both terror and magnificence, without any half-measures. Too much for most of us, maybe?

Are many members of Puccini's sizeable Western audience aware that they are watching disguised versions of a biblical story? Probably not. Yet the same subtext holds for many other works. Judith is incarnated not only in her historical avatars but in her disguised replicants, which at once conceal from us the uncompromising counter-cultural myth and throw sideways, tentative, partial light on what it reveals to us. For they either dare not or will not tell us frankly.

Murder Most Female

The secularization of the story necessary to escape censorship and public offence permitted free commercial exploitation of a sensational plot. But it could also have the effect of actually facilitating its contemporary resonances for 'real life'. Removed from the biblical envelope, it was more easily accommodated to an audience's perception of its own world. And uncoupled from antiquity, it had more evident relevance to current social issues. In short, it permitted audiences to see what their imaginative incapacity might otherwise have obscured: what was already there in the apocryphal Book.

Henry Chorley's preface to the published libretto of his oratorio *Judith* reflects his own anxieties and attempts to pre-empt those of his audience. 'I cannot present [the libretto] without some explanation', he says, because whilst the Testamental stories carry morals of universal application, the Apocrypha consists of merely 'picturesque legends'. The Book of Judith in particular displays a heroine doing something that under normal circumstances would be immoral, and therefore must not be taken as an example for 'universal instruction . . . It is no lesson' for Christians. Thus Chorley carefully distinguishes his work from the versions of those who have exploited the story's 'picturesque contrasts', by which he means its homicidal and sexual aspects. He admits that '"Judith" has often . . . been handled for the foreign stage, in which guise it has always been, of necessity, more or less objectionable.' Such condemnation presumably guarantees that he himself has nobly ignored its sensationalist possibilities; yet Chorley says that these aspects must nonetheless emerge 'of necessity'. Perhaps this observation promises that Chorley's audiences may still hope to savour the inherent sensationalism of the plot despite the author's modesty in its handling. This strange apologia, grammatically and logically distorted by its own ambivalence, is equally confused by the story's sacred/non-canonical status. Having insisted upon the unauthoritative character of the Apocrypha, Chorley ends by confirming that he has used no words not present in it, not wishing to adulterate 'the lofty and lyrical language of Scripture'.[13] His preface is a splendid instance of the attraction of Victorian culture to precisely those themes in the Book of Judith that it found most 'objectionable' and whose contemporary application it sought to frustrate. Yet it was of course precisely contemporary interests that were served by such works.

In both English and American culture the representation of murderous women becomes more common from the mid-nineteenth century onwards, especially in the publicity given to scandalous cases. One such was the ambivalently adjudicated case of Madeleine Smith, a Glasgow woman accused of murdering her lover in 1857. Indeed, by the 1890s there had evolved a cultural myth that there was a high incidence of wives poisoning unwanted husbands, and that female homicides' preferred method was poison because it was a remote, physically unaggressive method of murder: 'from the very earliest period in the world's history, women, when resolved upon committing murder, have generally had recourse to the phial.'[14] Moralizing this supposed preference, misogynistic commentators suggested that the secretive operations of poison were best suited to the natural duplicity of women. Subsumed into the popular Victorian myth of the poisonous wife, these ideas remained current well into the twentieth century, reflected in media coverage of murder trials and endorsed by the definitive studies of criminologists. By the 1920s there was a fashion for histories of notorious women criminals and homicides.

Horace Wyndham's *Feminine Frailty* (1929), for example, perpetuated the view that the homicidal wife typicalized fundamental feminine traits, especially their excessive 'passion'. As he recalled, 'Catherine Hayes chopped off her husband's head to live with her paramour.' In fact, this eighteenth-century case was a popular staple of Victorian collections of criminal histories, retold for instance in the long-popular Newgate Calendar.[15] The head-chopping wife was one of the titillating bogies of popular culture, emblematizing women's atavistic compulsion by passion, greed and revenge. Deferring to the authoritative Victorian criminologists such as Cesar Lombroso would lead one to believe that 'A desire for vengeance is responsible for many appalling acts in women'.[16] That was what head-chopping and poisonous wives represented: wives revolting against their masters. This is the trace in late Victorian and early twentieth-century culture of what seems to be a bad conscience about marriage, an implicit acknowledgement of Mill's contention that it was a relation founded upon coercion. If sufficiently provoked, the slave might rise up and slay the master, the intimacy of their relationship within the home actually facilitating revenge.

That this myth should have taken hold in the mid-century seems significantly coincidental with the establishment of the women's movements on both sides of the Atlantic. It was as if fear of women's unfamiliar self-assertion was displaced onto the tradition view that they were deceptive and manipulative. Paradoxically, it was when women began publicly to voice dissatisfaction, that the fact that they had been forced to exert influence indirectly and privately was reinforced by the myth. It was as if, in order to reassert that women's influence was best exerted by private influence upon their spouses, misogynists were busy inflating the supposed power of that influence.

The poisonous wife was the validating negative complement to the domestic angel; the one nourished and succoured her man, both literally and metaphorically, whilst the other fed him death. As Wyndham darkly observed, toxic 'fly-papers are still common objects of every domestic pantry . . . One of these days it may possibly occur to the authorities that this circumstance calls for attention'![17] Poison was the demonic sign of women's domestic role.

One of the early examples of the theme in its mid-Victorian guise was *Old St Paul's* (1841), a bestselling historical novel by the popular writer William Ainsworth. An outstandingly inept novelist, Ainsworth nevertheless remained popular into the twentieth century. In 1928, in a foreword to the Book of Judith, the academic M.R. James could casually mention the novel's villainess, Judith

Malmayns, with the expectation that readers would immediately recognize the allusion.[18] Ainsworth's Judith does not merely murder her husband: murder is her trade. Set in the 1660s, at the time of the Plague and Fire of London, the novel attributes the fire itself to the incendiary activity of Malmayns and her accomplice Chowles, who intend to take advantage by looting people's abandoned homes. Malmayns has already profited in a similar way from the plague. Having acquired a reputation as a nurse specializing in the disease's treatment, she habitually kills her incapacitated patients in order to rob them. When she and Chowles are trapped by the fire they set, the obvious moral point is one of poetic justice, not least because they are storing their loot in the church crypt at the time. When a firestorm swallows up the two malefactors, the imagery suggests that this is the Inferno in which they will burn eternally for their many crimes. (Ironically, Judith's burning alive echoes the marricide's old punishment, burning at the stake.)

Malmayns's demoniac aspect does suggest that her ruthlessness, however much attached to avarice, is that of the serial killer. When she murders her own husband she is the poisonous wife. The way in which she haunts the sickbeds of the dying, expediting the process by such methods as poison and smothering, hints that she is an angel of death, negative image of the domestic angel. In an unsubtle series of elaborations upon her villainy, crudely emphasized by authorial comment, it becomes clear that her forename is not more adventitiously chosen than her surname ('evil hands'). She is Judith as the murderess in the bedroom. Presumably this was what was in M.R. James's mind when he attributed the unpopularity of the Christian name to Ainsworth's notorious villainess. By 1928, the association of Judith with homicidal evil was well established.

The cultural matrix of anxious iconology into which Malmayns inserted herself so successfully became increasingly elaborate as the century progressed. In the 1860s the 'sensation novel' became the predominant popular genre, and murder was its *sine qua non* – not to mention bigamy, impersonation and incest. Dominated by women writers, the genre's popularity was also ascribed to female readers, some male contemporaries ruminating anxiously upon its corrupting influence.[19] Such strictures were often directed at Mary Braddon, the most successful of the sensationalists, whose *Lady Audley's Secret* (1862) epitomizes the genre. (Since its protagonist is a marricide, and Braddon's novel has a feminist subtext, it is apt that the translator of her novels into French was known by the sobriquet Madame Judith.)[20] Braddon's heroine points to something about the Victorian Murderess that will help us to understand their compound of Judith-Jael: the way in which this Romantic Criminal exposed the intolerable 'machine' of bourgeois society.

Lady Audley's story is one of an apparent domestic angel who is unmasked by her enemy and marital relative, Robert Audley, as a poisonous wife. Her double life as angel/demon reflects the Victorian fear of the secret enemy in the marital home. The narrator reflects that 'We hear every day of murders committed in the country ι . . . slow, protracted agonies from poisons administered by some kindred hand.'[21] Whilst Lucy Audley is the poisonous wife concealed within the domestic angel, the misogynist Robert thinks that her simpering perfidy is actually characteristic of all women, whose secret maleficence is indefatigable: 'They are . . . Joan of Arcs, Queen Elizabeths . . . [who] riot in battle, and murder, and clamour, and desperation.' (Just as Elizabeth and Joan were called Judiths in their day, essentially they are the same figure here too.) That is, homicidal urges are a natural constituent of the secret mental life of women because of their 'desperation', their passion. Excluded from formal positions of power, women's will to power is driven into the private realm: 'If they can't agitate the universe . . . they'll make mountains of . . . domestic molehills . . . To call them the weaker sex is to utter a hideous mockery. They are the stronger sex.' Of Robert's misogynistic rant ('"I hate women," he thought savagely') the ironic outcome is a capitulation to New Women's demand for emancipation, a conviction that it is easier to give in to them: at least then they will stop murdering their husbands. Through Robert's mouth Braddon is actually suggesting how far women's energies, distorted and driven inwards by the constriction of their domestic role, have produced within them a secret revolt. Lady Audley's double life as angel and murderess is presented as a melodramatic metonym for all women's lives, outwardly conformist, raging with resentment and frustrated energy within.

Nor is this secret hysteria confined to women. Braddon suggests that it is the customary mental state of everyone who lives in bourgeois society, for its social conventions and the 'machine' of everyday Victorian life imprison and distort the passions fundamental to human nature. When these are roused 'We want to root up gigantic trees in a primeval forest', yet 'the utmost that we can do for the relief of our passion is to knock over an easy chair.' It is this silent frustration of 'primeval' passion that makes Lucy Audley and Robert alike, and his 'savage' hatred of women is his equivalent to her homicidal urge. Both are victims of the social machine which represses human instincts.

Braddon implies that at some level everyone, under these conditions, is mad to a degree (even if it is only Lucy who ends up in a madhouse). This psychic violence is a social problem, not purely a gender problem. However, women's domestic circumstances are such as to compress their passion into more extreme channels than Robert himself would be driven into, because as a man he has outlets for his impulses that are socially acceptable. Indeed, the way he expresses his resentment against life is to resent women; the way he takes arms against it is to destroy Lucy. Onto women his misogynistic rant projects his own human capacity for the 'savage' and for 'destruction'; and in ruining Lucy he repudiates the truth about himself, simultaneously attributing his own secret urges to her and symbolically destroying them in her person. Indeed, his implacable vendetta against her itself expresses his own destructiveness, but in a way that he and others can regard as socially acceptable and even laudable. In exposing Lucy's crimes Robert becomes the personification of society's revenge upon women who are secretly rebellious. But he is simultaneously expelling a disturbing likeness of his own inner passions. Robert is Lucy's psychic (as well as marital) kin. By acting as her nemesis he acts as social authority itself, punishing one who transgresses. In Lucy he punishes in fact his own desire similarly to transgress.

Thus the real 'Secret' of the title is that all Victorians are incipiently mad because of the stresses of modern life's machine. As Romantic Criminal, Lucy is the exception who proves the rule, the one who carries that secret anarchy into action. A very similar psychic pressure was at work in another Victorian Lucy. The heroine of *Villette*, who envisioned her own daily self-murder as Jael killing Sisera, identified partly with the murderess, as the Law of the Father internalized. In *Lady Audley's Secret* a similar drama is played out, but its roles are distributed between protagonist and antagonist. Robert plays the Law of the Father, and Lady Audley plays the Sisera role, as the raging and transgressive id that must be punished. But because Robert's 'savage' emotions are identical to hers, he is enacting their repression in himself.

Thus, whereas in Brontë Jael represented the Law of the Father as murdering the authentic self, in Braddon it is the murderess Lucy who represents the authentic self. It is suggested that the New Woman and the Victorian marricide are identical, and their identity consists not in their maleficence but in their grievance. It is a grievance that any normal human being feels under the civilized constraints of a society that denies all the primal urges. The Murderess figure (so often Jael-Judith) is a sign not of abnormality but of normal identity. She is at once transgressive (Lucy Audley/Joan of Arc) and repressed (Lucy Snowe/Jael). As we saw in Brontë and *The Woman's Bible*, Jael is a sign of the socialized self. Her 'secret', and Lady Audley's, is that the murderess, the wife and the social avenger are all the same person, in whom the Law of the Father and the ultimate crime cohabit.

What Judith-Jael brings with her into the Victorian Murderess is the spirit of the Old Testament Law, 'an eye for an eye'. That is not simply confined to 'women's revenge', but of necessity the Judaeo-Christian tradition of capital punishment itself. Of judicial retribution women's revenge was a transgressive counterpart. When figured as a Jael-Judith, the murderess retains a trace of her authority (as in Renaissance paintings of Judith as executioner). This is why, as we shall see, those novels that invoke Judith-Jael as an archetype for women's deviance also invoke her challenge to easy distinctions between criminality and normality, self-repression and the rage it does not quell. Unlike the author of *Old St Paul's*, sophisticated writers recognized the ambiguity in the figure and that 'Romantic Criminal' might simply be a more courageous or desperate version of the law-abiding citizen.

In Braddon's novel this norm is of course represented by a man, since in this society masculinity is self-defined as the norm against which femininity represents the Other. Thus Robert defines his own rectitude by persecuting the vicarious enactor of his own repressed urges, Lucy, who represents women as the 'stronger sex', the violent Other. That Victorian suspicion was most effectively represented in the murderess as 'masculine woman', Judith-Jael, the Other who could figure men's repressed violence within that of women. She could embody the counter-cultural emotions seething underneath normal social relations.

The Other Self

The sensationalist genre of the 1860s conceals an analysis of social organization in what purports to be a description of the unexpected and the deviant. The familiar is invested with the thrill of the unusual. As it happens, this is the central characteristic of the uncanny, Freud's definition of which was itself a product of nineteenth-century ideas. He explained the uncanny's apparently impossible combination of the frightening (*unheimlich*) and the familiar (*heimlich*, homely) as a product of the repressed wish. In the doppelgänger, a figure recurrent in Victorian fiction, Freud finds the most instructive instance of the uncanny. In supernaturalized form, the double of the protagonist comes to represent 'all our suppressed acts of volition which nourish in us the illusion of free will': all those primitive and instinctual urges that the superego, and the society it labours under, suppress. The double is a product of the individual's 'primary narcissism', that which he shares with the child and with primitive man. Since it is Freud's conviction that all such psychic problems have their origin in infantile experience, he suggests that this displacement of repressed wishes onto the double includes a 'duplication of the genital symbol' representing castration.[22] Since the child fears castration by the father, the fear that first socializes him as one who internalizes the 'laws' under which he must live, the double in Freud's analysis seems to suggest an image of the wish conflated with the image of its punishment.

We may conclude, then, that as uncanny, the self and not-self, the liberated and punished, the sign of the wish and of its repression, the double might most suitably be envisaged as female. For Freud, the norm of psychological development is male, the Oedipal complex its key: women are abnormal because they have to pass through an indirect, mediated version of the Oedipus complex, a process that for Freud means that they must be immature, incompletely developed human beings. Similarly, women (lacking the penis which is the prerequisite of Oedipal development) are biologically incomplete. They are the image of the male castrated, as lacking. There is no need to take Freud's normative masculinism seriously as an account of human psychology: rather it is a mythic description, within the cultural terms that defined Freud's thinking and made it so ultimately successful and appealing to the very culture that it described. Freud's psychoanalysis is brilliantly symptomatic of his own culture's pathology. One instance of this is his definition of the uncanny, which corresponds rather closely to the cultural pathology of the Victorian Murderess. The repressed wishes represented by the criminal Lady Audley duplicate and parallel those of Robert. They are the 'primeval' 'chaos' that the social 'machine' constrains and imperfectly contains. Female, Lucy Audley is at once one of 'the stronger sex' – wreaking its willfulness in the world – and the punished, 'castrated' sex. The real Lady Audley is also the id of the apparent Lady Audley: the rebellious Jael behind the Ruth of the domestic angel. She is the familiar (domestic) secreting the unfamiliar (criminal).

Freud's own attitude to Judith as an instance of 'penis-envy', of the female's attempt to replicate the male's Oedipal experience, can be interpreted as a repressed recognition of the two myths as competing.[23] In a sense, Judith is the uncanny double of Oedipus in mythology. In Freud's account of the uncanny, the other person who is the double is a projection of an internal doubleness, an externalization of the primitive self. Reading mythology counter-culturally, then, we could suggest that Judith is the uncanny double of Oedipus, so that the real, repressed self of the archetypal Man is Woman.

In the Victorian fictions, Lady Audley as murderess is the repressed double of Robert's own rage; whereas in Brontë's novel, Lucy Snowe's internal division is imaged as Jael murdering Sisera, her primitive wishes represented as masculine. As in Robert's definition of the 'stronger' alternative, however, the dominant actor is the feminine figure. When Lucy Snowe later empathizes with the rage of Vashti, her instinctual and aggressive impulses are reinscribed from the internal Sisera onto the female theatrical performer. Lucy's hysterical reaction to this 'acting out' of her own suppressed aggression is simultaneously fascinated and fearful, because of her Vashti is the uncanny double.

Moreover, in Lucy's psyche the recurrent murder of id (Sisera) by Jael (superego) corresponds to Freud's description of the relation of the uncanny to the individual's 'compulsion to repeat'. Repetition-compulsion is the obsessive need to replay an infantile crisis, a compulsion dominating the unconscious mind and 'proceeding from the instinctual impulses'. According to Freud, 'whatever reminds us of this inner "compulsion to repeat"', this re-encounter with the repressed wish, is uncanny. In this proposition Freud relies on an earlier account of the uncanny which locates it in the paradox animate/inanimate. When something that is inanimate comes to life, it becomes uncanny. He sees this effect manifested in the folkloric character of the 'living doll'. Again, if we compare *Villette*, Vashti as uncanny reminder triggers Lucy's habitual response, which is to suppress recognition and categorize the actress/role as 'evil'. Deliberately confusing the identities of actress and role, this episode also replicates the uncanny effect of the double's animate/inanimate nature: Vashti is long dead, but resurrected by the actress who re-embodies her.

In the uncanny, the familiar returns as the unfamiliar or frightening, fearful response acknowledging how transgressive is the wish it embodies and the punishment that looms over it. Lucy Snowe's internal scene, endlessly replaying the murder of Sisera, suggests a variation of this imagistic pattern. As herself she repeatedly kills herself, vainly hoping that on some unforeseen occasion the murder will not be necessary. The scene of murder as self-repression is, like that of murder as self-expression for Lady Audley, a scene of doubling. Indeed, as the most transgressive of interpersonal actions, murder may be, perhaps, the most effective instance of the uncanny's liberation of a repressed wish, since it so fully implies the assertion of the self in defiance of taboo and law.

Freud himself refuses to speculate on the evident relationship between the uncanny and aesthetics. We must, however. If the Victorian woman reader, Braddon's target audience, recognized in Lady Audley the actor of her own domestic frustrations, her response recognized the uncanny. But in Lucy Snowe's reaction to Vashti the heroine herself perceives the uncanny. The reader's response to the uncanny is mediated through the heroine's first-person narrative, which merges description of Vashti's performance with her reactions. Although not mediated through first-person narrative, we might speculate that the victorians' mania for iconic representations of women – as Ruth/Judith, angel/demon – commonly performs this function. For the male subject (and it is always the male subject whose point-of-view determines Freud's analysis of the uncanny), we might deduce, the gender of the 'living doll' is significant. If the uncanny represents a 'dissociated complex' of the subject who observes it, then its dissociation from him by gender would be the most facile form that this repression of identification might take. In other words, it is possible that the Freudian uncanny is at root a mode of perceiving gender-difference, that he suggests the uncanny attributes castrated lack to the double. In which case, woman *as* woman encodes the punishment of castration as well as the Otherness of the double, the subject's resistance to identification with his transgressive self.

If we then universalize this subject as 'male gender' perceiving 'female gender' as uncanny, the paradoxical familiarity/unfamiliarity of the uncanny becomes the recognition that woman is the same (human) but different (feminine) from man. The fear evoked by this phenomenon may not necessarily be attributed to fear of castration; it may be a timorous recognition of the supposed 'mystery' of the woman. It is, after all, the traditional view of a masculinist culture that woman represents a mystery that baffles empathy.

On the other hand, how could woman represent the male subject's transgressive alterity, the more liberated version of his own primitive instincts? First, traditionally women were perceived as more 'natural', that is more animalistic, beings than men. The processes of female reproduction underpinned this prejudice, since men's reproductive function was 'invisible' and hence supposedly capable of sublimation. Women were more clearly allied to 'animal' functions. In the nineteenth century, the production of pseudo-scientific theories by practitioners of biological sciences, medicine and psychiatry was exacerbating the biological distinctions between the sexes. Darwin professed to find in evolutionary theory indications that women were less developed than men.[24] In effect, his suggestion that women's place in the evolutionary process was retarded by comparison to men's makes them anachronistic, just as orientalism regarded the East as a relic of an earlier stage in civilization. Women in this view represented the survival of the primitive in the modern human race. (The orientalist Judith-Jael, for instance.) Given this consensus of advanced pseudo-scientific Victorian authorities, woman could readily represent the instinctual urges of the male subject, and hence embody the uncanny.

Similar ideological supports for such an identification were provided by a whole spectrum of secularist philosophies. Darwinism was only the major exemplar of the late Victorians' submission to a materialist view of humanity and the universe. Materialism valorized biology as the reigning epistemological paradigm. Like the other 'human sciences' of this period, criminology regarded biological explanation as the proving ground of its theories. Regarded well into our own century as a definitive work, Cesar Lombroso's *The Female Criminal* claimed that criminality could be scientifically deduced from physiognomy, by an 'anatomico-pathological method'. Lombroso's analysis assumes that biology, chemistry and psychology are identical. Asserting that 'the primitive type of a species is more clearly represented in the female' (which is of course the basis of Freud's view of gender also), Lombroso concludes that there is 'wickedness latent in every women': they are criminal by nature.[25] We may deduce from this assertion that the converse is also implied: criminality is feminine. In Lombroso we see how Victorian culture transmuted the Romantic Criminal into something 'culturally' female. No wonder, then, that the Romantic Criminal would so often be seen as a Judith.

Lombroso states that when women are good, it is because the maternal instinct had overridden their capacity for evil. That is, good women are essentially as bad as bad women, but their natures have been efficiently suppressed. As the more atavistic sex, women's crimes manifest 'refined, diabolical cruelty'. Murderesses revel in torture and agonizingly slow modes of killing (poison is one of the methods he intends to emphasize here). For the same reason they enjoy mutilating or dismembering their victims. This claim might well remind us of the cultural interpretation of Mary Hobry as a Judithic surgeon of the corpse, just as the 'refined, diabolical cruelty' was manifest in Judith Malmayns.

When Lombroso seeks an instance of the political criminal, he selects Charlotte Corday, the famous 'Second Judith' of her day. Corday is his key example, and this is precisely because of the Judithic construction that could be placed upon her homicide.

Whilst invoking the Judithic paradigm of women's vengeance, he wants to deny the alternative of Judithic heroism. What Lombroso desires is the central cultural image of the Judith Murderess without its exculpatory baggage. Thus, boasting of having examined Corday's skull, which is illustrated by three plates, he pronounces himself satisfied that it betrays the same 'anomalies' as those of other female offenders. By this example Lombroso intends to deny the possibility that women might kill for altruistic rather than atavistic motives. In fact this is for him the distinction between male and female criminals, since the latter are motivated by jealousy, instead of those noble motives, 'such as love and honour, which drive men to crimes of passion'. And in any case, Lombroso adds, most of the offences committed by men were caused by women! In fine, the pathology of criminality is primitive reversion, and hence feminine. Men's crimes are impelled by 'love and honour', civilized concepts that presumably reflect their higher state of development. Lombroso's need to verify this by specific reference to female 'assassins', typed by Corday, is urgent because of the immediate contact: obliquely, he is addressing the fact that anarchists, including women terrorists, were active in 1890s Europe. In effect he offers the consolation of dismissing them simply as irrational and evil.

Just as Lombroso's 'method' is biological, so his view of criminality identifies it with sexuality. Prostitutes and fallen women are treated as the same, as the normative type of female criminal. Characteristically Lombroso fetches his explanation from human origins: 'the primitive woman was rarely a murderess; but she was always a prostitute, and such she remained until semi-civilized epochs.' Consequently, we should notice, women's essential 'atavism' must make them all prostitutes by nature too. (Again, Victorian feminists were clearly right to contend that society viewed all women this way.) Since women's utility has always been sexual, they must be by constitution indiscriminately so, says Lombroso. After the sentimentalized fallen woman of the mid-century, we see in his work how in subsequent decades the old conviction of women's animalistic voracity had re-emerged, fortified by pseudo-scientific authority. His phrenological claims also re-authorize the view that female criminals are 'singularly virile', like 'brutal men'. Subtextually, this phallic interpretation of the female criminal suggests that they are envious (that being their normal emotion, remember) of the male. Here Lombroso's overdetermination of his thesis stumbles on contradiction, since he has insisted that criminality is essentially a feminine characteristic: why, then, should criminality involve masculine characteristics? The answer, probably, is that Lombroso's 'brutal men' are envisaged in class terms, as the unwashed proletariat who are primitive in any

case. The masculinity of the Murderess – Judith and Corday being, traditionally, 'masculine women' – is part, then, of what made Judith an archetype of the
Victorian Murderess.

Lombroso's distinction between male and female criminals is the qualitative
difference between civilized and savage motives. There is a suggestive correspondence here with his contemporary Freud's analysis of the uncanny, as
reminder of primeval instinctual urges suppressed by the civilized ego. As both
men's analyses are very much products of their time, their complementarity is
not surprising. And we may deduce from that complementarity that representations of the Victorian Murderess are uncanny, that they are instances of its
familiarity/unfamiliarity, primitivism/repression, liberation/punishment. As
uncanny, she represents the male subject's forbidden transgressive desires,
vicariously liberating them. At the same time, though, she represents the punishment he dreads. (It is no accident that Lombroso's reflections on murderesses assume that their victims are male.)

Hence Judith-Turandot, who is simultaneously the ultimate object of desire
and the aberrant princess who commands executions. This radically ambiguous
uncanny Murderess would logically assume Judith-like incarnation whenever
that ambiguity was fully comprehended. Apart from the customary ambiguity
of Judith as icon, the mid-century had registered a more acutely uneasy
sensitivity to her moral ambivalence, as we saw in Chorley's libretto of 1858.
Moreover, a representation of the uncanny should, by Freud's account, register
both the potency of instinctual drives and the Law (the ego/society, that
renders them forbidden). As simultaneously murderess, siren and divinely
appointed avenger, Judith registers precisely this combination of the instinctive
with the punitive. She represents, indeed, the people of the Law – as did Jael,
instrument of the Judge Deborah. In this respect the Victorian Murderess is
immersed in the Arnoldian Hebraism of her culture. In this form Judith's
counter-culture myth was, then, ironically necessary to the *normalizing* mythology of Victorianism. She represented the culture's uncanny.

Uncanny Arts: Trollope and Realism

Once Arnold had articulated to that culture its Hebraic self-image, that self-
consciousness became part of the representation itself. One of the effects of
Arnold's influential essay was in fact to alter the representation of the Romantic
Criminal, which began to acknowledge a Hebraic/Hellenic context. We can see
this at work in a novel by Anthony Trollope, one of the most widely read novelists of the 1860s. In *The Last Chronicle of Barset* (1867) the uncanny, as Judith-
Jael, is portrayed through the role of art. Paintings represent the uncanny in this
realist novel, which refuses to be highly coloured or melodramatic. Paintings are
the secret life of this bourgeois world which is Trollope's forte, portraying the

passions and primitive archetypes that animate the people who move decorously through Victorian drawing-rooms. In short, art is revealed as the vehicle
of the uncanny.

Trollope's difficulty here is representative of a problem intrinsic to the
Victorian realist novel. In sensation novels, the melodramatic idiom allowed for
a high colouring of events and characters in which the figure of the Murderess-
Jael might be easily accommodated, whereas in the realist tradition writers
acknowledged that the received concept of heroism seemed inappropriate to the
mundanities of modern society. For the realist George Eliot, fiction's 'Romantic
Criminals' were a fantastic construct, denied by experience.[26] Similarly,
Trollope's characters are associated with the primitive, atavistic Romantic
Criminal only through the medium of art, which emblematized a level of experience otherwise inexpressible in the realist novel. Symbolic forenames and
ekphrasis (the description of works of art) are used to import idealizing elements
into the depiction of its characters. Icons such as Judith-Jael could either
enhance the reader's perception of an obscure but remarkable character, or
measure the distance between the glamorous 'falsities' of the Romantic
Criminal and the less obvious moral 'truths' of everyday life.

As simultaneously material and 'unreal', paintings become in realist fiction
an intimation of the uncanny. They signify that melodramatic inner psychic life
that human beings are accustomed to suppress when going about their daily
business. At the same time, they reify the fantasies that normal social relations
both deny and promulgate. *Ekphrasis* registers both the expression and the
repression of desire effected by the uncanny. In other words, paintings/icons
become the uncanny of the realist novel, investing it with an image of the unfamiliar that it can tolerate despite its commitment to the mundane.

In Trollope's popular *Last Chronicle of Barset*, coeval with Arnold's essay
'Hebraism and Hellenism', the romantic subplot significantly depends upon a
contrast between Hellenic and Hebraic icons of femininity. It is here that
Trollope describes the 'Romantic Criminals', 'the Judiths and Charlotte
Cordays'.[27] The novel follows the relationship between a fashionable, philan-
dering artist, Conway Dalrymple, and Clara Van Siever, heiress to a fortune.
Conway is already involved in a flirtation with a married woman, Mrs Dobbs
Broughton. In many ways the latter is presented as the archetypal Victorian
wife. Her marriage was arranged, and she is in no way surprised or dismayed by
its lovelessness and lack of intimacy, which she compensates by fantasizing that
Conway is hopelessly in love with her. Hers is the vacuity of mind and distortion of personality that the social ideal of femininity requires, an ideal iconized
as Hellenic by the classical Graces, the guise in which Conway paints her.

To this compliant feminine role-player Clara is a complete contrast, a candid,
authentic personality who, merely by being herself, implicitly challenges the
hypocrisies and bad faith of others. Himself something of a role-player like Mrs

Broughton, Conway is as fascinated by Clara as he is repelled by her frankness and formidability. His first reaction to her indicates a complex reaction-formation of attraction and defensiveness towards the challenge of her masculine, Judithic personality. There was 'about her nothing of feminine softness . . . He [Conway] certainly could make a picture of her . . . but it must be as Judith with the dissevered head, or as Jael using her hammer over the temple of Sisera.' In contrast to Mrs Broughton, Clara is iconized as Hebraic woman, Judith-Jael. At once compelling and mysterious to him, her nature immediately requires classification in familiarizing terms: Conway contains his disturbed response to her by referring her nature to iconography. Her personal impact is one of authenticity, unmitigated by social pretences, leaving him 'to consider whether he could say or think of himself that he was not a sham in anything'. It is this sense of menace to his self-esteem that makes him resolve upon painting her portrait: upon, that is, confirming her conformity to his image of her, but also his superiority to her. For Conway a painter's artifices become a way of simultaneously assimilating and mitigating Clara's unsocialized integrity. In the same way her *nouveau riche* class is ironized by Trollope as, far from the disability that the fashionable characters imagine, symbolic of that integrity. She has not been assimilated to genteel ideas of what is feminine. At one level, then, Conway's compulsion to paint her as Jael is an attempt to slide the 'sham' in himself over the authenticity in her, to recalibrate her personality in conventionalized terms. At once familiarizing and defamiliarizing, evoking and repressing, her character, Conway's sketch of her as Jael produces the Murderess as uncanny. Concurrently, the sketch is art as the uncanny.

Given the role of the Jael-Murderess as a mutivalent icon in Victorian culture, it is perhaps inevitable that Conway would choose this image to formulate, control and repress his response to Clara. Ironically, his reaction-formation indicates that the Jael-Murderess is a sign of the authentic woman for Victorian culture. Shorn of social polish and the submissive ways of conventionalized femininity, Woman would be, apparently, a 'tiger' and manslayer. What Conway sees in Clara is an image of his own fears, involving a tacit acknowledgment that the normal genteel woman is a repression of her own nature, a Ruth disguising her natural instincts from the observer. By contrast, Clara's countenance makes no concession to its observers: 'it seemed to declare that she could bear any light to which it might be subjected without flinching from it.' The fact that Conway is a philanderer leads us to infer that it is not simply unfamiliarity with women that inspires his habits of mind. This is a sophisticate's recourse to the prevalent ideology of intersexual relations, and to this degree paradigmatic of the unacknowledged truths represented by a Victorian Jael-Judith. Precisely because Clara is unsophisticated and frank, she herself is symbolic of what woman could or would be if social pretences failed. Thus her counter-cultural character must be 'interpreted', both visually and verbally, as Jael. As a society portraitist, Conway himself personifies the formal accommodations, the habits of representation, that allow Victorian society to ideologize itself as normative and natural. Faced with a tigress, one paints her into the Old Testament: anachronizing, formalizing, reifying and alienating an exception to the rules.

Whereas Mrs Broughton has a compulsion to romanticize herself as a martyr to intense, frustrated passion, Clara, who is truly exceptional, resists Conway's romanticizing construction of her. So compulsive is his need to iconologize Clara that, when she refuses to model, he sketches the Jael-Sisera scene in her absence. The image is independent of the woman herself, a fact that underscores Clara's objection that he 'can paint his Sisera without making me a Jael.' Conway's motive is the need to see himself as Sisera, under threat, and this dictates that Clara must be a Jael: the sketch is narcissistic in intent, and thus Jael-Clara is also *his* uncanny recognition of Sisera in himself. Only a psychic violence can breach his repression, so that he can only manage to propose to Clara when he rips up her portrait as Jael.

Conway's persuasion of Clara to model as Jael had covertly conveyed his fascination with her capacity for passion: 'artists in all ages have sought for higher types of models in painting women who have been violent or criminal, than have sufficed for them in their portraitures of gentleness and virtue. Look at all the Judiths . . . and the Charlotte Cordays.' In this invocation of the Romantic Criminal, Conway's disingenuous flattery nevertheless suggests a truth about Clara. Unlike the fantasies of Mrs Broughton, Clara's potential for intense feeling and antinomian action is authentic. She is strong enough to be something other than the Victorian Ruth; therefore inevitably she is the Victorian Judith. The Jael-Murderess, as Clara, is revealed in this novel as the sign of authentic passion as well as of common sense. That contrast valorizes the Jael-Murderess as desired and desirable Victorian icon of transgressive womanliness.

Trollope's novel exemplifies that the Victorians' Judith-Jael was not simply a cultural Other but a cultural Self, an image of the true self underlying social formations, and hence equally loved and repudiated. In demystifying the uncanny image of Judith-Jael, Trollope deliberately unmasks the true menace disguised by the Victorian icon of the Murderess: the unwelcome news that in the form of the uncanny his society has alienated the integrity of women, and precluded that of men. The Jael-Murderess is authenticity ideologically distorted as transgression. That is, of course, precisely why she is uncanny. What this icon achieved was a 'painting over' of the contradiction in Victorian cultural myth, that any authentic personality was socially deviant. A society that depended upon rejecting personal integrity was, of course, asking for trouble.

How far any society can afford too many human beings of integrity and authentic personality is a good question. The Mrs Broughtons oil the wheels of social intercourse, whilst the Clara-Judiths put a spoke in them. The rejection of authentic identity was therefore not just a Victorian problem, although society's rapid collectivization first precipitated a neurotic consciousness of what this repression might mean. Judith-Murderess was the essential image of a repression upon which modern society depended for its subsistence.

The Fallen Angel

The writer best equipped to explore the massive ramifications of this repression of the authentic personality was the American Nathaniel Hawthorne. His peculiarly intense romances reject realism, imbuing the nineteenth-century present with intimations of the past and of a visionary future, of legend, metaphysics, and the needs and desires that he reckoned universal to human beings in all times. Unlike most English Victorian writers, Hawthorne did possess the theological sophistication and the intense religious sensibility that could regard the Judith-Murderess as more than the repressed wish and the Law that punished it – though he saw that too. It is possible to see Hawthorne's whole œuvre as dedicated to one subversive but immensely consequential idea: that Anglo-American Christian culture has consistently failed to understand its own religion. Consequently, Hawthorne's vision is inevitably counter-cultural.

The Marble Faun (1860) is his most complex, risky and difficult exploration of society's spiritual inadequacy. The novel does not wholly succeed because it strikes a point at which Hawthorne himself finds it difficult to disengage from cultural norms. It reflects a crisis in his imagination: his encounter at first hand with European antiquity. A product of New England Puritanism, Hawthorne reacted ambivalently to his experiences as a cultured American tourist in Italy.[28] In particular he found Rome deeply dispiriting, and his consequent depression suggests the culture-shock of discovering that the European culture with which he had felt himself to be familiar was in fact profoundly alien to him. Rome was the city in which antiquity made itself present to the senses, in the ruins and museums that represented the long span of history from the ancient empire to the present. At the same time, it was the Eternal City of Catholicism. What Hawthorne's journey brought home to him was the Otherness of Europe for an American, especially one so conscious of his own origins in the early Puritan society of Massachusetts. In *The Marble Faun*, product of his European tour, Europe is represented in the manner of orientalism: America becomes the occident, Europe the anachronistic, powerful, yet in many ways repelling locus of fascination, where human beings are still driven by secret, atavistic, original urges to good and evil. Europe is the East of Hawthorne's imagination.

Here his fascination with the lineaments of evil takes on a greater chiaroscuro, darkened by a sense of Italian decadence. As America's progenitor, Europe becomes the uncanny: familiar yet unfamiliar, antique yet modern, richly spiritual yet evil. This uncanniness in his portrait of Rome becomes focused on the figure of the Romantic Criminal. Artists and *ekphrasis*, mediating European culture, symbolize the uncanny.

In his notebooks, that recognition of an alien culture is symptomatized when he sees the famous painting of the Judith Beatrice Cenci, then attributed to Guido Reni, which was recommended to tourists as a highlight of their itinerary. Hawthorne was fascinated by it, just as Shelley had been, and for the same reason: its radical ambiguity, that in fact of the Judithic Romantic Criminal. In *The Marble Faun* this painting is copied by the visiting American artist, Hilda. Twice in his notebooks Hawthorne attempted to describe its compelling qualities, but was disappointed by the results: 'the picture is quite indescribable, inconceivable, and unaccountable in its effect; for if you attempt to analyze it, you can never succeed in getting at the secret of its fascination', its radical ambiguity of innocence and sin. Cenci, 'a being unhumanized by some terrible fate',[29] is the face of the uncanny. In *The Marble Faun* she is transmogrified into the Romantic Criminal, Miriam, an artist whose past conceals a terrible secret of familial crime. Although we are never told what is is, its tenor is explicitly compared to Cenci's, and like Caravaggio Hawthorne perceives his Miriam/Cenci as the Judithic Murderess.

Beatrice arouses in Hawthorne a sense of affinity, absolute 'sympathy', which is attended nevertheless by a sense of her being absolutely 'inaccessible' to normal human perceptions. For him she is both double and alien, the uncanny criminal. In Miriam the same effect is achieved by her oscillation between the beautiful aesthete and the tortured sinner, the dark beauty who contrasts with the fair and innocent Hilda, the American WASP. For Hawthorne, Miriam is a cut above innocence as in the head-cutting Judith, because tortured guilt has sensitized her to her own soul. Like Cenci, in Hilda's words, she is a 'fallen angel'.[30] Thus her paintings compulsively reproduce scenes of the great Hebraic murderesses – Judith, Jael, Salome – and her self-portrait, orientally Judaic, is in the guise of Judith.

Each murderess is an avenger whose crime also punishes herself. As in Brontë, Jael is both the sign of transgression and the sign of the Law that represses it. Miriam's painting of Jael is animate/inanimate ('actually lifelike and deathlike'), and hence uncanny; but also made real in Miriam, 'as if she herself were Jael, and felt irresistibly compelled to make her bloody confession in this guise.' The double is liminal and rendered by art, the uncanny medium; but most important, this is Miriam's true self. Simultaneous sign of Law ('stern', vengeful) and crime ('vulgar murderess' and thief), Jael is the transgressor who both liberates Miriam's secret wish and evokes self-revulsion. The murder of Miriam's persecutor will in due course activate her secret wish. Her portfolio of Hebraic murderesses materializes her repetition-compulsion, the obsessive replaying of the same scene of crisis. The central example, Judith, is the epitome of feminine beauty as the uncanny: a 'woman, such as one sees only two or three, if even so many times, in all a lifetime; so beautiful, that she seemed to get into your consciousness and memory, and could never afterwards be shut out, but haunted your dreams, for pleasure or for pain.' Radically ambiguous yet compulsive, she possesses 'your inner realm as conquered territory, though without deigning to make herself at home there.' As possessor of the psyche, she is *heimlich*, as independent of it, *unheimlich*, not 'at home there'. She is Woman as the uncanny Other.

Yet Miriam has internalized the Law that condemns her as transgressive woman, an internalization signified by Judith/Jael. By final, ironic touches she renders her Hebraic paintings bathetic, expressing her consciousness that society would adjudge her merely a 'vulgar murderess'. She attempts to 'cancel' her authentic, Judithic self because the culture imprinted on her consciousness demands it. This motif allows Hawthorne's male sensitivities to contain his Miriam, a bride-turned-murderess of the paranoiac Victorian kind. Hence she is Judith, who 'vanquished Holofernes with her beauty, and slew him for too much adoring it.'

The spiritual paradox of Miriam's being – that one may only become an angel by committing a crime devilish enough to transpose one into the realm of radical spirituality – makes her, as it were, a throwback, orientalist, Hebraic, belonging to the dark secrets of the Old World: hence Miriam's Hebraic fore-name, the 'Jewish aspect' of her beauty and the redolent naming of her lover, Donatello, after the Renaissance artist who sculpted the most celebrated of Italian Judiths. The use of antique names symbolizes the eternal recurrence of the great universal, timeless contest between good and evil, at their most vivid and immoderate in this Old World. Miriam personifies Hawthorne's character-istic theme, that only sin may convert us into spiritually conscious beings, living in a different sphere, like Cenci/Judith, beyond the illusions of the everyday – and hence in the timelessness of a present that constantly announces itself as the past, beyond the measures of time.

In effect, human beings must be banished to the uncanny if they are to become fully spiritualized. Yet this fate is reserved only for an elite, the Romantic Criminals. Like Hester/Esther in Hawthorne's *The Scarlet Letter* (1850), the Judithic Miriam signifies a truth that is wholly unpalatable, that social morality is hopelessly out of step with spiritual truth. The authentic per-sonality, Judithic, is a criminal and a fugitive in nineteenth-century society. Above all, and this is Hawthorne's obsession in all his work, Anglo-American society has wholly failed to understand its own religion. Christianity is for Hawthorne a realm of dark, bitter, yet nobly romantic mystery, and its most pro-found secret is that only Lucifer – only a fallen angel – knows how to love good. To a contemporary readership Hawthorne could only convey this extravagantly heretical theme through the uncanny of art, by doubling Miriam as Judith. His was the most antinomian version of the conviction that this was the face of authentic human personality, the one that God would recognize.

That society could not afford to recognize it, must repress it by every means at its disposal, was the other unpalatable truth that Hawthorne secreted in *The Marble Faun*. For him society was entirely at odds with the true nature of good: not only for pragmatic reasons, for criminals are *ipso facto* anti-social, but because the social mind cannot comprehend either good or evil. As T.S. Eliot averred in another context, 'humankind cannot bear very much reality.' Judith as the return of the repressed implicitly reveals what her Victorian cultural mythology was so effortfully obscuring. Her icon provides the leverage that allows us to see Victorianism's underside as what it secretly valued most. It tended to love what it feared. Such is the character of a modern society so highly organized that it must criminalize its individualists. They are its atavistic self, but it is a self envisioned only to be hurriedly cancelled. Hence the Victorian Judiths, embodying both the true Self and the Law that hunts it down.

10

Framing the *Femme Fatale*
Sexology in the *Fin de Siècle*

If viewed negatively – from an irreligious perspective, for instance – Judith's isolation, chastity, widowhood, childlessness and murderousness would epitomize all that is morbid, nihilistic and abortive. Not surprisingly, then, in the 1890s a cultural mood of what might be called decorative despair remade her in its own image. As the century wound down and the confidence of high Victorianism waned, a malaise of hopelessness was the ambience in which the Decadent movement emerged. The writer Ford Madox Ford remembered the *fin de siècle* as a time of 'mental exhaustion', of a self-consciously despondent passivity: 'During these years the words *fin de siècle* were forever on the lips and were universally applied . . . No matter what happened in those days you said "That is typically *fin de siècle*", even if it were no more than your breakfast milk's appearing to have been watered. And, *fin de siècle* connoting "decadent", you did nothing about it.'[1] This resignation to entropy inspired a kind of art in which fatal women were commonplace, a host of Circes, Delilahs, Salomes and of course Judiths, as 'idols of perversity' who embodied a morbid pathology in female form.[2] If life and fate were nihilistic, misogyny proposed the fatal woman as its symbol. Whilst art critics have effectively diagnosed that misogyny, its underlying logic has not been fully recognized. Whilst I have discussed that elsewhere, for our purposes here the key point is these images' subtext of abortiveness. Woman, actually the site of fertility and birth, becomes the most striking index of entropy if she is recast as the death principle.

The Death of Love

Whereas in Christian tradition Judith had once figured resurrection – death-into-life – Decadent aesthetics jettisoned her regenerative aspect in order to bring her into line with the monotone villainesses of legend. They were all, of course, highly decorative – that was why they were *femmes fatales* – and thus embodied also the beauty of Decadence. The doctrine of 'Art for art's sake' was in essence a declaration of independence from socio-moral canons of value. Aestheticism had declared that art had no utility and no function outside its own production: it existed simply in order to be art, without any intention of 'improving' the spectator or indeed reflecting realities. Art captured the beauty of transience, and that response to a work of art itself represented the ecstatic momentariness of sensation. Essentially, the new Aestheticism owed much to a reaction against the dominance of the art critic John Ruskin, best expressed by the high priest of the new religion of art, the aesthete Walter Pater. Like Arnold, yet less candidly, Pater felt that Victorian England was too 'Hebraic' – behaviourist and moralistic – and Ruskin's values were the Hebraism to his Hellenism. In Pater's seminal work, *The Renaissance* (1873), the genealogy of Western art is represented as pagan and epicurean. It applies the Victorian mania for origins to the question of what is truly aesthetic and locates the answer in ancient Greece. Evidently, then, the Hebraic Judith, who had iconized so much for the Victorian psyche, would require reimagining in this system of thought as an unbuttoned Hellene. And that is precisely what Pater does to her.

Long undervalued, Botticelli's work was only in fact accorded its modern reputation in the nineteenth century, flourishing in the cultural conditions that produced decadence. Of Botticelli's Judith Ruskin had observed, fastidiously, that she was free of the prurience that marred so many representations of the subject.[3] For Pater, however, what Botticelli's art represented was a marvellous freedom from religious and moral intrusions. Rather it epitomized transience, hesitancy, momentariness: in a word, feeling without reflection. His art is 'undisturbed by any moral ambition . . . [preoccupied] with men and women . . . in their mixed and uncertain condition, always attractive . . . but saddened perpetually by the shadow upon them of the great things from which they shrink. His morality is all sympathy.' This characterization of Botticelli as melancholically 'sympathetic' is so salient to his larger theme that Pater repeats it almost verbatim a little later.[4] By 'sympathy' he intends a susceptible generosity of feeling, emotive, spontaneous and uninterrupted by judgement. In effect, Pater's view of art takes refuge from the exhausting processes of modern thought, its scientisms and nihilism, by substituting a materialist economy of feeling for a moral economy of thought. And he sees this as a return to the Hellenic origins that Botticelli had recaptured in the Renaissance.

Consequently, Pater's brand of antiquarianism leads him to insist that Botticelli's Madonnas are Venuses, deliberate paganizations of the Christian icon – indeed, repudiations of draconian ethics in favour of human sympathy. Pater's humanism, like his account of Botticelli's, is originary, pre-Christian, materialist. The 'freshness, uncertain and diffident promise' that he ascribes to Botticelli's art is uncertainty, feeling without object or origin, indeterminancy, rejecting acting in favour of simply being. For such an anti-active, involuntarist programme, the figure of Judith was too wilful and too busy. Moreover, as a traditional icon of wisdom, judgement, justice – qualities of cerebration and moral decision – she too fully represents the Hebraism which Pater's Hellenism is designed to deconstruct. Thus Pater needs to reinterpret Botticelli's *Judith* and *Justice* as contradicting Hebraism and the Law.

Having pointed out that Botticelli's model for the Madonna was reputed to be a Medici mistress (carnal indeed), he notes that the same model was used for Botticelli's Judith, 'when the great deed [was] over, and the moment of revulsion come'. Judith has been belatedly overwhelmed by human sympathy! That process of reversing signification, Madonna into Venusian sexuality, Judith into melancholy repentance, is all too clear in his next example, where Justice, with the same model's features, is 'sitting on a throne, but with a fixed look of self-hatred which makes the sword in her hand seem that of a suicide.' Pater's interpretation fantasizes that the feminine allegorization of Justice – metonymy for all law – is seen as self-destroying. Social and moral law erases itself. This is also the aestheticized subtext in his interpretation of Judith. She too must repent her own legalistic nature and thus artistically represent an indiscriminate kind of mercy. This underplot of aesthetics slaying Society reaches its climax in Pater's subsequent remark: that the same model is portrayed as Veritas, truth, 'in the allegorical picture of Calumnia, where one may note in passing the suggestiveness of an accident which identifies the image of Truth with the person of Venus.' Disingenuously casual, this 'observation' in fact closes the subtextual narrative of Pater's chapter on Botticelli. For him all these icons are in truth Venus, and Venus is truth, and truth beauty. Judith and the Madonna signify moralistic illusions impressed upon the intellect of Western civilization, whereas Venus as the carnal body signifies the secret truth of instinct. Materialism erases false consciousness, as art erases morality.

In this aesthetics beauty and art anaesthetize pain. The disenchantments of nihilism are translated into images of beautiful deaths. In paintings of mans-layers, the fatal woman brings her beauty to bear upon the scene, as the male victim brings his agony. Between them are distributed the attributes of Beautiful Death. Sensation is rendered extreme by the idea of expiring in it, an agonizing pleasure which is actually highlighted and defined by its being also the end of sensation itself – a terminus which gives it its high-resolution imaging. Consequently, the extremist pains of sadism and masochism are crucial ingredients of the aesthetic recipe.

In Klimt's popular paintings of Judith, typical products of *fin de siècle* Vienna, she is fetishized. In *Judith I*, her face registers an orgasmic joy in symbolic castration of the man. One breast is bare, its tinted flesh reified by the hard gold plating that transmogrifies her clothes and jewels. All the surfaces are textures of a high density, as if of the inanimate kind suggested by her gems. In a dimension where the body is a technology, this almost literally reflects the dominance of biological determinism at the time. This is orgasm as both brilliant and cruel, symbolized as the female body itself. In *Judith II*, the effect of cruelty is inten-sified into a voracious malice, the hands are talons. Both express Decadence's fatalizing of the female, and the paintings' subsequent popularity has in turn rendered them symbolic of Decadence to us.

Because inanition is so central to Decadence, it is not accidental that Decadent paintings of Judith (such as Constant's in 1885), tend to show her after the event, a standing figure, naked or half-naked, either holding the head or with the corpse lying in the background. She is not portrayed at the ener-getic moment of action, but wrapped in the envelope of flagrant cruelty and sexual antagonism. Her stillness, as in Klimt's first picture, is crucial to the Decadent economy of morbidity.

Klimt's *Judith II* is of the same stripe, but in *Judith I* sadism is complicated by the collision between voluptuousness and the resistant, blankly gorgeous surfaces of gold. Her flesh and its decorations share a reified quality, an animate/inanimate uncanniness, replicated in Holofernes' head, which is both accessory and inert flesh. It is as if this detumescence is held in stasis with the orgasmic twitch in her own face. Together, Klimt's paintings suggest two poles of Decadent perversity. The one, cruelty of such ruthlessness and unreflective-ness that it is almost transcendent in its energy. The other, a sado-masochism which finds its intensity in the moment of tension between stasis and ecstasy, in the coming-into-being of pain, in dying as the point of transition between phys-icality and inanition. *Judith I* is a snapshot of the sado-masochistic moment, the finely judged point at which pain becomes ecstasy. Decadent melancholy trans-formed the traditional icon of action and determination to signify the only form of energy accessible to it – cruelty.

Since it has to be abortive, in the Decadent economy of feeling this energy for sadism must be met by a paradoxically enervative response, masochism. Thus a circuit of as it were unproductive sensation is closed. Rather than the Renaissance image of orgasm in her acteme, sex as death, we have here death as sex. Loving death and hating women, Klimt's paintings revolve the Victorians' uncanny Judith into the Decadents' uncanny sex.

Willing Bondage: Sado-Masochism

As we saw, Judith already had a long if tacit history as a sado-masochistic symbol. In Decadent art this became explicit, just as a new term would be derived by the new 'science' or sexology from Leopold Sacher-Masoch's novel, *Venus in Furs* (1870). It remains the classic text of sado-masochism. As for Pater, here Venus and Judith are compounded. Respectively Body and Pain, they merge into one sexual dominatrix.

The novel's epigraph quotes the Book of Judith. And its protagonist Severin rhapsodizes, 'I envied the hero Holofernes because of the regal woman who cut off his head with a sword, and because of his beautiful sanguinary end.'[5] As an antique text, and biblical at that, to Sacher-Masoch's very Catholic imagination Judith's triumph represents the original scene of sado-masochism, sanctifying sexual aberration. (Doubtless the same religiose frisson was at work when a modern Valentine's Day message in *Private Eye* quoted the epigraph, and attributed it to 'VENUS IN FURS/THE VULGATE' – both bibles in their own way.)

Severin's obsessive fantasy is of a woman replicating Venus/Judith, her nakedness swathed in rich furs, and brandishing a whip over her cowering, adoring lover, who aspires to an ecstasy of pain. This central icon is repeatedly represented through paintings – a repetition-compulsion in every sense – with the customary uncanny effect. Severin/Sacher-Masoch has a Pygmalion complex, a need to re-create his lovers in the image of his pre-existent ideal. When he falls in love with a woman named Wanda, he persuades her to live out his fantasy. They draw up a contract in which he formally and willingly becomes her slave. But in time she gladly exchanges her mastery of Severin for her real desire, which is subjugation (hence reverting to Weiningerian type) to a 'beautiful' and 'animal' man. The story ends with a lament that men and women simply can't understand one another, but this is in fact one of Severin/Sacher-Masoch's (for there is little distance between author and protagonist) consoling fantasies, a theory to match his morbid view of sexuality.

Caught up in this characteristically abortive sexual fantasy is a pattern of racial attitudes that, again as in Weininger's theories, treats Jewishness as a 'faultline' that defines the boundary between Anglo-Saxon self and orientalized Other. Severin's most important alter-ego here is a German painter, who can paint the fantasy that Severin cannot quite manage to bring into being. His rival is a brutally exciting Russian, portrayed as dangerously animalistic because he is a Slav. As a Pole, Sacher-Masoch's national positioning between these two powers, which dominated Poland, makes him aspire to what he sees as the Superego of Germanness and fear the Id which is Slavic. It is not only Wanda whom he wishes to materialize as his fantasy, for the other characters are also projections of himself. As his masochistic sexuality is an attempt to achieve satisfaction through fear, so his fear of sexuality becomes his defeat by the Slav.

Whilst Sacher-Masoch is anti-Semitic, nevertheless his alter-ego Severin acquires his ideal painting of Venus through 'a Jew dealing in photographs'. Jews are for him the conduit of the primitive, low racial exemplars of the savage surviving. When he acts out the role of Wanda's servant in public, he has to travel third-class, like 'Jewish peddlers', like indeed the retailer who sold him his sexual fantasy. Feminized by his abject role, Severin is also de-classed and Judaicized: in effect a Romantic Criminal, yet in the Decadent passive mood. Subtextually, he acts out the role of those precious to Jehovah and therefore punished by him, as the old Israelites had often been. In the Book of Judith,

Achior had told Holofernes that he could only win if God wished to punish Israel, and the novel's epigraph is the culmination of the punitive theme: 'But the Almighty Lord hath struck him and hath delivered him into the hands of a woman' (16:7). Thinking of Judith, Severin asks, 'What shall I do so that He will punish me?' Implacable Jehovah of the Old Testament becomes for Severin the sadistic God, and to be abject to Him, the original he, would be to confirm that Severin is very special – a chosen one. As a man, Severin can identify with Judith as a projection of divine phallicism; and he can simultaneously identify with Holofernes as the punished. Thus Judith becomes an image of God's punitive love for him, the uncanny sign of the doubling of his desire in its punishment. That signification is carried through to its most extreme conclusion, as the psychopathology of sadism.

Wanda's real-life counterpart, Mrs Sacher-Masoch, wrote her own *Confessions* (1907) as an antidote to *Venus in Furs*.[6] In this she relates how she came to see herself as a victim, for by coercing her into sleeping with other men by emotional blackmail and her economic dependence, her husband had degraded her. Eventually she concluded that Sacher-Masoch was a pathological liar – the debunking obverse of his attempts to turn life into his fantasy – and thus her narrative unwrites his, step by step. She left him, after a decade. In the meantime, however, she became a feminist of the 1890s kind, the mother-worshippers, and this is the only ideology through which she can manage to challenge Sacher-Masoch's and valorize herself. Repeatedly she insists that she stayed with him only because of her children. Finally, she makes an impassioned plea for recognition of woman as equal, because on her mothering, nurturing presence depends the progress of humanity. Mrs Sacher-Masoch could take her vengeance on Sacher-Masoch's reputation as freethinking progressive artist (one that she herself had formerly credited) only be casting herself in the sacrificial maternal role approved for women who claimed independence. 'It's not for myself' was the only acceptable excuse for the assertion of integrity. It is her desire for that ('the whole soul') which closes her *Confessions*. In real life she had lived out her husband's Venusian fantasies and suffered their consequences; and then, escaping those, she lived out the competing ideology which once again committed her to self-sacrifice. It was simply a matter of substituting 'the race' for 'man' (two terms that patriarchy had always confused in any case), and the job was done. Iconic lenses are not merely media of perception but also hidden persuaders.

Similarly, it was possible to encode the image of Judith as Decadent death-bringer even into a more conventional woman's romantic history, if this were inserted into a Freudian 'family romance' of revenge upon the Father. In August Strindberg's *The Father* (1887), it is the wife who subverts his sanity in a malignant campaign of spite. In *The Dance of Death* (1900) another father is ruined by the alliance of his estranged wife with the daughter who had been the apple of his eye, but who now betrays him or the rival parent in a sex war.[7] The daughter's name is Judith, with intentional reverberations. Her second 'betrayal' of the father is to fall in love: Strindberg's way of ensuring that she has to acknowledge that masculinity, at least, is necessary to her. In this weirdly incoherent play the clearest strand is the Judith/Electra complex – the revolt of the daughter – which nevertheless masculinity can recuperate, if the woman's intended husband acts as Oedipus towards her father.

In the rising science of psychoanalysis, Freud performed a double-handed manœuvre with Judith's icon that was not dissimilar to Sacher-Masoch's religiose irreligion. Although also Austro-Hungarian, Freud was Jewish, and hence his irreverent impulses were Judaically inclined; against the Old Testament, as in his iconoclastic *Moses and Monotheism* (1934–8). The antique and the biblical were to be investigated, debunked and refashioned into icons for the new religion of sexology. Freud used Hebbel's Judith as a 'proof' that female frigidity/hysteria was owing to the 'taboo of virginity', an unconscious trace of the primitive tribal fear of the man's defloration as desecration. The woman is hostile to the man because he deflowers her (even though she desires him). Thus Judith's virgin widowhood in Hebbel's play is for Freud an instance both of the taboo and (when she kills Holofernes) the hostility it generates in woman towards man. For Freud the paradoxical virgin widowhood of Judith, as both technically deflowered by marriage and yet intact, symbolizes woman's hysterical state, in which she resents precisely what she wants, and hence is driven to penis-envy.[8] In this way the apostle of modern sexual psychopathology interestingly seems to repeat the Church Fathers, who had imposed upon Christian culture the view that widows were the next best thing to virgins, were indeed a sort of outgrowth of the virtue of virginity insofar as they were celibate. They were secular monks, since of course women could not be monks in the true and formal sense. *Mutatis mutandis*, Freud attributes women's supposed hysteria to biological destiny, as revealed by primitive rituals and suppressed by civilization. Deploying the new anthropology, he effectively naturalized patristic diktat as taboo and the unconscious, thus bringing it into line with the reigning episteme of biological determinism. Although Freud himself would have hated to think so, he simply ratified the authority of Genesis, where the woman's punishment is to desire her husband and pay for desire by pain, in labour. Mystified within the codes of self-sacrifice, labour is a subtextual image in the 1890s idolatry of sacred motherhood.

Freudian sexology maintained its hegemony even when avant-garde art passed from Decadence into French Surrealism. Despite its often more energetic desire to shock its audience, the fundamental convictions of Surrealist art remained masculinist in a similar way. Devoted to the antique and scientistic, the Surrealist writer Michel Leiris was curator of an anthropological museum in Paris. Anthropology also motivated his transcription of sexuality into an abstract ritual. His psychoautobiography *Manhood*, begun in the 1920s was not published until 1939.[9] It is an astounding record of his fantasy-life, in which the dominatrix Judith is compulsively reproduced and her varied disguises – as the opera heroines Tosca, Carmen and her other analogues, as even his own 'Tant Lise', for him a Judith by nature who personated those analogues on stage – are identified, categorized and labelled as the one fundamental true woman, the Judith of the Apocrypha. She is the goddess who intimidates and tortures Leiris in the only psychic scene in which he is at home. Her sadism he actually interprets as nurturing (like his aunt's love), and if only in onanistic wish-fulfilment, it transforms him into the virile *Matador* of his subtitle in a ritual that is comfortingly predictable. The frontispiece, Cranach's *Judith* and *Lucretia*, merges the former with the passivity of the latter, her detumescent sword comparable to the self-sacrificing knife. Sadism as onanism, feminine nurturing as destruction, form patterns that close the circle of Leiris's self-love. His psychic Judith is the guarantee of his self-esteem: a reassurance that he can love himself, even if perhaps no one else does.

A less timid fascination with woman as instinct is evinced by other Surrealists. Jean Giraudoux's *Judith: Tragédie en trois actes* (1931) intensively psychologizes the heroine, whilst Jean Cocteau's tapestry of Judith in 1950 portrayed fatal woman as tiger-woman, as the point of confluence between human and beast. This, from the director of the film *La Belle et la Bête* (*Beauty and the Beast*), spoke volumes about the savageries concealed within human sophistication. That bestiality meets technology in René Passerson's collage *Judith* (1965). Pure harpy, exultant over the (significantly) gigantic head of Man, Judith's body moves in two directions simultaneously: a Surrealist twist on Judith's duplicity, but also (since physically impossible) registering her inhumanity. Use of photographs for the faces implies the *verité* of inveterate intersexual antagonism in the human species. If in some sense abstract reason and the animal body – man and woman – pull the human being (man!) apart, the torn-up medium of collage and the deliberately contrasting materials deployed here also suggest the uncanny. In this representation of a masculinist psychic scene, in which desire disorders him, woman is an instinctive engine or natural technology of destruction.

Some women Surrealists eventually woke up to the misogyny implicit in such works. Max Ernst's quondam lover, Leonora Carrington gradually moved to a more feminist and politicized stance both in life and in art. In her later work she attempted to recuperate this primitivist reduction of 'woman' by depicting female instinctualism as a form of magical power, tapping hidden forces. Thus her hallucinatory story 'Judith' (1961) recasts the biblical narrative as a brutal tribal myth. The heroine is trapped and violated by patriarchy: 'her great bearded father', self-styled 'the Man . . . my Word is Law'.[10] As Man Judith's father hands over control to her rejected suitor Esrom, who rapes her at his instigation. In effect, these two add up to a collective 'Holofernes' representing social coercions inflicted upon women. Only an unbeatable will can withstand them, which is why this Judith decapitates her father and drives Esrom to suicide. Freed, she may now 'ride . . . the . . . heavens', merged with the horse that symbolizes her own banned desires. She has no fear of flying, that is. The story's Freudian 'family romance' motifs are clear enough, but they are also being violently, even angrily, compelled to metamorphose into a feminine power able to elude and even destroy them.

The original Judith's cool rationalism has become a penetrating intuitive cognition. Clearly Carrington recognized that Judith's is a myth of psychic autonomy, and recast it in modern anthropological terms as one of necessary, ritual sacrifice. Since Carrington's horses usually symbolize imaginative creativity, this story is also about how a woman can become an artist. It is Leiris's sex/art ritual reversed – a counter-myth for Freudian Surrealism.

By the early twentieth century the combined influences of Freud, Weininger and Sacher-Masoch had typed Judith for sexology as aberrant woman: phallic, masculine (that is, denatured), perverted, barren dominatrix. What would become one of the most powerful ideologies of the century, implicated even in the rational fear of neurosis itself, had typed her as a sign of neuroses. Professing to offer a new revelation, psychoanalysis in fact ratified Oedipal patriarchy and labelled Judith's counter-cultural myth deviant. When Freud effected his revolution he kept it nice and canonical, assuming his own place as an Oedipus who had stolen the Father's cultural throne.

Suffragette versus Superman

The fundamental premises of nihilistic determinism necessarily affected perspectives not only on personal relations but also on the public world of history and politics. By contrast to the entropic mood of the arts, though, this public, political world was rendered turbulent by a turn-of-the-century urge to effect change. Whilst in early twentieth-century Britain fear of anarchy would focus itself most neurotically on the Suffragette campaign for women's rights, European radical groups and anarchists had already given the *fin de siècle* a more destructive tincture.[11] The philosophy of history that proved able to supply determinism with an air of bravado was that of Friedrich Nietzsche, whose vision of the Superman supplanted Carlyle's Victorian model of the individual heroes who make history. In the Nietzschean doctrine of eternal recurrence, history is a repetitive cycle of growth and decay: regenerative energy is supplied to humanity only by the rise of a Superman, a tribal Messiah.[12] Whereas Carlyle's heroes were active and dynamic (like the Apocrypha's Judith), Nietzsche's are mystically instinctive, a crudescence of the life-force. The Superman beautifully answered the need to project biological determinism onto history – the hero as universal sex-drive. Of course, the more Carlylean Judith was thoroughly unsuited to this historicism, not least because sex-drive was regarded as a male monopoly. If women were frigid, fatal hysterics, this divide gendered historical decline as the female entropic principle, and historical rise as male tumescence. Underlying turn-of-the-century fictions was the conviction that history was sex on a grand scale.

In Flaubert's *Salammbô* (1862), the decline of the ancient Carthaginian empire becomes a paradigm of historical entropy.[13] Exquisitely decadent, the fabulously wealthy city has become fatally distanced from the instinctive energies that, embodied in the 'savage' form of the black slave Malo, now threaten it with a revolt from below. This insurgence of basic primitive instincts against the city of Civilization is only defeated by the city fathers' deployment of an unconscious, pre-rational version of Judith as Salome. The priestess Salammbo almost accidentally seduces her Holofernes, the besotted Malo, in his tent in the rebel camp, and then absconds with the magical totem of the city which, stolen by Malo, had become the symbol of its doom. Yet, although the frigid, fatal, instinctively destructive female may appear thus to have saved her city without quite intending to, the final destruction of Malo – intentionally copied by Flaubert from the French Judithic execution-rituals of the Renaissance – proves to be hers too. That is, a civilization's denial and corruption of ineradicable instinct renders it impotent. At such a juncture history's sex-drive becomes a death-drive.

Deracinated in the masculinist versions of history, philosophy and anthropology, Judith's myth was faring no better in the feminist philosophy of the Suffragettes. This was ironic, since Judith's claim to public political activity might seem (as it had been for Cristine de Pisan in the Middle Ages) a highly appropriate role-model for demanding the right to vote. But the women's movement was suspicious of the religious underpinnings of patriarchy, and in any case the Pankhursts encouraged an expropriation of the fervour of faith for what amounted to the new religion of women's rights. Thus Emily Davidson was hagiographized as a Suffragette martyr to the 'Faith'. Even though the movement had a logical rationale for their neglect of biblical icons, it is no coincidence that the image of Judith as a proximal Suffragette kept recurring during the years of Suffragette militancy. For their own propaganda constantly reiterated the theme of activism, that no campaign of public persuasion would succeed independently of more coercive tactics directed at the government – iconoclasm and violence represented, indeed, in the myth of Judith and its assault upon the patriarch. 'Deeds, not words!' as Emily Davidson herself had insisted. When, on 'Black Friday', 18 November 1910, the Women's Social and Political Union had besieged the House of Commons, clashing with the police, one of their banners proclaimed that 'Who would be free themselves must strike the blow'. Similarly, Margaret Robinson, who was imprisoned during the

10. *Judith with the Head of Holofernes* by Antiveduto Grammatica.

11. *(right) Judith with the
Head of Holofernes* by
Antiveduto Grammatica.

12. *Judith* by Artemisia
Gentileschi.

13. *(left) Judith* by Jan Sanders van Hemessen.
14. *Judith and her Maidservant with the Head of Holofernes* by Orazio Gentileschi.

17. *Judith and the Boy Hercules* by the Master of the Mansi Magdalen.

facing page

15. *(top) Judith* by Jan Metsys.

16. *Woman at her Toilet* (Judith Beautifying Herself) by unidentified
Netherlandish painter after van Eyck.

20. *Judith with the Head of Holofernes* by Johann Liss.

21. *(right) Judith Holding the Head of Holofernes*, attributed to Giovanni Antonio Pordenone.

22. *Mary Aubrey*, engraving from the series *The Crimes of Mary Aubrey* by J. Caulfield.

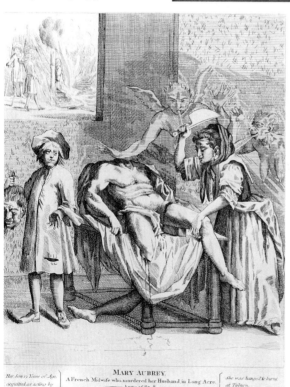

Her Son 13 Years of Age. acquitted as acting by compulsion.

MARY AUBREY.
A French Midwife who murdered her Husband in Long Acre.
——— ANNO 1687-8. ———
Published Jan 1 1795 by J. Caulfield.

She was hanged & burnt at Tyburn.

23. *(left) Saskia as Flora* by Rembrandt.

24. *Heiligenmartyrium* by Jaspar Woensam von Worms.

25. *(right)* 'Westerwald' jug.

26. Cabinet, French, *c.* 1675.

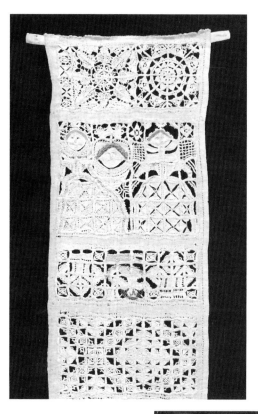

27. *(left)* Whitework sampler (detail).

28. *The Story of Judith of Bethulia*, a detail of a marble pavement in Siena Cathedral by Matteo di Giovanni.

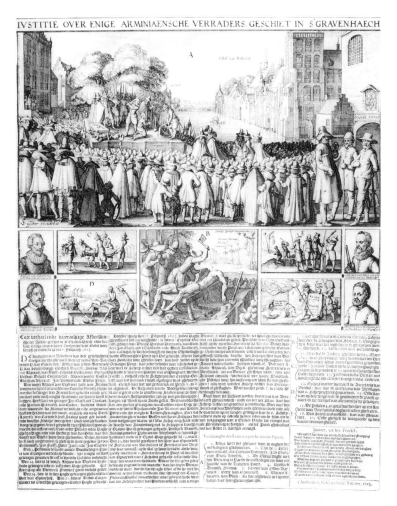

31. *Justitie over enige Arminiaensche verraders* by C.J. Visscher.

32. *(right) Charlotte Corday* by Paul Baudry.

33. Cartoon by Nick Newman, from *Private Eye*, issue 838.

"Oh my God — Judy's cut off Mr Punch's penis!"

34. *(left) Judith* by August Riedel.

35. *Judith of Bethulia*, a still from the film by D.W. Griffiths.

36. *Judith with the head of Holofernes* by Mattia Preti.

window-smashing campaign of 1911, recalled that the attitude was not emotional but pragmatic: 'I just remember that we were there to do it. I'm a practical person . . . If you have the courage of your convictions, you do it.'[14] To do the job, to have the courage of your convictions, to strike the blow yourself, to risk everything for the faith: all phrases that might equally describe the biblical Judith. And that subterranean myth ran through the years of Suffragism.

One of its most effective conduits was, in fact, Meredith's *One of Our Conquerors*, in which as we saw the New Woman's muse was the biblical heroine, explicitly re-embodied as 'Judith' Marsett. Although Meredith was regarded as an ally of the women's movement, more important for the currency of his political fable was his seminal influence upon the generation of intellectuals dominant by its second decade. In 1911 H.G. Wells saw the novel as prophetic of the political disillusionment that made his contemporaries impatient for radical change, for which the time had come at last. Indeed, in the year that Wells's novel was published the national mood was more than restless, for there was a new king, a new government launching a major programme of legislative reform, and Suffragette violence would reach a crisis in the window-smashing of November. Endorsing Meredith's assertion of women's rights, Wells emphasized the issue's urgency: 'Woman insists upon her presence . . . She comes to the politician and demands, Is she a child or a citizen?'[15] As if on cue, another fashionable writer, the now deservedly forgotten poet Lascelles Abercrombie, published his verse-drama of *Judith* in 1912.

Abercrombie's qualifications to author a radical modern interpretation of a religious theme were, in his contemporaries' view, impeccable. The fashionable Georgian poetic movement that he dominated was regarded as the literary equivalent of the radical political mood: iconoclastic, frank, dedicated to revising old myths in ways that reinterpreted them against the grain of old authorities. As D.H. Lawrence contended, the project of Georgian poetry was to hurl down the ancient totems of authority and erect new versions of 'faith' and 'love' adequate to the modern recognition that anthropology and primal drives were the key to humanity. Only by recognizing this, Lawrence and his contemporaries thought, could the sublimated ideals of religion and love be resurrected in their true guise.[16] Therefore Abercrombie favoured religious subjects, doubtless because it seemed daring to apply 'realism' to its apparent opposite, the supernatural. Yet Georgian iconoclasm shared that primitivist ethic that was desperate to recover old authorities in new guises and plundered myth as the record of an 'original' humanity.

It is, in fact, this prevailing primitivist ethic to which we can attribute the burgeoning of biblical drama in the first two decades of the century. Like Georgian poetry, the new biblical drama was part of a somewhat desperate cultural attempt to retrieve traditional values from the wreckage of the old authorities. If, as the contemporary enthusiasm for comparative mythology suggested,

the Old Testament was such a repository of the myths of the collective unconscious, then it was a prime candidate for 'daring' modern reinterpretation. For
this purpose the most hospitable Testamental stories were those of spicy
intrigue, illicit passion and murder. The adultery and homicide of David and
Bathsheba were treated with the appropriate mixture of bombast and eroticism
in Stephen Phillips's *The Sin of David* (1904) and C.W. Wynne's *David and
Bathshua* (1903). Of course, Judith's story was similarly alluring. In America
Thomas Aldrich's play *Judith* (1904) was both immediately successful and later
revived in the cinema by D.W. Griffith, whilst Thomas Sturge Moore's *Judith*
was published in London in 1911. There was an Italian film version in 1906,
and a French one in 1909. That combined Judith-Salome, *Salammbo*, was
filmed in Italy in 1911 and 1914 and in France in 1911. On Judith's alter-ego,
Jael, there were at least seven plays in the twenty years after 1901. It was even
recognized, not long afterwards, that the prolonged fashion for 'female' biblical
drama in some way centred on Judith. Whilst in many ways deferent to contemporary ideals of womanhood, in her choice of subject for an academic thesis
– 'Recent Judith-Drama and its Analogues' – a provincial American student in
the 1920s intuited as much. Listing fifteen plays on Judith alone, R.E. Glaymen
concluded that dramatizations of another six antique heroines were also in fact
versions of 'the Judith type of woman. Similarly she reappears throughout
world history. The Judith type of woman is perennial.'[17] She spoke more accurately than she knew, for the biblical drama of the early twentieth century was,
I suggest, a cultural programme designed to cope with the insurgence of the
'Judith type of woman': as anarchists hurling bombs, out on the streets, as the
Rosa Luxembourgs of radical groups, as Mrs Pankhurst and her riotous
cohorts. This was what conservatives greeted as 'the modern spirit of social
anarchy'.[18] It should be remembered that a number of the most famous radical
women – including Luxembourg and Eleanor Marx – were Jewish, and the
association of political agitation with Jewish intellectuals provided a topical
subtext for Judaic heroines on stage.

   The genre acknowledged the cultural prominence of the New Woman-
Suffragette by female-centred dramas, most obviously of all in their Judiths,
since only she iconized both political demand and the violence required to
achieve it. Yet the heroines of these biblical dramas remain 'womanly', essential-
ized by the concept of primal femininity. The Bathshebas are pulp-fiction
romantic heroines, whilst Judith, not an obvious candidate for the eugenicist
view of womanliness, was refashioned in ways at once awkward and fascinating.
Thomas Aldrich's is a virago constructed to address this epiphenomenon in the
audience's mind, and thus was specifically written for a leading actress of truly
Brunnhildean aspect. But if formidable and successful, his heroine is nevertheless remorseful: because even a virago is also a woman, fundamentally compassionate and tender, biologically programmed. Involuntarily responsive to

Holofernes' 'heathen beauty' – for which read archetypal masculinity – she discovers her emotions: 'O God! have I a heart?'[19] Given the ideology of sublime
motherhood, it is stressed that 'a hand moulded to press a babe against her
breast' commits murder instead, denying her own nature. Indeed, naturalness
symbolized as the universal human sexual instinct runs rampant in the play, for
not only Holofernes but also Achior and the eunuch Bagoas are obsessed by
Judith. Having put herself beyond the pale of natural femininity, however, at
the final curtain she flees from them all, crying 'Let no one born of woman
follow me!' This curiously redundant phraseology of childbirth provides the
closing image because of Aldrich's subtext, which is intended to recuperate the
independent virago for a lesson in woman's true destiny, marriage and motherhood, as her only route to fulfilment. To make Judith, proximal Suffragette,
subserve this moral was to absorb her into the eugenicist vision. This embodied
contradiction, formidable/vulnerable, responded to the cultural bogey of the
emancipated woman precisely by templating her as the originary 'phallic
woman' and then revealing (as it were) her soft underbelly. The tendency to
costume stage Judiths as semi-armoured but with bare navels encoded both
terms in the contradiction, the navel and belly being signs of Woman's reproductive function.

By positing the antique as originary yet remodelling it, these works resecured
gender as a binary opposition anterior to all historical and social developments.
Which was to say that it could not be revised by innovations such as the call for
women's rights; nor could such innovations do other than deny and frustrate
women's own true instincts.

But in this worship of instinct there was also a fear. If humankind were still
essentially savage – as Nietzschean materialism and the Freudian unconscious
proposed – the civilized personality might break down, and the social order
predicated upon it dissolve. Continental anarchism and the British Suffragette
movement both presented such nightmarish possibilities on the political scene.
It is in obliquely addressing and reassuring these fears that Abercrombie's
Judith achieved its *succès d'estime*.

Abercrombie was one of Nietzsche's earliest English admirers.[20] The ancient
form of verse-drama permits him to suggest that his *Judith*'s (for the time)
unusual emphasis on sex and violence springs from the timeless roots of modern
pathologies and politics. The play dramatizes a breakdown; of peace, of government, and of personal identity. On the surface, Judith is a valorized virago: like
the Suffragette Margaret Robinson, she announces that 'I have done what I
must do'.[21] Here, too, Ozias as the city's governor is transformed into her pro-
tector and her unrequited lover, perturbed by her project only because he fears
for her, and suffers torments of jealousy about her time with Holofernes. He is
not wrong, since the Assyrian camp is presented as an orientalized bacchanal of
debauchery, of which the Israelite men are pruriently envious; and when she

returns Judith, previously a serene exemplar of 'Virginity', has been raped. Her political action polluted by her personal revenge on Holofernes, and her body polluted by him too, she is so traumatized that she attempts suicide with his sword. Preventing this metamorphosis into Lucretia, Ozias saves Judith from herself in every sense. He reassures her that purity resides in the mind, not the body; that her action has nevertheless saved the city; and issues an edict that rewrites squalid history: an edict that is, in effect, what will become the 'official version' in the Apocrypha. Having acquired the sword, subordinated the heroine to his own sagacity and dictated the event to posterity, Ozias has acquired her achievement for himself, and of course for the patriarchal government and Testament. Under siege, it is not the old order, but the Suffragette, who has suffered psychic breakdown.

It is a happy ending for everyone except Judith, predicated on psychoanalysing the situation in order to achieve the *soi-disant* brutal realism for which Abercrombie was renowned. This was of course crowd-pleasing, since it was titillating, brought the story up-to-date and flattered the audience's modern assumptions. Rewriting the story as the struggle of human idealism with its well-nigh irresistible primitive urges, Abercrombie's subtext subverts the overt celebration of 'Virginity'. His Judith is a desexualized Suffragette forced by violence to recognize her real constitution as a woman, whereas Ozias is a Superman whose virility has been sublimated.

This is why Holofernes, portrayed as brutish sexuality, never appears in the play. His sexual vigour is in fact a projection of Ozias's and it is in Ozias's jealous, voyeuristic fantasy that we are told what Holofernes must be doing to Ozias's beloved: 'blood so loaden with brute lust of being . . . / with an immense phantasma of desire, / An unsubduable stream of unknown pleasure' subdues Judith. It is not just that antique verse-drama leaves the violent moments offstage; Ozias's indirect narration is a verbal orgasm simultaneous with the event of rape. Thereby Ozias's masculinity expropriates Holofernes's orientalized, savage energy, whilst his place at the head of the civilized city contains this as the history-making virility of the Superman. Strangely, he is the central character. All the energy of Abercrombie's overwrought verse goes into Ozias's unrequited passion for Judith and his Nietzschean idealism. Energized by the primordial drives of sex and ego – 'desire' – Ozias imagines the emergence of the will-to-power, which produces the Superman. Through the flesh and instinct it is possible to reach an ideal selfhood: 'Man hath his nature of the vehement world; / He is a torrent, like the stars and beasts / Flowing to answer the fierce world's desire.' Force of will enables him to 'Deny the mastery' of fate and become a hero, 'man's frail scabbard filled with steel'. The sword – which, incidentally, was obtained by Judith, at some personal cost – is thus as it were ingested by Ozias as his primal energy. In short, heroic power is a masculine principle.

What Old Testament drama offered the audience was access to a primordial state of humankind, the certain ground and Genesis of things. And if 'man and woman created he them', then gender must be a certain ground too, its very primality a source of reassurance as well as provoking the unease that must be reassured. To find a citizen Suffragette in the original, Testamental world, they returned to Judith. One could subdue by rewriting her, and thus totemistically quell those modern women inhabited by her spirit. Ancient authority and progressive modernity colluded in a defensive cultural myth of aboriginal woman.

From Woman to Woolf

In 1919, women in Britain were enfranchised to vote for the first time. A reactive, flourishing cultural industry now battened on 'the battle of sexes'. Bennett's *Our Women* (1920) was typical in that it conceded that women were now regarded quite differently from the way they had been in the bad old days before suffrage, yet reinforced the words of a fashionable psychologist, that 'sex dominated all [Woman's] activities from the cradle to the grave'.[22] Thus Bennett's next projected Judith was the displaced, domesticated version in *Punch and Judy*, for which Hitchcock asked him to prepare a screenplay;[23] and his libretto for Goossen's opera of *Judith* (1929) perpetuated a sexist sexual theme. A stream of sex-war publications appeared after the Great War because it was necessary to persuade women to return to domesticity from the occupations that war work had made accessible to them for the first time, and to discourage the lesbianism into which the lost generation's brides might now be tempted.[24] Finally, and not least, now that they had the vote women had to be persuaded that their intrinsic nature had not changes (and would not therefore vote for change). When there was widespread fear of another war, Judith's métier was not to be war but a repression of it, the homely 'battle of the sexes'.

Thus there was also a rash of interwar publications on biblical women, which attempted to modernize them by the canons of sexology. Thus, for example, Kuyper's *Women of the Old Testament: Fifty Devotional Messages for Women's Groups* (1934), a Dutch evangelical publication which was translated for the American market, is in fact a moral conduct-book for modern women. Ruth is offered as a model of woman's 'quiet, humble service'. Having revived this Victorian domestic angel and, in her mother-in-law Naomi, the eugenic mother-goddess, Kuyper asseverates that women are subordinate to their husbands. The demonic alternative of rebellious womanhood is Jael, who 'reminds us of Judith . . . who drove a sword through Holofernes' throat as he slept.' This implicit disapproval of the biblical murderesses is made explicit when Kuyper condemns, not Jael's role as God's instrument (that would be difficult in a religious textbook), but the means she used, 'foul and reprehensible'. She should have combatted Sisera openly, not as 'an assassin'.[25] Doubtless this open physical combat is recommended because women are now supposed to be equal, independent characters; but because of the disparity in physical strength between the heroines and the generals, God's handiwork would surely have remained undone – and that is Kuyper's preference despite his piety. Equality was a good thing just as long as it remained ineffective.

That women's new freedoms were not to be defeminizing was a message reinforced by images of pulchritude designed to connote both independence and objectification; the 1920s flapper's bobbed hair and short skirt were the sartorial language for this combination. The independent–erotic combination could be extended to the Judith icon, which had always carried both implications. But her iconization of autonomy was now privatized and trivialized as a licence only for hedonism.

At a time when women were being programmatically biologized in terms of erotic licence, Cranach's tendency to produce Judiths for erotic specularity was ripe for revival, just as the Victorian resuscitation of Botticelli had been linked to contemporary tastes in femininity. In 1928, the art magazine *The Connoisseur* published a full-page plate of a Cranach *Judith* from the Metropolitan Museum in New York, with an editorial commenting that she 'here looks but a lightsome heroine'.[26] (It is telling that Leiris's psychobiography, originating in the 1920s, focused on Cranach's Judith and Lucretia.) To revive Cranach's images was to speak to the postwar taste for supposedly autonomous, yet seducible, images of femininity.

Contemporary representations of Judith offered the same pleasurable combination. In the same year appeared M.R. James's limited edition of the apocryphal text, with four fine colour plates. James attributes the decline in popularity of the given name Judith to such associations as the psychopathic Judith in *Old St Paul's* and emphasizes the original's 'associations of war and bloodshed':[27] a concession to the contemporary cultural hostility represented by such writers as Kuyper. But the illustrator's thesis is wholly contrary in spirit. With James's and the text's political and martial heroine the plates juxtapose one who is sexualized and privatized. Each centres on an eroticized moment in the story, but not one portrays the murder itself. Like other artists of the time, the illustrator W. Russell Flint is overtly interested in occasions of specularity rather than in the narrative. The murder is merely a background datum, an inflection of eroticism for the plates. In the first, Judith's bathing (a rare scene in artistic tradition) is revived for an Art Deco version of orientalism, as she is pampered by an Indian female servant. Imitating such pairings in Victorian orientalist bathing scenes, it also offers a similar hint of lesbianism. Showing Judith returning to Bethulia with her maid, in a reversed version of Botticelli's composition, the fourth plate picks up that hint and implies a conspiratorial feminine triumph over the male. The absence of Holofernes from all four plates – *Hamlet* without the prince, as it were – underscores this autoerotic

feminine mood. Yet these displays of the female body are nevertheless offered
to the specular gaze of a *male* spectator. Thus in the second plate, Judith appears
before Holofernes, whose position as an observer is occupied by the spectator.
She herself is presented in willowy 1920s guise as a dancing harem-girl. In the
third plate Holofernes' absence is drawn to our attention when Judith reaches
for the sword, for to do this she draws the bed-curtain, concealing his body from
us, but revealing her own naked back: and with it the deduction that intercourse
has occurred. (Here the artistic tradition of early modern Judiths, which
encoded in her turned back both duplicity and promiscuity, is revived for a time
when laxer mores made the image less irreverent – and thus actually less
provocative. There is something pallid about Flint's eroticism.) All four plates
are designed either to position the spectator within Holofernes' appreciative
gaze, or to suggest voyeuristic access to autoerotic and lesbian privacy. This is
women's independence rendered conducive to masculine pleasure. The lesbian
threat is not condemned but, more subtly, absorbed into its opposite.

The most lurid version of Judith's role in the sex-war appeared in the *grand
guignol* of the Hungarian composer Béla Bartók's celebrated opera *Bluebeard's
Castle* (first performed in 1918). Here the long-feared figure of Judith as
Poisonous Wife was superseded by the Serial Killer Spouse, a paradigm of
resurgent masculinity. Bluebeard has murdered three wives before marrying a
romantic, truth-seeking Judith who insists on knowing too much. For this challenge to Bluebeard's right to unquestioned domestic dominance she joins her
precursors as another skeleton in his closet. Inquisitive wives, or indeed those
seeking real intimacy in marriage, might well have taken warning from this
Bluebeard's ukase, that Judith must love him – literally – unquestioningly. A
new psychodrama retrieved old sexual politics. Could this have been in the
millionaire J.C. Drewe's mind when in the 1920s he built another throwback,
the spanking new, but deliberately archaic, Castle Drogo, and furnished the bil-
liard-room – that male space – with a wall-size Renaissance Flemish tapestry of
Judith and Holofernes? This was at once a titillating and a respectable artwork,
and one way of reminding chaps to keep the ladies in their places.

These were progressive steps in the defacement of the Suffragette/Judith's
access to politics too. For decades, only the Swiss composer Arthur Honegger's
Judith would focus on her political value. Indeed, a transition from the political
to the personal realms is suggested by Flint's first plate. For this might be a
daughter of the Raj, preparing to seduce a hostile Maharajah on the frontier of
the British Empire; the kind of premise so popular in interwar Hollywood films.
Judith was being moved sideways into exotic romance.

At the same time, the displaced Judith of the 'battle of sexes' received her
most fashionably sophisticated personation in Noel Coward's hit comedy, *Hay
Fever* (1925). Its central character, the celebrated actress Judith Bliss, is a fascinating monster who enjoys striking melodramatic attitudes, vamping every man

she meets, provoking artificial domestic crises of sexual intrigue and sparring with her long-suffering husband, David. This biblically named pairing is one of Coward's subtler jokes and reflects his traditionally, if covertly, homosexual attraction to conflating the two icons. Similarly, the domestic furore that Judith provokes translates the Freudian 'family romance' into brittle comedy. Spinning off the original's duplicity is this Judith's talent for histrionics. An actress celebrated for tragedy who lives in a comedy, she personifies both the superficial likeness and the distance between a legendary heroine (such as her original) and a *grande dame* celebrity. Here be Judiths, but no one comes to any harm.

Another naturalized English Judith had a more lasting impact. Shortly after M.R. James mourned the given name's desuetude, it revived to become one of the more popular names for girls in the mid-century. Anecdotal evidence suggests that the initial trigger for this amongst English-speakers was the best-selling novel by Hugh Walpole, *Judith Paris* (1931), for women of the appropriate age often cite their parents' enthusiasm for the novel as the explanation for their names. Walpole's heroine is not biblical, but her formidability and determination suggest why he chose to name her thus: not least because many of the characters in the *Herries Chronicle* series of novels, in which she is the dominating figure, have biblical names. And as in the case of the apocryphal heroine, Walpole did link the woman to the nation, explicitly announcing that the family chronicle is really one of 'England' itself, and its heroine a patriotic exemplification of native English virtues[28] – a reverberation of the Victorians' Judith as Anglo-Saxony. Yet this motif does not really repoliticize Judith's name. The *Herries Chronicle*'s nostalgic intention, its containment of the heroine within a romantic family saga, and its placement of her as matriarch/romantic heroine combine to produce a privatized Judith very palatable to postwar gender mythology.

Further romanticization and domestication of the public heroine are neatly implemented in the plot of Puccini's popular opera, *Tosca* (1926), which Leiris had recognized as Judithic. Although Puccini is influenced here by the massive iconic political value of Judith's story in Italy, the opera's politics are subservient to its melodrama. In fact, *Tosca* entirely romanticized the Judith plot: the passionate, apolitical, tempestuous heroine stabs the lecherous tyrant Scarpia, not to save Italy but to save her love, Cavaradossi, who is the active patriot. No wonder this romantic angle eclipsed the musical adaptations by Goossens and Honegger, which atypically recalled her political value. *Tosca*'s plot invoked politics only in order to intensify the portrait of tragic passion.

The trend of postwar gender attitudes to retract women's emancipation did not escape Virginia Woolf, who satirized the pompous authors of tracts on Woman in her feminist classic *A Room of One's Own* (1929). One of their favourite strategies in their depreciation of women's intellectual abilities was to stress that female artistic achievements had been rare. Against this Woolf argued that women's lack of education and independence, whether political, economic or domestic, had precluded the 'room of one's own' – that is, the autonomy – necessary to artistic production. Now such opportunities were accessible to women who had the will to seize them, and they might take as their icon an imaginary 'Shakespeare's sister' of equally splendid talents – Judith Shakespeare. Woolf's feminist tract was written in 1928: possibly she had seen the Cranach in *The Connoisseur*, or James's reissue of the Book of Judith. Certainly Shakespeare's daughter was named Judith, and (as we have seen) for significant reasons. Woolf's choice of the name recalled, surely, the feminist icon who was progenitor of these christenings, and contained an implicit riposte to the masculinist Judith portrayed by her literary antagonist, Arnold Bennett. In rewriting his version she was implementing the radical women's writing that she was recommending. Woolf's Judith Shakespeare reunited the personal and the political in Judith's icon of autonomy and urged women to possess the same audacity. It was a benign instruction to 'seize the day'.

You're in the Army Now

If Woolf was reminding women that they must have the will to make emancipation count, the psychology of contemporary masculinism and the reigning episteme of psychoanalysis were fighting an aggressive rearguard action. It was a particularly tortuous one, especially in Nazi Germany, where Judith's culturally central role had been established by Hebbel's and Nestroy's dramas, and her role in psychoanalysis was assured by Weininger's and Freud's responses to these inviting role-plays in gender. As the Second World War approached, Judith's icon became a revealing symptom of militarist male hysteria.

As we saw, Freud was himself engaged in Oedipally eliminating the 'elders of his tribe', the patriarchs of Judaism. In making the Oedipus Complex the ruling paradigm of his system of thought, Freud needed to erase the competing revolt of the Daughter. If Moses had to go, so did Judith. Hence Freud's neglect of the Apocrypha's counter-cultural myth in favour of interpreting Hebbel's version. It was not only that his German-speaking readers knew the play intimately, but that Hebbel's Holofernes was heroized as an Oedipal Romantic and his Judith a hysteric. As for the Judith of the Surrealists and the Great War iconoclasts, this was an image that impinged *because* they needed to repress it, to conjure it in order ritually to defeat it. (Carrington's 'ritual' narrative is the obverse of this process.) Freud's strategies for eliding, reimagining and marginalizing the Judaic Woman par excellence are as complex as the difficulties he faced in doing so. He did not wish to discredit patriarchy, rather his Oedipus Complex endorsed the system as an involuntary and universal psychic necessity. As I have suggested, it is this closed system of power that

Judith's daughter-myth refuses. After the Great War his readers thought that Freud had decisively altered human beings' cognition, of themselves and their civilization. And so he had, but his conferment of reground mythic lenses actually enhanced the lineaments of masculinity as a cultural norm. In the Freudian universe women were not just the 'second sex' but defective men. Therefore it followed for him that, as reduced by Hebbel, Judith's was a defective Oedipus myth.

After the Great War, however, the defeat of a central masculine institution – the German army – seemed to require his explanation; and that once again required that masculine identity be re-secured by the elimination of the Daughter who had destroyed an army. So important had the army been to Austro-German society, however, that now Freud's expulsion of the Judithic threat had to be more ingenious than in his first contest with her. *Group Psychology and the Analysis of the Ego* (1921) claimed to discover the root sexual motives of sublimated behaviour. In this, Freud is attempting to account for the way in which collectivities are able to counteract the basic human instincts for self-preservation and short-term gratification. Loyalty to a general and neglect of personal risk in the service of the group were, he argued, phenomena rooted in homosocial and homoerotic love for the central male, fixations attributed to his charisma. Whenever such a relationship breaks down, for instance if the leader is killed, the group inevitably dissolves because its love-object has disappeared. As a 'proof' of this Freud cites the occasion in Nestroy's *Judith* when, hearing that Holofernes is dead, the Assyrians scatter in confusion.[29]

Writing for a Germanic audience, Freud does not bother to explain Nestroy's plot because it is well-known to them. But the peculiarity of Nestroy's version of Judith is vital to Freud's illustration, and hence anyone unfamiliar with that play will find Freud's point difficult to grasp. It is that although Holofernes is not dead, he might as well be, because his men believe that he is: their group morale is destroyed because the love-object that is its centre has been removed. Ironically, it is seeing the (fake) head that convinces them of this: the image of the authority-figure itself dissolves his power. Freud believed that group-bonding is not attached to the authority-figure as intrinsic being, but rather as authority's icon. This was proved by the magical operation of authority even in the absence of the authority-figure. (We may compare the Renaissance king's absence from the scene of power, the scaffold, an absence that rendered potency as magical.) Whilst this suggests that authority is a figment of the collective mind – an idea in which Freud is consciously irreverent – it also mystifies the idea of authority. That mystification is the more pronounced because Freud compares the leader as love-object to Christ (interestingly for Freud's Oedipal fixation, Christ of course is, to coin a phrase, the Son incarnate). In other words, whether Holofernes lives or dies is of no consequence, cannot compromise the power that is patriarchy. Freud's psychologization of Nestroy's drama subtextually denies that Judith's icon contests patriarchy, because her victim is not commensurate with it.

In fact, Freud's own use of Judith's story is as ambivalent as the fake head of Holofernes. His allusion is averted from the heroine to the homosocial group psychology of the Assyrian army. So determined is this averting of the heroine's icon that Freud draws on a doubly displaced derivative, Nestroy's travesty of Hebbel's play: an interpretation of an interpretation, successive layers intervening between the counter-cultural myth and the patriarchal institutions that he is re-masculinizing as necessarily homosocial. The moral is that, had Germany sustained instinctive masculinity, the army's moral would have prevented defeat. Nestroy's Judith is a male impersonator, whose trick exposes the homoerotics of an army culture as the basis of its military efficacy. In Nestroy it is not a woman who defeats the army, but a male who encodes Judith's 'masculine' character as understood by Freud in his 'Taboo of Virginity'. Thus employment of Nestroy's version indicates how homoeroticism can be subverted, 'proving' Freud's point about sublimated illusions. But at the same time it satisfies Freud himself, who can thus portray the subverter as male too. A woman (we may assume) could not achieve this disruptive effect upon the basic dynamics of culture.

Freud attributes this power to himself. As male impersonator/Judaic infiltrator, Nestroy's 'Judith' is used here as an exegesis for the collapse of the Austro-Hungarian Empire, 'Holofernes'; and Freud's own experience of anti-Semitism in its institutions contributes an element of revenge-fantasy to his analysis of their ruin. Yet even in Freud's allusion it is not possible to evacuate the original Judith. Freud's own Jewish revenge upon Austrian institutions is actually reliant (as Nestroy's was) on Judith's significance as 'the Jewess'. Thus it is possible to interpret Freud's own interpretation in a manner that slips his bonds.

In explicitly eroticizing the army, *Group Psychology* is in fact an attempt to codify the heightened sexuality that is fundamental to wartime consciousness. Memoirs of the Great War, as well as poems and novels, repeatedly displayed homoerotic responses to comrades, corpses, superiors, subordinates and antagonists, which reveal narcissistic identification and sublimated sadomasochism.[30] Because Freud spoke so aptly to wartime paranoia and postwar disenchantment, his time for lionization had come. His twentieth-century reputation is in fact a reflex of the war.

Simultaneously with Freudianism's assault on the Daughter Judith, the proto-Nazi remnants of the old German military cadre were also suppressing Judith's liberating political significance. In the light of Nazi anti-Semitism, this synchronicity with Freudianism is ironic indeed. If Freud either disguised her as a man or made her invisible behind prioritized males, the forerunners of Nazism demonized her as the enemy, socialism. As in Freudianism, that projection was Judith repressed, present/absent.

The Freikorps's masculinist fantasies were crucial to the bonding mechanisms and self-affirming strategies that formed the ideology of fascism. From its members' memoirs, diaries and novels it is possible to reconstruct the psychosexual narrative of Nazism as a refinement of Prussian ideology, which produced a fanatical desire to harden the boundaries of the self. This overreaction to profound fears focused most obsessively on the idea of gender-boundaries, upon definition of masculine invulnerability confronting female processes of ingestion, dissolution and the interpenetration of bodies. A psychological if not necessarily physical frigidity was the Freikorps's ultimate line of defence against all the forces that their paranoia fed upon, from women to race to communism. In a sense, for them any intersexual relation was miscegenation, a confounding of distinctions that they required to be absolute. One of the consequent reaction-formations was their risible (but vicious) attitude to Bolshevik women. These female soldiers were all their fears incarnate, and in their literature the multivalent threat posed by 'gunwomen' is repeatedly evoked and mastered. Fantasies of rape, torture, killing and dismemberment enact their terrors as revenges upon the Bolshevik female's body. In her most terrifying aspect, the enemy riflewoman is the woman with a penis.[31]

As iconographic expression of this fear is the fifth-columnist woman iconized by Hebraic images. A 'reversion' to the Old Testament allows misogyny, fear of the 'savage' Slav and orientalism to flow into the same channel of hatred. This iconography is not discussed by the Freikorps's psychohistorian Klaus Thareleit, but one of his examples of their fictions is nevertheless rather striking. In Friedrich Ekkehard's *Storm Generation* (1941), an account of streetfighting in Berlin in 1919, a woman shouting from a window becomes harbinger of an ambush, the sign of impending death: 'Her fear makes her stunning. She seems strangely familiar . . . Images return to him: the old woodcuts in the . . . family Bible . . . They look like this, those Old Testament women. Ruth, Esther . . . Salome . . . he can see . . . dark and inexorable fate.'[32] Woman here is the very sign of fear, as in Freikorps imagining generally. An Old Testament origin, which is also its origin in his race-memory, signifies that they are originary, fateful and primitive. Moreover, as a repository of family records – his own birth would have been recorded in it – the 'family Bible' also signifies his own identity, what is under threat. This is the proto-Nazi equivalent of the Victorian uncanny Judith. Searching for a way of codifying his fear, he reverts to images too familiar to be understood except in childlike fashion.

The striking thing about this passage is the way it jumbles the images it retrieves from memory. There is nothing threatening about Ruth, unless a married woman holds terror: perhaps this is a significant misremembering of her story, for Freikorps's men did manifest the reaction-formation of simultaneously fearing and depreciating their wives. Esther is more explicable: although not personally aggressive, through her husband she became a Jewish heroine. Perhaps both women are subtextually marital opponents as well as Jewesses, anti-Semitism reinforcing misogyny. But neither of these biblical heroines lured her man to his destruction, which is the fear envisioned here. Almost as inappropriate is the next image, of Salome, since although a fatal woman she is not 'Old Testament'. Perhaps he is unconsciously repressing her location in the gospels because he is at this very moment relying upon a distinction of Christian from Judaic. A further repression is suggested when he sees the woman again, 'Salome, Ruth, Esther . . . above him. Tight, tucked-in-skirt . . . right hand brandishing a pistol. The woman who enticed them.' For this phallic gunwoman none of the three icons is apt, for none used a weapon. The image of 'The Jewess' that he really needs for his mental refuge in atavistic myth is the murderous Judith-Jael, who destroyed the Teutonic general in Hebbel. After all, even if his knowledge of the Bible were hazy, Hebbel's Judith was famous amongst German-speakers. He represses her name, if not her image, because she would blur the vital boundary between masculine/efficient and feminine/disorderly, upon which his militaristic *mentalité* depends. An antidote against his fear of ambush requires both the swelling of hatred and repression of a sense of true menace.

Looking back on the Great War in 1923, and influenced by the Germanic mysticism of Nietzsche, D.H. Lawrence asserted that 'woman' must be 'held, by man, safe within the bounds of belief' or 'she becomes inevitably a destructive force'. He saw the sexual war as the universal one, transcending the territorial boundaries between Germany and the Anglo-American side.[33] Significantly, it is in the same work that Lawrence describes James Fenimore Cooper's Judith Hutter as racial and sexual Other of American Puritanism, although he does not recognize the consanguinity between her and the woman whom he and the Freikorps wished to imprison within the boundaries of atavistic belief. Despite the fact that they would soon be at war again, both sides used the same mythic lenses because they still had a common cultural mythology.

Within that mythology Judith occupied a peculiarly problematic position. In this respect we are contemplating a late outgrowth of the nineteenth-century ethnic mythology of Anglo-Saxony, in which as we saw Judith's positioning blurred the boundaries that this ideology was constructing. The place of the Bible in Nazi ideology was itself problematic. They were willing to exploit the charge that Jews crucified Christ, but much of Christianity was anathema to them. After all, the Bible contained Judaic as well as Christian books – and this was supposed to be the religion of peace, not warmongers. Some Christian pastors died in the camps because of their resistance to Nazism. In fact, the secularizing character of Nazism was fundamental to it. It chose Nietzschean superracialism in preference to the Christian god because, as a contemporary observed of fascism, 'The threat to religion, inherent in the totalitarian state, comes not only from the dictator's unwillingness to brook a rival power within their realm, but in the tendency to turn the dictator himself into a kind of tribal god.'[34] Essentially this rivalry for 'tribal' power parallels the situation in the Book of Judith, in which the dictator Nebuchadnezzar wishes to eradicate worship of gods other than himself.

For fascism's anti-religion Judith herself became an obstacle. For many years Hebbel's plays had been favourites of German audiences: under the Weimar Republic they received almost six thousand performances between the autumn of 1918 and the beginning of 1933. The Nazis also admired Hebbel, regarding him as the bard of Nordic race-memory, and his political ideas provided convenient propaganda for their own worship of the Reich. However, his *Judith* posed problems: a Jewish heroine, with a strong role also in Christian tradition, which Nazis regarded as largely a displaced version of Judaism, and in any case morally effete. Thus the influential critic Adolf Bartels, in *Hebbel und die Juden*, set to work to prove that actually Hebbel's Judith is really Germanic in character – more, a model of the true stoic Nordic spirit. In 1939, Franz Bielfeldt went further, claiming that both Judith and Holofernes were types of the Germanic Superman! On the other hand, Hebbel's play also presented the central conflict of German with Jew, according to Bielfeldt, because Judith was a double representation, German-stoic and Jewish-perfidious.[35]

This is perhaps the most ironic and even ludicrous version of Judith's Janus-face, a remarkable instance of her intractability for those who attempted to maintain her Teutonic nationalist iconography whilst repudiating her ethnicity. For this was to attempt to split an ethnic value from an ethnic value within a single figure, an impossible task when ethnicity itself was the object of this 'purifying' effort. For us in hindsight, Judith's positive/negative contradiction for Nazi mythology can signify Nazism's malignant irrationality. The mania of mass murder was foreshadowed in the irrationality of this sign. As I have suggested, Judith signified what they feared, what they hated and what they wanted. In effect, she was a counter-culture myth to Nazism, yoked by violence to its machine. If she was the assassin in God's hand, she could not be that of the tribal god Hitler, which was precisely why such earnest effort was expended on wresting her from Judaeo-Christian tradition.

On the other side the concept of Anglo-Saxony was also resurrected, not in its Nietzschean guise, but as the Judith of Anglo-Saxon 'Liberty'. In an edition of Ælfric's homily on Judith, published in 1940, the editor S. Harvey Gem used a quotation from the Anglo-Saxon abbot on Judith as his epigraph. Encouraging American sympathy, it was intended to symbolize Allied resistance to the Führer's onward march. The heroine had returned from her repression as the soldier's antagonistic Other to assume once again her epic mantle as Just War. At this time began her long and gradual recovery from the repressions of the early twentieth century, until in the 1980s and 1990s she would again become established as a recurrent, ubiquitous, profoundly significant cultural icon. (Thus in another edition of the Anglo-Saxon poem on Judith published in 1992, the American translator would allude to the Gulf War as Gem had alluded to the world war.)[36]

The new cultural authorities of psychology, sexology and eugenics had repressed Judith's myth in order to reconstruct and reinforce the gender-boundaries effaced by war; and where militarism continued its course – in the Freikorps's frontier war – the same pathologies persisted independent of psychiatric dogma. Only after the outbreak of the Second World War did the politics of Judith's icon re-emerge from behind this sexualized smokescreen, because only then did Anglo-American culture begin to discern that the assumptions it shared with Nazi Germany – especially ethnic eugenicism – were ultimately dangerous and evil when myth became Final Solution. One can say of Judith's counter-cultural myth that it proved its worth in its obduracy to Nazification.

11

Judith's List
Identity and the Final Solution

As eponymously 'The Jewess' and a paragon of Judaic piety, invoking for her heroic act an immutable faith in God's special care for his chosen people, the original Judith's significance was first and foremost as a personification of her nation. When his captain Achior warned Holofernes that Israel was guarded by a powerful god, his colleagues scoffed that 'we will not be afraid of . . . the children of Israel: for, lo, it is a people that have no strength nor power for a strong battle' (5:23). In the course of Hitler's Final Solution, similarly, the Jews were cast as quiescent victims of their own eradication. What followed from this, for postwar Zionists, was the conviction that Jewish survival could only be safeguarded by placing the new state of Israel on a permanent war footing. Israeli militarism, the ruthlessness of the secret service, Mossad, and the government's commitment to swift revenges upon terrorism were products of a determination to survive against all odds, and of a national self-image that regarded the fledgling state as a David defying the Goliath, or a Judith defying the Holofernes, of the Arab world. Judith's modern Zionist image is an embodiment of this spirit of 'Never Again'. More generally, through her myth, the Holocaust, its aftermath and its universal meaning have been explored in ways that probe the most disturbing aspects of human psychology. If, as I have suggested, Judith's myth has often been a focus of ideas about human identity, it is in the modern experience of Jews, for whom she can most comprehensively signify personal, ethnic and religious identities, that the issues of human freedom that are implicit in her myth are most dramatically enacted.

Zionism

Judith's modern icon is profoundly implicated in the trauma to Western liberalism dealt by the Holocaust and the Arab–Israeli conflict. Horror at the Holocaust's revelation of genocidal anti-Semitism and liberal sympathies with the Jews' desire for a homeland have had to contend with an equally strong unease about Israeli militarism and the 'hawks'[1] anti-Arab vehemence. At the very point where sympathy meets unease, Judith's icon is positioned, for the moral questions raised by Judith's myth could both signify and question militant Zionism. Her ruthlessness, her transcendence of human laws justified by her people's chosen status, could iconize the survivalist philosophy that drove Israeli politics, especially in the 1960s and 1970s, and the Machiavellian covert activity of Mossad. Just as Renaissance Judiths had been implicated in the propelling ideologies of war, civil unrest and assassination, so modern Judiths iconize those of 'theatres of conflict' and contemporary terrorism.

The moral problematics and anxieties of international politics in the late twentieth century are exposed by the ways in which her icon has been used since the Second World War. And as cultural myth has altered and contorted under the pressure of international events, her *mythos* has been symptomatic of the ways in which political and gender myths have colluded, and collided, in our attempts to make sense of the world we inhabit. We are often told, and we often think, that the world changed out of recognition in the second half of the twentieth century. But the behaviour of Judith's icon in Western culture demonstrates that the phenomena that we strive to understand and to judge are, in fact, the same fundamental issues that occupied our predecessors, in fresh and to us still puzzling guises. Understanding Judith's role in these phenomena is one way of beginning to understand how far the power of cultural myths over our minds is shaping our own perceptions of contemporary problems. Her icon provides a vehicle through which we can explore and, at another level, distance ourselves from the myths that stand between us and our experience – obscuring it even from ourselves.

Just as in the Counter-Reformation the Jesuits had produced Judith ballets for topical reasons, so in modern Israel and America she and Jael have inspired modern ballets, such as the Batsheva Dance Company's *Tongues of Fire* and Martha Graham's *Judith* ballet, produced in collaboration with Israelis in 1962. Those produced in Israel have signified the Israeli state's posture, within its encirclement by Arab states, of permanent alertness to incursion and of recurrent military aggression. Since the stories of Judith and Jael concern invasion of the Jewish lands, they also imply the self-perception of modern Israel that it is aggressive only in the cause of self-preservation. Unlike some earlier representations of Jael in this century, in Israeli imagery her so-called 'deceitfulness' and bad form were reconstituted in their Old Testament image by an official policy of counter-terrorism by stealth. The Machiavellianism of a Judith-Jael chimes with that of Mossad and is, as in Mossad's operating criteria, entirely bent to what is seen as the higher good of national survival.

Postwar Zionism early turned to Judith's story for a mythic prototype. In 1946, two years before the formal institution of Israel, a limited edition of the apocryphal text, *Judith, the Widow of Bethulia*, was published in London as a showcase for illustrations by Philip Ziegler. Seizing upon such pretexts as Judith's toilette and her allusion in prayer to the rape of the Israelite woman, its drawings are blatantly pornographic. Just as disturbingly, their depictions of Holofernes, his lustful sentries and the 'rape' of Israel all suggest grotesque orientalist stereotypes of the Arab. It is hard to avoid the impression that this is a product not only of the smart London art world but, less genteelly, of coarse racist propaganda.

Before the war, in the Hollywood Western *The Texas Ranger* its heroine 'Judith Alvarez' had mythologized the USA as the ethnic 'melting pot'. After the war, Hollywood cinema revived biblical epic partly as a medium for celebrating and sanctifying Israel's role as the melting pot of diaspora Jews. Cinematic images of Jewish refugees and emigrants travelling to another 'promised land' would replicate Old Testament narratives in modern dress, most notably in *Exodus* (1960). Cinema offered itself as the readiest and most globally influential vehicle to generate pro-Zionist feeling. One of the animating motives in the production of filmed biblical epics was the powerful Jewish presence in Hollywood. By the war, the Holocaust and the establishment of the state of Israel Jewish studio moguls and film-makers were motivated to assume a more committed attitude to Zionist themes.[2] Hollywood exerted itself to explain Jewish experience and to support the alliance between the USA and Israel.

That one of these cinematic treatments should be of the story of Judith was natural enough, in the context of a reasserted ethnicity and its identification with a religion, and *Judith* (dir. Daniel Mann, 1965), although a mediocre film, was a complex reflection of her problematic role in modern Zionism. Amongst other things, Judith's story was one of a decisive battle in which the Israelites defended both homeland and Judaism. Whereas Griffith's 1913 film had interpreted Judith's Israel as allegorical of America, the 1965 *Judith* revived its specificity to Jewish identity. By modernizing the story (which many viewers do not recognize in the film), this version returns to its nationalist context and the theme of persecution.

This Judith (Sophia Loren) is an Austrian refugee smuggled into British Palestine at the end of the war. As such she represents the return from the Jews' long diaspora, scattered across the world. Because this is the film's theme – remaking the nation against the odds – this Judith is not in fact a figure for resistance: on the contrary, she is made an instance of the process of assimilation to nationhood, for Israel is resistant simply in the nature of becoming itself. The propaganda point is precisely this, a justification of all political/military action espoused by the new state.

At the extremist end of Zionist ideology, the central assumption is that a chosen people has licence to do *anything* because of its special status. Judith's icon can signify this precisely because such a conviction underlies her assassination of the enemy. Ironically, however, this film is so anxious to portray the Israeli guerrillas in British Palestine positively, that it becomes a story of 'chosen ruthlessness' obstructed and prevented. The ideology is presented in the form of a Judith, but repudiated by representatives of the new state, the guerrillas who become its army and intelligence service. A bitter refugee from the European camps, driven by an obsession to assassinate her Nazi husband – who has escaped to Syria – Judith is actually prevented from achieving her aim by the wise guerrilla Aaron, who believes that revenge for the past must be abjured in favour of defending the Zionist state. The Nazi nevertheless dies: now advising the Arabs on military tactics against Israel, he is kidnapped by the guerrillas and killed by Syrian bombs during a raid on a border kibbutz. This poetic justice substitutes for Judith's intended homicide.

In this way the film attempts to have its cake and eat it, by at once presenting a justification for Israeli action and refusing to accommodate its more problematic aspects to the portrait of official policy. Its Judith personified the mindset of aggression and revenge, whilst its guerrillas and kibbutzim represent the forging of a new national identity. Therefore this Judith fails in her vengeance, whilst they educate her into the new ideas requisite to building the state. This is a way of invoking a bitterly fanatical version of Zionism in Judith, whilst representing the state of Israel as more pragmatic and less bloodthirsty than that might suggest. Thus the kibbutz becomes a vision of communal and national values, enshrined in a Zionist pastoral, agricultural work alternating with the courageous repulsion of Arab attacks. Not surprisingly, the way in which the plot therefore jettisons Judith's successful homicide robs it of the necessary climax and exposes its ideological contradictions.

The trauma of the Holocaust, which precipitated the foundation of Israel and motivated the determination that Jews would never again be victims, provides the film's sole emotive power. (Some war criminals did escape through Arab routes, as for instance Adolf Eichmann, who had been executed in 1962. And he had been betrayed by Mossad by his discarded mistress. Both facts underlie this film.) Rightly this modern mythification of the state begins with the refugees' experience, source of the Zionist ideal which the film attempts to represent in terms culturally familiar. With the nightmare of the Holocaust in Europe is juxtaposed an Israel envisioned in the rural/paradisial image that to Western consciousness most readily signifies innocence and utopia. The refugees' sufferings are reflected in Judith/Loren's previous life, as an inmate of Dachau, and her bitterness becomes the initial stage in the film's *Bildungsroman*: the transformation of an alienated European into an Israeli, redeemed by Zionism. To this end Judith is made a very unsympathetic character, self-absorbed, manipulative and immoral, a monster created by persecution. The military epic of the Book of Judith is reinterpreted as a pastoral romance, and this ironic tone wholly de-energizes the film's representation of a frontier war on the kibbutzes. But if in this film Judith's icon is recuperated from its own aggression, it cannot at the same time effectively justify militarism.

The reason why the film shies away from its own rationale for using Judith's icon is in part a matter of sexual politics. This Judith is a harpy whose revenge motive is exclusively personal, whereas Aaron (his priestly forename is intentionally significant here) must tutor her in political idealism. From his point of view, the modern Holofernes is not this maverick Nazi but the Arab forces to which he has attached himself. Thus the plot splits the theme of the Book of Judith from the executive agency of its heroine; and feminine aggression, it is implied, lacks the cool rationalism of the Israeli underground. In this respect the film is true both to the militarism and to the masculinism of the Israeli resistance, for its own women guerrillas complained bitterly of the way in which their role in the struggle was omitted or downplayed in later accounts, and of the misogyny of their comrades.[3]

In the 1960s, the popular image of the Israeli woman soldier was far from the reality. Such famed soldiers as Yael (Jael) Dayan might have been aptly named for the militant Old Testament heroines, but the Israeli army did not in fact abandon the traditional tenet that women should be non-combatants. They were confined to back-up and training roles, the Israeli army's attitudes combining Judaic convictions about women's roles with the masculinism endemic to any military institution. Thus, apart from her foiled attempt at homicide, Loren's Judith is not required to do much more than pose fetchingly in khaki shorts, her habitual pout conveniently combining stereotypical vampishness with Judith's sulky dissatisfaction at living with the kibbutzim. Nor is this supposed *femme fatale* even permitted to seduce anyone successfully, a British officer nobly rejecting her sexual payment for the secret information he betrays to her. And a romance with Aaron remains inchoate because it would interfere with the film's proposition, that it is Zionism, not love, that heals and redeems. Judith's husband is a cardboard figure, because his function is to suggest a consanguinity between Nazis and Syrians. Indeed, the Arabs are 'absent' in the film, because of its desire to suggest that the Middle Eastern conflict is still against the Nazi threat, and the audience is expected to recognize in Nazism an unambiguously evil antagonist. This is a way of eliding the Arabs' point of view.

Victim or Victor?

In postwar Zionism, Judith as the Good Jewess is a specific ethnic icon of her already long-established symbolic value, as an individual human being's personal autonomy. It opposes that ultimate symbol of totalitarian tyranny, the Third Reich. In order to recognize the mythic continuum between the politics of Nazism and the politics of 'normal life' we have to understand how cultural myth envelops every aspect of human experience.

A survivor of the concentration camps, Bruno Bettelheim explained the inmates' quiescence as the result of trauma, which deprived them of the ability to regard themselves as autonomous beings, and hence of the capacity for resistance. As an exception to this rule, he tells the story of a woman prisoner who rebelled, shooting an officer with his own gun, for which she was herself immediately shot.[4] Translating this into iconic terms, we can see that the Jewess who killed her persecutor with his own weapon was a Judith killing Holofernes. Her will to resist – her resumption of her own identity – overcame the mass apathy of the camp mentality. In the same way, the Book of Judith had juxtaposed the demoralized Bethulians, and their urge to surrender to Holofernes' army, with Judith's will to resist, and the Victorians had regarded Judith as an icon of the authentic and autonomous self.

The camps revealed 'a new reality', one naked of the reliable structures of normal behaviour in society. To quote Bettelheim, 'when a world goes to pieces, when inhumanity reigns supreme, man [sic] cannot go on with business as usual. One then has to radically re-evaluate all of what one has done, believed in, stood for . . . one has to take a stand on the new reality.'[5] Or, as we might say, re-evaluate our myths and decide what they really mean when their bones are exposed by that 'new reality'. Because the situation is so extreme, one in which death is ever-present and moral significance so vivid, the concentration camp can manifest for us the fundamental issue at stake in the Judith myth. It is one of autonomy and courage for which the ultimate price must always, *inherently*, be death. That is, anyone who is a Judith is one in consciousness that, in certain circumstances, she is inviting death as the price of refusing to compromise her own identity as a human being. Had every concentration camp inmate been a Judith by nature, the Nazis would have had a hard time of it. They did not, precisely because the costs of Judithic action are so high that few can contemplate them. The Holocaust is thus a vivid and atrocious instance of what full humanity requires of us.

Justice or Revenge?

The issues raised by the Holocaust are not easily accommodated by conventional mass-media representations, which depend upon simplistic symbolic codes and inert language. Such a poverty of means is inadequate to the case. Before examining an example of popular representation of the Holocaust, it is as well to understand that the difficulty of representing the event has to do not solely with its scale as an instance of inhumanity. The problem is also to do with the 'new reality' with which it menaces the audience as much as the camp inmates. Remembering Bettelheim's description of this, we should recognize that he is implying that in such extreme circumstances survival is dependent upon being able to jettison the cultural lies upon which one's previous existence has depended for its psychic comfort. Viewing this trauma from the perspective of Judithic significance, we could say that survival as an autonomous being depends upon being able to abandon pro-cultural myths and cleaving to a counter-cultural one. Any fiction about the Holocaust confronts the epiphany in history of a counter-cultural *mythos*.

However, by their very nature populist fictions are committed to replicating and reinforcing the prevailing cultural myths, the ones that their audiences inhabit. Like the 1965 *Judith*, most such representations prefer to approach the subject indirectly and selectively. In order to achieve the 'Medusa Effect' of a refracted image of horror, most films on the Holocaust have a more recent setting, which distances the event. An example of the problems they encounter is found in the television movie *The Execution* (1985, dir. P. Wendkos). What this attempts to address is the issue of revenge: whether it is morally acceptable to hunt down and assassinate war criminals, as Israeli teams have done. There are those who doubt whether it is even worth prosecuting war criminals so long after the event, to which it is riposted that the will to execute justice should not be subject to erosion by time. The issue is one of the nature of justice, which in fact Judith had traditionally personified.

In *The Execution*, a group of female survivors, now living in the USA, recognize a restaurateur as the former Nazi Walter, a doctor who had inflicted sexual abuse and sterilization upon them. Believing that the prison sentence he has served is wholly inadequate to his crimes and the trauma that has blighted their lives, they become convinced that true justice – what the official law will not dispense – will only be fulfilled if they kill him. Yet the film ultimately side-steps the issue of just retribution. It transpires that, contrary to what they think, he is killed not by the one chosen from their own number, but by another former camp inmate. They escape punishment, but this finale is denuded of moral significance by their technical innocence of the homicide.

Similarly, the relationship between Marischa, the chosen assassin, and Walter is handled in a way that evacuates meaning. In effect she is set up as the Judith of this plot, to seduce and then shoot the Nazi. But the film wants to exploit a romantic as well as a moral dilemma: so Marischa is misled into thinking that Walter is not in fact the former Nazi doctor before she sleeps with him. Since she has fallen in love with him, she is mightily relieved, but the next morning his true identity is confirmed. Thus she is exculpated from knowingly sleeping with the enemy, but she still has to kill him. Yet the film will not allow her to be guilty of doing that, either, so it resorts to the old cliché whereby he is accidentally shot as they struggle for the gun. Because Marischa is not really guilty of anything much, the moral ambivalence of vengeance is sidestepped. Moreover, it is then revealed that unlike her female associates she is not Jewish,

which neatly prevents the audience from identifying her with the publicly controversial character of Israeli policy towards war criminals. She is set up as a
Judith but the blandness of telemovie ideology cannot permit her to inhabit
that role.

Similarly, Marischa's irrepressible sexual passion for Walter and her remorse
become her punishment for what she has not, in fact, actually done. Exerted
even from beyond the grave, the charisma of her wicked lover thus contradicts
the feminist transgression implied in a Judith's role. By the end of the film, we
can still sympathize with the traumatized women because (this is how TV
network executives think) they are still victims. They are exculpated from the
supposedly central issue because of the chasm between their homicidal intention and the homicidal event. In erasing its own Judithic premise, this film is a
demonstration of how to evoke the Holocaust's problematic moral consequences in order to close one's eyes to them. This is the Medusa Effect become
denial.

Most of all what the women confront is the acknowledgement of their own
primitive desire to punish, that the child within remains permanently inconsolable at the horror to which it was too early exposed. It is the paradox of pre-
meditated, pitiless and unrepentant murder as sanctified assassination that lies
at the heart of the Judithic theme. Her remorselessness suggests a flickering
identity between her and her enemy, just as the murder of a war criminal might
be portrayed as making the avenger evil too. (We may recall the Judithic alter-
egos, tyrant/tyrannicide, of the Renaissance.) What Francis Bacon called
revenge – 'wild justice' – might be adequately imagined for the case only if it
evoked both the 'wild' primality of retribution and the super-humane values of
monotheism. This is a conundrum almost beyond resolution. Since the
problem of achieving a just attitude to war criminals is central to the cultural
bequest of the Holocaust, the issue of retribution that is central to the Judithic
myth stands for a major moral problem of the twentieth century. For representations of the Holocaust, her emblematization of justice has assumed a new
and immeasurably difficult role.

God Is Not as Man

Even in the original Book of Judith, God's sanctification of deceit, seduction
and murder implied that his justice was of a different order from humankind's.
Conceiving of him in anthropomorphic terms, the elders underestimate this
difference. Judith reminds them that they have no hope of understanding his
intentions, 'For you cannot find the depth of the heart of man . . . then how can
ye search out God . . . and know his mind, or comprehend his purpose?' (8:14).
God does not merely work in mysterious ways: he may well work in ways that
shock or outrage human beings, as Judith's acteme suggests. Indeed, as we saw,

Judith's femininity symbolizes the Otherness of the divine: that he isn't a man. By definition, the supernatural being is not natural or human, and to anthropomorphize God is (as Judith informs the elders) a form of hubris. The whole point of God is that he is not man, but more than man.

A fortiori this applies to his form of justice in the world, which is probably, as the most sophisticated of theologians have acknowledged, unlikely to be comprehensible in human terms. The Holocaust raises that central issue for Judaeo-Christian belief: How can a good God permit such evil? Why do human beings suffer as they do?

One of the Holocaust novels that have attempted to address this issue is André Schwarz-Bart's *The Last of the Just* (1959), which won the Prix Goncourt. Tracing through history the lives of God's Just Men, individuals selected in each generation for martyrdom to the sufferings of the chosen people, the novel moves through medieval massacres of Jews in Europe to modern pogroms and, ultimately, the Final Solution. Each of the Just Men is, in essence, a victim of his special status as one of God's elect. The wiser ones groan aloud at the discovery that they have been chosen, for they know that this probably means that an atrocious death awaits them. In fact, what this represents is the equivalence of autonomy and death that Judith's story shared with concentration camp heroism.

In the novel's relentless black comedy of suffering, Schwarz-Bart intimates that the destiny God has planned for his chosen people is an elevation that is proved in misery, degradation and death. Of course, this in many ways of orthodox Judaic view is reflected also in the Book of Judith, where the heroine is told that 'thou hast not spared thy life for the affliction of our nation, but has revenged our ruin' (13:20), because willing to pay the price of death.

Similarly, God makes the Just Men heroes so that they will be able to bear the horrible fate that it is their function to undergo. Spiritual election is, *mutatis mutandis*, always a cross, not a privilege, and imposing the extremity of suffering is God's way of demonstrating whom he loves (In the Book of Judith, we recall, the heroine's fate is a cheerful compound of bereavement, grief and perpetual solitude.)

Consequently, the Last Just Man is the only one of his cohort at Auschwitz, as they walk into the gas chambers, who fully comprehends what awaits them. He is built to perceive inhumanity for what it is, because others cannot be expected to bear such a perception. That, the novel suggests, is the secret of God's compassion, that he spares all others full knowledge of the horror of evil. In short, we might say, the heroes appointed by God are the only human beings not permitted the comfort of the Medusa Effect.

The Just man Mordecai Levy, a Pole, marries a woman named Judith, as the Good Jewess. When it is borne in upon him that he is indeed the fortunate/unfortunate Just Man of his generation, he knows perfectly well that this destiny is a poisoned cup. One very considerable gift God has given him, however, a gift whose value will be demonstrated more and more emphatically as the novel proceeds, is his wife Judith, a sensual beauty with whom his relationship is one of extremes between passion and hostility. As matriarch of the modern Levys, 'Mother Judith' is earthy also in the symbolic sense: an indomitable realist, a Mother Courage for Jewry under Nazism. Emphasis upon her maternal fecundity, generosity and physicality renders her symbolic of the essential humanity that the Holocaust outrages.

This Judith's dominating sexuality is the first clue to her prototype. That her resolution, realism and status are Judithic is confirmed when the Levys' village is attacked by Cossacks and most of its inhabitants perish in the pogrom. Although Judith and Mordecai escape, they are discovered in the woods by a rumbustuous Cossack of almost comic machismo, who is himself amused by Mordecai's terror of imminent death at his hands. Far from terrified herself, Judith is impatient with Mordecai's passive acceptance of slaughter and furious with the Cossack. Whilst the latter remains enervated by his own laughter, she seizes his sword and kills him. The episode's comedy, surprises and reversals catch the spirit of those in the Book of Judith, the black comedy forewritten by God's cruel love.

It is of course Judith Levy who tutors her grandson, the Last Just Man, in the individualism that will enable him to undergo his terrible test. Her striking qualities, robust irreverence and fierce realism, and her beauty are of the charismatic kind that produces extreme reactions in those who know her, of admiration or hostility. That charisma facilitates heroic survival of the inhumanity represented by the Holocaust. But Schwarz-Bart's matriarchal Judith suggests deference to the view that God's chosen ones are always male. There are orthodox Jewish women who contend that in Judaism femininity is 'different and equal', but Jewish feminists have argued that gender-subordination is endemic to it: 'There is an element of paradox in the low status of women in Judaism. A woman confers Jewishness on her children while a man does not. There are plenty of jokes and anecdotes about the powerful Jewish mama . . . But, overall, the image of Jewish womanhood is a glorification of servility.'[6] There is a similar paradox in Schwarz-Bart's novel. Although Mother Judith is the conduit of essential Jewishness to her grandson, she remains the servant of his destiny. That Mother Judith is the most memorable character represents a triumph of imagination over gender-stereotyping. It may unbalance the novel, but that is all to the good. Why indeed should the biblical Judith's own personification of Justice be relinquished to a male protagonist, simply because of his gender? The Good Jewess should simply have been perceived as the Good Jew, a role not gender-specific. In such a context, masculinism exposes its own limited conception of humanity, and partakes of the inhumanity that the novel was written to purge.

Never Again

Symbolically, the Cossack episode's contrast between Mordecai's passive victimhood and Judith's furious retaliation mythologizes the difference in *mentalité* between the camp inmates' passive acceptance of genocide and the postwar militance of Zionism. The episode stands for a climacteric in Jewish consciousness, a move from quietism during the European diaspora to the spirit of 'Never Again'. Judith's icon epitomizes this spirit. For instance, whereas a British greetings card, reproducing Klimt's *Judith I*, has tactfully cropped(!) the severed head, a similar card produced in Israel retains it.[7] For the British consumer this is simply a fashionable artwork, whereas in Israel it is profoundly meaningful.

Similarly, Mordecai's passivity symbolizes a Jewish past of pogrom and genocide, Judith's aggression the Jewish present, sworn never to submit again. A postwar Jewess has contended that 'there isn't a Jew alive, be she religious, atheistic or betraying her roots, who isn't reacting to the Holocaust.'[8] Implicitly Judith's icon represents Jewry's modern character.

Indeed, the increased incidence of Judith as a girl's forename since the mid-century might be interpreted, I think, as partly a consequence of this alteration in the self-construction and reputation of the Jews. It was after the second World War that Judith's name became strikingly more popular, recovering from its low point early in the century and outstripping the popularizing effect already gained from Horace Walpole's novel. One prompt to this popularity was the celebrity in the late 1940s and the 1950s of two Hollywood actresses, Judy Garland and Judy Holliday, both Jewish as it happens. There are no available figures for the proportional rise in the name's popularity amongst Jews specifically, but the very strong Jewish presence in the professions of academia and of psychiatry/psychology may provide an informal sample of this proportion. For instance, the index of *Feminism and Psychoanalysis* (1992) manifests a high incidence of professionals named Judith.[9] Popular fiction is a symptomatic record of widespread received ideas, even if in simplistic form. In Joseph Amiel's *Deeds* (1989), an example of the romantic 'family saga' fictions so popular in the late 1980s and 1990s, we can see these modern associations of Judith's name. The heroine, Gail, perceives herself as Judithic because of her parental inheritance: 'She had an inner vision of herself as a Joan of Arc or, because she had bound herself so tightly to Judaism . . . the single tie she could manage to her orthodox father – as a Judith, setting out alone with only her faith to cut down the powerful, the rich, the corrupt.'[10] In the emotional turbulence of her life, her cleaving to a Judithic myth of the self secures her identity, as a modern young Jewess supporting the militant causes of her generation in America. From these symptoms of the forename's modern associations, one may surmise that the rise of Zionism and of a self-consciously more extrovert ethnicity, in the spirit of

'Never Again', encouraged Jewish parents – whether consciously or not – to choose for their female offspring a name that itself signifies an assertive Jewish identity.

The contest of good and evil in the Book of Judith was carried into history in the most horrific manner by the confrontation of her descendants with the Final Solution. In many ways, Judith symbolizes the meaning of the Holocaust for the universal struggle between good and evil, slavery and autonomy.

12

Woman with a Gun
Terrorism, Power and Paranoia

The modern remakings of Judith have not been confined to her Zionist face, which revived her ancient status as a militant ethnic heroine. Other modern versions have re-embodied her in ways that reflect the political perturbations common to Western society in general. Her role within our perceptions of late twentieth-century urban life throws searching light on our contemporary anxieties about issues that we are still struggling to understand and resolve: issues thrown up by the nature of the giant modern city and the superpower state.

We can see how the biblical heroine is reincarnated on the streets of New York, for instance, if we return to the heroine of *Deeds*. This Jewish-American woman is an instance in popular fiction of the radicalism and feminism of a modern generation. In her self-imposed role as a Judith she threw herself into 'the women's movement, the antiwar movement, the environmental movement, the disarmament movement . . . unleashing almost indiscriminately at whatever authority she sensed was doing evil the fury she felt at the forces that had ravaged her own life.'[1] This romantic heroine, angry, feminist, radical, activist, is in fact only one example of a pervasive figure in the cultural myths prevailing from the 1970s into the 1990s: a figure we may sum up as the Woman with a Gun. By the mid-1990s she was ubiquitous in all forms of mass entertainment, from pulp fiction to Hollywood cinema. The timing is, I think, significant: this icon represented populist reaction to the rise of the contemporary women's movement in the 1970s.

At the same time, more obliquely, it represented a popular reaction to a more general perception of the character of contemporary life. For some time in the West we have lived in a society increasingly fearful of violence and urban breakdown, as well as of the depredations of terrorism. Whereas the latter irregularly obtrudes into urban life, the ambience of violence and criminality in major cities has seemed to suggest a normalization of fear. Whether or not this has been intensified by paranoia, fear of violence has become part of the accepted myth of modern culture. As we have seen, Judith long ago became a symptomatic sign of assassination and terrorism, in the Renaissance; and since the irruption of Joan of Arc in the fifteenth century she has also been associated with the militant or military woman. Representative of a populist perspective on her generation, Amiel's Gail is explicitly constructed as both Judith and her avatar Joan of Arc: of the prototype of political feminism *and* of an extraordinary Judithic politician. Joan's success is treated as proof that it is possible to be a Judith in real-life politics. In contemporary feminism, the key issue is a demand for equality with men in the public conduct of life, and the protest movements are precisely claiming the right to act upon the institutions which determine its conduct, politically and economically. Judith's icon already represented both militant feminism and violent politics. It is not surprising, therefore, that the rise of feminism and the increase in urban paranoia should have coincided with a marked and rapid revival of Judith's image in our culture. The next chapter will consider feminist uses of her myth, but here we need to discover her function in culture more generally. In her figure is concentrated a number of linked modern myths.

Judith in Hollywood

In the wake of the modern women's movement, women with guns have become a staple feature of mass entertainment. Whether these are soldiers, spies, terrorists, assassins, murderesses or rebellious women, the Judithic prototype is never far away. This is because a twentieth-century descendant of Judith, unlike Joan of Arc, reflects the advances in modern weaponry by using a gun rather than a sword. Of course, the gun can replicate the same phallic significance. But to wield a warsword required rather more physical strength than holding a gun, and hence privileged male force over female: it took the biblical heroine two strokes to sever the general's head. By contrast, the equivalent modern weapon is effective irrespective of the physical strength of its owner. It makes a person's capacity to exert force independent of that person's gender. And this is a crucial alteration in the sexual politics of violence. In the final analysis, the enforcement of any political system, including patriarchy, depends upon the ability to coerce those who cannot otherwise be governed, by physical violence if necessary. Within modern states police forces and armies perform this function, whilst within everyday social intercourse the greater physical strength of men backs up their ability to intimidate women when need arises. But the existence of guns, to which women also have access, removes this male advantage. If male violence towards women is the extreme point at which patriarchy can coerce women, the gun jeopardizes patriarchy by equalizing their ability to be violent. For this reason, Judith with a gun is a much more intimidating image than Judith with a sword, and her modern incarnation is more obviously menacing to male dominance.

Judith with a gun also implies a different moral pattern to her murder than did Judith with a sword. In the past, the easiest way to devalue and denigrate the biblical heroine was to portray her as fighting dirty. She got her victim drunk and incapable, despatching him when he could not fight back. Consequently, Kuyper in the 1930s complained that she could not be a hero, unlike her male biblical counterpart David, because he had faced his enemy fairly and squarely in open combat. In single combat, though, the physically weak biblical Judith would have failed utterly, whereas a modern Judith with a gun might win even in a face-to-face shoot-out with Holofernes. Unlike her biblical ancestor and prototype, the killer-woman need no longer resort to guile before acquiring and wielding the phallic weapon. This collapses the old simple distinction between Judithic/feminine and Davidic/masculine violence and puts them on a level playing-field. If she need no longer resort to dirty tricks but can depend upon honest-to-goodness firepower, her story need no longer be quite so morally ambiguous. In this respect Judith can be more emphatically heroic than in her past guises, more readily justified in her action. Her moral ambiguity having disappeared, she becomes an even more potent image of feminine dominance, uncompromised and uncompromising. And her equality in weaponry, depriving the male of his physical advantage, can make her seem more emphatically a feminist figure as well. Her heroism and her violence can thus exponentially reinforce one another, an armed woman facing an armed man on equal terms. This is feminism starkly portrayed as literally a duel of the sexes. This in itself is an intimidating image of feminism's effect on the balance of power. Simultaneously, though, equality on the physical plane is the more intensely challenging if one cannot simply dismiss the gunwoman as morally culpable. Both the physical and the ethical problems that bedevil Judith's story are simplified in her favour. She can now be counter-cultural without being counter-ethical, and consequently a more potent, positive image for women's domination. The more potent she is in these terms, the more menacing she is to male anxieties.

Or so it seems. Whilst the Woman With A Gun appears more shockingly confrontational than her predecessor with the sword, her image actually mitigates the phallic anxiety evoked by the original Judith. The latter's killing method, decapitation, was more obviously castratory than a bullet to the head. In fact, the implication that Judith had acquired phallic power, symbolized twice over by the sword and the severed head, is reduced in the image of the Woman With A Gun to the less shocking of the two symbols – the weapon. Apparently more intimidating to the male because more obviously equal in force to him, in symbolism the Woman With A Gun is actually only half as frightening as the biblical Judith.

An instance of Hollywood's rising trend of representing Women With Guns is *Private Benjamin* (1980, dir. H. Zieff), in which a Jewish-American princess enlists in the army as a combatant, a recently instituted career opportunity for women. Her Jewishness provides a cultural bridge for the audience between the familiar and the unfamiliar, acquainted as they are with the popular repute of Israeli women soldiers. The protagonist's forename and surname do similar conceptual work, for she is called Judy: Jewish and martial. From *Handgun* (1983, dir. T. Garnett) to *Thelma and Louise* (1991, dir. R. Scott), the Woman With A Gun has become an increasingly prominent sign of the cultural impact of feminism. Even that rumbustiously masculine genre, the Western, has been feminized in films such as *Bad Girls* (1994, dir. J. Kaplan). In 1977 Hudgins's poem *Holofernes* had seen Judith's acteme as 'a man of merely great power / finds a woman with a gift for doing what must be done'.[2] This is the Western hero's manly 'what a man's got to do' translated to his female counterpart. The films' protagonists also personify women's emergence into feminism, from the oppressed to the resurgent: they are signs of popular culture under the stress of social change.

At one level, Hollywood films have simply pandered to their female audiences by recognizing that they want to see feisty heroines ('positive role models'). This underlies the nomenclature of Private Judy Benjamin and Gail/Judith, for the name has been indelibly stamped with feisty/perky and glamorous associations. In late 1930s Britain, I am told, 'Judy was a name you gave to dogs', but by the 1960s that had altered. The actress Judi Dench helped to popularize the name in Britain, and the popular girls' comic *Judy* associated the eponym with teenage wish-fulfilment fantasies about ballerinas and the like. Identified with perky young womanhood by the star images of Judy Garland and Judy Holliday in the early 1950s, the name had been given on international fillip.[3] When one young woman, christened Judith, came up to Oxford in the 1950s, she reinvented herself as a more *soignée* personality named Judy. Since the rise of the women's movement, associations of attractive, modern, self-assertive femininity are invoked when the name is conferred on appropriate characters in popular fictions and mass entertainment. As in Judy Benjamin, this both encodes the Judithic sign of feminism and moderates it by glamour: played by Goldie Hawn, she was a dizzy blonde and a very reluctant woman soldier. The sign in the name thus accommodates popular entertainment's need at once to evoke stereotypes (emancipated womanhood) and extract their teeth. Popular entertainment does not achieve mass-market appeal unless it both represents current cultural bogeys *and* consoles its audience that these do not really require a complete overhaul of their mental furniture. Even women soldiers, shocking innovation though they are, are just charming blondes who don't really know what they have let themselves in for.

The conservative, recuperative character of popular fiction is particularly marked in the romance aimed at female readers. As literary critics have argued, their highly conventionalized plots and characters reinforce, both emotionally and ideologically, the romantic myths that discourage women from questioning the patriarchal values expressed in their personal relationships. Such fictions console women that the romantic myth to which they are emotionally committed is not just desirable but possible of fulfilment; equally, they discourage psychically disruptive recognition of their own discontents. Under pressure from the social effects of the women's movement, even the pulp romance adjusted itself during the 1980s in order to seem to acknowledge new motives in women's lives: but the adjustment was both uneasy and cosmetic. Indeed, it has been suggested that in essence the archetypal plot of popular romances mimes and reinforces the Oedipal view of human relationships.[4] For our purposes, we might deduce that the pro-cultural reinforcement of pulp romances is at the other extreme from the Judithic, counter-cultural myth and its feminist implications.

Judith's Given Name

In this light it is instructive to look at the role of both forename and *mythos* in these popular fictions, symptomatic as they are of prevailing ideologies. The glamorous associations of the name as 'femininity' in the 1960s are reflected in the eponym of Brian Cleeve's historical/romantic novel, *Judith*. In the 1980s, as the forename became imbricated in the cultural cliché of the 'sexy, independent woman', it became suspiciously common as the (usually pseudonymous) forename of blockbuster novelists – such as Judith Krantz, Judith Gould, Judy Blume and Judith Rossner. Its favouring is particularly significant of its associations in the popular mind during the 1980s, because popular authors are consciously treated as 'brand names' within the pulp-fiction market. Their names thus deliberately evoke associations to which potential purchasers are expected to respond and assure them that the product they are buying is precisely the glamorized/modernized romantic ideology they wish to 'buy into', quite literally. Judith's *nomen* represents a myth of the modern woman as 'having it all', as the woman constructed by *Cosmopolitan* magazine. In proferring an image of independence (but not feminism, which was widely viewed as extremist and excessive) *and* sex-centred happiness, the blockbuster and the woman's magazine suggest that women can possess the advantages demanded by feminism without demonizing themselves in the eyes of men, who remain their route to emotional fulfilment. Romantic fiction's exploitation of Judith's forename is part of a disingenuous marketing strategy, designed to preserve an anti-feminist fantasy-genre: immunizing its readers against feminism by using small doses of it, like a vaccine. Thus the Judiths of romantic fiction are much more culturally important and effective than intellectual snobs would be prepared to imagine. They are in fact symptoms of the massive conservative reaction against the impact of the women's movement, a reaction often subtle and insidious. It is at its most effective when using feminism's influence against itself, a classic ideological strategy of assimilating the enemy to one's own purposes.

Within the fictions, this contradiction (independent/romantic) is carried through in the deployment of Judithic female characters, often so named. In the conservative romantic world of the Mills and Boon novel a potential adulteress and suspected murderess is *A Girl Called Judith* (D. Orridge, 1988): a novel punctuated with dreams about totemic heads. In the romantic heroine's paranoid jealousy, Judith represents the Scarlet Woman who preys upon her husband, thus reflecting the name's associations of sex, death and duplicity. This storyline might seem to suggest the powerful, glamorized Judith, though demonized, and hence not endorsed by the novel. But it goes further than this in its recuperation of the bogey of murderous woman, for it is revealed that in fact this Judith is no *femme fatale*, but herself a victim of marital tragedy. Thus the rampaging murderess/adulteress is conjured away like a nightmare (nightmares figure in the plot), from which the 'normal' and very passive heroine wakes up. It is as if the cultural monster of this Judith/Woman With A Gun has been repudiated by both text and heroine as an aberrant archetype. Supposedly, the heroine is now able to recognize a fellow-woman, a sympathetic colleague in marital insecurity, and this is tacitly offered as sub-feminist. But the heroine's release from Judith-paranoia to restored marital harmony and security suggests rather that domestic happiness depends upon the absence of Judiths from one's home and one's own psyche. This Judith is the feminist bogey, banished from the pro-cultural fantasy that consoles women inhabiting romantic ideology.

The need simultaneously to recognize and deny feminist possibilities has led to a surprisingly high incidence of Judithic figures and allusions in popular culture. A dated but anxious-to-be-modern portrayal of a resilient young woman motivates the eponym of another Mills and Boon novel, *Judith* (B. Neels, 1982). In Pamela Belle's more intelligent historical romance, *Wintercombe* (1989), a young Puritan girl impulsively shoots a Cavalier colonel who has requisitioned her home. Afterwards guilty reaction sets in, but she is reassured by her stepmother's and grandmother's approval. Reassurance only takes effect when her stepmother 'remembered suitable biblical examples. "Think of the story of Jael and Sisera – or Judith and Holofernes. Both women killed their enemy – and used far more guile and deceit than you did. Yet they're hailed as great heroines."[5] In a society at war, both patriarchal and violent, the women are victims of military coercions, but a subversive, modern feminine independence is attributed to them by the novel. The Judithic incident and its invocation of the biblical prototype is the one occasion when their subversion becomes aggression and thus imports into the novel an image of feminist recalcitrance. However, since this is generically a pro-cultural fiction, the image is evoked only to be dispersed: the colonel survives, and no harm is done. One way or another, mass-market fictions sustain the contradictory acknowledgement/repudiation of the Woman With A Gun/feminist of which Judith is mythic prototype.

Judith Lets Rip

Flanking this contradictory conception of Woman With A Gun are two versions of her that are much more comfortably accommodated. The demonized version is seen in the genre of *film noir* as revived in the 1980s and early 1990s. The psychotic, murderous and adulterous *femme fatale* of the film *Shattered* (1991, dir. W. Petersen) is of course named Judith, in a simple revival of the Victorian sign of Judith as Murderess and Poisonous Wife. The latter was replicated in travesty by *Beetlejuice* (1988, dir. T. Burton), when a ghostly couple attempt to scare off their home's new owners. They appear in a masquerade version of the Judith acteme, the 'homicidal' wife holding her husband's severed head in one hand and a knife in the other. This image is summoned up to prove its opposite, that the couple's collaborative masquerade in the acteme actually demonstrates their marital harmony. Hollywood product is just as conservative about cultural myth as other popular fictions, which is why its Women With Guns are often merely deranged criminals (as in *Basic Instinct*, 1992, dir. P. Verhoeven). The very title of *Romeo Is Bleeding* (1994, P. Medak) conveys the essential concept: romantic man is betrayed by the rapacious Woman With A Gun, a deviant from the tradition ideology of romantic myth (Romeo and Juliet). Possessing the phallic gun and its metonymy for masculine force and mastery, Woman With A Gun has acquired the phallus as symbol of patriarchy and wreaks havoc with it. Figured by the gun, feminine empowerment is represented as inexorably dangerous and disorderly. This is feminism projected as the hostile image of phallic murderess – motivated by penis-envy to steal Oedipus's myth from him. As Oedipus's myth signifies patriarchy, it represents his penis-envy of his father as more than a merely sexual competition. Oedipus's acquisition of the phallus (killing his father and marrying his mother) is also his acquisition of the power of the Father (his throne). Oedipus is both a political and a sexual symbol. As we have seen, Judith's is the counter-cultural equivalent, the myth of the daughter's theft of phallic power. This is why the Woman With A Gun is prototypically Judith in representations, because hers is the competing myth to that of Oedipus.

However, modern Freudian representations of Judith as penis-envy expel the political dimension of her myth. The Freudian analysis of her story made her fit his view of sexuality's development as a male process which the female imitates, necessarily incompletely and ineffectively because she is not in fact male. In other words, attributing penis-envy to women immediately characterizes them as lacking, incomplete, ineffective. To see Judith *as* Oedipus, then, is to reduce her to a defective simulacrum of male sexuality. Defective sexually, she must be defective politically too, since the two processes are successfully conjoined only in Oedipus's acquisition of patriarchal power. In the Freudianized popular mind the Woman With A Gun is read as a personification of penis-envy, because our culture obsessively identifies the gun with the penis. Perceiving her in this way thus sexualizes her (as a pervert or as a sado-masochist fantasy), whilst suggesting that she is politically disabled. She cannot be Oedipus because, unlike him, she cannot achieve a sexual identity with power itself: she cannot do so because patriarchy has contrived to identify power with the penis, the biology with the politics. Further, the gun's symbolic confirmation of the Woman With A Gun's penis-envy confuses the issue of political rights (what women are demanding) with sexual deviance. They don't realize, the thought runs, that what they really want is what they just can't have because that's biology, isn't it?

That a gun is a penis-substitute is precisely the point: it is not the real thing. A man toting a gun is seen as doubly phallic, a Woman With A Gun as aspirant to what the man already has anyway. She seems more emphatically to lack the penis *because* she is brandishing the substitute for it that she seems to need. If anything, the myth of penis-envy makes a Woman With A Gun seem more, not less feminine, and the penis more desirable. That, ultimately, is why she is an erotic image for the male viewer. The political (phallic) disability of the Woman With A Gun is precisely symbolized by her weapon.

These are not merely abstract or decorative cultural images. Just as the Woman With A Gun is a hostile image of feminism as threat to patriarchy, so the gory fictions of these films are fantasy-projections of urban reality. In the myth of urban paranoia, the individual and the home are under constant threat from violence and intrusion. The corrupt policeman/intruder/rival of the husband in *Unlawful Entry* (1992, dir. J. Kaplan) cannot be repelled by the efforts of the husband himself, who is an 'unmanned' New Man. Instead it is the Wife With A Gun who kills the intruder who threatens to usurp his place, both in his prosperous suburban home and in his wife. Like the wife in *Fatal Attraction* (1987, dir. A. Lyne), this Wife With A Gun posits a recuperation of the phallic woman for a function that protects normal domesticity. She uses the gun not to challenge her husband's role but to bolster it, to declare extreme allegiance to him by killing what threatens him. The feminist implication of the Woman With A Gun is thus redirected to the old romantic myth of the wife who stands by her man. If aggressive, she is only so for his sake. More, she has helpfully relieved him of the necessity to do anything violent himself. He can stand by, the wronged victim, while she shoulders the burden of homicide-guilt. This is an extremely important feature of such films. Feminists have, after all, accused men of being the violent sex, but these husbands cannot manage to do

violence, so that charge falls by the wayside. Even more satisfactorily, it transpires that women themselves are the violent sex.

The gun held by the Woman With A Gun signifies a great deal about trans-
actions in social values when feminism impinges upon culture. The most interesting feature of such films as *Unlawful Entry* and *Shattered* is that they position
the Woman With A Gun within the prosperous suburbia that is menaced by
urban breakdown. From the cultural myths that they encode it is possible to see
that the many lurid, melodramatic and romantic images of the Woman With A
Gun express urban hysteria as well as masculine anxieties. Had the wife in
Unlawful Entry succumbed to the seductive intruder, suburban man would have
lost everything. Conversely, the 'bad' Woman With A Gun (as in *Shattered* and
Fatal Attraction) signifies *both* feminist menace and pandemic urban crime. In
effect, the Woman With A Gun is a displaced image of cultural neurosis about
urban life. As violent, she represents a menace similar to the intruder into the
home – worse, she is already in the home. In her image is concentrated the
fearful ambience of the modern city.

Like the Judith-Murderess in Victorian sensation novels, Woman With A
Gun is a paranoiac projection of the everyday. This is important for several
reasons. In her image that of the feminist is rendered hyperbolic and alienating,
a cultural reinforcement to alienizing feminism as excessive and disruptive. The
mass media of the early 1990s tended to characterize feminism in precisely this
way, as inappropriate in a 'post-feminist' world. Susan Faludi contended that
post-feminism was an imaginary but deliberate deterrent, because feminism
had not yet achieved its goals; whilst Robert Bly reasserted the virtues of
masculinism against the emasculating threat of feminism.[6] In such a polarized
and paranoid atmosphere, it should come as no surprise that the image of
Woman With A Gun encodes masculine anxiety and then redoubles it by
identification with society's major fear, urban violence. A subtext of this double
identification is that too many people have guns, therefore women have guns,
which is a sign of how unnatural it is that so many people have guns, for women
and guns are not supposed to go together; and the fact that women and guns
now go together is a sign of the deviance of society as a whole, which is why feminism and urban violence are the same thing. Similarly, the melodramatic cinematic images of Woman-with-a-Gun are signs of a paranoia not simply about
women but about society as a whole. She is an image of and for a society consciously in crisis, which is why her figuration is Judithic, Judith's icon customarily reviving at such junctures in history.

Women Terrorists

This is as true of the non-fictional Women With Guns as of the Hollywood and
romance versions. The Women With Guns of the real world are just as consti-

tutive of, and constituted by, the urban Judithic myth as their fictional counterparts. They are the modern versions of the Renaissance's Judiths – assassins, guerrillas and terrorists. Like the Woman With A Gun of urban melodrama and romance, they are mythic figures for an age of anxiety in the developed world, a world in fear of degeneration, decay and reversion to disorder. On the public stage, the most glamorized yet fearful image of the Woman With A Gun is the female guerrilla/terrorist, toting an Uzi. That icon was instituted in 1970, when the PFLP hijacker, Leila Khaled, became a media star. Representations of her established the popular image of the beautiful, fanatical woman terrorist, customarily regarded as more ruthless than her male comrades.[7] This variation on the myth that 'the female of the species is deadlier than the male' seemed to be confirmed when a botched undercover Mossad mission in Sweden brought to light the fact that their most efficient counter-terrorist was a female agent. The images of terrorist and counter-terrorist shadowed each other, alter-egos of fatal femininity. From the 1970s the most significant reincarnation in the popular mind of the *femme fatale* has been the woman terrorist as Woman With A Gun.

When she was a senior woman guerrilla during the Cuban revolution, Vilma Espin, Fidel Castro's sister-in-law, adopted the codename Deborah: in a formerly Catholic country, the name readily signified female radical militancy. But the closest mythic prototype for the woman guerrilla/terrorist is Deborah's more violent and seductive analogue, Judith. In this guise she is the female antagonist implied by the cover of Michael Baldwin's thriller, *Holofernes* (1990), which portrays a glamorous, predatory female hijacker. In David Edgar's play *Ecclesiastes* (1990), a trendy radical English vicar is a devotee of the Liberation Theology which, in Latin American Christian guerrilla movements, replicates the Jesuit, Judithic tyrannicide ideology of the Renaissance in modern form ('A Christian view of gelignite', as a conservative scoffs).[8] The vicar's wife is Judith, 'a toughie', whose name characterizes her role as the voice of integrity, chiding her husband when he compromises his radical religious principles. It is she who truly represents (Old Testament) liberation theology, whereas her soft-minded son Luke represents passive unworldliness, what we might call (New Testament) resignation theology. In comic guise, a similar character appears in the Monty Python film of *Life of Brian* (1979, dir. T. Jones). Brian's life in ancient Palestine is a bathetic analogue of Christ's, and his paramour is Judith, the most militant member of an incompetent and rebarbative guerrilla movement, the 'People's Front of Judaea'. When Judith urges her idle male colleagues to stop their incessant talking and do something revolutionary for a change, their leader dismisses her challenge with smug condescension, as 'another little ego-trip from the feminists'. In comic form, this episode reflects an archetype of the feminist Zionist guerrilla, aptly named. This mythic icon is the essential Judith of our times. The woman who intervenes in history has become the woman who blows it up.

Nor can this Woman With A Gun be detached from the coincidental impact of the women's movement. Women's claims to equal rights, public roles and political recognition all base themselves upon the fundamental claim for as much public *effectivity* as men have traditionally possessed. Terrorism itself represents a seizing of the ability (legitimate or not) to enforce political change. Feminism is analogously demanding and subversive of the prevailing power structure. Like terrorism, it flies in the face of what is accepted as the given order, and also like revolutionaries its adherents can be either suddenly violent or gradually fifth-columnist. If government is a patriarchy, a masculine power, then in assaulting it terrorism is in mythic terms the feminist subversion of global politics. Both feminism and terrorism are subversive of accepted authority, both demand radical political change. It is a short step to seeing the supposed extremism of feminism as the image not only of urban violence, but of urban terrorism. In Judith's icon as both feminist and terrorist, Woman With A Gun, this parallel is signified within our culture.

When this mythic image is projected onto the international scene in popular thrillers, terrorism itself is characterized in feminine terms, assaulting the legitimate masculinity of the state. In exploring the gendered *mythos* within which international politics is conducted, we need to begin with the mythology of the modern assassin. As illegal and covert intervener in history, the assassin is a colleague of the terrorist and guerrilla. Since the killings of Mahatma Gandhi and J.F. Kennedy, assassination has become an ever-present fear, not only for politicians but also for celebrities (for instance, John Lennon). Accompanying that fear has been a greater public consciousness, for the rapid acceleration in communications and news technology has conferred on the assassin greater prominence and notoriety than ever before. Indeed, the later twentieth century might almost be dubbed the age of the assassin. In this respect it replicates the Renaissance and also consequently its Judiths. A few years after the assassination of Kennedy, popular culture marked the advent of this terrifying modern myth of arbitrary and unexpected death-by-a-stranger. In the comic-caper film *The Assassination Bureau* (1968, dir. B. Dearden), the concept was reassuringly distanced, because the action was set in the years prior to the First World War. One episode involved the hero (a professional assassin) playing dead, supposedly the victim of a fatal woman's machinations. A witty comment on the trick, and the way in which it played to misogynist preconceptions, is provided when the camera glances at one of the frescoes on the wall behind, which represents Judith with the head of Holofernes. By alluding to Judith as prototype of the assassin and fatal woman, this moment reinforces the implication that the hero's German enemies fell for the trick because it so precisely fitted their mental attachment to the myth of fatal femininity.

Similarly, the fact that the assassins of modern leaders have usually been male has not precluded a recurrent reversion to the same cultural myth in modern representations of the assassin. For, as in the Renaissance, female gendering of the figure underlines that the assassin is deviant, an Other alien to the normal (viz male) person, and an invader of the customary order of things in a patriarchal society. Also as then, female gendering suggests the assassin's invisible and mysterious origin, the fact that by this act a nonentity becomes a demonic celebrity, achieving a prominence parasitic upon the victim's fame. In this respect he is like a woman aspiring to maleness, like the Woman With A Gun in fact. Kill the man, and you possess what he has got: this is the lure of assassination for the socially inadequate. As traditionally subordinate and publicly obscure, 'the second sex' is symbolically imported into the cultural myth of the assassin.

Similar reference of such acts to religious justification persists. The *fatwah* declared against Salmon Rushdie, sanctified by the theocratic rulers of Iran, is comparable to the Renaissance papacy's homicidal fiats against Elizabeth I and William the Silent. Like Counter-Reformation Catholicism, the *fatwah* incites an Islamic counterpart of Judith. It similarly assumes that the act of murder becomes something else when regarded as the human defence of God. Most Western states no longer accept this theocratic view of politics. Thus in 1989 a work dedicated to Rushdie was inspired by the bicentenary of the French Revolution to invoke Charlotte Corday's voice: 'Votre siècle abonde en arrogants prédateurs à étiquettes diverses; quand en face un humble, une humiliée, un offensé s'insurgent, retrouvez Charlotte Corday.' Corday is explicitly invoked as both a 'Judith' and a 'tyrannicide', model of resistance to all forms of compulsion and coercion.[9] The anonymous author thus offered Judith/Corday as a paradigm for defence of liberty against oppression, as a type for Rushdie's freedom of speech. Yet, as in the Renaissance, the Judithic idea encodes a doubling of the perpetrator and the victim. Judith/Corday was an assassin, Rushdie is a target, yet the author cites Rushdie as a Corday. As in the past, the icon of the ambiguous Judith encodes the collision of moral absolutes: French 'Liberty' versus Islamic doctrine, both of which can appeal to the image of sanctification for quite antipathetic ends. In Judith's icon is signified the difficulty of repudiating one ideological system in favour of another: that one ideology's terrorist is another's freedom-fighter.

In all these respects there is very little difference between the Renaissance sign of the assassin and the modern, and this is itself significant of the tenacity of traditional cultural myths, even in a professedly progressive age. *The Assassination Bureau* deliberately travestied the myth, but it did so within a plot that tamed the fatal woman/spy. Another film shows the myth in full spate, albeit in modernized guise. Affected by contemporary feminism's claims for women's equality and the cultural rise of the Woman With A Gun, both the CIA and Hollywood implicated themselves in the sexual politics of assassination. The question of female competence is fundamental to the modern version of the assassination myth. In the 1976 Hollywood film *The Next Man* (dir. R.C. Sarafian), for instance, Cornelia Sharpe played a professional assassin hired to kill a Saudi Arabian politician by interests hostile to his attempts to resolve the crisis in the Middle East. Her customary method is to seduce her target and then to kill him *post coitus*. By such Judithic behaviour her extreme ruthlessness is established, confirming misogynist myths about women's sexual duplicity and outraging male sentimentalities about the act of intercourse. Since the politician is played by Sean Connery, the film's suspense is generated by the audience's wondering whether his sexual attractiveness and her responsiveness to it will ultimately persuade her to spare his life. Corresponding to the film's suggestion that the mutual attraction is genuine as its attempt to suggest that Connery's charismatic peacemaker may represent a genuine possibility of resolution for the conflict. In the end, however, despite several implied hesitations, she does shoot him. Since Sharpe is a distinctly uninteresting actress, it is difficult to empathize with her mental processes. In any case, the audience is unlikely to be in any doubt as to the outcome, for the alternative ending – her sparing him – would carry no shock-value. The intended outrage is that, unlike Charlotte Corday and other Judithic political assassins, she is motivated not by conviction but simply by money. It is Sharpe's character's very competence in her chosen profession that counts against her most, for no feminine compassion, and not even female sexuality, deters her. Had she been a 'natural' woman, the whole world would have been a safer place. In order to set up this portentous thesis, she is inevitably portrayed as the stereotype of 1970s glamour. In a similar fashion, however, the female assassin's political disinterest implies a kind of feminine irresponsibility: that amorality is in this film a function of women's inability to *understand* politics. As audience, apprized of Connery's supposed political value, we are superior to her and offended by her: the implication is that she cannot see the wood for the trees. Thus she is chilling, but her competence is a version of moral incompetence. In this way the figure of the assassin is doubly demonized, the efficiency of the killer made the more repellent by her denaturalized femininity.

On the other hand, the fact that the assassin is effective as an historical actor means that, if cultural myth wants to resist the viability of women as political agents, it must reinforce the myth that femininity is incompetent at political subversion. Thus there are two competing versions of the assassin as Woman With A Gun: the unnaturally competent and the naturally incompetent, the demon and the bimbo. She may be employed by either side in the conflict, the government or the subversives. Thus during the politically disenchanted 1990s, with its popular suspicion of government-inspired violence, the CIA's past covert operations became the subject of greater scrutiny. One such case concerned Cuba. In response to Castro's successful establishment of his communist regime, the CIA resorted to the customary modes of state-inspired violence. According to the woman in question, Castro's mistress Marita Lorenz was given the task of assassinating him by poison. Whilst her credibility has often been questioned, her claim that the CIA tried to use her against Castro has been regarded as reasonably substantiated.[10] True or not, the suggestion that in its many attempts to assassinate Castro the CIA had recourse to the traditional method of employing a female seductress/betrayer, or Poisonous Wife, is yet another instance of the way in which myth and actuality feed upon each other. The CIA think in mythic terms, just like everybody else. Most satisfying of all, if one appreciates the gendered coding of the assassination mythology, is the result: Lorenz's claim that she hid the poison capsules in a jar of cold cream and they disintegrated. It is a delightful way of accounting for one's inability to do the job. Symbolically, the jar of cold cream, with its cosmetic associations, represents her role as the irresistibly beautiful fatal woman (one self-elevating, of course). It also suggests that as a woman she was lamentably ignorant of simple chemistry, for it did not occur to her that the chemicals in cold cream would react with the chemicals in the poison. It all adds up to splendidly bimboesque femininity, such as the CIA, the public and indeed Lorenz herself would appreciate as a stereotypical story of female incompetence, no less than female duplicity. Whether successful or not, professional or amateur, the female assassin is simultaneously glamorous, naturally sexual, sexually transgressive, intimidating and trivial of mind.

Thus, whilst the modern assassin is mythologized as the Woman With A Gun, the image contains a contradiction in this context also. On the one hand, the female assassin imagistically intensifies the unnaturalness of the killer: male assassins are threatening enough, but the notion that the female assassin contradicts her femininity as well as her conscience puts her further beyond the moral pale. On the other hand, her glamorized and/or incompetent image proffers a subtextual consolation to society's fears of subversion, whether political or feminist. In the 1990s, both the very successful French film *Nikita* (1990, dir. L. Besson) and its rapid American remake *The Assassin* (1993, dir. J. Badham) reflected the cultural prominence of the assassination myth and the paranoia generated by widespread doubts about undercover activity by governments. Nikita's anti-heroine was an anti-social, drug-crazed killer converted into a professional assassin by a sinister government agency. Once professionalized, she became reluctant to kill, just as the agency transformed her into a socialized, feminine, seductive woman. Normal women are not capable of killing. The fact that the film was punctiliously retitled '*La Femme* Nikita' on its American release seemed to emphasize this message: that if only women would remain as they should be, governments would revert to legal propriety as well. The image selected for the publicity poster was of the actress Anne Parillaud in a tight, short black dress and high heels, her gun at the ready. If the gun suggested the deadly Woman With A Gun, her clothing and her awkward pose suggested her physical restraint by glamour wear: the practical difficulties of running, ducking, etc, whilst balancing on heels, and of squatting self-protectively when one's clothes resist it. In the Hollywood remake, the dark beauty of Parillaud in a black dress (signifying death) was replaced by the all-American blondeness of Bridget Fonda, in a décolleté red dress (signifying blood as sex). In both cases the gun is more sexual than fearful, a fetish. These programmatic eroticizations of the female assassin were actually reinforced by the colour-code, since both red and black are colours associated with sexuality as well as death, linking *eros* and *thanatos*. Neither avatar of the assassin myth as feminine is in fact threatening, because so eroticized. As in the case of Castro's mistress and the Judith on the cover of the novel *Holofernes*, the Woman With A Gun is a contradiction. Whilst iconizing a cultural paranoia about subversion/feminism, her image also consoles and reassures that fear by transmuting it into traditionally seductive femininity. The male specular gaze is invited and indulged by the eroticized Woman With A Gun. She thus at once encodes and dispels prevalent fears. Whilst the proliferation of images of gun-toting women may seem to recognize women's equality or dominance in a supposedly post-feminist society, such images actually perform the reverse function: recognition cancelled by reassurance. Woman With A Gun is an ideological double-bluff.

This should be clear enough if we consider actual female assassins. Despite the cultural prominence of fictive Women With Guns, the popular mind remains obstinately resistant to the idea that real women perform real assassinations. After Rajiv Gandhi's assassination it was suggested that the perpetrators were two young girls who had presented him with bouquets. No one had anticipated that juvenile females would pose a security risk. This suggests that the myth of the female assassin is recognized as precisely that – a decorative fiction 'safely' discounted in actual political situations. Similarly, the glamour of the Woman With A Gun is not often replicated in actuality. In 1990, the middle-aged woman who stabbed a German politician also had no difficulty reaching him, because the same mental block was in operation; and the media audibly breathed disappointment and surprise that she seemed to be an ordinary housewife. Whether in public consciousness or in fact, the Woman With A Gun is not acknowledged as traversing the boundary between pretty fictions and mundane life. That is, the threat she supposedly represents is not taken seriously, however ubiquitous in popular culture: which means that this is a strikingly successful double-bluff, efficiently reassuring. The popular mind does not credit the Woman with a Gun as symbol of woman made powerful, only her glamour as sexual fantasy.

Similarly, if the threat of subversion to the efficient modern state is encoded into the Woman With A Gun, this too can become a way of reassuring us about the phenomenon of terrorism generally. Although the Renaissance assassin also challenged the view that state order was natural and secure, this challenge is the

more vivid when juxtaposed with the giant security apparatus of the late twentieth-century state. Even this, it appears, is not proof against either assassins or
terrorists – indeed, these phenomena have never been more marked. That
effectively *exacerbates* anxiety, since it is demonstrable that political order is
never secure, no matter how heavily protected by advanced technology and
manpower. We will return to the character of this anxiety presently, but for now
it is helpful to explore its moral dimension. As in the Renaissance, the moral
ambiguity of the relations between state and subversion is very effectively
encoded by that of Judith's icon. Just as it was then, so in modern times it is
difficult to make a secure moral distinction between terrorism/freedom-fight-
ing and state counter-terrorism. Both constitute illegal uses of surveillance,
conspiracy and violence. As in *Nikita*, the Judithic assassin may be employed
by either side, and her nationalist significance be used to justify either. By the
same token, both sides may be morally dubious. In the Middle East, Israel's
admission that, as long suspected, its secret service regularly deployed
assassination squads was, apologists for Mossad argued, simply a recognition of
the need for pragmatic solutions to the problem of terrorism. As in the religious
struggles of the Reformation, so in that between Israel and the PLO, both sides
fetched their authorization from the absolutes that are supposed to transcend
human laws. Hard-line politicians in Israel adhered to the Old Testament's code
of vengeance, 'an eye for an eye', as the religious concept that parallels the pragmatic: the thought goes that if each atrocity provokes a retributive atrocity it
will be clear that 'terrorism cannot win'. The moral ambiguity of Judith as
assassin (enemy of the Assyrians, saviour of the Israelites, fifth columnist or
freedom-fighter) embodies this uneasy doubling of terrorist and counter-terrorist, authority and subversion.

Fictional Heroines

The moral ambiguity that identifies terrorism with counter-terrorism is
explored within a Judithic scenario in John le Carré's proficient and popular
thriller, *The Little Drummer Girl* (1983). Its heroine, a relatively unsuccessful
English actress known as Charlie, is recruited to work for Mossad by a mysterious man known as Joseph. Neither Jewish nor an activist, Charlie is nevertheless one of those actresses who fancies herself sympathetic to all good causes
and especially revolutionary ones: as a result she has encountered the fringes of
a Palestinian group. Seduced by love of Joseph rather than Zionism. Charlie
agrees to impersonate the mistress of a Palestinian terrorist, Michel, in order to
lead Mossad to his brother Khalil, mastermind of a terrorist group operating
successfully in Europe. When Michel is killed by Mossad, Khalil seduces her,
as planned. Having followed Charlie, the Israeli hit squad is now able to ambush
Khalil in his own bedroom. That this is the Judith myth translated into the

modern Arab–Israeli conflict is implied by the novel's repeated invocation of biblical models and Zionist ideology. A Mossad agent is compared to the biblical David, and Joseph is explicitly identified with his namesake in the Old Testament. There Joseph was presented as a striking exemplar of resolute chastity, because he resisted the blandishments of his master Potiphar's wife. In art Joseph and Judith have been counterparts, as resisters of orientalist lust, which is why Charlie complains of Joseph's fascinating 'chastity' in the novel.[11] Both were also representatives of their people. Charlie, unlike her Joseph, does not replicate this traditional imagery because her role is as the Judithic seducer in modern guise – modern representations refuse to take the notion of Judith's chastity seriously, because this is counter-cultural to prevailing permissive values. Thus Charlie's version of Judith's guile requires her to be a promiscuous woman, who is happy to sleep with her Holofernes in order that he may be killed.

On the other hand, she experiences moral disgust at his killing and suffers a nervous breakdown. In this, le Carré depicts a political naïf's arrival at the consciousness that no political objective justifies murder and mayhem. Both Charlie and Joseph express sympathy with the Palestinian enemy, conveying le Carré's point that the political situation is so complex and intractable that neither side is right or wrong. Evocation of Palestinian terrorism is balanced by the novel's detailed depiction of Israel's counter-terrorist operations. Le Carré knows less about Islam than he does about Judaism, but he attempts to suggest the way in which their faiths become the protagonists' guarantee that everything they do (murder, massacre, torture, atrocity) is ultimately justifiable: necessary measures in a godly war. Ultimately the two sides are portrayed as consanguineous in ideology and guilt, despite their antipathy. The novel thus dramatizes the disturbing ambiguity in political ideologies of terrorism, whether governmental or subversive.

In the face of this problem, the novel retreats into a sentimental depiction of romantic love as the personalized alternative to political resolution of the conflict. In the final melancholy reunion of Charlie/Judith and Joseph, private love becomes the only sure ground of humanity in a world determined by impossibly compromised values. Against the masculinism of both Arabs and Israelis, le Carré offers Charlie's femininity as a counterpoint and reproach. Precisely because she is ruled by her emotions, she cannot abrogate compassion in the way that they so readily do. Both her sex and the Judithic plot are vital to the novel's theme, as an exposure of the identity between the two sides. On the other hand, this psychic history means that Charlie/Judith is another demotivated Woman With A Gun figure. She may not be incompetent like Castro's mistress, but her femininity becomes identified with political illiteracy as well as with apolitical compassion. Its thematic value is thus bought at the price of castrating the Woman With A Gun, transforming her into femininity-as-pacifism. At this level the novel revives and positivizes an old cliché about 'the second sex' as Romantic Love and Tenderness, emerging *out of* the Judithic assassin herself.

Despite the biblical ambience and the mythic identity of Charlie as a Judith to Khalil's Arab Holofernes, unlike Joseph's her typing is never made explicit in the text. Perhaps le Carré was not familiar with the Book of Judith, only with the cultural myths that feed upon it. Or perhaps in order to exculpate Charlie he did not wish to confuse her with the image of the resolute assassin. In the Middle Eastern theatre of war Judith's emphatically Zionist resonance would also have associated Charlie too closely with the cause here represented by Mossad. Le Carré needs the Judithic ambiguity to evoke the terrorist/counter-terrorist identity, but must suppress its nationalist signification.

As with the cultural myth of the assassin, sexual politics are fundamental to the mythology of terrorism. The existence of the woman terrorist has been taken to imply that modern feminism and terrorism are related phenomena, because both impel a rejection of the given order of things, which is identified with political stability. The view that the woman terrorist would have been an impossibility prior to the women's movement is, however, nonsense: as we have seen, women terrorists predate modern feminism. Equally, the view that women terrorists are personifications of female rebelliousness is also a cultural myth far from the fact. Herself formerly a member of a subversive group, Robin Morgan argued in *The Demon Lover* that the modern male terrorist was a recrudescence of the 'demon lover' figure of folklore. Mad, bad and dangerous to know, he is romanticized by his doomed heroism in 'the cause'. This roman-tic stereotype accounts, she thinks, for the magnetic attraction exerted by terrorists upon their female acolytes, and for the fact that most women terror-ists are recruited by their lovers. These women are not subversively mascu-line/phallic in character but subordinately feminine, handmaidens of their demon lovers. (Morgan adds that they often find a vicarious outlet for their own rage through their lovers' actions.)[12] If this is so, we might conclude that in fact the woman terrorist and Judith are actually antipathetic figures. Unlike the woman terrorist, Judith acts by herself and for herself, and it is crucial to her heroism that she loves and follows no man. Far from obeying a demon lover figure, she kills him in the person of Holofernes. If the biblical Judith is in effect a terrorist in the ancient world, the modern woman terrorist falls far short of her idealized image. To portray the woman terrorist as a Judith invokes a dis-ingenuous shadow of the real thing. The Judithic projection of Woman With A Gun implies a stronger cultural recognition of feminism than is really the case.

Equally, the fictional fascination with the woman terrorist tends to suggest that she is somehow characteristic of terrorism in general. This is important, because her deviance from feminine norms thus bolsters the view that terrorist conspiracy is wrong whilst governmental counter-terrorist conspiracy is not. By thus typing terrorism as anomalous/Other/feminine, it draws a false, gender-based distinction, as if governments did not employ precisely the same 'illegitimate' techniques. It also disguises the identity between terrorism and state power as official and outlaw forms of the same system, masculine dominance. The demon lover/terrorist and the spymaster (Nikita's boss, with whom she has a powerfully repressed sexual rapport) are simply alter-egos in the patriarchal system. The romantic myth that renders both figures equally charismatic bolsters masculine dominance generally, whether or not reinforced by formal positions of power. Indeed, insofar as the terrorist challenges a power, his own is seen as more unquestionably a matter merely of his sexual identity. Paradoxically, the more he rebels against authority the more he affirms that masculinity itself is potent enough without it. Masculine charisma – its destiny as powerful – is in the terrorist portrayed as independent of mere red tape, a natural force.

We can see this at work in le Carré's novel when he identifies the Israeli officer Joseph with the Arab terrorist Khalil. This effect, the exchange of Charlie between oppositional lovers/covert operators, is intended to subserve the theme that exposes the two sides' likeness in ideology and guilt. But it also automatically replays the romantic dynamics of the demon lover. Khalil's 'eyes . . . were Joseph's eyes, dark and purposeful and all-seeing'.[13] the dominant dark-hero not only of terrorist romance but also, of course, of popular romantic ideology in general. The Judaic Joseph and the Arab Khalil coalesce in the single figure of the sexually dominant dark-hero, the 'Holofernes' in the mythology of terrorism. When Joseph and Charlie are re-united in an embrace heavy with the discourse of romantic cliché, she is re-embracing Khalil as well. That idea is at the thematic level politically irenic, but at the level of cultural myth it maintains for the novel's readership the image of the terrorist as sexual hero. It cannot help but do so, because like the Woman With A Gun he is profoundly implicated in erotic fantasy. If masculinity is habitually envisaged by our culture as penetrative-aggressive, then the audaciously phallic-destructive terrorist is its dream lover. The distinction between him and normal masculinity is as insecure as the distinction between terrorism and covert state activity.

Despite this ambivalent identity, terrorism exposes something about its powerful antagonists. It feeds the paranoid insecurity of modern life in the developed countries because it demonstrates, just as the assassin does, the fundamental weakness even of superpowers in the face of guerrilla activity. In occasions both of assassination and of terrorism (activities often related to each other in any case), we can perceive a version of the David-versus-Goliath and Judith-versus-Holofernes scenario, in which the vast organization of the modern state is breached by limited but focused clandestine activity. Vietnamese guerrillas, the bombers of the World Trade Center and the IRA's attack on the City of London all manifested that the effect of terrorism precisely depended upon the ratio between its minimal means and the scale of its target, whether the latter was a massive military machine or a financial nerve-centre. All were instances of the vulnerability attendant upon efficient large-scale apparatuses. Similarly, to defeat the giant David only needed a pebble, and to defeat the mighty Assyrian Empire Judith only needed to disable one general. Their stories are the aboriginal myths that represent and explicate the fragility of institutionalized power. They signify its subversive secret of vulnerability, whether in the ancient Near East or in modern international politics.

Removing the Head

In the 1960s, Hannah Arendt theorized the politics of violence as manifested both in Vietnam and in the Paris riots of 1968. She suggested that it is necessary to distinguish between power and violence. Opposing those political theorists who had argued that all state power is founded on violence, she suggested that violence is in fact that which occurs when power is weak. It attacks declining power at its Achilles heel, its need to resort to force to protect itself. Directed against the state, violence exposes its weakness; employed by the state, violence symptomatizes its weakness. Unlike power, violence is simply an implement, a means-to-an-end. Therefore it cannot be revolutionary – revolutions use power – but only effect very limited short-term tasks of resistance, and the longer it persists the less effective it becomes.[14] That is, the most efficiently subversive violence is minimal but achieves maximum disruption.

If we recall the way in which Judith's action was interpreted by Freud in response to the first modern war, we can see that Freud's thesis supports Arendt's, if we apply both to the Judithic terrorist. In Freud's view, the killing of Holofernes attacked the group psychology upon which armies and empires depend to sustain themselves. It simply and economically removed the single lynchpin of the group's structure, its homoerotic object of collective desire, the leader. Indeed, in Nestroy's version of *Judith* even the homicide was unnecessary, for a fake severed head achieved exactly the same effect of imploding the institution. In the myth of Judith is represented, then, the political dynamics of the international conflict between terrorism and states, and the exposure of the superpower as inherently weak.

For precisely this purpose Michael Baldwin's surreal and clever thriller *Holofernes* (1990) radically reinterprets the myth of Judith. That the novel is consciously employing her myth is evident from the epigraph, which cites the Book of Judith and two Renaissance uses of Holofernes' name, Rabelais's pedantic tutor in *Gargantua and Pantagruel* and Tasso's chivalric knight in *Gerusalemme Liberata*. The vulnerable group psychology of the superpowers is manifested when a freelance terrorist named Dragout uses the international media to trick them into thinking that a major terrorist operation is under way in North Africa. Simultaneously he is duping his own Arab backers, who believe precisely the same thing, in order to embezzle the funds they have provided for an operation codenamed 'Holofernes'. Both the superpowers and their enemies are fellow-victims of Dragout, who has understood that both sides are effectively the same. Like Nestroy's Judith, he uses a fake Holofernes to defeat them.

He knows that he does not need to mount a real operation in order to achieve international disruption and terror: he just needs the *reputation* of a terrorist operation to implement terrorism. This wholly exposes the weakness of super-powers dependent upon reports, television film and covert intelligence, all of which confer on 'Holofernes' spurious reality. Telecommunications may seem to support the power of the modern state, but here they are revealed as equally subversive of it. The elegance of his con trick is evident only if we already understand the importance of the ratio of minimal means to maximal effect in terrorism. Dragout understands that violence and power are antipathetic, so he never uses it except when necessary. We might describe his as a textbook demonstration of Freud's exegesis of the political Judith myth, masculine group psychology projected onto the global scene.

That sexual politics are culturally crucial to this exploration of power-poli-tics is manifested in Baldwin's reinterpretation of Judith's sexual myth. The codename 'Holofernes' comprises both Dragout and his operation, identifying trickster and trick. Dragout embodies the accumulated significations of Holofernes in culture – such as those generated by the Book of Judith, Rabelais and Tasso. He is Holofernes as orientalist despot, empty pomp, patriarchal dominator, sexual predator, for he consciously plays these multiple roles as part of his operation's decor: it depends upon the manipulation of cultural myths. It also depends upon understanding the doubleness of perpetrator and victim, terrorist and state, which we saw demonstrated in the Renaissance. Just as the infidel Dragout killed the knight Holofernes in Tasso's Renaissance epic, yet in Baldwin's novel Dragout is Holofernes himself, so he is the terrorist as tyrant, the tyrant as terrorist. He is at once orientalist despot of his operation and sub-verter of superpowers; in both roles, replicating the overblown masculinity of Holofernes, as a mythic archetype of power.

To this role Dragout recruits as his Judithic antagonist the British agent Patrick Matson. He is formidable antagonist, but also one with an Achilles heel: his sexual identity. His existence in the macho world of covert operations has ossified his misogynistic attitudes whilst intensifying his sexual desires. Since the novel ironizes Matson's misogyny as a delusory myth that precludes successful relationships, if this delusion is dispelled the rest of his identity will disintegrate, for upon it depends his efficiency as a ruthless agent/soldier, the epitome of phallic aggression. Dragout thus disables the captured Matson by subjecting him to simultaneous torture and rape, using him as the Judith in his camp: precipitating a trauma from which after his escape Matson's only relief is a neurotically professional, 'masculine' behaviour. The classically masculine generic thriller hero is feminized, just as the Book of Judith inverted masculine epic into feminine romance. Matson is the victim of a terrorist demon lover.

If Matson is a Judith, he discovers that in effect the only course that will restore his gender-identity is actually to identify with the biblical heroine: to wreak her vengeance, identify with her in her 'masculine' act of homicide. When he asks a rape-counsellor if she has heard the word 'Holofernes' before, she explains that 'Holofernes is well-known in feminist circles . . . Read Apocrypha. He is the general who tried to rape Judith.' Since Matson is a literate man, he asks if this is the Judith of the Anglo-Saxon epic. This attribution of the feminist heroine to the masculine genre of epic is a metaphor for Matson's psychic re-integration: when his macho self returns he will again think of Anglo-Saxon epic, a way of achieving the mental transaction between himself and the original Judith's femininity. At this the counsellor replies, 'That's right. Only [instead of being raped] she got him drunk and chopped off his head with his own sword. We frequently advise it.'[15] This instruction in the nature of female anger and the need for revenge inducts Matson into the vengeance available to him: for it is indeed perfectly possible for him, as it is not for most women or most men for that matter, to kill his violator. His female psychotherapist urges him to do so. When the camp is taken, this is precisely what he does, in Dragout's exotic Holofernean bedroom. He has identified with female vengeance thus far, but afterwards reverts to learned masculine and professional behaviours. The solution to his riven identity is makeshift, just as is the superpowers' response to Dragout. At both levels, the contradictions in their identities make power and masculinity weak, dependent upon sustained violence to maintain themselves. Provisionally feminist for the sake of his virility, the contradictory Matson/Judith is just as ambiguous as the effeminate/masculinist Dragout/David. The way in which the illusions masculine/feminine meet is equivalent to the rapprochement between state and terrorist, power and its demon lover. There is an exact equivalence between what Matson 'learns' about gender and what the Rabelaisian 'tutor' Holofernes/Dragout teaches the superpowers about their own constitution.

Ultimately, then, *Holofernes* is an exploration of the Arendtian distinction between power and violence. Power/masculinity resides in the perceived need of its subjects to submit to it, which when weak becomes an 'illusion' of power shored up by violence. When weak it is vulnerable to counter-illusion, such as that practised by Dragout, and is repeatedly rebuilt by the exercise of force, which is itself a menace to the illusion. Illusions that are lived by are, *faute de mieux*, real.

This is a rather terrifying thought, but it is indeed fetched directly from the Book of Judith. The efficacy of Judith's forensically limited violence is precisely dependent upon the power of Holofernes himself: that to remove him is psychologically to defeat those who are accustomed to obey him. Without the one to whom power is attributed his subjects are indeed powerless to act; it is the behaviour learned under a power that makes that power vulnerable. And if the exertion of force is inadequate to the defence of power, then this too is conveyed by the metaphysics of the Book of Judith. The Assyrians, she says, 'trust in' their weaponry, 'and know not that thou art the Lord that breakest the battles . . . Throw down their *strength* in thy *power*' (9:7–8 [my italics]). Nebuchadnezzar's material strength is an illusion because the only absolute power is God's, absolute precisely because *immaterial*. The Arendtian distinction between violence and power resides in the fact that power is immaterial, the ability to command, whereas violence is a coercive materialist activity. In the Book of Judith Holofernes is weak because coercive, and violent because weak. The invisibility of God's power renders it independent of instruments and violence, though it may summon them as the delimited means to an end, for omnipotence is transcendent of means. The strong do not need to coerce, for they possess authority. Judith's is thus the strength of her authoritativeness to the elders, her ability to beguile Holofernes, rather than residing in the sword that she uses. On the contrary, it enables her to acquire the sword that signifies the limitation of his power to its instrument, force. The Judith myth configures the relation between power and violence.

As we have seen, sexual politics are profoundly imbricated in that relation. Popular culture reveals the way in which the mythologized codes of power and gender overlap real and fictional political scenes, as they overlap international politics and urban society's normalization of fear. In the modern cultural cliché of Woman With A Gun is compounded the image of terrorism and of feminism, threats to 'normal' masculinity and its position of power. Her bogey projects both urban paranoia and masculinist hysteria onto the feminine Other, the counter-cultural Judith: as if the destabilization of Western society were the fault of women, and as if to expel, exterminate or suppress feminism would permit the restoration of order. More immediately, the hostile image reinforces the masculinism it supposedly contests by provoking a consciously aggressive reversion in men to the masculinist stereotype that seems to offer them refuge and restoration. (Just as it does for Baldwin's Matson, reverting to type.) As cultural myth, far from acknowledging or heroizing feminism, the Woman With A Gun is deployed by reactionary ideology to instigate revalorized manhood in antagonism to it. She is not an image of women's having gained unprecedented power in late twentieth-century society. On the contrary, by skewing feminist aspirations into a masculinist thesis against them, the Woman With A Gun implies that feminism cannot get anywhere in practical terms. That is why she reassures those who most fear women's independence, by at once exaggerating and denying it. Exaggeration aggravates hostility to her, whilst denial reassures that surging hostility that it will overcome her in the end, just as it has always done in the past.

Thus masculinist morale is maintained. Her eroticized and trivialized image consoles the specular viewer that old stereotypes of femininity still hold good. A splendidly apt symbol of this double-bluff is the blowing up of the Uffizi in 1993 by terrorists, damaging Artemisia Gentileschi's *Judith*.[16] Impregnable the Woman With A Gun is not. The late twentieth century's bogey is only that. Like the dragons in fairy tales she represents a paranoid delusion, of feminine domination. She testifies not to feminist achievement but to masculinist hysteria. In that sense, she is most reliably a measure of how mightily society is mustering all its imagistic resources, to stem the tide of feminism before it really can achieve radical political change.

Even her gun, whilst attesting to the potential equalization of the genders through force, can be interpreted against the grain of feminist assertiveness. The image's secret weakness – its *appeal* to the paranoid viewer who fears it – is precisely that it holds a gun, signifier of violence, which is contraindicative of power. It thus works culturally to ratify hysterical masculinist complaints that women are dominating men, whilst signifying to men that they are safe enough. It is a perfected ideological double-bluff, at once false and true, yet in both respects masculinist.

At the same time, however, the gun's signifier of her secret weakness is itself a phallic symbol: it implies also the secret weakness of the myth of masculinity. If masculinity depends for mastery upon the superiority of its physical force, in Arendtian terms that would also signify its entropy. In part, Woman With A Gun is a cultural attempt to extricate embattled masculinity from the entropic implication of dependence on the phallic gun. Patriarchy is trying to free itself of the perception that masculinity both depends upon and is identical with physical force. Hence the cowering New Man shelters behind his Woman With A Gun, the replica of the old man's aggressive weakness. In order to emancipate itself from this disingenuous caricature of the sexes in the 1990s, feminism has to beware both the Woman With A Gun and the Man Without A Gun, for both images are attempts to disarm it.

The Woman With A Gun signifies both the assertion/contradiction that feminism is jeopardizing patriarchy, which is consoling, and the suppressed anxiety that it really is. Fear and reassurance feed upon each other in her image. She signifies for Western society what it fears, what it desires and also what it obscurely knows about the vulnerability of patriarchal power. Which is why the Woman With A Gun remains frightening despite the double-bluff encoded into her. Like the terrorist, hers is a mirror-image of the weak power. Maybe that mirror reflects an actuality, and patriarchy is indeed weak: but maybe (in this play of illusions) not. Time will tell whether, like Baldwin's superpowers in the terrorist era, patriarchy can rescue itself simply by blundering about in the realm of cultural mythology. After all, the Book of Judith already knew patri-archy's secrets twenty centuries ago, and yet (to adapt the eloquent words of a modern prime minister) 'It's still there'. We should never underestimate the power of cultural myth. Depending upon how she transmutes in future, the Woman With A Gun may reveal herself as prophetic of patriarchy's capacity to sustain itself, or revelatory of its doom.

13

Judy the Ripper
Feminists and Serial Killers

The man of power in the Book of Judith is a conscious player in the battle of the sexes, for 'he waited a time to deceive her, from the day that he had seen her' (12:16). Since she brings down patriarchy in his person, Judith's symbolic value should make her a natural icon for modern feminism. Thus, for instance, the American artist Cindy Sherman deliberately reworked Old Masters, casting herself as New Mistress of art. Just as in the Renaissance Artemisia Gentileschi had rendered Judith as a self-portrait of women's revenge on men's perfidy, so Sherman personated a composite of Judith and Delilah, with a severed head in one hand and scissors in the other. A traditional subject representing a male fear of women is inverted by this self-portrait, which puts the woman artist in charge of avenging power. And the scissors, utensil of the approved womanly household art of sewing, are diverted to the less pliant art of household homicide. Feminism's reappropriating traditional bogeys of embattled manhood as positive icons led to a revival of interest in Artemisia Gentileschi herself, re-imagined as a role-model for the Woman With A Gun: 'The Thelma – and Louise – of art', as *Newsweek* announced when a major touring exhibition of her work was mounted.[1] A feminist bookseller in Britain dubbed her operation 'Monstrous Regiment' and put Judith's icon on the cover of her catalogue.[2] Nor was it only feminists who recognized that Judith was an apt figure for women's independence in the 1980s and 1990s. Women's spending power increasingly inspired cultural organizations and the media to highlight images of powerful women, even if they often found ways of undermining the very images they peddled.

To the increasing prominence of women's issues we can attribute such phenomena on the London scene in the 1990s as a pair of *Judith* operas performed at the Almeida; the sale at Sotheby's of a very ordinary Renaissance painting of Judith, by a minor artist, for a quarter of a million pounds; and the poster advertising a rare public exhibition of the Queen's pictures, for which the painting selected was Allori's Judith.[3] All over Britain and tourist offices abroad, the image of the heroine bearing a man's severed head was disseminated as an attractive, authoritative image of official culture. It was notable, however, that unsuspecting commuters on the London Tube (for instance) often did not realize precisely what they were looking at; since the advertising text was printed over Holofernes' head. Unless already familiar with Judith's image, they did not tend to perceive her surprising accessory. Apart from this mollification of the image for public (male?) consumption, the poster represented the cultural ambience. It did so because it was by now recognized that 'women's imagery' had a commercial value on the market: it would attract the punters. But such acculturated appropriation of Judith's icon should not obscure the fact that *within* feminist thinking her sign does not function quite as simply to represent feminism as it does in the mainstream culture. If Judith can represent the militant face of feminism to the world outside, within feminism she is sited at points of ideological difficulty. As is so often the case with revolutions – and feminism has been dubbed 'the long revolution'[4] – they may be defeated from within, or corrupted by their own success. Since Judith, properly understood, is an icon of integrity, her placing in feminist culture can reveal both its strengths and its weaknesses.

You're on your Own

As the counter-cultural myth, Judith's Book – I suggest – effectively encodes the whole project of feminism. It offers an alternative, feminine cultural paradigm to the dominant cultural myth of Oedipal masculinity, because just as the Oedipus myth signifies all strata of patriarchy, so Judith's signifies all the strata of anti-patriarchy, as we have seen. Meanwhile, modern feminism is committed to a complete revision of culture and society to enfranchise 'the second sex'. To this end, feminist thinkers have contended, it is necessary to retrieve alternative, aboriginal myths of women's power, especially matriarchal myths of 'The Goddess', which have been lost in the male domination of culture. If feminism is concerned to retrieve a mythology against the received culture, and if as I have suggested Judith's is *the* counter-cultural myth, hers should be recognized as the sign of a new liberty.

Yet this has not invariably been the case in feminist art and thought. Feminism has a problem with God – at least as Judaeo-Christian tradition has perceived him: 'it is best to laugh at foolish women who think they can get their own way in a world where even God is a man and on the other side.'[5] Regarding him as the conceptual term at the apex of patriarchy, feminist theologians have attempted to re-imagine religion in a way that would make Christian feminism feasible.[6] The problem of religion is a crucial instance of disagreements within feminism about the means and ends whereby culture and society are to be reformed so that women could inhabit them as autonomous beings. Ultimately, autonomy – psychic, social and political – is the answer to the oft-repeated question 'What do women want?' Quite simply, feminism wants women to be themselves, without the unconscionable lets and hindrances imposed upon them by the way masculinist ideology construes them. However, a revolution that did not also liberate men from false mythology would be abortive.

In Victorian culture, as we saw, Judith-Jael was the sign of authentic personality, both for women and (in uncanny guise) for men. For women to live up to Judith as a role-model, they would have to eschew the mental conditioning that makes them susceptible to subordination. A distinguished and (more importantly) tough-minded novelist, Margaret Atwood, ran into flak from former feminist admirers when, in her novel *Cat's Eye*, she suggested that women permitted the traditional competition for men to poison their relationships with other women and to attenuate their own personalities. The novel's heroine Elaine's hostility to other women has been generated by their cruelties to her, in a vicious circle of mutual damage, because 'Forgiving men is so much easier than forgiving women'.[7] Precisely for this reason she refuses to be authentic to herself, a refusal encoded as her revulsion at paintings of Judith: 'Biblical subjects tilt towards violence: Judith cutting off the head of Holofernes is now popular . . . I don't like these shadowy, viscous pictures . . . I prefer . . . calm arrested gestures.' Her own personality is in fact 'arrested' and cold, fearing the uncanny and violent image that tells her to kill off her inner demons. As long as women hate each other, they cannot love themselves. If men are incapable of loving women, and so are women, then Elaine's rage is at the absence of love. The moral is that women must learn to love other women. I would go further than Atwood and suggest that they need to love most the Judithic women whose extraordinariness challenges their own servile psychology. Indeed, the element in the Book of Judith that is incredible, I suggest, is that Judith's maid is loyal to her mistress. A truly feminist woman might well alienate *soi-disant* feminists by making them feel less than adequate. Women thus help to imprison each other and themselves.

But then, would it be possible also to reform Holofernes, from tyranny, lechery, greed and cruelty? Is it possible for neither sex to play the role of slave? If it is not very careful, feminism too can generate myths that – by failing to acknowledge the courage required for authentic personality to sustain itself in anyone, irrespective of gender – will defeat its own ends.

As a woman who appropriates a normally masculine role, Judith can signify either equality or dominance: *The Female Man*, as in the title of Joanna Russ's novel (1985) about a woman of the future named Jael. But some feminists are suspicious of the idea that women should be like men or valorize qualities that masculinist society admires, for they regard this as compromising a fully alternative feminism. It is possible, as the critic Mary Jacobus has, to see Judith the 'phallic woman' as having defected to the traditionally masculine values of aggression, competition and domination.[8] In the 1970s, feminism was by and large committed to the view that women differed from men in that they were more compassionate and natural, nurturers – in short, mothers. A thorough-going 'essentialist' view of the female gender regards it as qualitatively distinct from the male. From that binary opposition ensues the repudiation by some feminists of 'masculine' mental qualities as well: logic, analytic rigour and rationality are rejected in favour of the intuition, instinct and creativity suppos-edly unique to the female gender. Of course, to such a philosophy of feminism Judith's resolution, ruthlessness, strategic forethought and rationalism are as repellent as her use of force.

Yet this version of feminism is fundamentally misguided. For it depends upon precisely that traditional binary opposition of genders – Intuition versus Reason – that it proposes to escape the ideological consequences of. It also sur-renders to masculinity ownership of rationalism, precisely what masculinism itself reserves to the male. Competitive chess is an instance of this contest for intellectual credibility. Whereas misogynist players contend that women lack the intellectual skill to achieve supremacy, the teenage girl who was once con-sidered the most likely to disprove this, the Yugoslavian prodigy Judit Poldar, in a *Sunday Times* profile cited her namesake as her role-model in this quest. Ironically enough in this context, feminism itself is an ideology born of (pre-cisely) the rational analysis, and hence the exposure, of patriarchy as ideology.

Even highly sophisticated feminist fictions can fall into the trap of indulging emotionalism, precisely because of a justifiable rage against culture's misprision of clever women. Sarah Maitland's *Telling Tales* (1983) sets out to reveal the truths submerged under biblical stories, 'snitching' on patriarchy as it were. The focus of Jael's story changes the significance of her homicide from her defend-ing a patriarchal tribe to a displaced act of rebellion against the husbands who have taken their wives too much for granted. Jael makes love to Sisera with joy and relish because, whilst she is accustomed to the daily round of waiting upon goatherds as if they were gods simply because they are men, she has never before served a man truly powerful, virile and beautiful: 'even asleep he carries his authority.'[9] She takes satisfaction in discovering a servitude that at least has the trappings of justification, given Sisera's splendour, when she is habituated to accepting a servitude all too visibly unjust. This ironic perspective conveys the daily frustration of women's coerced servitude. However, whilst men might need to be deterred from exploiting women, a Jael who seems sly and malicious is unlikely to convert male readers to the feminist cause. Maitland offers Jael as the icon of women's suppressed rage.

The only problem with this thesis is that it can be appropriated by its enemy, since misogynists do indeed think that feminists want to kill them, literally or metaphorically. Hence all the whingeing of misogynists that feminism has 'gone too far' and that men are now victims. This faction pounces gleefully upon images of women's vengeance. When the Virago Press celebrated its twentieth anniversary, for instance, the *Observer* illustrated its coverage with Artemisia Gentileschi's painting of Judith and her maid hacking at Holofernes, captioned as 'Women's Work'.[10]

An avenging Judith-Jael can iconize women's rage, and hence the psychic violence inflicted by patriarchy; but she cannot signify their enfranchisement into a new identity as progenitors. In her novel *The Tent Peg* (1989), Aritha van Herk recognizes this danger. Her J.L. (Jael) cross-dresses as a boy in order (like Judith) to infiltrate the enemy (male) camp, gradually dispels their illusions about women and spares the life of a would-be rapist (her Sisera). She chooses to educate mankind by patience, tolerance and good cheer, and her tent peg is not a homicidal weapon but a means of striking deep into the earth, staking a claim – in the book's mining metaphor – for natural human relations to replace the sex war. This plea for naturalness is a tactful version of an early feminist attraction to stereotyping women as nurturing earth-mothers. This has similar dangers to the Victorian feminists' eugenicism, for such stereotypes are as limiting as those they attempt to replace.

The Politics of Desire

More ambitiously, van Herk's prizewinning novel *Judith* (1978) does confront the difficulty of being a true Judith: on the one hand, possessing a power to emasculate patriarchy, and on the other, retaining the capacity to love. Liberation requires both.

Acknowledging that she must abandon a sterile, self-deluding way of life as the typical 'modern woman', van Herk's remade biblical Judith returns to nature and becomes a pig-farmer. The novel's central event is her castration of male piglets, in which her man, at first fearful of this symbolic activity, eventually co-operates, recognizing that her spirit is not mean but carnivalesque. (Here he plays Achior's role in electing for spiritual castration by Judith.) This is someone educable, capable of loving even a Judith, terrifying though her independence is. Having chosen potentially lonely self-reliance, Judith's life is transformed. Van Herk suggests that a woman can be a feminist and still have a happy ending: that, indeed, a happy ending is positively dependent on autonomy. In this way she assaults the reinforcement of patriarchy by romantic myth, women's fear that independence inevitably produces loneliness. In effect, van Herk is trying to reassure them that feminism will not rob them of romance, which is indeed the implicit reason why many young women denigrate feminism.

At the same time, though, iconizing carnivalesque feminine sexuality comes perilously close to accepting the traditional view of women as beings totalized by their sexuality. Like J.L.'s 'well-intentioned, nice men',[11] both women and men might mistake the old sexual politics for liberated equality of desire. Judith resisted and punished the masculinist, antagonistic desire of Holofernes for her, which had so much to do with power that it became a death-wish. It all depends upon the character of the desire, whether it be bond or bondage.

When male authors, however well-intentioned, treat Judith's story as a parable of sexual liberation they tend to stub their toes. Influenced by the 1960s vision of unlimited paradisial free love, Howard Barker's later plays sought to find the relation between the personal and the political by celebrating spontaneous human feeling as a liberation from ideology. Desire is the one positive force in the plays of his political disillusionment. Yet in his *Judith* (1990) this produces masculine boasting, feminine meretriciousness, abortiveness and – in Judith's desperate attempt to rape the corpse – necrophilia. (Reviewers found the play both bad and sickening.) The overt moral is that denying desire leads to ruin; yet the subtext seems to be that women ought to own up to their desire to submit to a dominant male. In Barker's previous version of *Judith*, a playlet within *The Possibilities* (1987), she loses motivation: 'I quite forgot the Israelites . . . I was in such a heat . . . I could not have cared if he dripped with my father's blood.'[12] Worse, she mutilates herself in self-punishment for betraying a host. Despite Barker's 1990s-style obscenities, his Holofernes is a throwback to Hebbel's fascistic portrait, and one has the uneasy feeling that Barker was unconscious of the masculinism in these cunning plays. Even as 'host' Holofernes is encoded as master-lover, the owner-occupier of a place that womanhood can only visit on sufferance. It is interesting that Barker has chewed on this particular story so determinedly. He achieved more in *The Hard Heart* (1992), in which Riddler is a matriarch defending her city and herself from (sexual) invasion. Dazzling trickery defeats her on both fronts. This gripping play is I think, also based on Judith's model, although Barker thinks not. For that very reason, he has produced an unconscious version that has managed intriguingly to address the problem of how to be a hard-headed woman without being hard-hearted.

Indeed, what would an emancipated consciousness be like? Can it even be imagined, if delusions pervade our culture? If imaginable, is it then susceptible of being written down, in the language that has been saturated in those delusions since time immemorial? Which is to say, can cultural mythology, and the language it permeates, be rewritten?

Nicholas Mosley's experimental postmodern fiction takes the disingenuousness of language as read, and 'reads' human behaviour itself as the performance of roles and lies, a thespian enterprise. In his novel *Judith* the eponymous protagonist is an expatriate in England, her foreignness enabling her to recognize role-playing as only an outsider might. She is living in a play, but the players do not all have the same script. Later, after a traumatic experience, she embarks on a journey beyond this analytic stage towards the discovery of how to live authentically as herself, even though 'people play games' all around her.[13] In the analytic stage, the prototypical myth for her experiences is the original Judith's story. The novel opens with her performance as maid in a West End play about Judith, in which the central roles are played by a famous actress and her estranged husband (they sound not unlike Elizabeth Taylor and Richard Burton). But the performance goes horribly wrong because of the subtexts introduced into it by the real-life relationship of the stars. Executing a travesty of his own desire for his wife, who had been abusing him backstage, Actor-Holofernes sets off a series of mishaps. When he becomes comically entangled in his costume, the Maid-Protagonist comes to the rescue by firmly hitching his private parts back into their proper place. Although the actors continue to go through the motions of seduction and murder, beneath these runs a different plot about their rediscovery of their own relationship, which Actor-Holofernes', half-deliberate ridiculousness had catalysed by evoking Actor-Judith's affectionate memories of her former partner's pratfalls. The unsparing quality of intimacy is revived. It is precisely the 'weird' gap between the hieratic tragic register of the play's sexual antagonisma and the comic register of the reconciling couple, reinforced by renewed sexual attraction, that makes the spectacle fascinating to the audience on this night, but makes it impossible to recover this atmosphere on other occasions. What is obliquely represented here is the way in which authentic behaviour may break through role-playing, in life as on the stage. More, in a sense it is the very deliberation with which roles are adopted (on the stage as distinct from life) that facilitates the sudden and indeed unnerving discovery that one is behaving authentically. Breaking through life's scripted forms – 'the games' and masks – is traumatic, but the only route to autonomous selfhood. Human relationships rely upon shared mythologies or codes, yet the only chance of authenticity depends upon the accident of involuntarily breaking them – as in the actor's mishap. In Mosley's novel the story of Judith thus becomes simultaneously the sign of authenticity (the play made real, the necessary code); and, as a myth, an instance of the oppressive behavioural patterns that human beings so resolutely inhabit. Judith's myth is both a measure of myth's hegemony and a sign of release from it.

What those mythologies preclude is intersexual intimacy, other than mutual desire. Vicki Feaver's brilliant poem 'Judith' asks itself a crucial question: 'wondering how a good woman can murder / I enter the tent of Holofernes.'[14] The answer is, in essence, that she can if her man desires her desire but repudiates her self. This Judith was trained in that betrayal by her husband, whose corpse, stiff and cold in her embrace, figures their relationship. His resistance to the mutual intimacy that she had generously offered him prevents her seduction by Holofernes, whose arrogant beauty is implicitly identified with Manasses's *rigor mortis*. Having dissected the politics of desire and their unconscionable price for her, she dissects him, as if he were a fish being gutted for cooking.

Feaver examines the meaning of the myth for feminine sexuality: a revulsion from the failure of intimacy in heterosexual relationships, which makes sexuality itself a problem for feminism. Between the sexes patriarchy has placed a barrier of alienation – an aggressive-penetrative view of sex – which for women can render intercourse not intimate but estranging.[15] The 'tent of Holofernes' that Feaver's Judith enters is the prison of patriarchy within which their bed has been made. Thus the poem becomes a parallel exploration of two forms of rage, against bereavement and against a male imperviousness that inevitably makes relationships exploitative. It is a genuinely feminist vision of the two essential constituents in Judith's myth, sex and death.

Since women's fate in sexual relationships can amount to a murder of their selves, the answer to the poem's moral question is that a good woman can murder because it is her defence against psychic suicide. The aggressive-penetrative, brutal view of sex makes homicide not alien to women's psychology but familiar to them (a domestic task like cooking); and to reverse it is to kill a would-be murderer. Consequently the poem's orgasmic image, releasing its sexual tension, occurs when Judith severs the head from his neck. And it is orgasmic not because Judith is a pervert, but because it consummates women's suppressed rage and liberates desire as a yearning for freedom.

In this respect the poem is a riposte to the simplistic view that desire is necessarily a heterosexual bond and that it can equalize relationships. Its moral is the reverse of Barker's. So-called 'sexual liberation' is not, then, necessarily a solution to any feminist quest for liberation.

Judithic autonomy thus exacts very high prices: an ability to reject all inducements (including that of her own desire), inducements to actions that seem natural but are rendered perverse by their social psychology. In life, however, it is very difficult for women to question relationships in which they have made such a heavy emotional investment. But the absolute coalescence of sexual celibacy and psychic autonomy encoded in the Book of Judith poses precisely this challenge. In Russ's *Female Man*, for instance, the difference between an autonomous and an enslaved feminine state is the fear of Judith-Jael expressed by someone who does not wish to surrender her delusions: 'I would like to be Jael, twisted as she is on the rack of her own hard logic [of resistance], triumphant in her extremity, the hateful hero with the broken heart.'[16] If that is the condition on which women would gain their freedom from the patriarchal ideology that they have internalized, is it one they are prepared to accept? Are they prepared to break their own hearts? Judith-Jael is the sign of the immense psychic difficulty of what real feminism would demand of women. It would be a wager on the fruits of freedom.

This is not, after all, a price exacted of men for autonomy, in a society that is ordered in such a way as to fulfil their desires. In *The Tent Peg* J.L. complains that men do not even have to bear the burden of knowing how much society protects and cherishes them, imagining that this comfort is simply perfectly natural.[17] Yet personal politics are supported by the whole public and private system, just as the sexual and political coincide in Judith's myth. (*Pace* Barker's Judith plays, in which he deliberately breaks this vital connexion.) Society is the collectivity of individuals. Which is why Judith's marriage is invoked – unusually in adaptations of the myth – in Feaver's poem: for it is the tie that formalizes the implication of every human relationship in the systematic rituals whereby society constitutes itself. For the same reason, personal choices of sexuality and celibacy are imbricated in society. Which is why, as I have suggested throughout this history, those versions of Judith's myth that have inserted into it a sexual relationship with Holofernes have always compromised her signification. By so doing they have tended to buy into a patriarchal mythology of sex. To 'modernize' the myth or 'make it more credible' by making Judith sexually available (as Hebbel did) is automatically to dispel her feminist implications. To take Judith into the mind, as Feaver's empathetic speaker does, is to take the step to freedom from an allotted role – in Mosley's terms, a stumble into the truth. The counter-cultural myth is the exit sign from patriarchy.

We might well ask ourselves why so many male artists have been determined to make Judith requite Holofernes's desire. This reflex implies the common masculinist view that a woman is actually obliged to requite masculine (that is, any man's) desire; more, that there is something unnatural about a woman who, once desire is conferred on her, will withstand it. As a would-be seducer says to Russ's resistant Jael, 'you're a beautiful woman . . . [therefore] you want me . . . This is what God made you for.'[18] Thus Judith's ambiguous myth of the erotic/celibate woman contests patriarchy at a particularly painful point, that at which masculine wish-fulfilment is denied. The usual result is that the woman is accused of frigidity or perversion, just as Freud typed Judith as an hysteric. Her myth counters that presumptuousness precisely because both her irresistible beauty and her celibacy are instigated by the ultimate Patriarch himself.

Heads and Hearts

In Ben Elton's witty radical novel, *This Other Eden* (1993), the male hero is FBI Special Agent Judy Schwarz. So named, he disrupts the reader's expectations of gender in a thriller, since far from being male and macho he is (a) 'a nerd' and (b) homosexual. Most of all, his name forces the reader constantly to adjust the naturalized mental relation between label and gender, constantly to break the circle created by ideology. Of course, this cannot be achieved without some concession that allows myth to mediate between automatic assumptions and radical alternatives, so the name chosen to evoke a coalescence between

244   JUDITH: SEXUAL WARRIOR

masculinity and femininity is Judith's, that of 'the female man'. Abbreviating it to Judy is both appropriate to the comic atmosphere and more girlish in effect. (As was the title of the juvenile comic *Judy*, known no doubt to Elton during his own youth.) It suggests that actually the nerdy Judy Schwarz is competent in ways that matter more than physique and aggression, values espoused by the bullies who are his FBI colleagues. Instead Judy is both clever and altruistic, motifs also supported by his nomenclature. A 'feminine' ideal of personality is slid over a male protagonist. Both Judy Schwarz and the original Judith possess a counter-cultural intelligence, eloquence and strategism that are normally appropriated by masculinist values. More counter-cultural than the Freudian bogey of emasculation is the radical Judy/Judith's monopoly on rationality, as a feminist perspective ought to recognize.

Judith contradicts the binary cultural opposition between femininity as id (physical and atavistic) and masculinity as superego (mental and masterful). Judith and Holofernes reverse this cultural opposition, for he is motivated by instincts, desires, delusions and presumptions, whilst she calculatedly uses those presumptions against him. In the counter-cultural myth, atavism is masculine, exposing the fact that patriarchal power is as much an unconscious solipsism as it is a conscious imposition of will. Indeed, if it were not so, *all* men would be able to recognize that patriarchy exists; and that it is so deeply embedded in the masculine unconscious, that this is precisely why it possesses psychic hegemony.

This is why, as I have suggested, feminism cannot afford to repudiate Judith's 'masculine' psychology. It is replicated in feminist fiction by Russ's heroine, named Jael Reasoner. In the Judithic icon is signified not only rationality, however, but also violence. That is why it so readily mythologizes feminist militancy. As in Feaver's poem, it can also be ingeniously interpreted as feminine sexuality. In both respects, it is an image of will and desire, cognates in that both are driven and determined qualities. As such they are expressed physically in sex and violence. Thus Judith's icon signifies both rationality and physicality, a complete personality. How important this is is clear only if we are conscious of feminism's repeated asseveration that cultural mythology has represented women as incomplete beings. Juxtaposed with the masculine, femininity has been construed in terms of lack: of the penis, of intellect, of will. Of course, this has been a compensation mechanism, for if we are really ruthless about attributing lack we can contend that it is maleness that is a lack, because it cannot give birth. As I suggested, the Book of Judith exacts a price from her – barrenness and isolation – which, we may now see, obeys the cultural imperative to subtract feminine physical productivity from a woman who possesses 'masculine' virtues. This motif as it were re-establishes a gendered equilibrium. However, its also the case that Judith's delivering her people is an analogue to the delivery of birth. Feminine creativity is thus subliminated by the narrative, but (like all the thematics of the story) it still depends upon her sex. (Thus we may note that in the 1990s one of the 'Mother Dolls' marketed by toy corporations, secreting a miniature baby-doll within her removable tummy, was named Judith. This marketing-man's choice suggests that the myth's 'reproduction' is being literalized, and the name's 'feminist' associations being expropriated to the cultural conditioning of little girls, learning their gender-roles. Notably, the doll has Barbie's figure despite her pregnancy.) Within the myth are both cultural compensation and counter-cultural identification of femininity with heroism as *creativity*. Her violence is the homicide of one in order to give life to many. Her sex and her violence thus are attributes of her human completeness, as rationality and physicality combined. Metaphorically, the act of violence stands for her capacity to carry through thought into action, motivated by feeling. That emotional capacity comprises both positive and negative forms, compassion for her people and anger at their 'rape' by the enemy (9:2). Thus her rage and revenge are typed as feminine yet not solely as 'women's vengeance'. Iconized as an integration of rationality, physicality and emotion, she may thus appropriately stand for that full humanity in women that has been denied them by cultural constructions. This is, I suggest, how to understand Judith's as a truly feminist myth.

Women Who Kill

Judith's violence is not merely atavistic because it is an instrument, used with the greatest economy, to achieve a larger goal. Her actions are worth exploring as an instance of the crucial distinction between violence and power. In the Book of Judith, as we saw, the weak oppressive power was patriarchy, the forensic guerrilla of God feminine. (And Jael Reasoner is 'an assassin' in 'Manland'.) Thus a similar ratio of violence to power holds for the patriarchal authority assumed for men in society. How does that ratio relate to the social revolution projected by feminism?

There is a feminist theory that holds that ultimately patriarchy is founded upon fear. If women *normally* conduct their lives in fear of attack, as van Herk's J.L. also suggests, then the ever-present apprehension of male violence is what keeps women in perpetual retreat: defusing tension, accepting domination, silently accepting unprovoked verbal abuse, using silence, diplomacy and guile to preserve themselves from harm. In which case, as Susan Brownmiller argues in *Against our Will*, rape is the crucial term in the maintenance of patriarchy. A woman need not ever be raped to live in constant fear all the same, a fear metonymic of all impositions of masculine will upon her. This is how the anti-heroine lives in Helen Zahavi's notorious bestselling novel *Dirty Weekend*. Terrorized by a Peeping Tom and obscene caller to the point where she no longer dare leave her flat, she finds no distinction between home and prison:

woman incarcerated in her own victimhood. If, as Brownmiller contends, rape is the guaranteeing sign of patriarchy, then in an Arendtian system it would represent the merely occasional violence characteristic of real power.

Zahavi's opening sentence warns us that 'This is the story of Bella, who woke up one morning and realised she'd had enough.' The novel's plot is a demonstration of what happens when a woman converts from classic female victim psychology to literal *femme fatale*. Bella metamorphoses from passive object into a serial-killer of predatory, insolent and thuggish men, until in the denouement she murders her male competitor, a Jack the Ripper figure. Brilliantly controlled by Zahavi's precise yet hypnotically repetitive prose, its fertile play of puns and one-liners, the novel celebrates Bella's repeated killing as a Revenger's Comedy. Of course Bella is mad, but the point is that she did not begin that way. On the contrary, 'she'd learnt to be a good loser',[19] the victim's (woman's) virtue, but when even her deprivation was not proof against male invasion, Bella discovered her breaking point. Zahavi is implying that whereas women generally bend over backwards under their domination, Bella's psyche is not supple enough to cope in this way: for her there is nothing between fear and psychotic aggression. She is the icon of what happens when you goad the afflicted too far: when they understand that there is no depth which their slavery will not plumb, no mercy no matter how much is relinquished to the conqueror.

This sexual politics is adumbrated in biblical terms, from the Old Testament that lays down law and ratifies vengeance. Significantly named after its ruthless warlord, the Iranian quack Nimrod advises Bella that there are only two states of being, and the choice is to be 'the butcher or the lamb'. Similarly, although the parallel is not made explicit, Bella murdering the voyeur Timothy is Jael reborn. (Publicity for the filmed version used a still of Bella carrying Jael's hammer.) This is the carnivalesque exuberance of an anti-mother to Timothy's infantile male, 'a dysfunctional mother's boy' whose misogyny is yet another thing for which women can be blamed because Timothy himself has no capacity for guilt or responsibility. 'She struck him with the hammer on his cheek . . . She hammered him again, to impress upon him that he was no longer dreaming. She hammered him again, to keep up the momentum. And she hammered him again, for the hell of it.' Much of Bella's work in her new profession is surreally jolly, not least because each of her victims embodies an aspect of the giant delusion perpetrated by patriarchy.

It is only in the act of murder that Bella can experience autonomy, for enragement reveals to men their presumption. Similarly, Russ's assassin Jael exults, 'with every truthful reflection in th eyes of a dying man I get back a little of my soul; with every gasp of horrified comprehension I come a little more into the light. See? It's *me*! . . . It is I, who you will not admit exists. Look! Do you *see me*?'[20] These surreal feminist visions suggest that only as the sword sinks into his neck do a man's eyes open to 'see' a woman's personhood, for at all other times the patriarchal *mentalité* makes him blind to it.

If we look back at the many paintings of Judith's acteme executed over the centuries, it should strike us that her victim is very rarely represented as looking at her during the murder. In Caravaggio's, for instance, Holofernes in his agony is staring out of frame. Unconsciously yet slyly, encoded into such representations is a masculinist refusal to recognize the authentic woman. We can compare a similar reflex in representations of Judith that portray her as suffering from guilt after the event. The crucial point about Zahavi's and Russ's avatars of Judith-Jael is that 'I am not guilty because I murdered. *I murdered because I was guilty*': of having so long submitted to victimhood and non-personhood. Equally, representations of Judith as remorseful, such as Hawthorne's, restore a patriarchal estimate of her, because a remorseless Judith is implicitly feminist. Thus feminist fictions can expose by contrast the vested interests that motivate any detachment of Judith's icon from Justice, whose retributions are not culturally defined as guilty.

For the punishment of gender-crime Zahavi's Bella actually exceeds the Old Testament: her 'justice is not biblical [patriarchal] justice. She could never take an eye for an eye, and a tooth for a tooth.' Momentarily gender-stereotypes cause the reader to wonder whether this means she will spare Timothy's life at least, but this idea is swiftly and comically dispelled: 'The weak and flaccid parity [of that] would make her nearly puke.' Subtextually the suggestion of a flaccid penis anticipates Bella's maternal pity for Timothy's shrivelled organ as he 'blubs', bringing castration into the metaphorical equation of Bella's justicial concept: 'an eye for a tooth, and a life for an eye.' Similarly, she kills Norman (Normal Man) after sexual impotence motivates brutality towards her. If we interpret this castration motif by reference to Brownmiller's analysis of rape as guarantee of patriarchy, something rather interesting emerges. If the sign of rape guarantees patriarchy, then its antithesis, the sign of castration, must similarly guarantee feminism. As we know, castration is implicit in Jael-Judith's icon. (As a male auditor of one of my papers on Judith once remarked to me, 'Who knows what she got up to while she was alone with his body in the tent?' That space in the text accommodates the possibility of literal as well as metaphoric castration of Holofernes.) In which case, Judith's instrumental violence signifies the necessary term in a feminist revolution, its coming to power.

And Zahavi's Bella – aberrant serial killer/castrator – we could interpret as the key to matriarchy's usurping patriarchy. Another of Bella's victims is Reggie, a petty-tyrant dentist who makes himself feel important by battery and sexual abuse, and whose death prompts the gleeful coinage 'Reggicide'. The implicit parallel with political assassination maintains the novel's consistent relation of sexual to public politics, and of Bella's surreal existence to social actuality. When she kills Timothy she is like the 'peasant' in revolt, with a 'prison-burning sort of grin'. As worm-Bella cowered behind the bars of her own home, the narrator commented: 'Putrid air and bars. Men riot over less.' Which is to say, if men had to live like women the revolution would happen in double-quick time.

If the seaside town of Brighton has long been the resort of hole-in-corner extramarital affairs, of the 'dirty weekend', Bella shakes the sexual kaleidoscope into a new formation, the *Dirty Weekend* of bloody mayhem. On the book's cover, stylized 'standard views' of Brighton as seaside playground are defamiliarized by their newly sinister significance. A bucket of brightly coloured plastic toy swords, for instance, and one of those cardboard flats with cut-outs through which holidaymakers stick their heads for comic photographs: the figures, of course, are Punch and Judy, and Judy (as we saw, a displaced marital Judith) is in the act of beating Punch over the head. She is like Bella, the seaside Judith who converts holiday fantasies of men's comeuppance – toy swords – into knives and hammers and guns. The wondrous and totally unfamiliar nonchalance that Bella feels when she first walks the streets with the gun in her possession is, in fine, her holiday from patriarchy. Judith is the sign of a woman enjoying herself as never before. Zahavi's anti-sentimental, confrontational, combative, unmitigated re-use of Judith-Murderess as serial-killer feminist avenger is what facilitates the novel's frank reduction of 'normal life' to its most unacceptable components, its covert brutalities. In fact, the essential sign of Bella's freedom is not her weapon but her laughter. This is crucial, because the gun as we have seen is contraindicative of power. Bella's feminist power is represented as her mirth. Over and over again she gets to laugh at the ludicrous posturings (physical and verbal) of her victims, whereas suppression of that laughter is normally enforced by the inequality at the core of social organization. Similarly, *Dirty Weekend* is a comic novel precisely because it is feminist, even though (or rather because) it is excessively violent and squalid. *Reductio ad absurdum* is Zahavi's way of exposing the character of masculinism.

Germaine Greer once said that 'Women have no idea how much men hate them', but a male reader of Zahavi might riposte that he had no idea how much women hated men. When in 1993 Michael Winner's film version was announced, apparently endorsed by the author, there was general puzzlement in Britain that a director associated with low-budget masculinist sensation movies should have elected to make it. In a confrontation with Winner on *The Late Show* the feminist journalist Joan Smith complained of both works' association of femininity with violence. Smith herself has written on the misogynist politics manifested in the case of the Yorkshire Ripper, Britain's most notorious modern serial-killer.[21] For her a fictional female serial-killer cannot be expressive of feminist values. But to interpret Zahavi's thesis in this way is to miss the point that it deliberately makes transgressively and excessively. The novel does not regard Bella as sane, nor does it recommend her as a role-model for women. On the contrary, Bella is intended as a lesson *for men*. 'Behave, or the Bella will get you': a counterblast to the bogeymen rapists already planted in women's psyches to keep them quiet.

If the ubiquitous images in film and fiction of the Woman with a Gun are expressions of anxiety about gender-roles and social anarchy, this also explains the glut of 1990s paperback publications about murderesses. The 'true stories of women who kill' is the teaser for one such compilation by Wesley Clarkson, who makes some effort to write from the woman's point of view. On the other hand, the titles of his books play directly – as such works usually do – into the mythic stereotypes enshrined in proverbs: *Hell Hath No Fury* and, of course, *Like a Woman Scorned* (1992). This thrifty distribution of a single adage over two titles aptly signifies the simplistic yet capacious nature of mythic stereotypes for the West's 'processing' of reality.

Clarkson describes, amongst others, Pamela Sainsbury, who for years had submitted to her husband's obsessive possessiveness and sexual sadism. In September 1990, after a sadistic session, she strangled him as he slept. Afterwards she scribbled on a calendar: 'This is the first day of the rest of my life.'[22] In order to dispose of the body she cut it up with a saw and a carving knife, dumping the remains; she did, however, keep the head, bagged, in a cupboard. According to Clarkson, she intended by this to reassure herself of the reality of her husband's demise. Some might think that she kept it as a trophy. However, if one is familiar with the semiotics of the Judith-Murderess it seems almost as if the pattern of Sainsbury's actions were dictated by her cultural myth. After a series of quasi-Judithic actions, the retention of the head can be interpreted as the *materialized* record of her husband's permanent absence. It perpetuated the moment of murder, and by retaining its memento Sainsbury kept the violent/authentic moment in her possession. But if violence is instrumental, it cannot be perpetuated in this way. Protracted need to recover its material reassurance is a sign of weakness, that Sainsbury had not really perceived her action as empowering her. For this is a divergence from the Judithic masterplot. The biblical heroine donated all her trophies to the temple, because (we may now perceive) *she did not need them*. She simply was (before and after, at all times) the person she had been when she murdered.

When Sainsbury was questioned by police she said that before she left in the police car she had dumped the head in the dustbin. One view might be that, panicked, she was trying to dispose of the evidence remaining in the house. According to Clarkson, however, she had already decided to confess and binning the head was a gesture of relief. If so, then presumably the head's materiality was not the reassurance she had imagined, but rather a sign of the psychic subordination still in place: signifying not her autonomy but her weakness. One way or another, it is an interesting case of how mythic semiotics translate themselves into actualities. Human behaviour conforms with its psychic myths. Nor does the coincidence of fiction with non-fiction end there. The Sainsbury's lived in 'the picturesque seaside town of Sidmouth, in Devon'. Bella-Judith lived in Brighton. Seaside towns and suburbs were where the Judith myth was played out in the 1990s, in hotels and marital bedrooms.

Whereas Bella fastidiously refrained from literalizing the symbolic castration in the plot of Judith (she doesn't hit 'below the belt'), actuality did. In the summer of 1993 an American woman's mutilation of her husband caused a media sensation.[23] Allegedly having been raped by her husband, Lorena Leonora Bobbitt castrated him whilst he slept. Male journalists reported that their wives had laughed at the news, or commented 'Good for her!', and female journalists joined in the approbation. Some commented upon the comic alacrity with which law officers went in quest of the severed member, which Lorena had discarded in a car park, and which doctors hastened to sew back onto her husband, who subsequently made a career out of public appearances as a remade man. Named John Wayne Bobbitt, and reportedly aspiring to be Jean-Claude Van Damme, he was a walking parody of redneck masculinity. Whatever else the Bobbitts did or did not do, they gave the public a striking instance of modern women's supposed emasculation of the male, made literal. And Lorena's vengeance evoked the gender divide in perceptions of violence and morality. Reports of female approval established that Lorena's action was regarded as vicarious of widespread resentments. It was not that women were eager to say that they would do the same, but rather that they did not hesitate to say (often with Bella-like amusement) that they knew why she had done it. Both the Monster-woman and the servile immigrant wife had 'had enough'. In the USA Mrs Bobbitt became celebrated by some women as a feminist heroine; in Britain, where the case spawned innumerable cartoons imaging 'women's vengeance', one in *Private Eye* finally excavated the archetype of the marital Judith – Mrs Judy castrating Punch. In essence the mythic archetype behind Mrs Bobbitt was well understood, indeed tacitly dictated the terms in which she was represented in the media and the public imagination.

This case was important because it finally translated the cultural cliché of the Woman With A Gun into what was portrayed as a representative instance of everyday realities, of women's insurgence as permeating normal suburbia and the mind of a woman not feminist, but dependent and 'orientalized' (poor immigrant wife).[24] This familiarized the fantasy Woman With A Gun as an ordinary and somewhat passive woman, and such a familiarization is much more disturbing to society than the fictions that it constructs to defuse its fears. Paradoxically, when myths become real in a way that divests them of their exotica they reveal themselves more intransigently.

That was precisely why the Judithic archetype for Mrs Bobbitt emerged in the form of Mrs Judy, because comic caricature at once acknowledged the bathetic setting of suburbia, and yet returned her to a stereotype that could be laughed at, relieving male tension. Competing with that, however, was another media phenomenon, for researchers immediately set about finding other examples of castrating wives. The American satirical magazine *Spy* listed a number of confirmed and reputed instances of women who had castrated their husbands in recent years.[25] This showed that the Bobbitt case of partner-castration was not unique, but a social quantity repeated across the USA and other nations. The publicity generated by the Bobbitt case stood on the verge of establishing an actualized social mythology of castration. Mrs Bobbitt was potentially a Bella-Monster, sign of castration as deterrence in a feminized society.

Similarly, the real point of Zahavi's novel is that women need to be not serial-killers but revolutionaries, massing for 'prison-burning riots'. Politics is of course the natural realm of Judith's figurations. An explicit instance of her deployment in public issues occurred in a poem published during the protracted controversy over the restructuring of the National Health Service in Britain. U.A. Fanthorpe's 'Clerical Error' (1993) was the dramatic monologue of an NHS bureaucrat at the cutting edge of this policy, its front office so to speak: 'What must I do when Job and his daughters / Cram into my office where they are not allowed, / . . . seeking comfort?' The biblical characterization of 'the poor and the afflicted' as the suffering Job is followed by the speaker's specious reassurance to another patient: 'Go to the nurses, Judith, / Judith, the nurses are looking for you (which is a lie).'[26] Judith the confused, homeless care-in-the-community person is the most marginalized, most acute example of a social organization hostile to weakness. But her biblical eponym implies that, unlike Job, this is one who will not accept her affliction patiently. She is the harbinger of social revolution.

The distinction between power and violence should be applied to the moral of *Dirty Weekend*. Its focus on the weak point of its enemy targets the typical confrontation of genders, in which Normal Man's capacity for violence defends the patriarchal order. But the confrontation exposes the weakness of this resort to physical force: masculinism is only powerful as long as women do not 'wake up one morning'. If masculinist society is based upon violence, which when exercised is not power but its failure, then by contrast the Bobbitt case, a rare act of violence inflicted by the underclass, is as it were a terrorism executed on the fragile superpower. As Mr Punch, wife-beater and murderer, was a cultural caricature of Man On Top, Mrs Judy/Bobbitt inevitably functions as a sign of Woman On Top. Judith and her avatars comprise all the central features of a feminist manifesto.

And precisely because counter-cultural, Judith's mythology can be traced as the clue to an alternative history of Western culture. (This book, that is.) When its various historical permutations are examined, they expose the vested interests embedded in that culture. The ways in which her myth resists pro-cultural assimilation have revealed the mechanisms whereby that assimilation is normally achieved. So to place her icon under surveillance is no less than to investigate what our cultural mythology has made us, and why. Ultimately that is the comprehensive meaning of her role as 'God's Assassin'. She is an image of the autonomy that is constantly being wrested from us all, and an icon of the way to recover it.

Notes

1 Beginning

1. Rebecca West, *The Young Rebecca: Writings of Rebecca West 1911–17*, selected and introduced by Jane Marcus (1928), 11.
2. Georges Bataille, *Eroticism*, trans. Mary Dalwood (1962: repr. 1987), 22.

2 The Gorgeous Gorgon

1. *The Bishop's Bible* (London, 1568), 10:4.
2. E.g. St Jerome, *Letter liv* Patrologia Latina, vol. 22 (Paris, 1864), paragraph 16 and St Ambrose, *De Viduis* Patrologia Latina, vol. 16, chs vii–viii, 196–9, paragraphs 37–50. For modern theological comment on the Book see e.g. Enslin's *The Book of Judith: Greek text with an English translation*, ed. with a general introduction and appendices by Solomon Zeitlin (Jewish Apocryphal Literature Series, vol. 7) (1972) and T. Craven, *Convention in the Book of Judith* (1983); for a literary and psychoanalytical analysis see M. Stocker, 'Biblical Story and the Heroine' in *The Bible as Rhetoric: Studies in Biblical Persuasion and Credibility*, ed. Martin Warner (Warwick Studies in Philosophy and Literature Series) (1990). For (inevitably very incomplete) bibliographies of Judith in English and German literature see Herbert Pentin, *Judith* (The Apocrypha in English Literature Series) (1908); and Edna Purdie, *The Story of Judith in German and English Literature* (Bibliothèque de la Revue de littérature comparée series, f.xxxix) (1927).
3. See Ch. 10, below.
4. St Jerome, *Letter liv*, 293, paragraph 16.
5. Sigmund Freud, 'The Taboo of Virginity' (see Ch. 10, below).
6. Hugh of St Victor, *Sermones lxxxvi*. On hubris see e.g. Philip de Haveng, Patrologia Latina, vol. 177.
7. See M. Stocker, 'Biblical Story'.
8. See Ch. 4, below.
9. For the general aesthetic term 'Medusa Effect' see Siegfried Kracauer, *Theory of Film: The Redemption of Physical Reality*, (1960), 305–6.
10. On Judith as humility see e.g. Hugh of St Victor, *Sermones lxxxvi*.
11. Simone de Beauvoir, *The Second Sex* (1949), trans. and ed. H.M. Parshley (1988), 170–229; on allegorical females see Marina Warner, *Monuments and Maidens: the Allegory of the Female Form* (1985).
12. *Les Règles de la Seconde Rhétorique* (c. 1430), ed. M.L.E. Langlois, in *Recueil d'Arts de Seconde Rhétorique* (1902).
13. See my detailed analysis of the Sainte-Chapelle's iconography, in papers delivered at the Courtauld Institute (1992) and University of Warwick; see M. Stocker, *Medieval Iconography*, forthcoming.
14. See my 'Biblical Story' and Paul

Joannides, 'Titian's *Judith* and its context: the iconography of decapitation', *Apollo*, cxxxv, no. 361 (March, 1992), 163–70.

15. For Esther's 'meekness' see Chaucer's 'Balade', ed. Geoffrey Grigson.

16. See esp. Chs 7–9, below.

17. Examples of feminist theology include *Feminist Interpretation of the Bible*, ed. L.M. Russell (1985).

18. For studies of Gentileschi see Germaine Greer, *The Obstacle Race: the Fortunes of Women Painters and their Work* (1981), 189–207 and Mary D. Garrard, *Artemisia Gentilieschi: the Image of the Female Hero in Italian Baroque Art* (1989).

19. See my 'Biblical Story'.

20. The key source for the story is Livy. For a brief but very interesting survey of Lucretia's representations see Ian Donaldson, *The Rapes of Lucretia: A Myth and its Transformations* (1982).

21. Augustine, *City of God*, I. 28ff.

3   Her Virtue Was Vice

1. On Judith's role in the Middle Ages see M. Stocker *Medieval Iconography*, forthcoming.

2. Ibid.; and Prudentius, *Psychomachia*, in *Prudentius with an English Translation by H.V. Thomson* (1949–53), 2 vols.

3. *Tractatus de Regimine Principum Ad Regem Henricum Sextum*, repr. in *Four English Political Tracts of the Middle Ages*, ed. J.P. Genet (1977), 133–4.

4. For a general study of portraiture, see J. Pope-Hennessy, *The Portrait in the Renaissance* (1966).

5. See the identification in Christopher Lloyd, *The Queen's Pictures: Royal Collectors through the Centuries, with an Essay by Sir Oliver Millar* (1991), 92.

6. For the identification of Donatello's sculpture see Stocker, *Medieval Iconography*.

7. See D. Freedberg in *Journal of the Warburg and Courtauld Institutes* (1971, 1982).

8. 'The Provenance of Van Eyck's *Woman*', *Harvard Library Bulletin* (1994).

9. Medieval bathrooms are described in *Revelations of the Medieval World* (general eds Philippe Ariès and Georges Duby), *Volume II: Revelations of the Medieval World*, ed. Georges Duby, trans. Arthur Goldhammer, (1988), 602–3.

10. For a history of the topos see Horst Schroeder, *Der Topos der Nine Worthies in Literatur und bildender Kunst* (1971).

11. For a general study of advice-books on marriage see Margaret J.M. Ezell, *The Patriarch's Wife: Literary Evidence and the History of the Family* (1987).

12. Paris Bordon (1500–71), 'Venetian Woman at her Toilette' in *The National Gallery of Scotland: Concise Catalogue of Paintings* (1997).

13. For a general study of the genre see A. Tapie et al. (eds), *Vanitas* (1990).

14. J.M. Synge, 'Queens', ed. Grigson.

15. For prostitution see B. Pullan, *Rich and Poor in Renaissance Venice: The Social Institutions of a Catholic State* (1971), 257–8, 374–94.

16. As in e.g. *Delle Belleza delle Donne* in *Prose di M. Agnolo Firenzuola Fiorentino* (Florence, 1545), ff.82ᵛ–83ʳ.

17. T. Wilson, *Ceramic Art of the Italian Renaissance* (1987).

18. Crispijn de Passe, *Le Miroir de Plus Belles Courtisannes de ce Temps* (Amsterdam, 1631).

19. For descriptions of furniture, see Peter Thornton, *The Italian Renaissance Interior, 1400–1600* (1991).

20. For an incident of beard-tugging see Pullan, *Rich and Poor*, 376.

21. E.g. as in Griselda Pollock, *Vision and Difference: Femininity, Feminism and the Histories of Art* (1988).

22. For Renaissance connoisseurship see e.g. R. Lightbown and A. McGregor (1989).

23. E.g. Hugh Broughton, *An Epistle to the learned nobility of England touching translating the Bible* (Amsterdam, 1609, repr. 1977), 25 and 34.

24. Cornelis van der Geest, located in the Mauritshuis, The Hague.

25. See e.g. R.C. Cudworth (1642), 4°C 21(2) Th. Seld; S.W. Hull, *Chaste, Silent and Obedient: English Books for Women 1475–1640* (1982).

26. For an analysis of the fresco see C.E. Gilbert, *Poets Seeing Artists' Work* (1991), *Instances in the Italian Renaissance*, 'Lettere Italiane' series, no.42 (1991), 89.

27. For further discussion see Ch. 3, below.

28. Petrarch, *Triumphus Cupidinis*, 363–4; exhibit at the *Age of Masaccio* exhibition (Florence, 1989).

29. Du Bartas, *La Judit*, Book II; Joshua Sylvester, *Bethulians Rescue* (1594); Henry Sponar's ballad, no. xxiv in *Songs and Ballads Chiefly of the Reign of Philip and Mary*, ed. T. Wright (London, 1860), 79–82.

30. See 'Imbibing Politics: Importation of German Stoneware', in my *Medieval Iconography*.

31. See e.g. C. Brown et al., *Rembrandt: The Master and his Workshop* (1991), 2 vols, vol. 1, 190–91.

32. Sigmund Freud, 'Medusa's Head' (1940).

4   Worshipping Women

1. For the medieval debate see F.L. Utley, *The Crooked Rib: an analytical index to the argument about women in English and Scots literature to the end of the year 1568* (1944); for historians' controversy over Renaissance women see Joan Kelly, *Women, History and Theory* (1984), 19–50; response by Mary Beth Rose (ed. and intro.), *Women in the Middle Ages and Renaissance: Literary and Historical Perspectives* (1986).

2. *St Botolph's Parish Church, Boston: The Misericords* (1994).

3. E.g. I.G., *An Apologie for Womenkinde* (London, 1605) and Filmer, *Patriarca* (?1638).

4. *Life of Christina of Markyate: A Twelfth-century Recluse*, ed. C.H. Talbot (1959), 76.

5. H.C. Agrippa, *A Treatise of the Nobilite and Excellencye of Women Kynde*, trans.

Clapham (London, 1542); L. Woodbridge, *Women in the English Renaissance: Literature and the Notion of Womenkind, 1540–1620* (1984); Ian McLean, *The Renaissance Notion of Woman: A Study in the Fortunes of Scholasticism and Medical Science in European Intellectual Life* (1980).

6. Examples of Judith cited for women's supremacy are J. Swetnam (see below), *Interlocucyon* (London, 1525), Edward Gosynhyll *The Prayse of All Women* (London, 1542). J. Swetnam, *The Arraignment of Lewd, Idle, Froward and Inconstant Women* (London, 1615), 23–4; E. Sowernam, *Esther Hath Hang'd Haman, or An Answer to The Arraignment of Women* (London, 1615).

7. Aemilia Lanier, *The Poems of Shakespeare's Dark Lady: Salve Deus Rey Judaeorum*, intro. A.L. Rowse (1979), 77–8, 125.

8. An example of the study of the theme in art is H. Diane Russell and Bernadine Barnes, *Eva Ave: Women in Renaissance and Baroque Prints* (1990).

9. A history of the theme is S. Meltzoff, *Botticelli, Signorelli and Savonarola: Theologica, Poetica and Painting from Boccaccio to Poliziano* (1987).

10. Examples are in the Walker Gallery Liverpool, the Château de Langeais and Cluny Museum, Paris.

11. This *salle* is mentioned in passing by C.E. Gilbert *Poets Seeing Artists' Work: Instances in the Italian Renaissance*, 'Lettere Italiane' series, no.42 (1991), 89.

12. For Mantegna's career see L. Gowing (general ed.), *A Biographical Dictionary of Artists* (1983).

13. A feminist history of needlework is Rozsika Parker, *The Subversive Stitch: Embroidery and the Making of the Feminine* (1984).

14. For a history of the syphilis epidemic see R.P.T. Davenport-Hynes, *Sex, Death and Punishment: Attitudes to Sex and Sexuality in Britain since the Renaissance* (1990).

15. A story reported by Simon Goulart, *Histoires Admirables et Mémorables de*

Nostre Temps (Paris, 1607) 2 vols, 362–3.

16. For Judith's previous history in this role, see Ch. 5, below, and M. Stocker *Medieval Iconography*, forthcoming.

17. E.g. Latimer, *Fourth Sermon* (Parker Society Edition), 378. For my study of his work and Catherine Bertie see my unpublished paper 'Merry Widows', first delivered to the 'Language, Culture, History' seminar at Oxford University in 1991. For Latimer's immense general influence on Protestant iconoclasm see M. Aston, *England's Iconoclasts* (1988), 172.

18. *Luther's Prefaces to the Apocryphal Books* (1934), 196–7.

19. For examples see Ch. 5, below.

20. For full discussion of this Netherlandish iconography see my unpublished paper, 'Imbibing Politics', first delivered to the British Archaeological Association European Conference, 1992.

21. Ibid.

22. An example of the type is now at Yarnton church, Oxfordshire.

23. D. Scarisbrick, *Tudor and Jacobean Jewellery* (1995), 48.

24. For the local context in Regensburg see K.E.S. Zapalac, *In His Image and Likeness: Political Iconography and Religious Change in Regensburg, 1500–1600* (1990), 131–4.

25. E.g. W. Heemskerck, *The Hebrew Heroine* (Amsterdam, 1647); for some thoughts on Netherlandish Judith-drama see Anne Marie Musschoot, *Het Judith-thema in de Nederlandse Letterkunde*, 107–43. For its context in iconography see my 'Imbibing Politics'.

26. *Holophernes* (perf. 1572): J. Payne Collier, *The History of English Dramatic Poetry to the Time of Shakespeare* (London, 1831), 3 vols I.xxi. Cf. Ch. 4, below.

27. Ralph Radcliffe (c. 1538); Sixt Birck, *Judith* (1536: repr. Augsburg, 1539); see also Ch. 4, below, and, for Schonaeus's influence in England, M. Stocker, 'Shakespeare's Secrets: Family, Politics, Religion, and a Source

for *Love's Labours Lost*', in *Shakespeare Yearbook VI*, ed. H. Klein and R. Wymer (1996).

28. E.g. Munich (1565), Vienna (1573 and 1590).

29. Purposes of Jesuit pedagogy are set out by Guarinoni (1610).

30. See Ch. 6, below.

31. Ibid.

32. Henry Parker, Eighth Baron Morley, *Dedications to the Exposition and Declaration of the Psalm 'Deus vitionum Dominus'* (1539).

33. For her biography see Nancy Lyman Roelker, *Queen of Navarre: Jeanne d'Albret, 1528–72* (1968).

34. For the dedication to Marguerite see Holmes's edition of Du Bartas's *La Judit* (1935).

35. T. Heywood, *History of the Reformation* (London, 1605).

36. T. Bentley, *Monument of Matrons* (1582), B2, B4, 43–6; M. Drayton (1591), I.2. See also C. Levin, 'Lady Jane Grey: Protestant Queen and Martyr', in M.P. Hannay (ed.), *Silent but for the Word* (1985), 92–106.

37. Alice Clark, *The Working Life of Women in the Seventeenth Century* (1919, repr. 1992).

38. For an extensive re-evaluation of Catherine Bertie see my 'Merry Widows'.

39. Lanier, *Shakespeare's Dark Lady*, 53–4.

40. See e.g. G.R. Potter and M. Greengrass (eds), *John Calvin*, Documents of Modern History Series (1983), 79–80, 2; P. Benedict, *Rouen During the Wars of Religion* (1981), 86–7; N.Z. Davis, *Women on Top* (1975), 65–95. For the wars see J.H.M. Salmon, *Society in Crisis: France in the Sixteenth Century* (1975).

41. On official Counter-Reformation attitudes to women I am much indebted to Nick Davidson's paper, 'Sexual Sin in Italy between the Fourteenth and Seventeenth Centuries', delivered in the Oxford University History Faculty in 1992.

42. Various views of women's social roles have been offered by e.g. Susan

Amussen *An Ordered Society: Gender and Class in Early-Modern England* (1988) and Ralph A. Houlbrooke, *English Family Life, 1576–1716* (1989).

5   The Monstrous Regiment of Judiths

1. A version of this chapter was first delivered to the Oxford University English Faculty Renaissance Seminar in 1988.
2. For early queenship, Rabanus Maurus and royal traditions see M. Stocker, *Medieval Iconography*, forthcoming.
3. For Caxton, Richard III, Villon and the medieval metrical *Judith* see M. Stocker, 'Apocryphal Entries: Judith and the Politics of Caxton's *Golden Legend*', in L. Smith and J.H.M. Taylor (eds) *Women, the Book and the Worldly* (1995).
4. F. Hotman, *Francogallia*, ed. R.E. Giesey and J.H.M. Salmon (1972), 479–95; see also Stocker, *Medieval Iconography*.
5. Christine de Pisan, *Book of the City of Ladies*, trans. Earl Jeffrey Richards (1982), Book II:31.
6. For some accounts of the succession issue see Mortime Levine, *Tudor Dynastic Problems, 1460–1571* (1973) and Constance Jordan, *Renaissance Feminism: Literary Texts and Political Models* (1990).
7. Pageant text quoted by Louise Olga Fradenburg, *City, Marriage, Tournament: arts of rule in late medieval Scotland* (1991), without comment on Judith's significance.
8. For opposing views of her abilities see John Ernest Neale, *Queen Elizabeth* (repr. 1958) and Christopher Haigh, *Queen Elizabeth I* (1988).
9. For their general activities see Christina Hallowell Garrett, *The Marian Exiles: a study in the origins of Elizabethan Puritanism* (1938).
10. David Lindsay, *The Works of Sir David Lindsay of the Mount, 1490–1555* (1931–6), 107–8.

11. E.g. John Knox, *The First Blast of the Trumpet against the Monstrous Regiment of Women* (Geneva, 1558), 41–42^v; cf. Christopher Goodman, *How Superior Powers Ought to be Obeyd of their Subjects* (Geneva, 1558), d2^v.
12. 'Ave Maria in Commendation of our Most Virtuous Queen', ballad repr. in H.R. Rollins (1920). The procession is described in S. Anglo, *Spectacle, Pageantry and Early Tudor Policy* (1969), 319–20.
13. Knox *Monstrous Regiment*, 41^r–41^v; John Poynet, *A Short Treatise of Politike Pouuer . . .* (1556).
14. Calvin, *Institutes*, 2:1512–16; *Zurich Letters*, 34ff.
15. Knox, letter to Cecil, *Works*, 2:20–21.
16. John Aylmer, *An Harborowe for Faithfull and Trewe Subjectes agaynst the late blowne Blaste* (Strassburg, 1559), D2–3, R^v–R2, A2, B2^v–B3, R2^v, E3^v–E4, Q.
17. Gertrude Marian Sibley, *Lost Plays and Masques 1500–1642* (1933), 76, lists this performance as apocryphal (!) but is underestimating tradition.
18. R. Barnefield, *Cynthia* (1595), penultimate stanza.
19. The Second Norwich Pageant, 1578, repr. In 'The Reception of the Queen at Norwich, 1578' in John Nichols, *The Progresses and Public Processions of Queen Elizabeth* (London, 1823), 2:145–9
20. T. Deloney, *The Overthrow of Proud Holofernes, and the Triumph of Virtuous Queen Judith* (c. 1593), in *Works* (1912), 355–61; E. Jenings (trans.), *The Famous History of the Virtuous and Godly Woman Judith* (1565); cf. e.g. *Ave Caesar* (1603). For W. Pekering's *The Historye of Judith and Holofernes* (1566–7) and *A Godly Ditty . . .* (1586), whose Elizabeth is 'a Judith just' see E.C. Wilson, *England's Eliza* (1939), 36–7, 43n. On the wide popular base of Protestantism see P. Collinson, *The Religion of Protestants: The church in English society, 1559–1625* (1982).
21. For official rules on her portraits see

R. Strong, *Gloriana: the Portraits of Queen Elizabeth I* (1987), 20.

22. See my 'Merry Widows'. Unpublished paper, first delivered to the 'Language, Culture, History' seminar at Oxford University in 1991.

23. See Marina Warner, *Joan of Arc* (1991), 204–5, 224–5.

24. See e.g. Philip Benedict, *Rouen during the Wars of Religion* (1981), 105, 260.

25. See my 'Shakespeare's Secrets: Family, Politics, Religion and a Source for *Love's Labours Lost*', in *Shakespeare Yearbook VI*, ed. H. Klein and R. Wynner (1996).

26. For the designs see Simon Bouquet, *Bref et sommaire recueil de ce qui a esté faict . . .* (Paris, 1572).

27. See e.g. the incident mentioned in Eleanor E. Tremayne, *The First Governess of the Netherlands, Margaret of Austria* (1908), 37–40.

28. C. d'Espence, *Oraison funebres es obseques de . . . Marie* (Paris, 1561).

29. See Ch. 5, below; and Frederic J. Baumgartner, *Radical Reactionaries: the Political Thought of the French Catholic League* (1975).

30. E.S. Taylor, *The History of Playing Cards* (London, 1865), 139.

31. See my 'Shakespeare's Secrets'.

32. Du Bartas's influence: e.g. R.A. Sayce, *The French Biblical Epic in the Seventeenth Century* (1955); Terence Cave, *Devotional Poetry in France c. 1570–1613* (1969), 23, 92. There were also translations into Dutch by Zacharias Heyns, *De weke wanden edelen* (Zwol, 1616) and into Polish by R. Leszczynski, *Judith* (Baranowie, 1629).

33. See Stocker, *Medieval Iconography* for Florence; for Marie de Medici's patronage, see Deborah Marrow, *The Art Patronage of Maria de' Medici* (1982).

34. Pierre Le Moyne, *La Gallerie des femmes fortes* (Lyon, 1667).

35. See e.g. Pierre Matthieu, *Histoire de Louys xi. Roy de France* (1610). On feminist themes in early seventeenth-century French literature see Ian

McLean, *Woman Triumphant: Feminism in French Literature, 1610–1652* (1977).

36. T. Heywood, *Nine bookes of various history concerning women* (1624; repr. Islip, 1640), 20–42, 184.

37. C. Marlowe, *Massacre at Paris* (London, c. 1593). For its French sources see P.H. Kocher, *Christopher Marlowe: a Study of his Thought, Learning and Character* (1962), J. Briggs *This Stage-Play World: English Literature and its Background, 1580–1625* (1983).

38. E.g. T. Petremand (1578), M. de Calages (1660).

39. James VI, Preface to *Uranie*, in *Poems*, 16; L.B. Campbell, *Divine Poetry and Drama in Sixteenth-century England* (1959), ch. 9.

40. William Camden, *Histoire d'Elizabeth Royne d'Angleterre, traduit du Latin de Guillaume Camden* (Paris, 1627), 172.

41. Helen Georgia Stafford, *James VI of Scotland and the Throne of England* (c. 1940), 14; P.J. Holmes, 'Mary Stewart in England', in *Mary Stewart: Queen in Three Kingdom's*, ed. Michael Lynch (1988), 195–218. Holmes thinks James was more than acquiescent, but I suggest that he was actively campaigning for her death, and at a much earlier stage than this.

42. E.g. *An Excellent and Materiall Discourse*, trans. 'S.B.' (1626); John Dove, *A Confutation of Atheisme* (repr. London, 1640), 4–5.

43. E.g. J. Lane's *An elegie upon the death of the high and renowned princesse our late soveraigne Elizabeth* (1603), repr. in *Fugitive Tracts*, 2nd series, 2 (London, 1875).

6   Hanging's Too Good for Her

1. Extended versions of this paper were delivered at the Institute of Historical Research, London (1990) and at Durham and Oxford Universities.

2. Philippe de Commynes, *Memoires* (repr. Honoré Champion, 1924–5).

3. Jean de Petit, *Apology*.

4 See M. Stocker, *Medieval Iconography*, forthcoming.

5. J.C. Burckhardt, *The Civilization of the Renaissance*, trans. S.C.G. Middlemore (revd edn 1929), 60.

6. See my 'Apocryphal Entries: The Politics of Judith in Caxton's *Golden Legend*', in L. Smith and J.H.M. Taylor (eds), *Women and the Book* (1995).

7. For the circumstances see Frederick Harrison, *William the Silent* (1897), 233; for the iconography see my 'Imbibing Politics: Importation of German Stoneware', in Stocker, *Medieval Iconography*.

8. Juan de Mariana, *On Kings and Kingship* (1599); Michel Roussel, *Antimariana* (Paris, 1610); Douai Bible (1609–10), 1011; Judith invoked for Gunpowder Plot, Thomas Morton, *An Exact discoverie of Romish doctrine in the Case of conspiracie and rebellion by pregnant observations* (London, 1605), 29. For history of political thought see Q. Skinner, *The Foundations of Modern Political Thought*, vol. 2 (1978); J.H.M. Salmon, *The French Religious Wars in English Political Thought* (1959), R. Mousnier, *The Assassination of Henry IV* (1973).

9. *Martine Mar-Sixtus, a second replie against the defensory and apology of Sixtus the fift*. Signed R.W. (London, 1591).

10. See Ch. 3, above.

11. For a general study of the massacre see A. Soman (ed.), *The Massacre of St Bartholomew* (1974).

12. M. Foucault, *Discipline and Punish: The Birth of the Prison*, trans. Alan Sheridan (1979), 23–4, 49.

13. Contemporary description in Jean François Ravaillac, *The terrible and deserved death of Francis Ravilliack* (London, 1610).

14. E. Scarry, The Body in Pain (1985).

15. Sir Edmund Skory (trans.), *An Extract out of the Historie of the Last French King Henry the Fourth* (London, 1610), D3.

16. BN, E. Hennin, n. 11148.

17. Hierosme de Benevent, *A Discourse to the Lords of Parliament* (1611), B2^r–B2^v.

18. E.g. Robert Persons, *De Persecutione Anglicana Libellus* (Rome, 1582).

19. On primitive notions of taboo, see M. Douglas, *Purity and Danger* (1966).

20. Orest Ranum, 'The French Ritual of Tyrannicide in the late Sixteenth Century,' in *Sixteenth-Century Journal* 11 (1980), 63–82.

21. Ben Jonson, *Sejanus His Fall*, ed. W.F. Bolton (1966).

22. Philippe Erlanger, *St Bartholomew's Night*, trans. P. O'Brian (1962), 252–3.

23. Ibid., 251–3.

24. 'Deploration of the Curel Murther', *Sempill Ballats*, 63.

25. *The French Herald* (London, 1611), 2, 8–9.

26. Skory, *An Extract out of the Historie*, D3.

27. J. de Bonestat, *Anti-Jesuites au roy* (Saumer, 1611), 60; *French Herald* (1611), 5; Pierre Matthieu, *The heroyk life and deplorable death of the most Christian King Henry Fourth*, trans. E. Grimeston (London, 1612), 105.

28. Virgilio Malvezzi, *Romulus and Tarquin*, trans. Henry Carey (1937), 16; Edward Sexby, *Killing Noe Murder* (London, 1659), 7–8.

29. Ibid., 15.

30. Roussel, *Antimariana*, 216ff; Michael Hawke, *Killing is murder, and no murder* (London, 1657).

31. *Vindiciae Contra Tyrannos*, trans. and ed. Julian H. Franklin, in *Constitutionalism and Resistance in the Sixteenth Century* (1969), 137–99.

32. John Felton, *The prayer and confession of Mr. Felton, word for word as hee spake it immediately before his execution* (London, 1628), 3.

33. Nicolaus Seravius, *Nicolai Serarii . . . in libros Regum et Paralipomenon commentaria posthuma* (Mogunt, 1617).

34. Sir Simonds D'Ewes, *Extracts from the MS. Journal* (London, 1783), 38–45.

35. Jean Boucher, *Apologie pour Jehan Chastel* (1610), 264.

36. Henri Estienne, *A mervaylous discourse upon the lyfe, deedes, and behaviours of Katherine de Medicis* (London, 1575), 55–9, 159–67, 175, 186, 194.

37. M. Bakhtin, *Rabelais and his World*, trans. H. Iswolsky (1968), 26–7; P. Stallybrass, 'Patriarchal Territories', in *Rewriting the Renaissance: the discourses of sexual difference in early modern Europe*, ed. M.W. Ferguson and N.J. Vickers (1986).

38. F. Hotman, *Francogallia*, ed. R.E. Giesey and J.H.M. Salmon (1972), 485–6.

39. S. Brownmiller, *Against our Will: Men, Women and Rape* (1976).

40. See Ch. 3, above.

41. For her life see Corrado Ricci, *Beatrice Cenci*, 2 vols (1925).

42. M. Merini, *Michelangelo Merisi da Caravaggio* (1987), 418.

43. Simon Goulart, *Admirable and Memorable histories containing the wonders of our time*, trans. E. Grimeston (London, 1607), 362–4.

44. *The Historical works of m. Adolphe Thiers*, trans. by T.W. Redhead, 3 vols (London, 1845–7), 174.

45. E.g. illustration to *Complainte sur la mort de Louis* (1793), BM, H.W. Martin Collection.

46. Simon Pierre Mérard de Saint-Just, *Judith et Holopherne* (1789).

47. For a history of the guillotine see Daniel Gerould, ed. *Gallant and Libertine: eighteenth-century French divertissements and parades* (Performing Arts Journal, 1983).

48. Thomas Carlyle, *The French Revolution*, 2 vols (1929), vol. 2, 295.

49. Joseph Shearing, *The Angel of the Assassination: Marie-Charlotte de Corday* (c. 1935).

50. Carlyle, *French Revolution*, vol. 2, 313.

51. Isaac Cruikshank, 'A Second Jeanne D'Arc' (1793), BM C 8335.

52. Carlyle, *French Revolution*, vol. 2, 310.

53. Earthenware figures, 'The Assassination of Marat' (1793), Fitzwilliam Museum, Cambridge.

54. Cf. Albert Soboul, 'Sentiment religieux et cultes populaires pendant la

55. Kenneth Clark, *The Romantic Rebellion, romantic versus classic art* (1973), 32.

56. Anonymous watercolour, at Vesailles.

57. Carlyle, *French Revolution*, vol. 2, 314, cites an eyewitness.

58. L. Jordanova, 'Medical Mediations: Mind, Body and the Guillotine', *History Workshop* 28 (1989), 40. S.Hist.Per 21.

59. See Shearing, *Angel of the Assassination*, 266–7.

60. Anonymous engraving (pub. Basset, Paris), at Versailles.

61. Cf. Neil Hertz on Tocqueville in 'Medusa's Head: Male Hysteria under Political Pressure,' in *Representations* 4 (1983). 27–54, and Gallagher et al.'s critique in *Representations* 4 (1983), 55–72.

62. Charlotte Corday, *Le Vol de la Guillotine* (1989), 43.

Révolution', *Annales Historiques de la Révolution Française* 148 (1957), 193–213.

7 The Dark Angel

1. See Ronald Paulson, *Representations of Revolution (1789–1820)*, (1983), 361–87 on Goya.

2. Harold Bloom, *The Anxiety of Influence: a theory of poetry* (1973); cf. Walter Jackson Bate, *The Burden of the Past and the English Poet* (1971).

3. Percy Bysshe Shelley, *The Cenci* (1819), 222–3, 233, 243, 256–65; J.W. Donohue, 'Shelley's Beatrice and the Romantic Concept of Tragic Character,' *Keats–Shelley Journal*, 17 (1968), 53–73, connects Shelley's Beatrice with his response to the 'psychological' acting of Eliza O'Neill.

4. Thomas Carlyle, *The French Revolution: A History*, 2 vols (1929), vol. 2, 264.

5. Anthony Trollope, *The Last Chronicle of Barset*, ed. Stephen Charles Gill (1980).

6. For a contrast between Catholicism and Protestantism see C. Crosby, *The*

Ends of History: Victorians and 'the Woman Question' (1991), 110–43, and R. Clark-Beattie, 'Fables of Rebellion: Anti-Catholicism and the Structure of *Villette*', *ELH* 53 (1986), 821–47.

7. C. Brontë, *Villette* (London, 1853, repr. 1909), 96–7, 234.

8. See Benjamin Jowett, *On the Interpretation of Scripture* (London, 1860); Lewis Henry Morgan, *Ancient Society, or Researches in the lines of Human Progress from Savagery through Barbarism to Civilization* (London, 1877); Joseph Ernest Renan, *Histoire des Origines du Christianisme* (Paris, 1863–83).

9. Matthew Arnold, *Culture and Anarchy* (1869), ed. by J. Dover Wilson (1950), 129–44.

10. Abraham Gilam, *The Emancipation of the Jews in England, 1830–60* (1982).

11. Edward W. Said, *Orientalism* (c.1985; repr. 1991).

12. L. Nochlin, 'The Imaginary Orient', *Art in America* 71 (May 1983).

13. Elizabeth Cady Stanton, *The Woman's Bible: the Original Feminist Attack on the Bible*, ed. and intro. by Dale Spender (1985), Pt 2, 15–16, 35, 20–21, 84–92.

14. For the Victorian's interest in typology see G.P. Landow, *Victorian Types, Victorian Shadows: Biblical Typology in Victorian Literature, Art, and Thought* (1980).

15. T.B. Macaulay, 'Civil Disabilities of the Jews' (1831) repr. In *Critical and Historical Essays* (1903), 291–302, esp. 296.

16. See esp. Havelock Ellis, *The Task of Social Hygiene* (revd edn 1927).

17. Otto Weininger, *Sex and Character* (London, 1906), 279; *Judith*, in *Three Plays by Hebbel*, trans. M. W. Sonnenfeld (1974).

18. U.H. Gerlach, *Hebbel as a Critic of his own Works* (1972), 79.

19. Freud, 'Taboo of Virginity'. S. Kofman, *Freud and Fiction* (1991), thinks Freud distorted literary texts. In this case, I think, the distortion was already there.

20. T.P. Peardon, *The Transition in English Historical Writing, 1760–1830* (1933); A Briggs, *Saxons, Normans and Victorians* (1966); J.M. Kemble, *The Saxons in England*, 2 vols (1849).

21. John Mason Neale, *Judith, a Seatonian poem* (Cambridge, 1856).

22. *Judith; or the Prophetess of Bethulia* (London, 1849).

23. In this paragraph's analysis of Nestroy I am much indebted to I. Barea, *Vienna: Legend and Reality* (1996), 230–33.

8 Judy and Punch

1. For two of the differing perspectives on marital relations in the eighteenth century see L. Stone, *The Family, Sex and Marriage in England, 1500–1800* (1979), ch. 8, and A. MacFarlane, *Marriage and Love in England: Modes of Reproduction 1300–1840* (1986).

2. For a history of the puppet-show see G. Speaight, *Punch and Judy: a history* (revd edn 1970).

3. For Joan as a plebeian name see e.g. the proverb, M.P. Tilley, *A Dictionary of Proverbs* (1950), 347, reference J57.

4. Horace Walpole, *Anecdotes of Painting in England* (4th edn, London, 1786), vol 3, 7, attribution, 19; enthusiasm for 'historical painting', F. Antal, *Hogarth and his Place in European Art* (1962), 143ff.

5. See e.g. M. Vicinus (ed.), *Suffer and Be Still: Women in the Victorian Age* (1972); N. Armstrong, *Desire and Domestic Fiction: A Political History of the Novel* (1987); M. Poovey, *Uneven Developments: The Ideological Work of Gender in Mid-Victorian England* (1988).

6. See e.g. L. Mahood, *The Magdalenes: Prostitution in the Nineteenth Century* (1990); L. Nead, *Myths of Sexuality: Representations of Women in Victorian Britain* (1988); E. Trudgill's juxtaposition of *Madonnas and Magdalens: The Origins and Development of Victorian Sexual Attitudes* (1976), 256–72.

7. She is the ideal wife in the *Woman's Bible*, II:38. John Mason Neale, *Ruth a Seatonian poem* (Cambridge, 1860). J.S. Mill, *Subjection of Women* (1869), in *A Vindication of the Rights of Women by MaryWollstonecraft and The Subjection of Women by J.S. Mill* with an introduction by Mary Warnock (1985), 248–9.

8. Hence the novel's epigraph: 'Drop, drop, slow tears!...', and the last word, 'tears' (E. Gaskell, *Ruth*, ed. A. Shelston (1985), epigraph and 458). The novel refers to the biblical Ruth, 313, and the Magdalen, 119.

9. E.g. A. Besant, 'Marriage' (1882), in *The Sexuality Debates*, ed. S. Jeffreys (1987), 391–445; F. Trollope, *Domestic Manners of the Americans* (1832), I:82–3.

10. On Madan see Richard Davenport-Hines, *Sex, Death and Punishment: Attitudes to Sex and Sexuality in Britain since the Renaissance* (1990), 36–7. On the treatment of the repentant prostitutes as objects of pathos in sermons see Ann Jessie van Sant, *Eighteenth-Century Sensibility and the Novel* (1993), 31–7.

11. *Judith. An Oratorio. As Performed at the Lock-Hospital Chapel, On Wednesday the 29th of Feb., 1764... Printed for the Benefit of the Charity, and to Be Had at the Hospital* (1764).

12. J. Fenimore Cooper, *The Deerslayer* (1841: repr. 1963), 499.

13. See e.g. R. Cecil, *The Masks of Death: Changing Attitudes in the Nineteenth Century* (1991), 19.

14. *No Trees in the Street*, dir. J. Lee Thompson (1959).

15. *The Judy* (1935); *Judy's Annual*, ed. C.H. Ross (1879).

16. 'The Ladies' (1895), in *Rudyard Kipling's Verse: Definitive Edition* (1940), 443.

17. B. Taylor, *Eve and the New Jerusalem: Socialism and Feminism in the Nineteenth Century* (1983), 162–3.

18. E.g. *An Exposition of the Books called Apocrypha... By a Layman* (1828), 15. For an account of the controversy see *The Cambridge History of the Bible*, ed. S.L. Greenslade (1963), 2:391; R.C.D.

19. Jasper, *Prayer Book Revision in England 1800–1900* (1954).

19. Voltaire, *La Bible enfin Expliquée* (1776), 434–5.

20. Sir William Smith, *A Smaller Dictionary of the Bible* (London, 1866, repr. 1907), 282.

21. These views are discussed in M. Stocker, 'Bennett and Modernism', forthcoming.

22. See e.g. I. Nowell OSB, *Jonah. Tobit. Judith.* (Collegiate Bible Commentary, 1986).

23. *Woman's Bible*, II:30–1; F. Swiney, 'The Bar of Isis or the Law of the Mother' (1912) in *The Sexuality Debates*, ed. Jeffreys, 468–88.

24. See e.g. A. Milbank, 'Josephine Butler: Christianity, Feminism and Social Action', in *Disciplines of Faith: Studies in Religion, Politics and Patriarchy*, ed. J. Obelkevich et al. (1987), 154–64.

25. See Ch. 9, below.

26. See H.M. Cecil (1894), repr. in *Meredith: The Critical Heritage*, ed. J. Williams (1971), 412–28; A. Woods, *George Meredith as Champion of Women and Progressive Education* (1937). On his conscious radicalism see D. Williams, *George Meredith: His Life and Lost Love* (1977), 167–9.

27. G. Meredith, *Rhoda Fleming: a story* (1910), 50–3.

28. *Saturday Review* (14 October 1865), repr, in *Meredith: The Critical Heritage*, 139–44.

29. *The Times* (18 May 1891), repr. in *Meredith: The Critical Heritage*, 352–5.

30. G. Meredith, *One of our Conquerors* (1910), 339–41.

31. H.G. Wells, *The New Machiavelli*, 132.

9   Reader, I Murdered Him

1. *An Exposition of the Books Called Apocrypha... By a Layman* (1828), 7.

2. For an excellent general study of female murderers see Ann Jones, *Women Who Kill* (1991).

3. *A Cabinet of Grief* (1688), *An Epilogue to the French Midwife's Tragedy who was*

Burnt for the Murder of her Husband, Denis Hobry (London, 1688), *A Hellish Murder* (1688), *A Warning-Piece to All Married Men and Women* (1688).

4. *Cabinet*, 2.
5. Ibid.
6. *Warning-Piece*, final line; *Cabinet*, 10; *Hellish Murder*, 39; *Epilogue*.
7. Examples of successful operas on the theme include Serov's *Judith* (1863), a great success in Russia.
8. G.B. Shaw, *The Complete Musical Criticism*, 3 vols, ed. Dan. H. Lawrence (1981), II:938.
9. G. Eliot, *Middlemarch* (1871–2), ed. W.J. Harvey (1965), 172.
10. The incident is described by J.R. Stephens, *The Censorship of English Drama 1824–1901* (1980), 103.
11. For the Italian context see M. Stocker, *Medieval Iconography*, forthcoming.
12. See Ch. 7, above.
13. H. Chorley and H. Leslie, *Judith: A Biblical Cantata: Words Selected from the Holy Scriptures by Henry F. Chorley, Music Composed by Henry Leslie* (London, 1858), 'Introductory'.
14. H. Wyndham, *Feminine Frailty* (1929), 14.
15. Ibid, 10; George Theodore, *The Newgate Calendar* (1816), new edition with an introduction by Christopher Hibbert (1991), 170–89.
16. Wyndham, *Feminine Frailty*, 11.
17. Ibid., 14.
18. *Judith*, intro. M.R. James (1928), xvii.
19. The best account of the sensation genre is by E. Showalter, *A Literature of their Own: British Women Novelists from Brontë to Lessing*, rev. edn (1982), 153–81.
20. Her real name was Julie Bernat: translation of *Lady Audley's Secret*, 1863.
21. Mary Elizabeth Braddon, *Lady Audley's Secret*, ed. D. Skilton (1987), 54, 205–7. On Victorian treatment of 'madness' in unhappy women see Elaine Showalter, *The Female Malady: Women, Madness and English Culture, 1830–1980* (1985).

22. S. Freud, 'The Uncanny' (1919), *Pelican Freud Library*, vol. 14, 335–76.
23. See Ch. 9, below.
24. C. Darwin, *The Descent of Man* (1874), III:19; G. Romanes, 'Mental Differences between Men and Women' (1887), repr. in *The Education Papers*, ed. D. Spender (1987), esp. 10–11. For medical developments see T. Laqueur, *Making Sex: Body and Gender from the Greeks to Freud* (1990), esp. 207–32; L. Jordanova, *Sexual Visions: Images of Gender in Science and Medicine Between the Eighteenth and Twentieth Centuries* (1989).
25. C. Lombroso and W. Ferrero, *The Female Offender* (repr. 1959), 2, 33, 95, 109–11, 147–9, 198, 267.
26. George Eliot, *Adam Bede* (1859) ed. F.R. Leavis (1961), 178.
27. *Last Chronicle of Barset*, ed. P. Fairclough and L. Lerner (1967). References: 395, 260, 633, 277, 278, 262, 540, 635, 861, 699, 48.
28. Nathaniel Hawthorne, *The French and Italian Notebooks*, ed. Thomas Woodson (1980). His fellow-novelist Henry James was struck by Hawthorne's 'detest[ation]' of Rome and thought it betrayed the 'occidental savour' of the un-Europeanized American (Henry James, *Hawthorne* (1879: repr. 1966), 139).
29. Hawthorne, *Notebooks* [1858], 294, 158, 520–1, 92–3, 520.
30. *The Marble Faun* (1860: repr. 1961), 308, 54, 39–40, 42–3.

10 Framing the *Femme Fatale*

1. Ford Madox Ford, *A History of Our Own Times*, ed. S. Beinfeld and S.J. Stang (1989), 186. For the decade see H. Jackson, *The Eighteen Nineties* (1913).
2. See esp. B. Dijkstra, *Idols of Perversity: Fantasies of Feminine Evil in Fin-de-Siècle Culture* (1986) and E. Showalter, *Sexual Anarchy: Gender and Culture at the Fin de Siècle* (1991).

3. J. Ruskin, 'Mornings in Florence', in *Works*, vol. 23, ed. E.T. Cook and A. Wedderburn (1906), 335–7. For Botticelli's reputation see M. Levey, 'Botticelli in Nineteenth-Century England', *Journal of the Warburg and Courtauld Institutes*, 23 (1960).

4. W. Pater, *The Renaissance* (1873: repr. 1959), 50–3, 47.

5. *Venus in Furs and Selected Letters*, ed. S. Lotringer (1989), 183, 67, 133, 68, 106, 180, 210, 172, 60.

6. W. von Sacher-Masoch, *Confessions*, trans. M. Phillips et al. (1990), 119.

7. A. Strindberg, *The Dance of Death: A Drama in Two Parts* [1900], repr. in *The Strindberg Reader*, ed. and trans. A. Paulson (1968).

8. Sigmund Freud, 'The Taboo of Virginity', esp. 208.

9. M. Leiris, *Manhood* (1968).

10. L. Carrington, *The Seventh Horse and Other Tales*, ed. M. Warner (1989), 193, 199–201.

11. For a history of the Suffragette movement see S. Kent, *Sex and Suffrage in Britain 1860–1914* (1987).

12. F.W. Nietzsche, *Thus Spake Zarathustra*, trans. A. Tille and M.M. Bozman (1958), 98–100 *et passim*.

13. G. Flaubert, *Salammbô*, trans. A.J. Krailsheimer (1977).

14. Reproduced in *Shoulder to Shoulder* (BBC Publications, n.d.), 34.

15. See Ch. 7, above; H.G. Wells *The New Machiavelli* (1911), 300.

16. D.H. Lawrence in 1913, quoted in *Georgian Poetry 1911–22*, ed. T. Rogers (1977), 102–3.

17. R.E. Glaymen, 'Recent Judith-Drama and its Analogues' (Doctoral thesis, University of Pennsylvania, privately printed, 1930), 120, 111.

18. F. Harrison (1913), 511, on Suffragettes.

19. T.B. Aldrich, *Judith of Bethulia: A Tragedy* (1904), 79, 83–4, 98. The play was written for Nance O'Neil.

20. Abercrombie was already familiar with Nietzsche's ideas. See P. Bridgewater, *Nietzsche in Anglosaxony* (1972), 117–19.

21. Lascelles Abercrombie, *Judith*, in *Emblems of Love: Designed in Several Discourses* (1912), 127–8, 132, 134, 162, 172, 185–6.

22. Bauer, *Woman*, 404.

23. For Hitchcock's request see M. Drabble, *Arnold Bennett: A Biography* (1975), 329.

24. On sexology's anti-feminism see S. Jeffreys, *The Spinster and her Enemies* (1985), 155ff.

25. A. Kuyper, *Women of the Old Testament: Fifty Devotional Messages for Women's Groups* (1934). Quotations from 75, 77, 88.

26. *The Connoisseur* (June 1928), 125.

27. *Judith*, intro. M.R. James (1928), xvii.

28. H. Walpole, *Judith Paris* (1931), 'A Prefatory Letter', and 135.

29. S. Freud, 'Group Psychology and the Analysis of the Ego' (1921: repr. in the Penguin edn of Freud, vol. 12, 1985), 127.

30. P. Fussell, *The Great War and Modern Memory* (1977), *passim*.

31. K. Theweleit, *Male Fantasies*, vol. I, trans. S. Conway (1987).

32. Quoted ibid., 77–8.

33. D.H. Lawrence, *Studies in Classic American Literature* (1923), 67.

34. G.T. Garrott, *Europe's Dance of Death* (1940), 318.

35. See W.J. Niven, *The Reception of Friedrich Hebbel in Germany in the Era of National Socialism* (1984), 99–103.

36. *Judith, Juliana and Elene: Three Fighting Saints*, trans. M. Nelson (1991), 206–7.

11 Judith's List

1. E.g. Batsheva Dance Co., *Tongues of Fire*; Martha Graham's 1962 ballet of Judith was in collaboration with Israelis. For a somewhat anecdotal work (confusing Jael with Judith), see G. Manor, *The Gospel According to Dance: Choreography and the Bible from Ballet to Modern* (1980), 52–3.

2. N. Gabler, *An Empire of their Own: How the Jews invented Hollywood* (1989), 328ff.

3. Women's resentment: Esther Fuchs, 'Images of Love and War in Contemporary Israeli Fiction: A Feminist Re-vision', in *Arms and the Woman: War, Gender, and Literary Representation*, ed. Helen M. Cooper (1989), 268–82.

4. B. Bettelheim, *The Informed Heart* (1991), esp. 230–1.

5. For some reflections on films' difficulty see Ronnie Landau, 'The Holocaust: The Unique and the Universal', in *Film, History and the Jewish Experience: A Reader*, ed. J. Davis (1986), 9–14.

6. 'Elizabeth', 'Growing Up Jewish', in *Walking on the Water: Women Talk About Spirituality*, ed. Jo Garcia and Sara Maitland (1983), 29–42. 'Woman', in *Walking on the Water*, 169.

7. Cards by W. Turnowsky Ltd, Tel Aviv; Graffiti Fair Ltd, Birmingham.

8. Maureen Gilbert, 'When Hitler Returns: The Impossibilities of Being a Jewish Woman', in *Walking on the Water*, 157–72.

9. *Feminism and Psychoanalysis: A Critical Dictionary*, ed. E. Wright and D. Chisholm (1992).

10. J. Amiel, *Deeds* (1989), 128.

12 Woman with a Gun

1. J. Amiel, *Deeds* (1989), 128.

2. A. Hudgins, 'Holofernes Reminiscences after Three Thousand Years', *Georgia Review* 31 (1977), 905.

3. Cf. the ingenue of *A Date with Judy*, dir. J. Pasternak (1948).

4. J. Cook, 'Fictional Fathers', in *Sweet Dreams: Sexuality Gender and Popular Fiction*, ed. S. Radstone (1988), 142–3.

5. P. Belle, *Wintercombe* (1989), 283.

6. S. Faludi, *Backlash: The Undeclared War against Women* (1992); Bly, *Iron John* (1994).

7. For a populist account of Khaled, see E. MacDonald, *Shoot the Women First* (1991), 97–132.

8. David Edgar, *Ecclesiastes* (1985).

9. *Charlotte Corday 1989*, dedication, 43, 34.

10. For various accounts of Marita Lorenz, see her *Marita* (1993); *Observer Magazine* (7.11.93); *Sunday Times Magazine* (21.11.93).

11. J. le Carré, *The Little Drummer Girl* (1983), 72. Despite much discussion of the novel, critics have not discussed its biblical motifs. On its politics see J. Diamond, 'Spies in the Promised Land', *Race and Class*, 25 (1984); T. Barley, *Taking Sides: The Fiction of John le Carré* (1986), 146–66.

12. R. Morgan, *The Demon Lover: On the Sexuality of Terrorism* (1989).

13. J. le Carré, *The Little Drummer Girl*, 500.

14. H. Arendt, *On Violence* (1970).

15. M. Baldwin, *Holofernes* (1990), 150, 277. Baldwin actually explores the issues of terrorism, whereas I. McQueen's opera on Judith, *Line of Terror* (1993), raised the identification only in its title.

16. 'Italians Blame Shadowy Powers', *Independent* (30.5.93).

13 Judy the Ripper

1. *Newsweek* (22.7.91).

2. Dream World Books, Colchester.

3. I. McQueen and I. Bergkwist, *Line of Terror*, and D. Lang, *Judith and Holofernes*, at the Almeida, London, July 1993; Sotheby's, London, 1991; National Gallery exhibition, London, *The Queen's Pictures*, 1991.

4. J. Mitchell, *Women: The Longest Revolution* (1984).

5. Sara Maitland, *Daughter of Jerusalem* (1978), 30, 83, 167–8.

6. E.g. M. Daly, *Beyond God the Father: Toward a Philosophy of Women's Liberation* (1985).

7. M. Atwood, *Cat's Eye* (1990), 267, 325–6, 359.

8. M. Jacobus, *Reading Woman: Essays in Feminist Criticism* (1986), 110–36. For a critique of feminist theory's 'Maternal Metaphor', see D.C. Stanton in N.K. Miller (ed.) *The Poetics of Gender* (1986).

9. Sara Maitland, *Telling Tales* (1983) 2, 3.

10. See L. Goodings's response from Virago, 'Call me Old-Fashioned', *Independent on Sunday* (20.6.93).

11. A. van Herk, *The Tent Peg*, 172–3.

12. Barker, *The Possibilities* (1987), 55–7.

13. N. Mosley, *Judith: A Novel* (1992), 28, 93, 97.

14. V. Feaver, 'Judith', *Independent on Sunday* (1.11.92).

15. For feminism's controversies about sexuality see S. Firestone, *The Dialectic of Sex* (1971), 142.

16. J. Russ, *The Female Man* (1985), 212.

17. Van Herk, *Tent Peg*, 172–3.

18. Russ, *Female Man*, 181.

19. H. Zahavi, *Dirty Weekend* (1991), 1, 4, 39, 56–8, 139.

20. Russ, *Female Man*, 187.

21. E.g. 'Much Ado about Lia', *Sunday Times Magazine* (12.9.93); Joan Smith, *Misogynies* (1990), 117–51.

22. W. Clarkson, *Like a Woman Scorned: True Stories of Women Who Kill* (1992), 21.

23. E.g. 'American Diary' (*Guardian*, 16.8.93); 'Your Penis or your Life' (*Guardian* (21.1.94); 'Wife's Graphic Story', *National Enquirer* (7.12.93).

24. Anxious 'this has gone too far' articles are instanced by 'Domestic Violence Should Be Defeated, Not Avenged', *Daily Telegraph* (19.1.94). Cf. 'Can you Handle the "Yes" babes?', London *Evening Standard* (1.2.94).

25. *Spy* (April 1994); 'One Minute it Was There . . .', *Guardian* (6.4.94).

26. U.A. Fanthorpe, 'Clerical Error', *Independent* (29.9.93).

Index